CREATING JUDAISM

MICHAEL L. SATLOW

CREATING JUDAISM

History, Tradition, Practice

Columbia University Press
New York

Columbia University Press
Publishers Since 1893
New York, Chichester, West Sussex
Copyright © 2006 Michael L. Satlow

Library of Congress Cataloging-in-Publication Data
Satlow, Michael L.
Creating Judaism : history, tradition, practice / Michael L. Satlow
p.   cm.   Includes bibliographical references and index.
ISBN 978-0-231-13488-0 (cloth : alk. paper) — ISBN 978-0-231-13489-7 (pbk. : alk. paper) —
ISBN 978-0-231-50911-4 (ebook)   1. Judaism.   2. Jews—Identity.   I. Title.
BM45.S226 2006   296—dc22
2006018056
978-0-231-13488-6

Casebound editions of Columbia University Press books are printed
on permanent and durable acid-free paper.

Printed in the United States of America
c 10 9 8 7 6 5 4 3 2 1
p 10 9 8 7 6 5 4 3

For Jacqueline

CONTENTS

ACKNOWLEDGMENTS

WRITING THIS BOOK has brought me far outside of my usual comfort zone, and I have turned to many colleagues, students, friends, and family for guidance. It is a pleasure for me to acknowledge their help and generosity.

The idea for this book, and the intellectual model underlying it, emerged slowly over long and pleasant conversations with former colleagues at Indiana University, especially Robert Orsi and Steven Weitzman. I benefited immensely from the comments that I received when presenting earlier drafts of the introduction at the Jewish Theological Seminary as well as to my colleagues in Judaic Studies at Brown University and the graduate students in the Department of Religious Studies. My colleague Muhammad Qasim Zaman helped me work through one important problem, and the trenchant comments of Shaul Magid and Charles Mathewes to yet another draft helped me sharpen my thoughts.

Several colleagues read individual chapters. Michah Gottlieb, Hindy Najman, and David Novak saved me from numerous mistakes. A series of conversations with Daniel Abrams was similarly helpful at a critical moment. It was my good fortune, as I began writing this book, to meet Moshe Rosman. Moshe not only read several chapters with extraordinary care, repeatedly correcting errors and pushing me to clarify and refine my arguments, but also has been a valuable dialogue partner. The extensive comments of the anonymous referees for Columbia University Press were extraordinarily useful. For all remaining errors and problems in this book, I have only myself to thank.

This book could not have been completed without the support that I have received from numerous institutions, especially the Department of Religious Studies, the Program in Judaic Studies, and the office of the Dean of the Faculty at Brown University. I completed this book while enjoying the hospitality of the Shalom Hartman Institute in Jerusalem; my thanks to Adiel Schremer for both his help with logistics as well as good conversation while I was there. Isaiah Gafni facilitated my access to resources at Hebrew University. The wonderful collection at the Jewish National and University Library at Hebrew University was invaluable; my thanks and apologies to the many colleagues in the Judaica Reading Room whom I regularly and frantically pestered.

The ideas in this book gestated in the classroom, and I thank the many students who graciously endured my attempts to make them comprehensible. Through their questions, blank stares, and spirited dissents, my students at the University of Virginia, Indiana University, and Brown University—whether they knew it or not—contributed actively to the development of this book. My teaching in the Me'ah program run by Hebrew College provided an additional opportunity for test-driving ideas and drafts, and the comments and critiques of my adult students led to yet another round of rewriting.

I am appreciative of the support of my sister, Vicki Satlow, who led me to Columbia University Press. I have been lucky to find in my editor, Wendy Lochner, an able and encouraging advocate for this project. My copyeditor, Susan Pensak, has been a pleasure to work with. Many individuals, and the institutions that they represent, generously and expeditiously responded to my requests for images and permissions: David Kraemer and David Sclar of the Jewish Theological Seminary of America; Robert Hill and Ruth Paige of Temple Emanu-El in Providence, in which is housed the Abraham and Natalie Percelay Museum; Elka Deitsch of Temple Emanu-El in New York; Rabbi Peretz Scheinerman of the Providence Hebrew Day School; and Tom Gilbert at AP/Accuweather.

The pleasures of teaching and research pale against those that my children give me. Daniel, Penina, and Jeremy enjoy seeing their names in print, and I am only too happy to be able to do this for them as a token of my love.

For reasons known only to her, my wife, Jacqueline, continues to put up with me. The least that I can do is dedicate this book to her.

CHRONOLOGY

CA. 1000 BCE	The united monarchies of David and Solomon
CA. 1000 BCE–586 BCE	Period of the Israelite monarchies
722 BCE	Fall of Northern Israelite kingdom
586 BCE	First Temple destroyed by Babylonians
CA. 515 BCE	Second Temple established
CA. 515 BCE–70 CE	Second Temple period
323 BCE	Death of Alexander the Great; beginning of Hellenistic period
CA. 200 BCE	Translation of the Bible into Greek (Septuagint), Antiochus III conquers Jerusalem
168 BCE–162 BCE	Defilement of Temple by Antiochus IV and Maccabean uprising
63 BCE	Entrance of Pompey, the Roman general, to Jerusalem
30 BCE–4 BCE	Rule of Herod
70 CE	Destruction of the Second Temple by the Romans
70–640	Rabbinic period
70–CA. 250:	Period of the *tannaim*
132–135	Bar Kokhba Revolt
CA. 220	Redaction of Mishnah
CA. 250–CA. 500	Period of the *amoraim*
CA. 400	Redaction of Palestinian Talmud
CA. 500	Redaction of Babylonian Talmud
CA. 550–1050	Geonic period
640	Muslim conquest of Near East
661–750	Umayyad dynasty

750–1258	'Abbasid dynasty
755	Abd al-Rahman (an Umayyad) declares his emirate in Cordoba (Andalusia)
928–942	Se'adyah ben Joseph serves as geon of Sura
929	Abd al-Rahman III declares himself caliph in Andalusia
1086	Rulers of Andalusia call on Almoravids for military aid
1135–1204	Life of Maimonides
1147	Almohads overthrow Almoravids
LATE 1200S	Authorship of Zohar
1492	Expulsion of Jews from Spain
1626–1676	Life of Sabbatai Zvi
1654	Portuguese expel Jews from Brazil; a boatload arrives in New Amsterdam
1656	Excommunication of Spinoza in Amsterdam
1698–1760	Life of Ba'al Shem Tov
1704	Foundation of Kahal Kadosh Shearith Israel, Spanish-Portuguese synagogue in New York
1729–1786	Life of Moses Mendelssohn
1817	Formation of the New Israelite Temple Association in Hamburg
1875	Hebrew Union College founded
1881–1914	Over two million Jews immigrate to the United States from Eastern Europe
1885	Pittsburgh Platform
1887	Foundation of the Jewish Theological Seminary of America
1894	Dreyfus affair
1897	First Zionist Congress
1898	Foundation of the Orthodox Union
1902	Foundation of Agudath Ha-Rabbanim
1948	Creation of the State of Israel
1967	Six-Day War

CREATING JUDAISM

INTRODUCTION

What is judaism? At first glance, the question itself appears either silly or arcane. Everybody, after all, has some working mental concept that they call "Judaism." Many committed Jews and Christians can provide a precise and articulate definition, drawing a clear bright line between what "counts" as Judaism and what does not. Many more people who cannot or will not provide such a definition nevertheless inherently know what Judaism is: "I know it when I see it," they might reply. For such people, to argue about a precise meaning is a mere academic exercise, an abstruse and meaningless game of words that in no way gets at Judaism's real meaning.

Maybe I am just drawn to silly and arcane questions, but the issue that lurks behind this bald and oversimplified question has been nagging me for more than a decade. Its roots, I suspect, are personal. I am a Jew who was raised in a largely nonobservant family that nevertheless emphasized the value of Jewish identity, of belonging to a people. The supplemental school of the Conservative synagogue that we joined shortly before my bar mitzvah reinforced this central message of Jewish identity, of *am yisrael*, the "People of Israel," basically a biological notion of an extended family, in which all Jews share the accomplishments, disappointments, and calamities of all other Jews. To a slightly alienated and awkward Jewish youth growing up in a very non-Jewish suburb of Boston, this was a powerful idea. It was also an idea that in college did not stand up very well to the experience of meeting actual Jews.

I was a fickle and eclectic Jew in college. I regularly attended religious services, but never the same one regularly. The Jews that I met in college were hardly representative of the American Jewish community, but even this narrow cross section was stunningly diverse. My struggle to integrate this enormous diversity with my notion of *am yisrael* was further complicated by my first trip to Israel. Riding in the middle of a planeload of Satmar Hasidim whose rebbe was making his first trip to the land of Israel—they refuse to recognize the sovereignty of the modern State of Israel, which they regard as a Jewish heresy—in short order I found myself learning Hebrew at Ofra, a settlement of religious Zionists on the West Bank. Soon after I returned to the United States the man who taught me Talmud at Ofra was imprisoned for bombing Palestinian officials. The United Jewish Appeal slogan at the time proclaimed "We Are One!" I, though, found myself increasingly wondering, "Are We One?" What actually links divergent Jewish communities?

The question, as I discovered soon after beginning my graduate studies in Jews and Judaism in antiquity, has a distinguished intellectual pedigree. I had come late to a question that has plagued scholars since the discovery in the early twentieth century of the synagogue mosaics from ancient Palestine and the wall paintings on the synagogue in Dura Europos, a Roman garrison town in Syria that was evacuated in the third century CE. As the archaeological evidence was making clear, the synagogues of late antiquity were richly decorated with representations of animals, humans, zodiacs, and even, perhaps, Helios and the God of Israel. Seen against rabbinic literature, which is virtually the only extant Jewish literature from late antiquity, these finds were jarring. Rabbinic literature, such as the Babylonian Talmud, leaves us totally unprepared to deal with synagogues ornately decorated with figurative representations.

In his massive, twelve-volume work, *Jewish Symbols in the Greco-Roman Period*, a Yale scholar, Erwin Ramsdell Goodenough, attempted to explain the discrepancy between the archaeological and literary data.[1] The archaeological evidence, he argued, is best interpreted against the thought of Philo (ca. 30 BCE–30 CE), a Jewish philosopher writing in Greek in Alexandria. Seen together, Philo and the archaeological evidence testify to a mystical, astral Judaism. This mystical Judaism, whose adherents sought direct experience of God, is to be contrasted with the staid Judaism of the Rabbis, with their emphasis on law and Torah as mediating a Jew's contact with the divine.

Goodenough, it turned out, was wrong. For a number of reasons, his neat division between astral and rabbinic Judaism cannot be sustained. His work, though, brilliantly opened up the field both by heightening awareness of what had until his time been an unproblematic concept, Judaism, and by putting the issue of Jewish diversity squarely on the scholarly table.

Goodenough's insistence that in antiquity there were two types of Judaism forced scholars to confront the assumptions that inform their use of the category Judaism. The word itself is surprisingly ill-attested in antiquity and first appears in Hebrew (as *yahadut*) only in the Middle Ages. Its origin appears to have been Greek. The author or editor of 2 Maccabees, a history of the Maccabean revolt (which occurred ca. 165 BCE) that was written in Greek and then condensed around 100 BCE, coined the word. For this writer, Judaism stood in opposition to Hellenism as the true religion of Israel. It was, above all, a *normative* definition, to be held by a community in order to define itself against other "outside" groups, customs, and beliefs. It is an insider's definition, meant to differentiate "us" not only from "them" but even from different groups of "us." Some groups of Jews thus become true defenders of "Judaism," against not only some outside enemy but even other Jews who in some way are seen as attacking the authentic religion.

This earliest understanding of Judaism, which continues to some extent to today, ultimately is an essentialist one. Essentialist definitions assert that there is an essence to the thing, usually marked by a set of defining characteristics. This might be a set of beliefs or practices or a supernatural essence. Without this essence—whatever it is—it is no longer considered Judaism. Essentialist definitions usually have a normative dimension. They are created and used by a community to define itself and thus also to set its boundaries.

The practice of defining Judaism both normatively and essentially has had a remarkable staying power. Paul, himself a Jew, turned this normative definition on its head. Judaism indeed had an essence, but that essence was the static, dead "law" against which Christianity would come to define itself as a religion of the spirit. In these formulations, Judaism became a Christian theological category that Christians could use for their own self-definition: We are not Jews.

The term *Judaism* never shed this theological baggage. As used commonly and academically in nineteenth-century Germany, there was always a defining essence to Judaism. Judaism had an essential core, a feature without which it was no longer Judaism. Only true Judaism contains that essential core; groups that claim to practice Judaism, but that appear to an outside observer to lack the essential characteristic of Judaism, can now safely be characterized as "inauthentic," "heretical," or simply not Jewish. This highlights both the normative nature of essentialist definitions as well as the importance of perspective. Those Jews that one essentialist definition of Judaism might classify as heretics rarely see themselves as anything but authentic.

Essentialist and normative definitions are useful for communal self-definition. Communities, of course, regularly define themselves in whatever manner they see fit. One Jewish group that wants to define itself against both non-Jews and other, competing Jewish groups will naturally try to cast itself as more "authentic." It will draw upon history to create a definition of Judaism to which it is the true heir and other claimants are not. Judaism's essence, not very coincidentally, becomes identical with that of the particular claimant. Such essentialist self-definitions help to reinforce group cohesion by giving its members an opportunity to unite as participants in some transcendent essence.

As good as they are for the creation and maintenance of group boundaries, essentialist definitions of Judaism have more limited usefulness outside the specific groups that use them. They are interesting to study as "first-order" definitions, the ways in which specific groups define themselves, but they fail to explain anything "real" about Judaism. Essentialist definitions of Judaism can never *explain* or account for the diversity of Jewish religious life, both today and through history. Those forms of Jewish life, practice, and belief that are thought to be in accord with the essentialist definition are the only data that are considered relevant, thus reinforcing the original definition. Such definitions of all religious traditions create circles that tend to put an objective academic imprimatur on one subgroup's self-definition.

The problem, as the study of Judaism in antiquity has made clear in the wake of Goodenough's opus, is that there were many Jewish subgroups, and that they were frequently at odds with each other. Until Goodenough, scholars almost uncritically considered the Judaism of antiquity to be that of the Pharisees, as imaginatively reconstructed by modern scholars. Goodenough forced scholars to take contemporary "renegade" and "marginal" Jewish groups more seriously, especially the group documented by the Dead Sea scrolls, which were just beginning to be published. The cumulative effect of this scholarly activity was to decenter the Pharisees; they did not represent "mainstream" Judaism, but rather were just one of many Jewish groups (albeit one that at certain times may have had more influence than others) competing for adherents until the slow rise of the Rabbis that began after the destruction of the Second Temple in 70 CE. Jacob Neusner, a professor then at Brown University, saw such diversity in this period that he tended to speak of the "Judaisms" of antiquity rather than of a single Judaism.

The term *Judaisms* seems to solve the problem created by *Judaism*. It implicitly assumes that there are many Judaisms, each one of which has integrity in its own right, thus rejecting a single normative definition. *Judaisms* became appealing to some scholars of modern Judaism, who use it to describe the enormous variety of modern and contemporary Jewish life. Jewish thinkers throughout history have offered theological positions that are at times mutually exclusive, and Jewish communities have at times differed so fundamentally from each other in practice that their members would not eat in the houses of, or marry, members of other Jewish groups. How can all of these groups, claiming to be Jewish, really constitute a single religious tradition? *Judaisms* usefully shifts our focus from essentialist definitions that classify some forms of Jewish life as more authentic than others to the tremendous diversity of Jewish practice and belief.

But *Judaisms* actually does not solve anything. Remarkably, and despite its common use by scholars, there is little extensive scholarly defense of the term; it has been used, but only thinly explained or argued. If *Judaism* suffers from its neglect of diversity, *Judaisms* neglects the aspect of unity. However diverse, Jewish religious communities understand themselves to be part of the same "tradition," and often recognize (sometimes reluctantly) some legitimacy to the claims of other Jewish communities. Even when wide theological or ritual gulfs separate Jewish communities, there often remain social relations, justified under the principle of *am yisrael*. There is a border, however fuzzy it might sometimes be, between religious communities that identify themselves as Jewish and those that see themselves as Muslim, Christian, or Hindu. Like Goodenough's pioneering work, *Judaisms* raises awareness to a problem without providing a clear solution to it.

The debate between *Judaism* and *Judaisms* is largely a matter of semantic emphasis, but points to a much more interesting and complex problem. How are we, not necessarily as participants within a religious community but as human beings who seek to understand and learn something from and about religion, to explain the enormous diversity of Jewish religious communities—or, for that matter, any group of religious communities—without losing sight of their unity?

This was the question that was very much on my mind when, a year out of graduate school, I was assigned to teach "Introduction to Judaism." I had never taken such a course in college and was at first overwhelmed by the quantity of the material that I felt I needed to cram into the semester. How could I possibly cover everything? This concern, however, soon gave way to the more pressing intellectual one: What is "Judaism"? What is the subject matter of such a course? The common textbooks turned out to be little help. Despite the wide scholarly recognition of the deficiencies of a unitary approach to Judaism, most modern discussions of Judaism tend to stay closely in line with the older, canonical model: Judaism traces a straight line from the Bible to the Pharisees to the Rabbis to their heirs. Judaism, in this model, is the textual tradition of the Rabbis, sometimes called "rabbinic Judaism."

This standard approach to the study of Judaism is to make exactly this division, between the "normative" tradition of rabbinic Judaism and all others. It assumes there is a single normative Judaism that unfolds like an independent living organism. It also requires some parochial preconceptions about what is truly "Jewish." Thus, Reform Jews might reject a congregation of humanistic Jews—a community that identifies itself as a Jewish religious community and yet explicitly rejects the existence of God—as inauthentic, just as some Orthodox Jews, especially in Israel, have rejected Reform Judaism—which does not accept Jewish law, or *halakhah*, as binding on all Jews—as an authentic expression of Judaism.

There is, however, another way to look at Judaism that avoids the inherent parochialism of first-order definitions. This book will argue for a definition of Judaism that can better account both for its immense diversity and its unifying features. More important, it will show how changing the way we approach the "problem" of Judaism can give us a much richer and deeper understanding of Jewish religious life and tradition.

Judaism, I will argue, is best seen not as a single organismlike tradition but as a family of traditions. Ludwig Wittgenstein, a twentieth-century philosopher, advanced the idea of "familial resemblance." He noted that family members can resemble each other in a variety of ways or not at all. I might have my mother's nose, and my mother might have her mother's chin, but I might not look at all like my grandmother. Wittgenstein is interested in the nature of this relationship for philosophical reasons, but it can profitably be applied to religion. Jonathan Z. Smith, a professor of religion at the University of Chicago, put the problem somewhat differently but, I think, drove at the same point when he argued for a polythetic definition of early Judaism (and, by extension, other religious traditions).[2] Polythetic definitions differ from essentialist ones in that they focus on sets of overlapping characteristics. Out of a list of characteristics that all members of a class might share, there will be large overlaps of shared characteristics, but some members will have nothing in common with others. There is no single shared component that is essential to a member's inclusion.

Biological metaphors for religion should not be pushed too far. Judaism is not a tangible living thing that inexorably unfolds over time. Judaism has no genes; it is the creation and recreation of human beings working in history. Each community of Jews creates its Judaism anew, reading and understanding their traditions through their own peculiar and historically specific worldviews.

Judaism, then, has no history. Jewish communities have local histories (I will leave it to the historians to debate whether *Jewish history* is a term that has meaning), and some patterns of thought and tradition have intellectual histories. Because Judaism, however, is not a single phenomenon that can be captured in a single, predominant narrative, it is misleading to talk of the "history of Judaism." Judaism, as a whole, does not have a story; any master narrative obscures the dynamic process by which communities continually recreate their Judaism. Indeed, even those elements of Judaism that can be traced historically infrequently develop in any kind of linear way. Jewish communities do not typically adhere piously to the ideas and rituals of the generations immediately before them, particularly when they live in different social and cultural traditions. Rather, they often skip back to previous texts and rituals in order to lend authority to practices that they find more concordant with their own society. A history of Judaism creates a history where none truly existed, drawing a straight line through a tangled web and thus almost arbitrarily declaring some things central to its story and others marginal.

Judaism's diversity is easier to explain than its unity. Although there may not be a singular tradition called Judaism, not every religious community can be called Jewish. This, of course, is obvious: Roman Catholics and Muslims do not identify themselves as practitioners of Judaism, and any definition that attempts to consider them as Jews against their will is ill-advised. More complex are the cases of contested self-identification, in which a group considers itself to be a Jewish community when other Jewish groups reject them. What of Messianic Jews (those who claim to be Jewish believers that Jesus was the messiah) or Black Hebrews? Without making normative judgments based on unjustified essentialist assumptions of what is to "count" as evidence for "authentic" Judaism, is it possible to explain the overlapping characteristics that unite these different religious communities into "Judaism"?

The fundamental argument of this book is that Judaism can be charted, polythetically, onto three maps. Here I use another metaphor drawn from Jonathan Z. Smith. A "map" is a scholarly, or second-order, rendering of a territory; it is a representation. Essentialist and normative definitions are appealing; they can usually be stated in just a few sentences, and the normative question they seek to answer—Does it or does it not "count" as Judaism?—is immediate. Maps are messier and the question that they seek to answer is inherently different. This book makes no normative claims about what is or should be considered Judaism by a religious community. Rather, its goal is to create and apply a non-normative model of Judaism that might help us to better understand how Jewish communities throughout history have been so diverse and yet considered themselves to be members of the same family.

The three maps onto which Judaism can be plotted are Israel, textual tradition, and religious practice. By Israel I refer to self-identity, the act of identifying as a member of *am yisrael* and the particular self-understanding of what that identification means. All groups that self-identify as Jews "count," and, however much other Jewish communities contest their identity, their own self-characterization puts them on the map. These communities identify themselves as Jews, locating themselves (or not) within a sacred narrative and a bloodline. The objective truth of this claim is less important in this case than the community's self-perception; being part of Israel begins with the claim to be, not with some outsider judging whether that claim is correct. At the same time, though, Jewish self-perception is hardly consistent or static. Different communities, and their individual members, use different strategies for identifying as Jews.

The second map charts the communities' canonical texts. Jewish communities throughout history have tended to ascribe authority of some type to a bounded and largely similar set of texts. Nearly every community from late antiquity to the present that identifies itself as Jewish has held in high regard the Hebrew Bible and the rabbinic textual tradition, although the precise nature of that regard and of the authority given to these texts is complex, contested, and varies from community to community. These texts constitute an ongoing dialogue that has been remarkably consistent, providing a set of resources upon which Jewish communities have drawn in order to authorize their understandings of Judaism.

Texts, however, are not the only vehicles of tradition. Jewish communities also transmit religious practices, some of which coexist uneasily with the textual tradition. On the one hand, by absorbing traditional practices and at times converting these ad hoc practices into scripted and meaningful rituals, rabbinic texts preserve them for later generations; even when the practices themselves fall out of use, later communities can recover them from the texts. Yet, on the other hand, these texts tend to structure the practices and ascribe meanings to them that do not always survive the test of time, and frequently a practice breaks from the texts that attempt to ritualize and interpret it.

In the following pages I flesh out and illustrate this polythetic model. It is worth noting, though, how this approach differs from the conventional one. Typically, Judaism is described in terms of its core beliefs and normative practices. This focus on belief arose from modern Western notions of "religion" that locate the value and function of religion in meaning and intention. The modern anthropologist Clifford Geertz drew upon this tradition when he offered his highly influential definition of religion as a system of meaning.[3] In this book the subordination of belief to tradition (as constituted by texts and practices) is deliberate, a consequence of a nonessentialist approach. Beliefs, of course, are important. But, I suggest, a more fruitful way to get at them is to mine the range of possibilities presented by the canon. I understand tradition as a wide and sprawling conversation that nevertheless does have some boundaries. When a community constructs its beliefs, it draws selectively on this tradition, with results that differ widely from other Jewish religious communities. By sharing certain conceptual categories (for example, God, Torah, and Israel) most Jewish communities find themselves in the same conversation, but the move from the conceptual categories to more specific beliefs is by no means uniform, linear, or predictable.

To chart a community's Judaism, then, requires sensitivity to how a specific community of Jews, embedded in its own social, economic, and cultural context, makes sense of its tradition. It means never to lose sight of the fact that "Judaism" is an abstract noun. Jews, not Judaism, believe and do things. Moreover, even within the twin constraints of historical circumstances and the deep, shared, but ultimately humanly constructed structures of meaning that appear natural to a given society, individuals have agency; they function not only in religious communities but also as idiosyncratic individuals. Any rich account of Judaism must balance the ways in which tradition might constrain a community with the ways in which a community and the individuals within it use tradition as a resource. This is a process that might be called negotiation, referring to the ways that Jews negotiate their traditions within their unique historical contexts.

To assert a Jewish identity is to locate oneself within the sacred history of the people Israel. To be a Jew is to make, primarily, a historical claim. It is to identify with a narrative (albeit one that different communities tell differently) that extends back to Abraham, "our father," and that is linked to God's covenant. It is to enter, to use Bennedict Anderson's felicitous phrase, an "imagined community," held together by a gripping narrative of origins that succeeds not only in providing a coherent past, but one that also generates value and meaning.[4]

As an objective account of the past, the Torah makes poor history. As a historical narrative, however, it brilliantly forges a national identity. Like many (or most?) stories of historical origins, it creates a common past rooted in struggle. To subscribe to this history is to identify with a distinctive people forged in the slave pits and harsh desert. Unlike many historical narratives, though, it also identifies the nation with a biological family. Because all sprung from a common ancestor, the people Israel are bound by blood. And if that was not enough, the Torah goes on to separate this people not only by history and biology but also by destiny: covenanted to God.

Later Jewish readers emphasized different aspects of this narrative. Following the historiographical explosion and vibrant romantic nationalism that permeated German culture in general, many nineteenth-century German Jews emphasized national history as a mode of identity. The earliest believers of Jesus deemphasized biology and used God's covenant with Israel as their primary mode of Jewish identity, whereas Judah Halevi promoted an almost racist ideology. Modernity has brought several other modes of Jewish identity, from Zionism to "Yiddishkeit," whether understood religiously or culturally.

Being "Jewish" is not simply a legal and technical matter. Communities become "Jewish" first and foremost because they say they are; they buy in to some model or story that links them to past and present Jews. Jewish communities may or may not accept the claims of "Jewishness" of other groups, but all draw ultimately on similar sources.

Those sources make up *tradition*. In Islamic thought, Judaism (like Christianity) is considered a "religion of the book" because Israel is thought to have received an authentic, divine revelation and recorded it in a book (the Bible) that they continue to revere. According to some Muslims, the Hebrew Bible is corrupt; the Jews did not faithfully guard what was revealed to them. Nevertheless, according to this line of thinking, the Jews earn credit (and, in fact, a somewhat privileged political position) for preserving this (albeit corrupted) record of revelation. This early Muslim evaluation of Judaism partially echoes earlier Greek and Roman evaluations, many of which grudgingly admire Judaism for the antiquity of its traditions, however peculiar they sometimes appear. It also parallels contemporary Christian views of Judaism that tended to see Judaism as stuck in the Old Testament, stubbornly and anachronistically hanging on to the literal meaning of a book and covenant that has been superseded by the death of Christ. The common belief today that Judaism is "the religion of the Bible" originated in these theological assumptions.

The problem is that Judaism cannot in any meaningful sense be called "the religion of the Bible." One need only read the Bible and then observe any living Jewish community to realize this. The Torah clearly and at length commands animal sacrifice; no Jewish group today sacrifices. On the Sabbath, many Jews go to synagogues to pray and listen to the reading of the Torah, but the Bible does not mention a synagogue and does not prescribe regular prayer or reading of the Torah. Jews who keep kosher today refrain from eating milk and meat products together, or even from cooking the one in pots that have been used for the other; the Bible contains only a cryptic command (thrice repeated) that one should not eat a kid in its mother's milk. The Bible is certainly important in Judaism, but only *as it is read through the lens of a textual tradition.*

Beginning with the Hebrew Bible itself, one of the defining characteristics of the sacred books of the Jews is that they build upon and enter into conversations with each other. The primary literary legacy of the Rabbis of antiquity, the Babylonian Talmud, is a massive combination of biblical commentaries, random stories and sharp argumentation, all presented as "Torah," and now understood widely as the content of God's revelation. Nearly every Jewish book that later Jewish communities accepted as "sacred" or "canonical" draws on both the Bible and the Talmud. For instance, in his twelfth-century code of law, the *Mishneh Torah*, Maimonides sought to strip the Talmud of all but its essence, which he saw as its legal rulings. The Zohar is incomprehensible without the Bible and the earlier rabbinic traditions; it is organized as a commentary on the former and draws liberally on the latter. Biblical commentators, who might be promoting radically new ideas, nevertheless claim authority for these ideas from earlier books. Tradition gradually accretes.

A comparison with Protestant movements sharpens the distinctiveness of Jewish tradition. In many Protestant denominations, especially those of the "low church," tradition does not hold a privileged place. Rather, only the Holy Spirit is thought to mediate between the individual and the Bible. Faith alone, scripture alone, as Martin Luther declared. An individual's direct confrontation with the New Testament is the path to connecting to the divine. At best, tradition here is irrelevant; at worst, it perverts that unmediated experience. This notion, incidentally, is the root of many modern understandings of religion, which see religion (or "spirituality") as innate and individual.[5]

This Protestant understanding contrasts starkly with the Jewish notion of tradition. For almost every Jewish community throughout history, "faith alone, scripture alone" is not nearly enough. Far from locating "spirituality" in the individual, many expressions of Judaism locate it in the community. The formation of tradition is, after all, a communal process. Unlike Roman Catholicism, Judaism has no central authority. Books enter into the tradition because many different communities accept them. The Babylonian Talmud became authoritative only because many Jewish communities accepted it as such. Some accepted the *Mishneh Torah* as authoritative shortly after it was issued, but the *Shulhan Arukh*, a sixteenth-century code of law, displaced it. Today very few Jewish communities (primarily Jews from Yemen) regard the *Mishneh Torah* as legally authoritative, but many Jews nevertheless study it as an important, sacred text.

As the example of the *Mishneh Torah* illustrates, traditional texts are not necessarily authoritative texts. Some Jewish communities regard the Zohar with utmost sanctity, while other communities loathe it. From the Middle Ages on, most Jewish communities hold the Babylonian Talmud in high regard, though not all consider it to be authoritative in all matters. Today, some Jewish communities punctiliously adhere to the *Shulhan Arukh*, but many Jews disregard it. Reform Judaism gives to tradition a voice, but not a veto—tradition must be taken seriously, but it never overrides the individual's conscience.

Textual tradition, then, is just barely powerful enough to hold together the diversity of Judaism, the centrifugal force that prevents the many different forms of Jewish religious expression from each flying off as independent religions. The willingness of Jewish communities to regard the same or similar books as "sacred," to take them seriously if not fully agreeing on their authority, links them. The textual tradition defines, as Talal Asad, a scholar of religion, might say, a "conversation."[6] These texts connect to and build upon each other, taking up similar sets of issues. In this sense, "tradition" is not automatically authoritative—it constitutes an organically growing engagement with the past.

Textual traditions are human products, created not only in reference to previous sacred books but also to the present in which those books are read. The Babylonian Talmud is a prolonged engagement with earlier Jewish traditions, but only as read by the Rabbis of Babylonia; there is nothing culturally or religiously "pure" about it. Maimonides's philosophical writings are explicitly in dialogue with Greek, Roman, and Islamic philosophy, while the Zohar might implicitly engage Christianity. Previous texts are always read through a contemporary lens, thus bringing these earlier texts into a continuing dialogue.

Focusing on textual tradition, however, can obscure the power of practice. In *Women as Ritual Experts*, Susan Sered tells the story of a group of older, illiterate Kurdistani women who in the weeks before Passover fastidiously sorted through the rice that they would use for the holiday grain by grain, seven times over. Just as they ignored the rabbis urging them to wash their hands before eating bread, so too they ignored their insistence that this sorting was unnecessary.[7] For these women, the ritual itself, passed down from their mothers, was more important than any textually based norm.

The latest National Jewish Population studies tell a similar story. A large percentage of those who identify themselves as Jews attend a seder on Passover and light the menorah on Hannukah.[0] They frequently do this with little knowledge of Jewish textual traditions; they would be mystified by "traditional" interpretations and norms of the ritual. In both of these examples the rituals seem to float independently of text. Students in my classes frequently and without a hint of doubt assert the "meaning" of a Jewish ritual although such an interpretation of the ritual is nowhere found in traditional Jewish texts.

According to Haym Soloveitchik, the independent force of ritual should not surprise us.[9] The authority of text within Jewish communities has been steadily increasing throughout modernity, exploding in contemporary America (especially within the Orthodox and Conservative communities). But this has not always been the case, nor is it even the case in all Jewish communities. In many communities, practices survived independent of, or existed even prior to, the texts that explain and regulate them. The practices move down through the generations, and their practitioners search for new meanings to make them relevant.

In fact, the very reason that many of these rituals have survived is precisely because they are underdetermined. They have no inherent meaning; they exist in a dynamic intertextual world in which Jews link them to other rituals, symbols, and texts to create transient meanings. Indeed, the more firmly linked a ritual is to a particular meaning, frequently the less successful it is. For this reason, most of the many Jewish holidays that commemorate specific historical events (e.g., creation of the Septuagint or specific catastrophes in the Middle Ages) failed to persist, as did those rituals too tightly connected to specific and changing assumptions (e.g., the geonic blessing over the bloodied sheet after a marriage). Yet many underdetermined practices, like the Jewish food laws (*kashrut*), persist even in a modern world in which they would seemingly be incompatible.[10]

To focus on "tradition" rather than "beliefs" does not suggest that belief is unimportant, but only that in anything other than a very broad sense specific beliefs are not essential to a notion of Judaism. It is, for example, relatively uncontroversial to assert that Judaism is "monotheistic," but there is no definition of monotheism that would have been agreeable to all Jewish communities. Such variation is only multiplied on the level of the individuals even within a particular Jewish community; two neighbors who observe kashrut may have radically different reasons for doing so.

Beliefs, whether of a community or an individual, frequently emerge from a sincere engagement with tradition within an embedded historical context. But the Jewish textual and ritual traditions are rich and multivocal; they can frequently be mined with equal effectiveness to arrive at mutually exclusive positions. Thus, a statement that begins "Judaism believes . . . " is doubly flawed: It assigns agency to Judaism rather than Jews, and it implies a single correct position when one can rarely be found either in traditional resources or, in fact, in real Jewish communities.

While there may not be specific beliefs to be found in all Jewish communities and texts at all times, there is a widely shared cluster of concepts that continually reappear in what I have been calling the "conversation" shaped by tradition. The German Jewish thinker Franz Rosenzweig (1886–1929) crisply identified these concepts as God, Torah, Israel, Creation, Revelation, and Redemption. These concepts are found as early as the Hebrew Bible and still remain very much a part of modern Jewish thought. Most Jewish communities might agree that there is one God, but that leaves open to debate everything from how to define "one" to how to define "God" to the nature of that "one God." That is, there can be wide and vigorous disagreement within a conversation while at the same time being engaged in the same conversation. The boundaries of tradition might be broad, but they do exist. Messianic Jews and Black Hebrews have, from a non-normative perspective, every right to call themselves "Israel," but through their rejection of the postbiblical Jewish literature they have largely ceased to engage in the same conversation as other Jewish communities. Similarly, secular and humanistic Jews, with their rejection of God, puts them outside the limits of the conversation as defined by the tradition.

Throughout this book I return to the ways in which different Jewish communities, both today and throughout history, have formed and justified their distinctive beliefs. What are the bounds of this shared conversation, and how and why does a Jewish community formulate its response to it? What emerges from this approach is not a set of the "essential beliefs" of Judaism, but yet another conceptual map on which we can plot a range of different and yet all "authentically" Jewish responses.

For example, the Hebrew Bible offers several answers to the nagging problem of theodicy, God's justice. The problem is that it is often hard to reconcile the idea of a just and all-powerful God with the fact of evil in the world. One biblical view is unnuanced: people get what they deserve and all that happens in the world must be just, for it reflects the will of God. The biblical prophets who sought to explain the destruction of the First Temple in 586 BCE commonly adopted this view. This event, in their eyes, was no ordinary tragedy. The Temple in Jerusalem was the very house of God—how could God allow its destruction? They answered by asserting Israel's sinfulness, for which God punished them by sending the Babylonians against them. But, for another biblical author, this line of argument was unsatisfactory. The author of Job threw up his hands at the problem, saying the presence of evil in the world must be just, for it is from God, but the explanation of this justice is a mystery. The author of Ecclesiastes offers yet another alternative: God is not involved with the petty details of human lives.

Throughout their history, the Jews have had many occasions to test these responses. The self-styled Hasidim, a group of ascetic Jews in medieval Germany (to be distinguished from the Eastern Europeans in the eighteenth and nineteenth centuries who appropriated this title), so fully embraced the idea of evil as just punishment that they engaged in harsh self-punishments to cleanse themselves of sin. The Rabbis of antiquity more or less subscribed to the idea that human misfortunes result justly from human sin, but this led them into a quandary regarding the related problem of human free will: If God is both omniscient and involved with the just punishment of individuals, do humans really have free will? If they don't, how can they justly be punished for an action about which they had no choice?

After the Holocaust, the issue of theodicy has become central to modern Jewish theology. Here again there are a wide range of answers, from the traditional ("the Jews brought it upon themselves because they assimilated") to the radical denial of God's historical involvement with Israel or in human affairs at all.

Theodicy and free will are just two theological themes that run through this book. Other themes include the nature of God; the concept of Israel as both a chosen, or covenanted, people and as a land promised in the Bible to Abraham and his descendents; revelation and the authority of the commandments; and redemption and afterlife.

Theology offers one kind of explanatory discourse about religion. Traditionally practiced, it creates coherent intellectual systems for faith communities. But theology is not the only means of creating religious meaning. For the Rabbis and most later forms of Judaism, physical actions rather than belief answer the questions "What does God want from me?" and "How am I to behave according to God's will?" In many forms of Judaism these questions are far more important than theological ones. Religious practice and theology, however, are best seen as complementary. Real Jewish communities combine theological positions and religious practices in ways that are both unexpected and yet seem, to them, to be coherent. Clearly, different Jewish communities put these pieces together differently, arriving at unique and distinctive systems of meaning, one tied to the next through a family resemblance.

Within the narrow circles of the academic study of religion, it is hardly necessary to justify a non-normative approach to the study of religion. As I have discovered in my classes and synagogue, though, the academy has done an exceptionally poor job of making this case outside of its walls. Many turn to the study of religion to gain insight into the ultimate questions of the human condition: Is there a supernatural force? What is the meaning of life, and what defines a life well-led? Is there life after death? These questions are outside the purview of a non-normative and nonessentialist approach to a religion. What good is it, then? By approaching religion with the a priori presumption that if there is nothing divine in it, am I not both denigrating religion and even making it irrelevant? Why should a nonacademic care about a polythetic approach to Judaism or, for that matter, any other religion?

For those accustomed to seeing religion as either reflecting some kind of divine and ultimate truth or an interior and subjective experience (e.g., "spirituality") that lies beyond critical analysis, the approach that I use in this book might seem jarring. Throughout this book I presume that religion is a human creation and thus subject to the same critical scrutiny as any other human phenomenon. Humanistic and social scientific approaches can thus profitably be brought to bear on religion; neither the sacred authority that some ascribe to it nor a sense of its subjectivity exempt it from analysis.

A *presumption* that religion is a human creation, though, is not an *assertion* of the absolute truth of this claim. Nor is such an assertion necessary to profitably engage the arguments of this book. To engage religion critically is not to deny the possibility that it truly does reflect some divine reality. This book remains agnostic on this point; it works outward from a premise but makes no absolute truth claims about that premise. My goal is not to challenge faith commitments but, by approaching the same set of material from a different perspective, to more deeply enrich our appreciation of the complex role that religion, specifically Judaism, continues to play in human society.

The idea that religion is an entirely individual choice, that spirituality can exist and be shaped by individuals outside communal institutions, is an entirely contemporary understanding. Deeply religious thinkers throughout history have critically reflected on their own traditions, rejecting the notion that religion lies in some protected zone impervious to scrutiny. Indeed, the modern university system arose from the desire to properly train clergy.

The appreciation of religion enabled by this approach can take a variety of forms. By understanding religion as being shaped and acted upon by human agents, rather than as inexorably unfolding as part of some predetermined divine plan, we can better understand the vital role that religion has played in history. I refer here not to the overly simplistic Marxist idea that religion is a tool to oppress the weak (although the issue of power and economics must always be taken into account), but to the more complex interaction between religious traditions and real people who not only mold but who are also shaped by their serious engagement with their traditions. Just as religion must take history into account, so too must history reckon with religion.

More important, perhaps, is the way in which this perspective can liberate us from the idea that religious traditions offer only simplistic answers that demand unwavering faith. Religious traditions can instead be seen as a testament to the astoundingly diverse and creative ways that human beings have responded to the challenges of being human. They can thus provide resources for those today who struggle with the same or similar problems. We wrestle with the same problems as our ancient ancestors. We too ask how we might live our lives in the best way possible, deal with interminable suffering, explain the death of a child. Religious traditions reflect sustained and serious attempts to answer these questions, and, while we might ultimately reject many of these answers and the premises upon which they are based, it seems to me foolish to ignore them. Religious traditions provide resources that can be engaged, analyzed, critiqued, and used even by those of different religions or none at all.

While the primary purpose of this book is to offer a fresh perspective on Judaism, it is by no means intended only for Jews. The goal of this book is neither to offer a normative definition of Judaism for Jews nor a defense of Judaism to non-Jews. It is meant not to challenge one's faith but to expand intellectual limits, helping us to see yet another side to religion. Although in the conclusion I will briefly discuss some of the implications of this model of Judaism, my hope is that this book will provide a set of intellectual resources that may be of use to us all as we daily confront the joys and challenges inherent in being human.

This book offers a series of snapshots of Judaism throughout time. Although arranged roughly chronologically, these snapshots do not constitute a narrative. Indeed, one of the arguments of the book is that Judaism has no history, although Jews themselves as well as the rabbinic textual tradition does. The scope and scale of this book have forced me to ignore, or only allude to, many large and fascinating Jewish communities such as those in medieval and contemporary Western Europe, in Turkey and most of the Middle East, and in modern Central and South America. My neglect of these communities is not meant in any way to marginalize them. The potential scope of a book like this is enormous, and the limits of space, time, and my own competence have forced me to make several painful and at times almost arbitrary decisions of coverage.

Each chapter focuses on a specific Jewish community, its history, and, most important, how it defines its Judaism. For each community, then, I pay special attention to the issue of self-identity (i.e., how it defines itself as "Israel"), the relationship to (or formation of) the biblical and rabbinic textual tradition as refracted through its own specific historical circumstances, and its religious practices, whether in accord or not with the rabbinic traditions that were thought to govern them. Throughout each chapter I especially highlight the processes by which each community molds the raw stuff of tradition to its own needs (and sometimes thereby even adding to that tradition) as well as the fundamentally human issues with which it grappled.

The next chapter, "Promised Lands," offers an account of Judaism in the United States and Israel. Both countries host stunningly diverse Jewish communities. Yet, despite the clear ideological and institutionalized differences between these communities, I argue that one can really speak of "American Judaism" and "Israeli Judaism" as distinctive religious families. Whereas Judaism in America, in all of its astounding variety, has been decisively shaped by American culture and society, Judaism in Israel is impossible to understand without taking into account the role of the state and the effects of political power. By also exploring the complexity of the gaps between institutionalized Judaism and Judaism as it is actually practiced, this chapter develops a lens through which the later chapters can be viewed.

Chapter 2, "Creating Judaism," jumps back to the period of the ancient Israelites and the formation of the Hebrew Bible. Although the religion described in the Hebrew Bible looks little like Judaism as it would develop later, the Hebrew Bible—known to Jews as a sacred text that would acquire the name *Tanak*, an acronym for its three parts—is a foundational document that initiates the "conversation" into which all later Jewish canonical texts would join. This chapter tells the story of the development of the Hebrew Bible into the form in which it now exists and explores the significance of this development.

During the "Second Temple period" (ca. 515 BCE–70 CE) Jews increasingly turned to the Hebrew Bible as a source of authority, even as they drew from it very different conclusions. Chapter 3, "Between Athens and Jerusalem," discusses the earliest Jewish engagements with the Hebrew Bible, occurring both within and outside the Land of Israel. How did the Hebrew Bible look through the lens of Hellenism, the complex and amorphous cultural and social outlook that permeated the Near East from the time of Alexander's conquest in 332 BCE? This chapter looks especially at the Judaism that wasn't, the many interpretations and texts that never made it into the Jewish canon.

Due to the critical role played by the Rabbis (ca. 70 CE–640 CE), I devote three chapters to drawing out their social and historical context, their literary heritage, their conceptual world, and their religious practices. Almost all forms of Judaism after antiquity spring from, or take part in a dialogue with, the Rabbis. "The Rabbis" (chapter 4) tells of the creation and role of these teachers in Jewish society after the destruction of the Temple and their often strained status within that society. The Rabbis left a large and innovative literary legacy, and this chapter discusses the nature of it. The next two chapters deal more with the content of this literature. Chapter 5, "Rabbinic Concepts" argues that the Rabbis never developed a theology, either in the sense of a coherent system or a set of doctrines. Instead, they organically developed conceptual maps that outline ranges of theological options—this approach would be critical for the ability of later Jewish communities to draw upon and make meaningful rabbinic ideas. In chapter 6, "Mitzvot," I outline the "commandments." Performance of these *mitzvot*, according to the Rabbis, brings one closer to the presence of God. My focus in this chapter is on both the tenuous nature between the mitzvot and their textual justifications as well as on the ways in which the mitzvot can function to create "sacred time."

The "victory" of the Rabbis was in no way assured in their lifetimes. It was primarily through the promotion of the Babylonian Talmud by the Geonim, rabbinic scholars who lived in Iraq from around 800–1100 CE, that the legacy of the Rabbis spread and gained authority within the wider Jewish community. Chapter 7, "The Rise of Reason," traces the geonic engagement not only with the "rabbinic project" but also with the Islamic culture in which they lived. No less than their opponents, the Karaites, they applied Islamic modes of thinking to their tradition.

The Karaites and Geonim were not the only Jews who saw their tradition through an Islamic lens. The Jews of Spain, living in what nineteenth-century German Jews valorized as the "Golden Age," flourished intellectually. Chapter 8, "From Moses to Moses," discusses the Jewish world that produced Maimonides and the ways in which Maimonides's own understanding of Judaism grew out of that world.

If Maimonides sought deeper knowledge of God, the Jewish mystics who responded to him sought to directly experience the divine. "Seeing God," chapter 9, explores the medieval Jewish kabbalists, especially their major literary production, the Zohar, and its ideas. The Zohar is at once deeply traditional, drawing on the Hebrew Bible and virtually every corner of the rabbinic tradition, and radically innovative. The Zohar's mystical ideas would become an important resource for later Jews.

Chapter 10, "East and West," focuses on the nineteenth century, in both Western and Eastern Europe. Jewish communities in these two areas were forced to confront similar conditions of modernity, although they formulated distinct responses. The communities of Western Europe invented the concept of Judaism as we usually use it today, standing for a coherent system of belief and practice that contains an essence. That society also gave birth to ideology within Judaism that would lead to the Jewish religious movements as they are known today. Ideologies never fully developed in Eastern Europe, which instead formed factions based on stances toward the newly emerging Hasidic movement. This chapter brings us back to the immediate historical origins of those Jews who would emigrate to America and Israel, setting the stage for the chapter with which this book began.

This book does not explicitly make a theologically constructive argument. I have no interest or stake in making Jews "better Jews" or in creating a new first-order definition of Judaism. At the same time, just as I have shaped the material that has gone into this book, the material has shaped me. As I noted above, this book does have constructive implications for Jews and non-Jews, religious and secular. I take up some of these implications in the conclusion.

In order to widen the accessibility of these pages, I have transliterated more according to popular usage than scholarly convention and have used light annotation. I cite simple primary sources (e.g., biblical verses) in the text itself; the sources for other citations can be found in the bibliographical essay and notes for each chapter, which also contain important relevant works in English that are accessible to a nonscholarly audience.

1

PROMISED LANDS

ON A TYPICAL Saturday morning in my neighborhood, the Jews start passing our house at quarter to eight. It starts with the men and older boys, all dressed in black suits and white shirts, black coats, and wearing black hats, walking to their yeshiva minyan. An hour later the crowd changes. Still men and boys, they now wear a variety of different suits and coats and instead of black hats don knitted *kippot*. By 9:45 AM these men and boys are largely already at their Modern Orthodox synagogue and the cars of nattily dressed families bound for a bar or bat mitzvah at the local Conservative synagogues and Reform temples begin to pass the women in their long skirts, wigs, and snoods pushing their children in strollers to join their husbands at the yeshiva minyan. The neighborhood Habad rabbi does not directly go by our house, but if we are out at about 10 AM we frequently pass him as he walks to the *mikveh* to ritually immerse prior to his morning prayers.

The synagogues and congregations to which these Jews are heading are correspondingly diverse. The yeshiva minyan meets in the auditorium of the local Orthodox day school, to which the minyan is tightly linked. The room is divided in half, with men sitting in the front and women behind them, separated by a tall barrier (or *mechitza*). Only men lead the prayers, which is done slowly and from the floor; the slightly raised platform in the middle of the room is used for the Torah reading. The minyan's rav and other dignitaries sit in the front of the room, but at floor level. Their liturgy derives from a traditional Eastern European prayer rite.

In many respects the Modern Orthodox synagogue is similar. It too separates men and women and restricts public liturgical functions to men. Both the yeshiva and Modern Orthodox congregations use substantively the same liturgy, although the latter includes a special prayer for the welfare of the State of Israel, which the former omits. It is, though, the differences that are more apparent. The Modern Orthodox have a synagogue rather than just a minyan—they comprise an institution as well as a prayer quorum. In contrast to the mechitza in the yeshiva minyan, the mechitza in this synagogue is made of a see-through lattice, is lower, and runs down the center of the room, so that during the processional of the Torah it passes close enough to the mechitza to allow women to kiss it. Prayers are led from a raised *bimah* (or dais), on which the rabbi and president of the synagogue typically sit facing the congregation. The dress of the congregants, the style (although not substance) of worship, and especially the weekly sermon all mark a significant difference with the yeshiva minyan. Although both congregations contain accountants, doctors, lawyers, and other professionals who received similar American educations, the yeshiva minyan exhibits more ambivalence toward modern American society. Whereas the members of the Modern Orthodox community are by and large comfortable with their dual identity as both Orthodox Jews and modern Americans, those in the yeshiva minyan typically feel a greater tension. For the former, there are truths located outside the Torah that are compatible with it, while for the latter the Torah (meaning the entire rabbinic tradition that is seen as flowing from it) is the sole source of truth.

The Conservative and Reform houses of worship are far more imposing structures, with each containing over one thousand member families. Both have enormous grand sanctuaries with no mechitzas (although the Conservative synagogue has a small upper gallery that is rarely used, and never in order to separate men and women) and raised daises that require electronic amplification. Both congregations employ cantors who lead the services in a relatively formal style that is punctuated with directions, in English, about when to stand and sit and which page to turn to. Most Saturday mornings each of these congregations hosts at least one bar or bat mitzvah ceremony, marking a child's attainment of the legal age of majority (twelve for girls and thirteen for boys). Typically, the guests at these ceremonies outnumber the congregational attendees; on a Saturday morning on which there is no bar or bat mitzvah or any other special occasion the Conservative congregation draws approximately 150 congregants, and a smaller, regular service at the Reform synagogue some two to three dozen. The vast majority of the members of both synagogues do not observe the traditional restrictions against work on the Sabbath, and unlike most of their Orthodox compatriots might

1.1 Auditorium of the Providence Hebrew Day School, set up for prayer. The Torah is read from the platform, called a *bimah*, in the middle; the women sit behind the *mechitza* in the back.   *Courtesy of the Providence Hebrew Day School*

follow their attendance at religious services with running errands or a trip to the mall.

The differences between these "liberal" congregations are more subtle. The Conservative synagogue, atypically of American Conservative synagogues, has an additional raised dais in the middle of the room from which most of the prayers (but not the Torah reading) are recited. They use different liturgies that are structurally similar to each other and to the Orthodox liturgies, at the same time modifying and abridging the traditional prayers in different ways. As might be expected, more English is used in the Reform service than in the Conservative one. Both synagogues are not only egalitarian but also employ women on their clerical staffs.

This very brief and superficial account of the congregations in my neighborhood does not, of course, even begin to do justice to the diversity of Jewish life today, even in the Rhode Island area and all the more so throughout America. I have lived and prayed in communities that have only a single congregation (almost always called a temple), in which they would conduct Reform services, in a high-classical style, on Friday nights and traditional egalitarian services Saturday morning. I have prayed in different minyanim primarily targeted to aging hippies, Hollywood moguls, investment bankers, gays and lesbians, and soccer moms. I have seen Jewish communities that did not know what a mikveh was and, if they did, would oppose having one in their neighborhood, and I watched a Habad family try to create one by digging out the cellar of their rental house. I know Orthodox men and women who are fastidious about their morning prayers, even after waking up in each other's arms after meeting at a bar the evening before, and Reform Jews who will not let any food or drink pass their lips without the appropriate blessing. During Passover several of my college classmates would skip the bread at dinner while taking a helping of the sausage. I know lesbian Reform rabbis, gay Orthodox rabbis, and female rabbis of every denomination—even Orthodox, although they are few, far between, and generally quite discreet. There are Jews for whom anything Jewish seems foreign, Jews who are as ideologically committed to living as full participants in modern American culture as they are to faithful adherence to the mitzvot, and Jews who attempt to sequester themselves in villages in upstate New York and in New Jersey, ironically invoking their constitutional rights and fighting for them in American courts and in local politics. This enormous diversity would seem almost staggeringly incomprehensible if it did not almost precisely mirror the diversity of America itself.

The magnitude of this Jewish diversity is matched in Israel, although its shape is very different. There are Jews who religiously light candles on Friday night before sitting down in front of the TV and others who are so stringent about Passover that they own two apartments, one of which they use only for the holiday. As Western ideological movements such as Reform and Conservative Judaism struggle for legal and popular recognition, streams of Sephardim and Eastern Jews make their way each year to the graves of the Jewish saints to pray for intercession. A Jew who attends religious services at the Great Synagogue in Jerusalem, with its choral music and Eastern European liturgy, would scarcely be able to follow the Yemenite service in Me'ah Shearim (an ulta-Orthodox neighborhood), not even a mile away. On Shavuot (Pentecost) it is hard to imagine observances as far apart as the throng at the Western Wall in Jerusalem, each group fighting for space and against other groups (or pelting with stones the women who come to form their own prayer groups, complete with reading from a Torah scroll), and the agriculturally centered rituals of the kibbutzim. One group of Orthodox Jews refuses military service on the West Bank because they believe it to be against their religious principles and others claim that it is a religious imperative to settle the West Bank and a sin against God to leave it.

America and Israel now represent the two overwhelmingly dominant centers of world Jewry. The demographic shift was tragically swift. In 1939 the estimated global Jewish population was 16.6 million souls, but by 1945 it had been reduced to 11 million, with European Jewry in ruins. In 2002 there were approximately 13.2 million Jews worldwide, with about 5.7 million living in the United States and 5 million in Israel. France came in a distant third, with 519,000; all of Europe (East and West) contained only slightly more than 1.5 million Jews. Between 1945 and 1950 Israel's Jewish population doubled from 500,000 to 1 million, primarily because of the influx of European refugees. While Israel has historically depended on immigration for its Jewish population growth, after the great Jewish immigration waves of the early twentieth century (with the exceptions of the much smaller immigrations from Europe after World War II and from the former Soviet Union in the late twentieth century) Jews in the United States have relied primarily on reproduction for their population growth.[1]

It would be logical to assume that the American and Israeli Jewish communities are more similar than they are different. In our age of mass communication and easy travel, the level of interaction between Jewish communities in Israel and abroad has never been greater. Television, publications, and especially the internet transmit in real time culture as well as religious assumptions and sensibilities. Within American Jewish communities, especially since 1967, Israel has consistently ranked high as a source of Jewish pride and identification, and some study of Israeli history and culture is common in most American Jewish educational institutions. American Jews frequently travel to Israel, either individually and in families or through tours organized and subsidized by Jewish communal institutions. Birthright Israel alone has sent over 80,000 young Jews to Israel for a free ten-day trip; many Orthodox Jewish youth spend a year or two between high school and college, or after college, studying at a yeshiva in Israel; and, according to the National Jewish Population Survey of 2000, 35 percent of the total American Jewish population has visited Israel. The flow is not unidirectional. Israelis visit and have multiple family connections to the United States. Many travel to the United States for pleasure, work, and study; in 2004, according to U.S. government statistics, 337,513 Israelis visited the United States. American Jews are not foreign to Israelis.

Yet as counterintuitive as it might seem, American Judaism and Israeli Judaism, in all their riotous variety, are more distinct than they are similar. There is, to be sure, overlap; perhaps the influence of Israeli forms of Orthodoxy on American Modern Orthodoxy and the struggling establishment of

American Jewish movements in Israel are the strongest visible signs of this interchange, and neither phenomenon is statistically significant at present. American Judaism is as distinctly American as Israeli Judaism is distinctly Israeli, and long-term visitors from one community to the other are continually baffled and frustrated by the gulf that separates their expectations from reality. Where Jews sometimes look for Judaism as common denominator, they find only a common numerator.

The story of Judaism in America has typically been told as one of history and institutions. In this telling, the ideological positions of the institutional movements (e.g., Reform, Conservative, Reconstructionist, Orthodox) are thought to encapsulate what it meant and means to be Jewish in America. Similarly, and from a more partisan and applied perspective, the "strength" of American Judaism is seen as tightly linked to membership in Jewish institutions, organizations, and movements. Scholars today are growing increasingly uncomfortable with this model. Jewish identification, they assert, occurs in forums outside established institutions, and a focus on ideological movements yields a seriously distorted picture of what it means to be Jewish today in America. This reservation is well taken, and later in this chapter I will discuss how American Judaism looks outside the movements. Nevertheless, the movements remain important for an understanding of American Judaism. Millions of American Jews continue in some way to identify with them, whether as members of their constituent institutions (e.g., the synagogue) or as selective beneficiaries of the ideologies that they have produced. To know the Jewish movements and institutions is not to know American Judaism, but any account of American Judaism that neglects them must remain incomplete. More important for this book, however, the history of the Jewish movements presents a case study in the distinctively American interpretation of traditional Jewish texts and practices. It can thus sensitize us to the dynamic filtering of tradition that occurs within both institutions and individuals.

The first Jews in the Americas were Dutch. In 1630 Holland expelled the Portuguese from Brazil. Jews—some 1,000 to 1,500 according to some estimates, constituting a third to half of the Dutch population there—flocked to the new Dutch colony, establishing businesses and trading outposts. In 1654, however, the Portuguese retook Brazil and expelled the Jews. Many attempted to return to Amsterdam and several took refuge in the West

Indies—one group founded a community in Curaçao, which today, number-
ing 300 families, prays in the oldest synagogue in the Western Hemisphere
(built in 1732) and houses a Torah scroll brought from the Great Synagogue
in Amsterdam. A single boatload of refugees found its way to New Amsterdam. Reluctantly allowed to settle there by Peter Stuyvesant, they soon pe-
titioned for land for a cemetery and formed a tiny community so small and
dispersed that by 1663 the community's single Torah scroll, borrowed from
Amsterdam, made the return voyage overseas; apparently New Amsterdam
could not sustain a minyan. The Jewish community would desire, and be allowed, public worship only at the beginning of the eighteenth century, then
under British rule.

The first synagogue in colonial America was founded in New York around
1704, and called Kahal Kadosh Shearith Israel, "The Holy Congregation of
the Remnant of Israel." It kept a close association to its mother synagogue
in Amsterdam, maintaining the Sephardic-Portuguese liturgical rites of
that synagogue and continuing to emphasize the use of Portuguese, even
as the community was increasingly unable to understand the language.
Sephardic congregations were soon established in Philadelphia (1740) and
Newport (ca. 1758). Small Jewish communities also organized in Savannah
and Charleston. These early Sephardic communities were so sparsely populated (often consisting of only one to two dozen families) that they were
soon outnumbered by the Ashkenazic Jews from Western Europe that had
begun to trickle into the colony.

Very few of these early Sephardic communities were able to survive the
arrival of the Ashkenazim. Shearith Israel and Mikve Israel, in Philadelphia, had strong and wealthy support that allowed these congregations to
maintain their Spanish-Portuguese heritage. Both synagogues, to this day,
continue to conduct their services in accordance with their earlier, if modified, distinctive customs. Both synagogues continue to insist on Sephardic
rabbis as leaders for their congregations. They use a modified version of the
old Sephardic liturgy from London and Amsterdam (*The Book of Prayers*),
printed with instructions and English translations. Shearith Israel insists
that its ushers wear tails and top hats, although the sermons are now delivered, and its minutes kept, in English. With a decreasing proportion of the
membership of these congregations today from non-Ashkenazic heritages,
they sometimes struggle to preserve their earlier identity.

The slow but steady stream of German Jews into America after the Revolution decisively changed the composition of the American Jewish community, as small and disorganized as it was. German Jews, mainly peddlers

and merchants, not only settled in the bigger cities but also struck out to the frontier, especially the South and Midwest. Many of these Jews were from "traditional" backgrounds, ritually observant but not ideologically affiliated. Some came from areas in Germany where Reform Judaism was gathering momentum. These Jews established small communities and synagogues, some traditional and others with a more "reformed" orientation, throughout early America. Many of today's small Jewish congregations in these regions trace their origins back to German Jewish founders in the nineteenth century.

Unsurprisingly, these early American Jews exhibited a diverse range of religious behaviors. Some, despite the hardships, continued to maintain "traditional" mores. They closed their businesses for Shabbat (which meant closing from Friday afternoon through the Christian Sabbath, opening again on Monday morning), they observed the Jewish holidays, and they observed the dietary laws (*kashrut*). None was particularly easy to do in this environment. Sabbath closing necessitated monetary losses, and holiday closings were particularly irksome to Christian business partners. There was no organized system for the ritual slaughter of animals, which led wealthier Jews to hire immigrants to slaughter animals for them. Many, probably most, Jews were eclectic in their religious observance. They did not feel that they could afford either to close their businesses on Shabbat and the holidays or a slaughterer for their meat.

One factor that contributed to this religious laxity was that the Jewish community in the early republic was by and large religiously rudderless. They did what their parents did, adapted for their new environments—the few rabbis in America were imported from Europe, confined to major cities, and only heeded sporadically. There was little Jewish education and few Jews had even minimal comprehension of Hebrew. The case of Rabbi David De Sola Pool, brought over from France in 1817 to serve as the rabbi of Shearith Israel, offers a graphic example of the state of Jewish education in early America: His tenure "was not destined to be a long one. While the community profoundly respected his Hebrew learning, parents were unwilling to entrust children to him because of his propensity for strong drink. By the beginning of 1821 he had only one paying pupil in addition to the five free pupils. In May of that year he ceased to be head of the school."[2] Correspondingly, there was little knowledge of Jewish sacred texts apart from the Bible, which was available primarily in the King James Version. Isaac Leeser, the hazan (or cantor, but here more properly the spiritual leader) of Mikveh Israel in Philadelphia (although he himself was Ashkenazic), retranslated the Hebrew Bible into English. The full version was published by the newly founded Jewish Publication Society in 1854 and quickly became popular in Jewish households and congregations. Other Jewish sacred texts, though, were scarcely to be found on American soil. The first full copy of the Babylonian Talmud might not have arrived in America until the mid-nineteenth century, and even then copies were rare. The Talmud (in its original language) was not published in America until the end of the nineteenth century—and this first edition, curiously, was a section of the Palestinian Talmud, which was hardly used in living Jewish communities. Otherwise, copies of the Talmud, codes, and commentaries were imported from Europe, and there were few in America who could, or would want to, read them.

A second, far more important factor was the American context within which these traditions had to root. The American shaping of traditional Jewish concepts and practices is clear from the very beginning of the community. At its founding, Shearith Israel emulated the model of governance found in the Amsterdam Jewish community, with the elders (*maamad*) holding tight reigns over the community. Under both ideological and practical pressures, though, this model soon broke down. There was simply too much ideological dissonance between this system of governance and the assault on the notion of aristocracy unleashed by democratic movements. American Jews did not want their status as democratic citizens to end upon entry to the synagogue. Moreover, unlike Amsterdam, early America offered more opportunities for Jews, thus weakening even further the threat of excommunication wielded by the synagogue elders. The idea of local communities governing their own local affairs, rather than a single and closed central authority dictating to the entire Jewish community, caused a movement from a "synagogue community" to a "community of synagogues."

These synagogues, in architecture and worship, also demonstrated their distinctly American context. Jewish women, like their Protestant sisters, wanted to attend a house of worship, and appeared to have attended in unprecedented numbers. Although barred from leading the service, they still wanted a view of the action, and synagogues were remodeled to allow women a clear line of sight to the men's section. Designed by the leading non-Jewish architects of their day, many of these synagogues drew far more architecturally on the styles of local houses of worship than they did on the "old country"—certainly not a new phenomenon.

As an institution, the synagogue was successful precisely because it was so American—Jew and non-Jew alike could understand and respect it as a

Jewish house of worship. The success of other Jewish religious institutions was directly correlated with their ability to be framed in the larger American religious landscape. Jewish women created benevolent societies and Sunday schools, modeling them directly on Protestant examples. Jewish men created fraternal organizations like B'nai B'rith (1842), which were no less indebted to non-Jewish communal organizations. On the other hand, institutions that did not translate well into this larger American religious idiom did not fare well. Many communities lacked a mikveh, the ritual bath most typically used for immersion after a woman's menstrual period, and those that did exist went largely unused.

The relative success of "Jewish" concepts and practices, too, correlated with comprehension and translatability in this larger American context. Belief in a single, universal, and awesome God was a given. Jews differed with Christians over the role of Jesus in the divine economy, but their basic conception of God came much in line with more prevalent notions. By the mid to late nineteenth century, American synagogue architecture and liturgy began to reflect this commitment to God's transcendent awe. The hierarchical space and soaring ceilings of synagogues like Congregation Emanu-El of the City of New York reinforced this notion, as did the English translations of the most popular prayer books.

The rituals that Jews did practice they infused with new meanings. Whatever the relative laxity of Shabbat observance among eighteenth- and nineteenth century American Jews, the idea of the Sabbath could readily be understood against the Christian Sabbath and its blue laws. Kashrut posed a more serious challenge and thus tended to be relatively neglected.

Similarly, the American Jewish acceptance of ethnic distinctiveness— their self-understanding as Israel—was varied and ambivalent. In the eyes of Christian Americans, most Jews were doubly marked, as an ethnic and a religious community. Their status was thus more complex than that of other immigrant groups. The "Hebrews" had a long-established place in Christian theology. On the one hand, it was a privileged place: They are the biblical people, covenanted to God, the "olive tree," in the words of Paul, from which sprung the branch of Christianity (cf. Romans 9–11). On the other hand, God rejected them for their obstinacy, rejection, and murder of Christ—a line of argument that pervades the writings of Luther and Calvin, the spiritual forebears of the Puritans. Throughout the eighteenth and nineteenth centuries, American Christians would emphasize one or the other side of this evaluation of Jews, but they would always regard the Hebrews as a distinctive people. Even George Washington, in his famous letter to the

"Hebrew Congregation in Newport" in which he expresses his commitment to eliminating bigotry from the new republic, refers to them as "children of the Stock of Abraham, who dwell in this land."

It was largely through these external eyes that Jews filtered their own self-understanding. Some Jewish communities and individuals were proud to be associated with the "Stock of Abraham," others, living in more difficult social conditions, were not. The idea of Israel as a genetically linked and divinely sanctioned family was at odds with the democratic ideals of citizenship. Where Jews felt barriers to full integration, as they did in the colonial period, they were more likely to find refuge with their own and with a stronger sense of identity with other Jews. By the late nineteenth century, though, universalism was a strong American ideal, with particularistic identifications discouraged. Many Jews in America, as in Europe, understood Israel to constitute a religious or spiritual community rather than a biological one. Essentialist notions of Jewish identity, such as those espoused by Judah Halevi, the Zohar, and in some parts of contemporaneous Europe, found no following in America. When J. A. Joel wrote in 1866 of his Passover seder four years earlier as a Union soldier in the field, he refers to the other twenty seder participants as his "co-religionists"—signaling an understanding of a community linked in a voluntary religious association.

Although this understanding of Israel was most likely widespread among Jews, the emerging Reform movement was the first larger institution to articulate and aggressively promote it. Reform ideology landed in America along with the Jewish immigrants from Germany through the nineteenth century, but until mid-century was largely confined to local practices in individual congregations.[3] In the 1840s it began to crystallize, in its American form, into institutions and an ideology. Large, well-funded Reform temples were built in major cities to compete with the "Americanized traditionalism" of spiritual leaders like Isaac Leeser. Isaac Meyer Wise (1819–1900), who was born in Bohemia but served as a rabbi in Albany, New York before moving to Cincinnati in 1854, saw in these local congregations an emerging trend. Grandly calling his prayer book of 1857 *Minhag Amerika* ("The Custom of America"), Wise set out to articulate an American Judaism. He introduced the mixed seating of men and women in his synagogue in Albany, and by the end of the century nearly all Reform synagogues had family pews.

Wise's most enduring legacy is the Hebrew Union College (HUC), which he established in Cincinnati in 1875. The first successful rabbinical seminary in America, HUC sought to train the rabbinic leaders of this new

1.2 Interior of the sanctuary, Congregation Emanu-El of the City of New York. Photo by Malcolm Varon. *Courtesy of Congregation Emanu-El of the City of New York*

American Judaism. Despite Wise's advocacy of HUC as a seminary for *all* American rabbis, the institution's appeal was more limited. Within the decade, it had become the institutional center of Reform Judaism in America. In 1885, the American Reform movement jelled further around a set of ideological principles known as the Pittsburgh Platform. The platform attempted to Americanize the ideas of the European reformers, and it is worth quoting in full:

1. We recognize in every religion an attempt to grasp the Infinite, and in every mode, source or book of revelation held sacred in any religious system the consciousness of the indwelling of God in man. We hold that Judaism presents the highest conception of the God-idea as taught in our Holy Scriptures and developed and spiritualized by the Jewish teachers, in accordance with the moral and philosophical progress of their respective ages. We maintain that Judaism preserved and defended midst continual struggles and trials and under enforced isolation, this God-idea as the central religious truth for the human race.

2. We recognize in the Bible the record of the consecration of the Jewish people to its mission as the priest of the one God, and value it as the most potent instrument of religious and moral instruction. We hold that the modern discoveries of scientific researches in the domain of nature and history are not antagonistic to the doctrines of Judaism, the Bible reflecting the primitive ideas of its own age, and at times clothing its conception of divine Providence and Justice dealing with men in miraculous narratives.

3. We recognize in the Mosaic legislation a system of training the Jewish people for its mission during its national life in Palestine, and today we accept as binding only its moral laws, and maintain only such ceremonies as elevate and sanctify our lives, but reject all such as are not adapted to the views and habits of modern civilization.

4. We hold that all such Mosaic and rabbinical laws as regulate diet, priestly purity, and dress originated in ages and under the influence of ideas entirely foreign to our present mental and spiritual state. They fail to impress the modern Jew with a spirit of priestly holiness; their observance in our days is apt rather to obstruct than to further modern spiritual elevation.

5. We recognize, in the modern era of universal culture of heart and intellect, the approaching of the realization of Israel's great Messianic hope for the establishment of the kingdom of truth, justice, and peace among all men. We consider ourselves no longer a nation, but a religious community, and therefore expect neither a return to Palestine, nor a sacrificial worship under the sons of Aaron, nor the restoration of any of the laws concerning the Jewish state.

6. We recognize in Judaism a progressive religion, ever striving to be in accord with the postulates of reason. We are convinced of the utmost necessity of preserving the historical identity with our great past. Christianity and Islam, being daughter religions of Judaism, we appreciate their providential mission, to aid in the spreading of monotheistic and moral truth. We acknowledge that the spirit of broad humanity of our age is our ally in the fulfillment of our mission, and therefore we extend the hand of fellowship to all who cooperate with us in the establishment of the reign of truth and righteousness among men.

7. We reassert the doctrine of Judaism that the soul is immortal, grounding the belief on the divine nature of human spirit, which forever finds bliss in righteousness and misery in wickedness. We reject as ideas not rooted in Judaism, the beliefs both in bodily resurrection and in Gehenna and Eden (Hell and Paradise) as abodes for everlasting punishment and reward.

8. In full accordance with the spirit of the Mosaic legislation, which strives to regulate the relations between rich and poor, we deem it our duty to participate in the great task of modern times, to solve, on the basis of justice and righteousness, the problems presented by the contrasts and evils of the present organization of society.

Here is a vision of a rational, universalistic Judaism rooted in its enduring preservation of the highest human religious truth, the God-idea, whose divine mission is to bring social justice to the world. Particularistic practices, rituals that fail to elevate the individual, superstitious ideas, and a desire to return to the promised land are all deemed foreign and alien. The community of Israel is notable and distinctive for its role in preserving the highest human truth, an idea that, as we will see later in this book, has deep European Jewish roots. Ceremonial laws, however, have no intrinsic or necessary link to that truth. Modern Jews are to observe those rituals and practices that result in "spiritual elevation." The platform implies that the decision as to what constitutes an appropriate ritual is to be left to the community, not—as in modern Reform Judaism—the individual. No matter how meaningful to an individual, for example, kashrut is rejected.[4]

To every action there is a reaction, and the ideological assertiveness of the Reform movement led to the formation and strengthening of other Jewish movements. The meeting at which the Pittsburgh Platform was adopted was itself a source of schism; several rabbis, upset with the nonkosher banquet meal served at the conference, stormed out in protest. Now alienated from the institutional structures of Reform Judaism, some of these rabbis sought to create a new institutional home for their own vision of Judaism in America. Reinvigorating the struggling Jewish Theological Seminary of America, these rabbis and their supporters created Conservative Judaism.

The Jewish Theological Seminary (JTS) was founded in New York in 1887. Led by rabbis from the Sephardic congregations of Philadelphia and New York, but joined by some Ashkenazic rabbis alarmed at what they saw as the radical turn of Reform, JTS was a response to the opening of Hebrew Union College. Its early years were rocky, short on both finances and students. When Solomon Schechter, then a distinguished scholar at Cambridge University, took the helm of JTS in 1902 he set out to fundamentally transform it.[5]

Schechter was the right man at the right time. The massive immigration of Eastern European Jews had begun. Between 1881 and 1914, over two million Jews would emigrate from Eastern Europe to America, with close to another half-million arriving between 1915 and 1931 (compare to the approximately 180,000 Jews who emigrated from Eastern Europe to Palestine between 1881 and 1931). These Jews were generally poor and more traditional (but not ideological) in practice and welcomed ambivalently, if at all, by American Jews. While many in the first generation of these immigrants sought to transplant their lifestyles from the Pale to this *goldene medina* ("golden land" in Yiddish), by the second generation they frequently struggled to integrate the world of their parents with their new life in America. Although by the second generation many of these Jews had abandoned most of the traditional rituals and customs, Reform Judaism left them ideologically puzzled and, as practiced in the wealthy synagogues in the bigger cities, socially isolated. It was to this large population of Jews, many of whom lived in New York, that Schechter made his pitch.

Schechter sought to appeal to these traditionally minded Ashkenazic Jews by maintaining the role and status of the commandments, the mitzvot. He asserted that these mitzvot are obligatory, despite the fact that many are "ceremonial." At the same time, they are not static. Judaism and its law (*halakhah*), he claimed, have always adapted to its historical setting. He thus centered himself on the ideological spectrum squarely between the more radical expressions of Reform Judaism and the idea, articulated in Europe by Samson Raphael Hirsch and his followers, that the halakhah is entirely divine and unchanging. Despite this ideological difference with those Jews who subscribed to Hirsch, they all formed a serious, if short-lived, alliance against Reform Judaism. Just as Wise sought to create an institution for

American Judaism, understood and writ large, so too did Schechter. The Orthodox Jewish Congregational Union of America (the Orthodox Union), founded in 1898, joined Schechter and JTS to oppose Reform Judaism.

In contrast to these ideological movements, which all subscribed to the idea that "Judaism" and life as an American citizen were compatible, a group of Eastern European immigrants banded together to create the Rabbi Isaac Elchanan Theological Seminary (RIETS) in 1897, now as a direct response to JTS. RIETS was to be a bastion of isolationism, an Eastern European yeshiva that happened to be on American soil. The foundation of RIETS was soon followed by the formation of the Agudath Ha-Rabbanim (the Union of Orthodox Rabbis) in 1902. Refusing to recognize graduates of JTS or even rabbinic seminaries from Western Europe as legitimate, the group cultivated a tense relationship not only with the more "liberal" Jewish movements but even with the Orthodox Union.

RIETS soon collapsed. The students themselves rebelled against its isolationism, demanding that they be taught skills that would allow them to compete for rabbinic positions in America. In 1915 the leaders of RIETS turned to a rich European immigrant, Bernard Revel (1885–1940), to help reorganize the institution. Revel, who married into the family that controlled Oklahoma Petroleum and Gasoline Company and was active in managing the business, saw no future for RIETS's isolationist outlook. Subscribing more to a vision of an Orthodoxy integrated into contemporary non-Jewish society, he ambitiously proposed to build an Orthodox educational institution on the American model. Yeshiva College was opened in 1928, to the dismay of the more conservative members of the Agudath Ha-Rabbanim. Yeshiva College, later renamed Yeshiva University, continues to exist today as a kind of standard-bearer of American Modern Orthodoxy.[6]

Most American Jews, of course, could not care less about the development of these ideological movements. Struggling to survive financially and to integrate culturally into the melting pot of America, most Jews simply abandoned Jewish affiliations and customs, a fact widely noted at the time by leaders of all of the nascent movements. Even by today's standards, the figures are arresting. Only 23 percent of Jews were affiliated with a synagogue in 1919; 75 percent of young Jews of New York had not attended a synagogue (presumably even once) in 1934; and only 17 percent of Jewish children in New York City received any kind of formal Jewish education in 1924. European rabbis looked with horror at American Jewry.[7]

These figures are especially intriguing when compared with contemporary measures of non-Jewish American religiosity. The interwar period saw a general decline of the standard measures of American religiosity, but no other American religious group comes close to equaling the Jewish neglect for their religious institutions. There are, no doubt, many and complex reasons for this dissimilarity. The ordinary struggles of an immigrant group to assimilate into a culture that was still tinged with prejudice against it must account for a large part of this Jewish neglect. While the ideological reconciliations of "Judaism" with American culture might have been reassuring to some Jews, it fell flat with most. Whether for the retailer trying to make sense of the "God-idea," the businessman who fears that he will lose the deal if he cannot lunch with the supplier, or the family whose child was rejected from a selective college because of their Jewish name, ideology was not terribly helpful on the street.

Unlike colonial times, through the nineteenth and twentieth centuries there were also burgeoning nonreligious avenues for Jewish identification. Jews could, and did, form secular alternatives to those institutions from which they were excluded. Political, intellectual, theatrical, and artistic expressions of "Jewish culture" thrived, especially in the bigger cities. Seen increasingly by non-Jewish Americans as an ethnic rather than religious group, Jews increasingly began to behave like one. Reform Judaism continued to preach that Israel was solely a religious group, but its voice was drowned out by the mass of Eastern European Jews whose Jewish identity was ethnic rather than religious. To this group, "kosher-style" was more important than kosher, even as the BLT remained taboo.

There were European roots to this form of ethnic identification, but even this cultural tradition soon assumed a distinctly American shape. Yiddish theatre and participation in socialist and Zionist causes soon grew to be primary sites of Jewish identity; being Jewish could be safely divorced from Judaism. Jewishness, in this understanding, became an ethnicity like, for example, "Italian-American," in which a religious connection is generally assumed but not strictly necessary. The understanding of Jewishness as ethnicity prepared the ground for American Jewish culture and arts. Jewish literature, music, and drama could remain disconnected from God, having only the most tenuous if any connection to the rabbinic "conversation" and traditional Jewish rituals, and yet still serve as a vehicle for Jewish identity.

World War II changed what it meant to be an American Jew.[8] Although the true horror of the Holocaust would not sink into the American Jewish consciousness for two more decades, its impact was felt almost immediately. The slaughter of Jews simply because they were Jews drove home to American Jews their need to organize as a community—national

Jewish organizations were created on an unprecedented scale, spurred even further by the creation of the modern State of Israel in 1948. Among non-Jews, it drove most overt expressions of anti-Semitism underground. While many clubs and educational institutions continued to discriminate against Jews (Yale University did not abandon its Jewish quota until the 1960s), the public discourse at least reflected an American society more open to Jews. For the Jews themselves, this rhetorical openness allowed them to begin to shape a different kind of ethnic and religious identity, one that was truly voluntaristic.

The Holocaust also had demographic implications for American Jews. Between 1945 and 1947 forty thousand Jews emigrated from Europe to America. Among the refugees and survivors were Hasidim (of which there were very few in America and no organized communities prior to World War II) and many staunchly conservative rabbis. They landed in a very different America than the one in which the Agudath Ha-Rabbanim emerged. Rather than vociferously engaging America, some of these groups attempted to isolate themselves, whether in parts of Brooklyn (the Satmar and Lubavitch Hasidim) or in Lakewood, New Jersey, where an "ultra-Orthodox" yeshiva was founded. These groups were well outside the Jewish religious mainstream.

The American context, however, had a far more profound impact on the shifting shape of American Judaism. The U.S. army was a great equalizer, during and after World War II. Jews were integrated into the fighting units; they were GIs like all other GIs, doing their patriotic duty; the notion of a "GI Jew" was born. When returning from the war they took advantage, like the other GIs, of the GI bill in order to go to college. And, like masses of other Americans, they were able to move out of their cramped city apartments into modest houses in suburbia, where they pursued the same American dream as everybody else.

Although it began before World War II, Reconstructionism was to a large degree shaped by these postwar trends. Reconstructionism traces its ideological founding to the writings and thought of Mordecai Kaplan (1881–1983). Kaplan was an Orthodox rabbi before joining the faculty of the Jewish Theological Seminary. Seeing what he perceived as the decline of Judaism in America in the 1920s and 1930s, Kaplan began to publish a series of essays in which he attempted to articulate why the Jewish institutions and movements of his day were so unattractive to American Jews. He refined his thinking in his magnum opus, *Judaism as a Civilization: Toward a Reconstruction of American-Jewish Life*, published in 1934.[9] Much influenced by the American philosophical movement known as pragmatism (of which John Dewey was a founder), Kaplan carefully critiqued the ideological and philosophical coherence of the other Jewish movements. His critiques remain incisive and surprisingly fresh, even to modern readers. Much more controversial, then and now, are his answers.

Kaplan was, above all, a rationalist. This led him to deny a place for nearly all supernatural elements within Judaism. Moving even beyond the God-idea of the Pittsburgh Platform, Kaplan defines God as "the force that makes for salvation." The definition is intentionally and uncharacteristically vague, as nowhere does Kaplan precisely define what he means by either *force* or *salvation.* It is clear, though, that both were rooted in human experience. To achieve their greatest potential, humans must actualize that which is already within them—an idea with perhaps unintended parallels to the pantheism of early Hasidism.

Denying the power of God as a supernatural force creates a conceptual domino effect. If there is no external supernatural God, there can be no covenant; Israel, as a holy or covenanted people, has no historical meaning or destiny. This presumption creates a sobering explanation for theodicy. There is no meaning or greater purpose to Israel's historical traumas. When Israel is persecuted or suffers natural calamities it is not the result of her "sins," but of human evil or unstoppable natural calamity. Without covenant there is also no place for the mitzvot as obligatory commandments; God does not command. Kaplan has great respect for the Hebrew Bible and the rabbinic tradition, but as entirely fallible human texts.

Given the radical nature of Kaplan's thought, his actual reconstruction of Judaism, how he thinks it should look on the ground, is surpisingly conservative. For Kaplan, although there are no obligatory commandments, there are Jewish "folkways." These are the practices and customs that define Israel as a civilization. Kaplan is very careful here not to define Israel as a nation. Nations, in his view, are parochial and, by definition, bad—a critique of modern nationalism that was not uncommon in the period between the two world wars. As an ancient civilization, Israel does have a greater mission, namely, to demonstrate to the world that civilization is not equivalent to nation, and that the former can serve as a better model than the latter. Israel's mission is to stand against modern state nationalism.

Israel's traditional folkways hold it together as a coherent people. Kaplan was a strong advocate of Hebrew and its revival as a living language. Civilizations have their own languages, and Hebrew is the historical language of the Jews. They also have their own ancestral lands, and Kaplan strongly advocated, in spite of his fear of nationalism, the establishment of Palestine as a Jewish state. In a Jewish state, he reasoned, Jews would be free to express themselves most fully, to allow their uniquely Jewish civilization to flourish. As for some thinkers from the Eastern European *Haskalah* movement, a Jewish homeland in Palestine was justified culturally rather than theologically. The Land of Israel was not the Jewish homeland because it was a land that God promised to the children of Israel, but because it was the historical homeland of the Jews and held out the greatest possibility for Israel's continued survival and cultural vitality.

For the vast majority of Jews who live outside of the Land of Israel, Kaplan equates adherence to folkways with religious revival. Jews should observe Shabbat, the holidays, and kashrut, and they should receive an extensive Jewish education. By seeing the mitzvot more as folkways than commandments, he is also able to appropriate aspects of Reform thought. Ideally, for Kaplan, Shabbat is a time for study, family and community renewal, play, and restraint from work. Some people, he recognizes, will have to work on Shabbat and the holidays, and what constitutes "play" for some will entail violations against the traditional mitzvot. Each individual is empowered to make his or her own decision, although that decision would ideally be made within the framework of the tradition. Folkways are dynamic, and both individuals and communities are free to eliminate or create new ones as the times demanded.

The "his or her" in the last paragraph is important. Among early twentieth-century Jewish thinkers, he was arguably the most forward thinking on issues of gender. The Reform movement had gestured toward gender equality, although it would be many decades until they fully acted on it. In some Conservative and Orthodox congregations women agitated for the right for increased participation in public worship, but these requests, which would have been seen by Jews and non-Jews alike as breeching a woman's proper station, were rare, sporadic, and largely ineffective. For Kaplan, though, gender equality was logical. He is credited with instituting the first bat mitzvah in America, of his daughter in 1922.

Kaplan's ideas found especially fertile ground in the Jewish community after World War II. While no other Jewish movement, and probably relatively few Jews, subscribed to his explicit rejection of a supernatural God, the idea of Judaism as a civilization that was at once proud, distinctive, and universal, was profoundly influential. It helped to foster a stronger sense of Jewish solidarity that was further strengthened by the Jewish community center movement. These centers, ultimately established in almost every area of significant Jewish population, were and remain places for Jews to socialize with other Jews; their connection to "Judaism" or Jewish folkways is often nominal if present at all. Frequently, in fact, Jewish community centers encounter some opposition from local synagogues, who see their largely secular activities as competing with and undermining their own more religious mission.

Kaplan's thought generally resonated with American Jewry. Many American Jews wanted "tradition," ethnic pride, and community, but they did not want obligation. They wanted the State of Israel, but also to be American. Ironically, the movement founded in 1955 around Kaplan's ideas, Reconstructionism, could not successfully deliver to this market. Rather, it was Conservative Judaism that was best poised to take advantage of the postwar needs of American Jews. Appropriating, sometimes tacitly, Kaplan's most appealing ideas but without rejecting God, the Conservative movement exploded in the postwar years. It was also able to provide an institutional framework, creating new synagogues to serve the expanding suburban communities. In 1950 the Committee on Jewish Law and Standards, a new Conservative committee formed to offer halakhic guidance to the movement, issued a responsum that permitted driving to synagogue on Shabbat. The responsum, which has been bitterly critiqued to the present day by some for its loose halakhic reasoning, was in fact largely symbolic. In suburban America most Jews would either drive to synagogue or not go at all, and they had little awareness of or interest in halakhic intricacies. The 1950s Conservative synagogue offered traditional-style prayer, respectable suburban-style religiosity, and not many demands. The movement remained politely ambiguous about its support of Israel, being careful not to prick the anxieties of the second-generation Jews who were just beginning to establish themselves as true Americans.

Conservative Jewish leaders were by no means alone in their ambivalent stance toward the creation of the State of Israel. While most Jewish leaders, in the aftermath of the Holocaust, recognized and supported the establishment of a safe Jewish homeland, their theological approaches were more complex. Conservative Judaism did not have a clear ideological stance toward the creation of the State of Israel, and their early responses tended to be based on pragmatic considerations. Both Reform and many Orthodox leaders were opposed theologically, although on very different grounds. Reform opposition was based on an understanding of Israel as a religious rather than national or ethnic community. The Pittsburgh Platform explicitly rejected the notion of an ingathering to the land of Israel, whether in present or eschatological times. Few American Orthodox Jews, on the other hand, were convinced by the reasoning of the new religious Zionists, who saw God's redemptive hand in the formation of the State of Israel. Instead, many Orthodox rabbis believed that God would ultimately lead the ingathering of Jews to the Promised Land, but for humans to take the initiative was, at minimum, presumptuous. The very notion of a modern Jewish state was compounded by the realization that it would be secular, led by nonreligious Jews and not governed by halakhah. After the Holocaust and the bloody Israeli War of Independence there was little vocal opposition to the state, although the theological issues remained unsettled.

These theological issues came to a head after the Six-Day War in 1967. Israel's defeat of the surrounding Arab countries was so swift and decisive that it transformed Israel's image. The unification of Jerusalem and taking of sovereignty over the Temple Mount captured the Jewish religious imagination. For the American Jewish community, the timing could hardly have been more fortuitous. America was, of course, undergoing a violent cultur al upheaval, which was shaking up the Jewish community in precisely the same manner as it was American society at large. In a society increasingly consumed with issues of ethnicity, race, and identity polities, the Six-Day War made Israel into a symbol of American Jewish pride. Israel, imagined as a small, weak, and besieged country that triumphed over its enemies because of the intelligence and courage of its soldiers, symbolized the American Jewish community's own evolving self perception. Jews rallied around this image of the State of Israel.

The increasing importance of the State of Israel as a site of American Jewish identity compelled the religious movements to deal with theological issues more directly. The "San Francisco Platform" of the Reform movement, entitled "Reform Judaism—A Centenary Perspective" and adopted in 1976, breaks with the Pittsburgh Platform, not only unconditionally supporting the State of Israel but even encouraging aliyah, immigration to Israel, "for those who wish to find maximum personal fulfillment in the cause of Zion." The Conservative and Reform movements opened organizational and educational institutions in Israel in order to show their support. The position of the Israeli religious Zionists began to gain adherents in Modern Orthodox circles in America, with many such congregations (along with Conservative congregations) adopting the "Prayer for the State of Israel" composed by the Chief Rabbinate of the State of Israel, which seeks the welfare of Israel, "the beginning of the budding of our redemption." As Modern Orthodox teens have increasingly spent a year or two in Israel studying at yeshiva (75 percent of American Orthodox Jews who are members of Orthodox synagogues have visited Israel at least once, compared to 57 percent of Conservative Jews and 44 percent of Reform Jews), the evaluation of the modern State of Israel as an important part of the redemptive process has gained strength. Even many ultra-Orthodox have moved from active hostility to the State of Israel to ambivalence—only a very small group of American Jews are now actively opposed, on theological grounds, to the existence of the State.

If identity politics was one of the defining qualities of the American sixties that had a decisive impact on the shape of modern American Judaism, the emphasis on individual autonomy and spirituality was the other. The sixties gave birth to the Havurah movement, a loosely organized network of small Jewish prayer groups that rebelled against the large, established suburban synagogues. Mainly from Reform and Conservative backgrounds (although there were also several who came from Orthodox backgrounds), its adherents eschewed the formality and professionalism that were inherent in the synagogues, preferring participatory services that emphasized individual spirituality. In line with their appeal to individual needs and the low financial costs of their maintenance (they often used a person's home or rented cheap space), they appeared in bewildering variety. There were havurot that recited a traditional liturgy in its entirety; havurot that used new liturgies, or created their own liturgy; havurot that replaced the liturgy entirely with meditation or creative movement; and havurot that developed a neo-Hasidic outlook, emphasizing long and joyful melodies. They did not share an ideology as much as they did a goal and a market.

The Havurah movement, although never statistically significant, forced the ideological movements to respond. Reform Judaism began to increase its emphasis on personal autonomy and to create new liturgies that would respond to different needs. Reform synagogues gradually replaced the archaic *Union Prayer Book* with *Gates of Prayer*, which itself offered multiple prayer options; today, that is being replaced with a yet another standard prayer book. The Reform youth movement aggressively sought to appeal to the desire for personally meaningful religious options and a desire to engage in social justice. Reconstructionism did a spiritual about-face, abandoning Kaplan's cold rationality for an explicitly spiritual approach, emphasizing mysticism through traditional texts as well as Hasidic legends. Even Orthodoxy responded to this swelling desire on the part of American Jews for spiritual connection. Savvy Orthodox leader, emphasized adherence to the mitzvot as personally and spiritually rewarding, deemphasizing (although never denying) their compulsory nature. Spirituality, not a rabbinic post or a divine reward in the world-to-come, awaited the student of Talmud.

Perhaps one of the most peculiar beneficiaries of this turn toward spirituality was the Lubavitch (Habad) movement. Transplanted from Europe to Brooklyn, New York during World War II and led by a dynamic rebbe, Menachem Schneerson, Lubavitch began to formulate for itself a mission that extended to all Israel. The movement sent emissaries throughout the American Jewish community. Forming Habad Houses, especially in college communities and aimed at Jewish college students, these emissaries often provided open and nonjudgmental support, along with some free food, to Jews who were seeking a spiritual connection they regarded as "authentic." The strategy of providing these small centers at which young adult Jews could learn and experiment with their Judaism was timely and turned Habad (unlike other surviving Hasidic dynasties, like Satmar and Ger) into a major player on the American Jewish landscape. Also never hesitant about using the modern media, including satellite video and the internet, Habad has projected its presence far beyond what one might expect from such a small group.

Underneath Habad's institutional strategy is a theology that emerges most clearly at the Mitzvah Mobile. This usually takes the form of Lubavitch Hasidim asking passers-by if they are Jewish. If a woman, they might give her some information about lighting Shabbat candles. If a man, they might invite him into their van where they instruct him to put on tefillin and recite the Shema. The purpose of this is not merely educational. Subscribing to a version of Lurianic Kabbalah, they believe that every time they succeed in getting Jews to do a mitzvah, they liberate a divine spark and thus move the world closer to redemption. While the individual Jewish participant in these activities may see himself or herself involved in personal, spiritual exploration the Habad emissary may understand the activities as having cosmic importance.

Habad's messianism, especially in recent years, has hardly been low-key. One of the most distinctive activities that often takes place in a Habad House at Shabbat dinner is dancing to the song (in English), "We want Moshiah now," using the Hebrew term for messiah. In 1994, with the death of the rebbe, this messianic strain erupted. Schneerson neither left a child nor appointed a successor. Throughout his last years he made a number of statements that suggested to many of his followers that he himself was the messiah, leading them into the messianic era. This led them to talk not of the rebbe's "death" but of his "concealment," as he waits to return to earthly life and openly reveal himself as the messiah. Thus, they argue, a new rebbe should not be appointed; the administrative structures (in which Schneerson was not in any case directly involved) should continue to operate, but Schneerson alone, even in concealment, is the spiritual leader. Habad adherents who share this belief continue to speak of the rebbe in the present tense, as if he never died.

Predictably, the belief in a "concealed" messiah that will return to earth to lead the world into redemption unleashed a storm of controversy both inside and outside Habad. The basic premise, although couched in kabbalistic terminology, is patently Christian. Within the movement, another group actively opposes the messianic group: the rebbe may have been saintly, but like every mortal he died. Tensely coexisting in the same organizational structure (the emissaries too adhere to different camps), these two groups are struggling to determine the future of Habad. Meanwhile, as a result of Habad's high visibility, what might have been a curious internal squabble of a small fundamentalist group has attracted widespread attention. A messianic doctrine that asserts that the messiah is something other than completely mortal, one prominent Orthodox Jew has argued, is nothing short of heretical. While this does not reflect the consensus of American Orthodox Jewry, it does point to the shifting place of Lubavitch within the wider Jewish community.[10]

The very willingness of some Orthodox Jews to label others as heretics points to the increasing Jewish factionalism born of identity politics. Jews have followed Americans generally in creating smaller communities with increasingly high walls. As fundamentalism, at least in its more mild forms, has gained ground in American thought and culture, so too has the Jewish fundamentalism nurtured by the European refugees and their descendents gained prominence. Over the last three decades the openness and halakhic flexibility of Modern Orthodoxy in America has been fighting, or adapting, the encroachment of "yeshiva Judaism." As Haym Soloveitchik has pointed out, the nature of Orthodoxy in America has changed. It has gone, in his opinion, from a mimetic "way of life" to a set of textual regulations.[11] In this phenomenon one can see a confluence of the American value on individual autonomy with the democratization of knowledge as available and accessible to all. Ironically, individual Orthodox Jews, who view themselves as obligated to follow the halakhah, now feel free to challenge their local rabbis on the basis of something they found in a book or on the internet. This tendency has led to an increasing stringency within the Orthodox community, and intra-Orthodox factionalism largely based on adherence to these new strictures.

One small but significant example of these Orthodox tensions is the case of *halav yisrael*. Classical halakhic texts are divided on the need for milk, in order to be kosher, to have been supervised by a Jew from milking to processing. Many Jewish communities have ignored this stringency; a well-known and respected ultra-Orthodox American rabbi, Moshe Feinstein, even wrote a responsum arguing for the (limited) permissibility of milk that is not *halav yisrael*. Until the last decade or two, *halav yisrael* was simply not a significant issue among American Orthodox Jews—very few thought it was important. Today, however, a small but growing number of Jews, primarily coming out of or adhering to "yeshiva" rather than Modern Orthodoxy, have turned to *halav yisrael*. The social ramifications are important. These Jews have ceased eating in the homes of other Jews who consider themselves Orthodox and kosher, although who do not themselves buy only *halav yisrael* dairy products. Kashrut, the very wedge that limits social interaction between Jews and non-Jews, is now being deployed not only between Jews, but between Orthodox Jews.

Halav yisrael, of course, is just a small symbol of a larger battle being waged in American Orthodoxy. The real issue underlying that battle, the openness to American society, is ironically a product of that very society. Such a battle would have been unthinkable forty years ago. Only the growth of fundamentalism in America, the public acceptability of a discourse that calls for segregation from secular and corrupt "values," has made possible the conditions that have led to the current state of American Orthodoxy.

Factionalism is not confined to the Orthodox. It is increasingly common within and between other American Jewish groups. American Jewish movements have sought to clarify their borders with each other. Perhaps the most common means that they have used to do so is, again, distinctly American—the issue of gender and sexuality. Gender and sexuality have been used in different ways by the Orthodox to define its line with the Conservative movement and by the Conservative movement to draw its own line in the sand with the Reform movement.

In theory and on an ideological level there is little difference between Conservative and Orthodox Judaism. Both fundamentally subscribe to the notion that the mitzvot are obligatory, that they derive from the same canon of sacred texts, and that halakhah is determined through similar methods of argument. There are, of course, some ideological differences, such as assertions about the divine or historical nature of halakhah, but these are by and large secondary to this shared core. On paper, the halakhic requirements for both Conservative and Orthodox Jews are also quite similar. Again, to be sure, there are differences: Conservative decisors have permitted the use of electricity on Shabbat, the consumption of swordfish (which begins its life with scales and then loses them in adulthood) and gelatin, and a triennial Torah reading (i.e., the entire Torah is read in the synagogue over three years rather than one year). The Conservative movement has allowed the eating of cheese that uses rennet, a curdling agent that may be derived from nonkosher animals, as well as the consumption of some wines that are produced by non-Jews.

Orthodox Jewish groups seized few of these issues to mark their own boundary with Conservative Judaism; for a time there was a mild focus on the use of electricity on Shabbat. Instead, their boundary line was that of gender. Until the feminist movement in the 1970s, Conservative and Orthodox (and even Reform) congregations were not very far apart in their treatment of women. Many Conservative synagogues seated men and women separately, and some Orthodox synagogues seated them together, but in neither were women allowed to lead prayer services. Gradually, under the pressure of changing gender expectations through the 1970s, Conservative synagogues moved toward mixed seating, allowing women to count for a prayer quorum (minyan), and even the (nonsanctioned) participation of women in ritual roles. In 1983 the national movement began to ordain women as Conservative rabbis.

While it was a response to the changing social conditions and the grassroots activities that were taking place in local synagogues, the decision of the Jewish Theological Seminary to ordain women as rabbis (and the decision of the Rabbinical Assembly, the professional organization of Conservative rabbis, to accept them) was justified halakhically. The primary halakhic objection to women serving as rabbis was their inability to lead prayer services; because they were not obligated to perform that class of mitzvot, they could not help those who were (i.e., men) to fulfill their obligations. The halakhic solution accepted by the movement was to allow women to voluntarily assume the same halakhic obligations as men. This is the same principle that the movement deemed operative in allowing other women to fulfill public ritual roles—agreeing to perform such a role is considered an implicit acceptance of the obligations of all the mitzvot. The full inclusion of women in the synagogue service became known as egalitarianism. By any reading, the halakhic logic was strained, although probably not more so than that found in many other responsa, both Conservative and Orthodox.

The decision to ordain women caused an uproar both within the Conservative and Orthodox movements. A small number of faculty members from the Jewish Theological Seminary resigned, with one founding a small splinter organization, the Union for Traditional Judaism. An alternative nonegalitarian minyan continued to meet at the Jewish Theological Seminary for over a decade after the inclusion of women in the rabbinical school. Orthodox Jews held egalitarianism up as an example of the Conservative break with halakhah. The Conservative movement, they claimed, was hypocritical, claiming to be a halakhic movement but really twisting halakhah and simply going along with the tide.

The elevation of the Conservative ordination of women from a halakhic dispute into an Orthodox boundary marker has created problems for Orthodox women who are themselves seeking greater ritual acceptance and participation. The issue of egalitarianism is so charged in the Orthodox community that women who broach it are often accused of challenging the very basis of the community. The problem is compounded by the tensions between the modern and yeshiva wings of Orthodoxy; some Modern Orthodox Jews are afraid that accommodating the demands of these women would provide ammunition to the conservative Jews more closely affiliated with the yeshivot. The result has been a relatively cool, and sometimes hostile, response. Some educated Orthodox women find themselves in powerful, highly-respected professional careers but increasingly marginalized in their synagogues, which are frequently raising the mechitza. Because the issue of feminism remains so charged in the Orthodox world, nearly all attempts to reconcile changing gender attitudes and expectations with the conditions of Orthodoxy have been controversial.[12]

It is not only the Modern Orthodox who have solidified their boundary on the left while looking over their right shoulder. There is a clear ideological divide separating the Conservative and Reform movements: the former regards halakhah as binding and the latter does not. On the ground, however, things are murkier. Most Jews affiliated with the Conservative movement (through, for example, membership in a Conservative synagogue) are not in any meaningful way ideologically Conservative. They neither observe halakhah nor see themselves as obligated to do so. Nor are they, as a group, any more Jewishly educated or committed than their Reform brethren. And as Reform Judaism has moved toward reintegrating and reinvigorating traditional rituals and practices, including kashrut and Shabbat,

Conservative Jews can less be distinguished by their level of practice. With both movements ordaining women, the Conservative movement had to seek other boundary markers.

One such marker was intermarriage and the status of the children within intermarried families. Intermarriage has always been an ideological problem for Reform Judaism. On the one hand, the movement has never condoned intermarriage; on the contrary, it has always officially been against it. Yet, on the other hand, the movement had an ideological commitment to personal autonomy, which only strengthened in the 1960s and 1970s. Shouldn't the individual Jew be free to make his or her own choices? And shouldn't the individual rabbi be free to decide whether he or she wants to officiate at such a marriage? Reinforcing the ideological problem are practical considerations. A significant minority of married Jews in America today is intermarried, and Reform synagogues typically contain a larger share of such intermarried couples than their Orthodox and Conservative counterparts. In order to remain welcoming to such families and to uphold the ideological principle of personal autonomy, the Reform movement muted its criticism of intermarriages, and while it discourages its rabbis from performing them, the Central Conference of American Rabbis (the professional organization of Reform rabbis) makes the matter an issue of rabbinic discretion.

Before the other large American Jewish movements, Reform recognized the complex issues created by the high rate of Jewish intermarriage. According to the halakhah, a Jewish child is one born of a Jewish mother. As the children of intermarriages increased, synagogues faced some difficult choices. Should they welcome the families and thus encourage the family to "be" Jewish, or should they exclude the family and drive them away? If they welcome the family, how should they treat the non-Jewish spouse? Could they really make a distinction between the children of Jewish women married to non-Jewish men (Jewish, in all respects) and those of Jewish men married to non-Jewish women (non-Jewish, in all respects)? The answers to each of these questions have very human costs.

The Reform movement attempted to address this issue boldly through its adoption of a resolution on "patrilineal descent." In 1983 the Central Conference of American Rabbis issued the following declaration:

The Central Conference of American Rabbis declares that the child of one Jewish parent is under the presumption of Jewish descent. This presumption of the Jewish status of the offspring of any mixed marriage is to be established through appropriate and timely public and formal acts of identification with the Jewish faith and people. The performance of these mitzvot serves to commit those who participate in them, both parent and child, to Jewish life.

Depending on circumstances, mitzvot leading toward a positive and exclusive Jewish identity will include entry into the covenant, acquisition of a Hebrew name, Torah study, Bar/Bat Mitzvah, and Kabbalat Torah (Confirmation). For those beyond childhood claiming Jewish identity, other public acts or declarations may be added or substituted after consultation with their rabbi.[13]

Unlike the traditional halakhic definition, in which status as a Jew is defined according to an objective criterion, this definition combines objective and subjective criteria. Either parent may now be Jewish, but in no case is the child of an intermarried couple automatically considered Jewish. All such children must now undergo "appropriate and timely public and formal acts of identification"; it is neither necessary nor sufficient to have a Jewish mother.

This change in the definition of Jewish status arguably achieved its goal. Today 65 percent of the children of intermarried couples of whom one spouse identifies as a Reform Jew are being raised as Jews; the figure rises to 98 percent of the children of intermarried couples who have joined a Reform synagogue. It did not come without costs, though. The subjective element of the creation of status is open to debate, and within the Reform movement itself a child might be deemed Jewish by one rabbi and non-Jewish by another. Children who grow up believing that they are Jewish, when moving to a different community, may find their identity under attack.

The greater cost may have been in relations between Reform Judaism and the other Jewish movements. Prior to 1983, most rabbis in all the movements acted under a principle of presumption. If an individual claimed to be Jewish, she or he would ordinarily be trusted. The patrilineal descent resolution threw everyone's identity into question by creating a class of people that would not be considered Jews by all. A child of a Jewish father and non-Jewish mother raised as a Jew and who later adopts an observant lifestyle would be forced to convert before an Orthodox rabbi might officiate at her wedding, whereas that same rabbi might well officiate at the wedding of a child of a Jewish mother and non-Jewish father who was raised as a Christian but who did not formally convert to Christianity—although a Reform rabbi might not officiate in that case.

For the Conservative movement, here was the boundary marker. The movement not only firmly reiterated its commitment to the halakhic definition of a Jew as one born of a Jewish mother, but it even adopted a rabbinic "standard" forbidding Conservative rabbis from officiating at an intermarriage. This is one of the very few offenses that can lead to expulsion from the Rabbinical Assembly. "We," the movement clearly states, do not in any way sanction intermarriage and continue to define a "Jew" according to the halakhah.

This boundary, though, has faced steady grassroots pressure. The complicated issues of identity as they actually get worked out in local synagogues are not easily addressed by stringent ideologies. The United Synagogue of America, the Conservative movement's union of synagogues, prefers an inclusive stance toward intermarried families, thus generating the same kinds of problems that motivated the Reform movement to adopt the resolution on patrilineal descent. While statistics are not available, a relatively sizable proportion of the memberships of many Conservative synagogues might in fact consist of intermarried families. These social facts are forcing the Conservative movement to tone down (but not drop) its hard-line stances on these issues.

With one boundary marker weakened, another had to be strengthened. This time the boundary marker was homosexuality.[14] In 1990 the Central Conference of American Rabbis began to accept openly gay rabbis. Throughout the 1990s both the Central Conference as well as the Union of American Hebrew Congregations (now the Union of Reform Judaism, the union of Reform synagogues) have issued resolutions that edge toward acceptance of same-sex marriages or unions; the latest resolutions leave officiation at such marriages a matter of rabbinic discretion, but call on Reform rabbis to be supportive of their colleagues who do perform them.

Soon after the Reform movement accepted openly gay rabbis, the Conservative movement issued a responsum that forbade homosexuals from becoming Conservative rabbis. As the Orthodox did with the women's issue, the Conservative movement transformed a halakhic matter into a boundary marker, with analogous results. Many gay members of Conservative synagogues feel disenfranchised, and the movement has less flexibility to address their concerns. As in the case of intermarriage, the movement's institutions are just beginning to return to the table to discuss how they might respond to this situation.

The very fact that these American movements have turned issues of gender and sexuality into boundary markers—and not, for example, swordfish, *shatnez* (the combination of wool and linen in a single garment), or social justice—is telling. American movements create distinctly American-style borders, and in so doing they share the same rhetorical space. A rabbi associated with Agudath Ha-Rabbanim writes an articulate column that is syndicated in some (non-Jewish) daily newspapers in which he occasionally approvingly cites the opinions of Reform Jews—although his movement in 1997 declared, "Reform and Conservative are not Judaism at all. Their adherents are Jews, according to the Jewish Law, but their religion is not Judaism." Sometimes those groups who understand each other the best (or at least think they do) condemn each other the most. Perhaps, in fact, the increasingly rigid and shrill boundaries that some Jewish movements are erecting today are a condition of their dependence on a shared American culture. The more they fear their similarity, the harder they work to differentiate themselves.

This is why ideological divisiveness tends to be stronger in larger Jewish population centers. A large Jewish population allows for increased niche marketing and creates the need for synagogues and movements to define what makes them unique. Because the movements themselves are mostly headquartered in New York, this local need seeps into national positions. These positions might have resonance in other large urban communities (e.g., Chicago, Los Angeles, Boston, and Cleveland) but they ring hollow in smaller Jewish communities. In effect, the "official" platforms of the big three Jewish movements—Reform, Conservative, and Orthodox—despite all their differences, constitute a kind of American urban Judaism. Orthodox, more specifically, is concentrated in the Northeast; about two-thirds of all American Orthodox Jewish adults live in that region of the country. Smaller Jewish communities cannot afford such rigid boundaries. Many "one-congregation" communities offer some combination of liberal and more traditional services, striving for inclusiveness. Even medium-sized Jewish communities are now more frequently forming community day schools in order to gather the critical mass necessary for a single day school. On the ground the rigid ideological boundaries dissolve or at least become more permeable.

Some ideological boundaries, however, have grown impermeable. All Jewish movements categorically reject "Messianic Jews," formerly more commonly known as Jews for Jesus. A loose confederation of independent congregations, the Messianic Jewish Alliance declares that "Messianic Judaism is a Biblically-based movement of people who, as committed Jews, believe in Yeshua (Jesus) as the Jewish Messiah of Israel of whom the

Jewish Law and Prophets spoke." Generally comprised of (or at least targeted to) Jews, "Messianic Judaism" subscribes to the dual ethnic and religious notion of Israel, apparently rejects the rabbinic tradition as well as the rituals that its members see as growing out of it, and asserts that the biblical prophecies of the messiah have been fulfilled in the person of Jesus. Because most of these beliefs find parallels in other accepted Jewish groups (e.g., some ethnically identified Jewish groups also reject the rabbis, and some Lubavitch Hasidim think that the biblical messianic prophecies have been fulfilled, but in the person of their departed rebbe), Messianic Judaism raises troubling issues of Jewish identification. What makes Messianic Judaism so outside the institutional Jewish pale that, in his comprehensive guide to Reform Jewish living, Mark Washofsky can state "in no uncertain terms that the religion of these 'Jewish Christian' groups is *not* Judaism but Christianity and that a Jew who adopts their doctrine becomes an apostate"?[15]

The widespread Jewish rejection of Messianic Judaism as "Judaism" is based on ideological, historical, and social factors. The other Jewish movements fight fiercely among themselves, but their fights are all based in a common tradition. All parties, to use a legal metaphor, stipulate to more or less the same tradition, although they differ significantly on its authority and interpretation. By refusing to stipulate to this shared tradition, Messianic Jews put themselves outside of this "conversation," and by joining in their rejection of Messianic Judaism the other Jewish institutions reinforce their own sense of shared identity. Although the rejection of the rabbinic tradition ideologically distances Messianic Judaism from the other Jewish movements, more significant is the historical freight implicit in the affirmative acceptance of Jesus. As structurally similar as the messianism of Messianic Jews and some Lubavitch Hasidim might appear, Jesus is not the rebbe. In American Jewish historical memory, especially after the Holocaust and despite the almost complete assimilation of Jews into American society, Christianity remains a somewhat frightening other, a perpetrator of horrendous violence against Jews over the last two thousand years. For a Jew to accept Jesus as the messiah is to assert that the many Jews who were killed precisely because they refused to make this assertion were foolish rather than courageous; it is to render a mockery of Jewish martyrs. This possibility repels many Jews.

At least as powerful a factor for the widespread rejection of Messianic Judaism by American Jewish organizations is the particular sociological position of American Jews. Major Jewish institutions over the last fifty years have developed an alarmist message of assimilation—Jews have done too good a job assimilating and thriving in American society, to a point that threatens their ethnic and religious distinctiveness. If the driving question among Ashkenazic Jews two or three generations ago was "How can we be part of America?" today it is "Why be Jewish?" All Jewish institutions support some kind of distinctive Jewish identity, which means sharpening that Jewish identity by contrasting it with the identities it is not—most easily and commonly, Christianity. By blurring that line, Messianic Judaism is seen as promoting the end of a distinctive Jewish identity.

Perhaps there is no greater evidence of the distinctively American character of all of these institutions, movements, and ideologies than the simple and obvious fact that they have had limited appeal outside the United States. Even in Canada and South America, Jewish movements affiliated with or based on American institutions have had only limited and local success, and some have gained none at all. Far from preserving some essential and pure tradition, these movements have all actively filtered and shaped various aspects of their tradition in accord with their unique social circumstances.

Whether among Catholics, Jews, or any other religious group, the beliefs and rituals of individual practitioners rarely line up in any consistent or predictable way with the norms of the "official" institutions to which they might even belong. Not surprisingly, then, the Judaism of most American Jews reflects that of the ideological movements only slightly if at all. While there are legitimate criticisms of the National Jewish Population Survey of 2000 and the conclusions drawn from that data, the statistics provided by the survey offer a fascinating snapshot of some aspects of American Jewish life.[16] According to this data, only 40 percent of American Jewish households belong to synagogues. Of this group, 39 percent belong to Reform synagogues, 33 percent to Conservative synagogues, 21 percent to Orthodox synagogues, and 3 percent to Reconstructionist synagogues. These figures diverge from institutional self-identification: 35 percent of American Jews consider themselves to be Reform, 26 percent to be Conservative, and 10 percent to be Orthodox. This simple measure of identification raises more questions than it provides answers: What is the "Judaism" of all those who identify with a movement but are unaffiliated with one of that movement's synagogues? How is the Judaism of the 60 percent of American Jewish households that do not belong to synagogues to be accounted for?

While this survey data does not ask about matters of beliefs, its questions about ritual further reveal the complexity of American Judaism. Of the entire American Jewish population, 77 percent hold or attend a Passover seder, 72 percent light Hannukah candles, 59 percent fast on Yom Kippur, 28 percent light Shabbat candles, 27 percent attend synagogue monthly, and 21 percent keep kosher at home. Those who align with Jewish ideological movements are not always with the program. "Orthodox" Judaism distinguishes itself by its commitment to halakhic norms, including refraining from business dealings on the Sabbath, regular attendance at religious services, and maintenance of the Jewish food laws. According to the survey data, among self-identified Orthodox Jews, 78 percent refrain from handling money on Shabbat, 58 percent attend religious services once a week or more, 75 percent keep kosher outside the house, and 86 percent keep kosher inside the house. Recognizing that most Conservative Jews diverge from prescribed Conservative ritual practice (which is actually much in line with that of the Orthodox), the survey's authors presented self-identified Conservative Jews with a somewhat different set of questions. Within this group, 89 percent attended or held a Passover seder in the prior year, 85 percent attended services at least once in the prior year, and 26 percent (30 percent of those who are also members of Conservative synagogues) keep kosher at home. Modifying the questions, again, for self-identified Reform Jews, the survey found that 82 percent attended or held a Passover seder in the prior year, 72 percent attended services at least once in the prior year, and 57 percent (70 percent of those who are also members of Reform synagogues) fasted on Yom Kippur. These, of course, are only the surveyed behaviors, which cannot begin to capture the wide and unpredictable variety of Jewish life in America.

Even more so than the American Jewish institutions and movements, individual Jews read and practice their tradition in American terms. According to one recent study by Steven Cohen and Arnold Eisen, individual Jewish identity in America largely takes for granted the American value of individualism, or "the sovereign self." American Jews "aim to make Jewish narratives part of their own personal stories, by picking and choosing among new and inherited practices and texts so as to find the combination they as individuals can authentically affirm."[17] It is not enough to say that a certain percentage of Jews "attended" a Passover seder; it is far more revealing to note the license they feel free in taking to conduct that ritual, "skipping those acts or scenes that carry little obvious personal meaning or significance, and adding or emphasizing others."[18] Most American Jews connect with each other ethnically rather than religiously, and despite their frequently deep commitment to God they do not, according to Cohen and Eisen, expect to find spirituality in the synagogue. Their religious life, rather, is patched together from incomplete snippets of knowledge of the textual tradition and rituals to which they have often nostalgic connections, most commonly enacted within familial settings.

Judaism in America, whether on an institutional or individual level, is hardly simple to describe. Jews subscribe to notions of the people Israel that range from a "faith-community" (classical Reform Judaism) to the tribalism of ethnicity. The Jewish movements nearly all participate in a conversation whose shape is determined by traditional texts, but most American Jews have little if any knowledge of these texts. American Jews practice an overlapping set of rituals, but do so in different ways and with understandings of them that have little to do with their "canonical" interpretations. Yet, despite these differences, American Jews and their movements remain identifiably American, linked by their shared cultural assumptions. Jewish diversity mirrors in quantity and quality that of America itself.

Historical context, however, can only account for local similarity. It leaves open the question of how American Judaism is linked to other non-American or noncontemporary Jewish communities. In what meaningful sense can we speak more globally about Judaism? To gain some leverage on this question, we must turn briefly to Israel.

"To your offspring," God declares to Abraham, "I assign this land, from the river of Egypt to the great river, the river Euphrates" (Genesis 15:18). As welcoming as America (as Spain many years earlier) has been to the Jews, the "golden land" is not the "promised land," the land that God promised to the children of Abraham. In one respect, "Zion" was a mythical land, a land that signified God's blessing and redemption, at whose center stood "the place that I will show," as the author of Deuteronomy constantly intones. The biblical treatment of Zion is at times so ahistorical and unanchored to a specific piece of real estate that the Puritans, and then American settlers in the nineteenth century, felt no discomfort in applying the concept to their own settlements in North America.

Zion, though, is not only a concept. It refers to a real geographical area in which Israelites established their kingdoms in the first millennium BCE, and in which, later, Jewish life would thrive. With the loss first of political power in the first century BCE, and then the slow erosion of Jewish self-autonomy through the Middle Ages, the Jewish community in the land of Zion lost both numbers and vitality. Despite the amazing vibrancy of Jewish life in the sixteenth century in some cities in the Land of Israel, by the nineteenth century the Jewish community had dwindled; there were about twenty-four thousand Jews living in Palestine in 1880 under Ottoman rule.

These Jews remained through the community's decline primarily because they saw the land not as a political state—indeed, the political arrangements over the territory were seen as entirely irrelevant—but because the promised land was seen as holy land. The small and relatively poor Jewish community living in Jerusalem through the Ottoman period saw themselves as living closer to God. Their strong notion of sacred space was shared in kind, if not degree, by the many other Jews who made pilgrimages, or who desired to make pilgrimages, to the holy land. Even the rationalist rabbi and philosopher Maimonides, who seems to deny that holiness could inhere more to one location than to another, desired to travel to the holy land—although not enough to vacate his cushy palace job in Egypt.

Zionism was a late-nineteenth-century political movement that owed more to emerging ideas of European state nationalism than it did to the Hebrew Bible or religious ideas of sacred space. The first Zionist immigrations to Palestine in the late-nineteenth and earliest twentieth centuries (they are conventionally referred to as the first to fifth *aliyot*, the plural of aliyah, deriving from a Hebrew verb that means "ascent") were composed primarily of secular Western European Jews. As in America, though, these Central and Western European Jews were soon overwhelmed by Jews from Eastern Europe—about 180,000 Eastern European Jews arrived in Palestine between 1881 and 1931 (compared to about 2.5 million Eastern European Jews who immigrated to America during this same period). A flood of refugees and concentration camp survivors (again, mainly Eastern European) arrived after the end of World War II.

Sketched very roughly, the Jewish population in Israel in 1948 was divided between three primary interest groups: older and established families who were far more impressed with Israel as holy land rather than a political state, radically secular Western European Jews, and more traditionally minded Eastern European Jews. These divisions were hardly all inclusive, but they capture a dynamic that would be etched on the religious formation at the establishment of the state. Although vastly outnumbered, the Western secularists took the lead in the political constitution of the State of Israel. The political arrangements that they made with the more traditional

Jews were characterized by pragmatic accommodation. While the State of Israel was to be essentially secular, it was to be informed (phrased in a brilliantly vague and ambiguous way) by Jewish law and customs. Moreover, following the Ottoman model, personal and status law was to be handled by the appropriately recognized religious communities themselves. Marriages and divorces, for example, were to be administered solely by religious communities; there was (and remains) no option for "civil" marriage or divorce. For Jews, the "recognized" religious authority was that of the Chief Rabbinate. Its financial support would come from the governmental ministries that traditionally, per the original agreements at the foundation of the state, have been controlled by the more religious factions.

As this ambiguous and tense arrangement was being worked out through the 1950s, the Israeli demographic profile began to shift. In 1949–50 some 52,000 Jews of Yemen were brought to Israel, followed almost immediately by the emigration of about 125,000 Jews from Iraq. Through the decade, Jews from Turkey, Syria, Egypt, Libya, Tunisia, Algeria, and especially Morocco flooded into the state. While the foundations of the state were decidedly Ashkenazic, its population was tilting to Sephardic and Eastern. Like some Eastern European counterparts, these Jews were "traditional" in the sense that they followed the customs of their families and communities. Yet while there was some overlap between the basic shape of European and Mediterranean Jewish traditions, they also differed significantly. The country encountered another demographic jolt around 1990, when almost 200,000 Jews from the former Soviet Union, the vast majority of whom were secular and who had been totally isolated from anything Jewish, emigrated to Israel.[19]

Demographics tell only part of the story and in this case the less interesting and important part. America too supports a demographically diverse Jewish community. The difference between America and Israel, though, is the state. The Jewish State, with its politics and power, fundamentally shapes Jewish religious life in Israel.

The history and demographics of the state never created the conditions that in Western and Central Europe and then America led to modern Jewish ideologies. Indeed, these movements, which were at best ambivalent about the formation of the Jewish state, largely absented themselves from the state and its politics. The result of these factors, along with the institutionalization of the Ottoman system of religious administration, was the development of a single ideological split within Israeli society between "religious" and "secular," rather than that of an ideological spectrum as seen in America. It is embedded in the legal and administrative structure of the state, which divides, for example, its public school system into "official" and "official religious," and in granting all authority over Jewish religious matters to the office of the Chief Rabbinate. It is also much a part of the social and cultural consciousness of the Israeli public, the majority of whom descend from families who have had little connection to the Western ideological movements. The exemption from military service (normally expected of all citizens) that "religious" teenagers can receive for studying at a yeshiva, and the resentment and bitterness that that engenders among the "secular," further reinforces this basic fault line.

The line between secular and religious, it should be noted, is not strongly marked by issues of gender. Israel never had a "sexual revolution" like the one in America; issues of feminism, gender, and homosexuality never rose to the status of boundary markers. In part this is due to the socialist ideology on which the state was founded, which explicitly affirmed gender equality. While there are, of course, passionate Israeli advocates for both feminism and gay rights, feminism as a movement has been pushed to the ideological margins; its very existence sits in an uneasy tension with a basic part of Israeli self-understanding. At the same time, in contradiction to this ideology of gender of equality, the Sephardic and Eastern Jewish communities were far more comfortable living with gender separation than their European counterparts, and in the past these women were far less likely to agitate for equality. This is not to say that there was (and is) less sex discrimination in Israel than America—despite relatively progressive legal protections, women and homosexuals probably suffer more social discrimination in Israel than in the United States. But, unlike the hot-button issue of military service, until very recently Jewish religious communities in Israel did not use it to help define themselves.

Ideological lines, here as always, fail to capture the true texture of religious life. According to a recent survey, about 10 percent of the Israeli Jewish population identifies itself as hard-core secularists, and another 20 percent as "religious." This leaves 70 percent of the Israeli Jewish population seeming to float between these two poles. These Jews often categorize themselves as "traditional," somewhat eclectically blending together different traditional elements in ways that are meaningful for them and their families. They might, for example, have a Shabbat meal on Friday night in accord with the customs of their ancestors before the teenagers head out to the disco. Or, on Yom Kippur, they might fast, but instead of going to synagogue will take their children out to ride their bicycles in the nearly deserted streets. An otherwise "secular" man might insist that his girlfriend immerse in the mikveh after her menstrual period so that they can resume sexual relations. Along strictly ideological grounds, this normal religious texture of Israeli religious life seems incoherent.

There is, though, logic behind the incoherence. Some Israeli societal institutions as well as its foundational ideology drive toward Jewish unity. This trend, working directly against the forces that split Israeli Jews into "secular" and "religious," ultimately keeps Israeli Jewish society from tearing at the seams. In order to absorb the different Jewish ethnic communities, Israeli society developed a Jewish "melting pot" approach to culture. Unlike the mosaic model of modern America, Israeli culture drove toward, as an ideal, the eradication of Jewish communal differences. Instead of being Russian Jews, Moroccan Jews, Iraqi Jews, and American Jews in Israel, the logic goes, "we" are all Israeli Jews. This single model of Israeli Jewish culture, of course, is a highly contested ideal. Originally the "Israeli" was to conform to an ideal created by the Ashkenazic secular elite. More recently this model has been challenged by the Sephardic and Eastern communities, who correctly see it as only paying lip service to a universalistic ideal; the "we" is based on Ashkenazic models. It also never fully applied; Jewish communities continued to adhere to some of their distinctive practices and ideas. Nevertheless, there is a strong (if, perhaps, declining) push to see all Israeli Jews as constituting a single cultural unity.

The most significant institutional force for promoting this ideology is the military. Aside from the small fraction of religious teenagers that avoid the military completely, all Israelis, men and women, can spend anywhere, on average, between two and four years in active service, followed by annual reserve duty (for men only) for the next twenty years. Aside from a few units that are distinctly "religious," most of the units are mixed, and the pressure to get along with fellow-soldiers is strong. The military has long been seen not only as necessary for defense but also as a vehicle for social, cultural, and religious integration of disparate Jewish immigrant communities. It is also in the military that a more or less distinctive Israeli "Judaism of the middle" is forged. The military provides an environment that allows for most of the basic conditions for halakhic observance, but the observance is tempered by pragmatism and a spirit of accommodation. Basic Jewish practices, such as kashrut and commemoration of Shabbat and the holidays, are part of the unthinking texture of life; it is as much a part of religion as it is of culture. This approach to religious ideas and rituals is reflected outside the military in a culture that largely sees Jewish customs as voluntaristic but not ideological. Unlike, for example, the Reform and Reconstructionist movements in America, Israeli Jews have not developed an ideology to justify their nonhalakhic approach to Judaism.

This set of conditions accounts for the relative unpopularity of these Western religious movements in Israel. The Reform and Conservative movements have been trying for years, mostly unsuccessfully, to establish themselves in Israel. They correctly complain that they are working at a legal disadvantage—the Chief Rabbinate refuses to recognize their rabbis as legitimate Jewish authorities, and thus deny to them the right to officiate at marriages and conversions. The movements also rightly note that they offer ideologies that would justify the practices of the bulk of the Israeli Jewish population. They have far more problems, though, arguing to the very Israeli population to whom they appeal why they actually need these ideologies. For many Israelis who when outside Israel might easily identify with one of these movements, within the Jewish State these movements fail to speak to them.

The fact that 20 percent of Israeli Jews identify themselves as Orthodox should not obscure the many significant fissures that divide this "Orthodox" community. Unlike in Europe and the United States, where divisions within the Orthodox world frequently revolve around approaches to modernity and the relationship with secular and Christian societies, the divisions within Israeli Orthodoxy are rooted in both ethnic origin and the state and its politics. Traditional Jews from Sephardic and Eastern origins (e.g., Morocco, Yemen, Iraq) continue to maintain local synagogues, are represented on the national level by the Sephardic chief rabbi, and have their own political party. Not surprisingly, the distinctive religious customs of these individual communities have weakened as succeeding generations integrate into Israeli society.

One intriguing example of this process of integration is explored by Susan Sered in her book, *Women as Ritual Experts*.[20] Closely observing a community of elderly Kurdistani women in Jerusalem who regularly attended a municipal day center, Sered observed that these women maintained many of their distinctive customs and beliefs, which often related unpredictably to halakhah. They continued, for example, to sort their rice, grain by grain, seven times over, prior to Passover despite the assurance of local rabbis that this was unnecessary. Just as stubbornly, they ignored the rabbis who asserted that they needed to ritually wash their hands prior to eating bread. They saw a link between many of their rituals, such as lighting Sabbath candles, visiting the graves of Jewish holy men, and saying blessings prior to consumption, to the health and fertility of their family members. Their children, on the other hand, maintained few of these distinctive practices and beliefs.

The more significant split today within Israeli Orthodoxy ultimately is informed by its adherents' theological stance toward the state. The problem goes back to the beginning of the Zionist movement. In the late nineteenth and early twentieth centuries many traditional Jews opposed the creation of the State of Israel as a theological affront to God; God, they asserted, will return the people Israel to their land during the period of redemption—to anticipate this divine return through human action is to deny faith in God. The spiritual heirs of this position who today live in the State of Israel fall along a spectrum, from those who utterly deny the legitimacy of the state and refuse to have anything at all to do with it to those who actually participate in the government but refuse to serve in the military. Although this group is the face of Orthodoxy that is at the center of the division between "secular" and "religious" Jews in Israel, it is small relative to those who would identify as "religious Zionists."

Theodor Herzl's secular Zionism in the late nineteenth and earliest twentieth centuries soon found some supporters among traditional Jews from Eastern Europe. The intellectual justification for this support was still very much in formation throughout the early twentieth century. The earliest religious Zionists justified their support of a Jewish state along both theological and practical grounds. Theologically, they saw the foundation of a Jewish state in the land of Israel as a move toward redemption. Because Zionism was created by God, these thinkers cleverly (but somewhat illogically) argued, it too must be good and part of God's plan. By creating a Jewish state, Jews are not going against God's will but in fact are acting as agents of it. This theological justification was deeply informed by contemporary optimistic views of progress, in which humans were seen as moving along a straight line toward "redemption" and "perfection," however conceived. For these early religious Zionists, the establishment of a Jewish state in Palestine was an enactment of the "ingathering of the exiles," seen as the first stage of God's promised redemption. Such an active eschatological theology primarily but indirectly draws upon kabbalistic ideas, in which humans play an active role in bringing redemption. When a new prayer for the State of Israel was formulated, it was no accident that, unlike the prayers for the welfare of the state upon which it was modeled and that Jews had included in their services from the medieval period, this new prayer included the assertion that the State of Israel was the start of the redemptive process.

There was also a practical side to the support of religious Zionists for the new political state. Several of its early leaders saw the State of Israel as holding the greatest promise for establishing the conditions that would allow for the fullest expression of a life according to Torah, as they understood it. A Jewish society, even a largely secular one, would be far more tolerant of Jewish religious life than that of Eastern Europe. Bolder thinkers had a more expansive vision of using a Jewish state to meld "Orthodox" Judaism with secular studies to produce a uniquely Jewish environment.

These lines of justification converged in the thought of Rabbi Abraham Isaac Kook (1865–1935).[21] Born in Latvia, Kook immigrated to Palestine in 1904 and became the first Ashkenazi chief rabbi in 1921. His mystical theology embraced secular Zionists, whom he saw as fulfilling the divine plan for redemption. He even designed educational curricula that integrated secular studies. This inclusive vision was critical in gaining secular support for the office of the Chief Rabbinate and the acceptance of a "place at the table" for Orthodox leaders and interests. Kook's vision, which was largely accepted by secular Jews in Palestine, was of a Jewish state in which religious and nonreligious worked side by side for redemption—although each group might understand the meaning of that term quite differently.

What Kook probably never did envision was the nationalist exposition given to this theology by his son, Rabbi Zvi Yehudah Kook. According to the younger Kook, the critical factor that would lead to redemption was not the building of state and the "ingathering of the exiles," but the actual settling of the promised land of Israel. He thus turned the focus to the physical land. It was no longer good enough to establish a Jewish state on *some* of the land, now it was a religious imperative to settle *all* of it. Conversely, it was against God's eschatological plan to unsettle, or to withdraw from, any of the promised land. The land became "holy space," and by reviving this thread of biblical and (to a lesser degree) rabbinic theology, Kook essentially reversed the long subordination within rabbinic tradition of holy space to holy time.

This theology of the land, previously marginal, found confirmation in the Israeli victory in the 1967 war. The Israeli conquest of the West Bank, and of the Old City of Jerusalem especially, brought theology, history, and politics into a fateful convergence. From the period shortly after the conquest it became clear, solely from a political perspective, that the need to occupy this land for reasons of security was counterbalanced by the practical, legal, and moral implications of occupying the territories and their over one million Palestinian inhabitants. The calculus, however, was not only political.

The drama of Jews gaining sovereignty over the site of the Temple Mount for the first time since the Hasmonean kings evoked extraordinarily powerful emotions. Suddenly, the distant hopes encapsulated in the Hebrew Bible and the prayer books were realized in a military victory that many saw as miraculous.

Zvi Yehudah Kook's version of religious Zionism exploded after 1967. The 1967 war was confirmation to his followers that the world was on the cusp of the redemptive age and that it was in the hands of the Jews to bring it to fruition by settling on land that was rightfully theirs. He expounded this theology through Merkaz HaRav, the influential yeshiva that his father founded. Shortly after the 1967 war, some of Kook's devoted students quickly put the theology into practice by settling in the occupied territories. At first creating illegal settlements, they organized themselves into Gush Emunim, the "Block of the Faithful," which found allies in the secular ultranationalist political parties. Under the Likud government led by Menahem Begin in the mid-late 1970s and their successors, many of the illegal settlements were recognized and new settlements encouraged.

This is not the place to discuss the charged and complex political and ethical issues involved in the settlement of the lands occupied by Israel since 1967. For our purposes, most important is the effect of this movement on Israeli religious life. By tapping into a deep historical consciousness and yoking naked nationalism to a redemptive, quasi-mystical theology, Gush Emunim successfully placed the issue of the promised land and its settlement as a defining issue of religious Zionism. Religion and politics have melded; political issues become religious quagmires. This is the religious logic that led (perversely, many have argued) to the assassination of Prime Minister Yitzhak Rabin, which the Jewish assassin justified with a halakhic argument. It is also the logic that has led and will continue to lead to the resistance on the part of settlers to the Israeli government's dismantling of their settlements. And it is the logic that drives extremists to seek the rebuilding of the Third Temple on the Temple Mount, the reinstitution of the sacrificial service, and the hoped-for ushering in of the messianic period.

The impact of the Gush Emunim movement and its theology on Israeli Orthodoxy go well beyond the relative few who actually decided to "settle" on Palestinian land. For many, to be Orthodox means to take a political stance against withdrawal. All other considerations, such as gender, take a decided backseat to the politics of withdrawal and the essential holiness of the land. Even the Israeli Orthodox Jews on the political left—a significant minority—in large part define themselves by their political position. On a larger scale, this theology has contributed to a sense of "holy space," that there is something not only promised but even intrinsically and eternally holy about the land of Israel. For an Israeli Orthodox Jew to deny the holiness of space in favor of divine omnipresence is to put oneself on the very margins of Israeli Orthodoxy.

Religious Zionists of all types differentiate themselves from non-Zionist Orthodox Jews by their dress, openness to modern culture, and, most important, their stance toward military service. While one might not expect to find a religious Zionist at the beach on Shabbat or in a nonkosher restaurant, there is little to distinguish religious Zionists from nonreligious Israelis. The men serve in the military and the women, who are able to gain an exemption because of the potentially corrupting influence of the army on them, often join an alternative (all-female) governmental program, Sherut le'am, "Service for the People," for a year or two.

Orthodox Jewish feminism, like religious pluralism, has only just arrived in Israel, and even then is primarily confined to immigrants from the United States and Western Europe. A few Orthodox congregations, mainly

1.3 Jews praying at the Western Wall in Jerusalem.

Copyright © AP/Wide World Photos, used with permission

in Jerusalem, experiment with integrating women into the prayer services. The "Women of the Wall" engaged in a decade-long legal and political battle to gain the right to hold women's prayer groups, with women wearing religious garments, at the Western Wall. Not only have they failed to gain this right, but in the interim the Orthodox establishment that has authority over the site has tightened its hold, demanding that women now conform to stricter standards of modesty even in the plaza behind the wall.

By and large, Israeli Orthodox women focus their religious life domestically. The growing difference between the roles of women in Western and Israeli Orthodoxy is in part due to social conditions. Whereas in the United States, for example, the push toward increasing female participation in religious services is primarily driven by highly educated, professional women who experience a gap between their high-status place in the secular world and their confinement behind the mechitza in synagogue, the achievement of higher education and high-status jobs by Orthodox women in Israel is far rarer.

When the early Zionists markedly contrasted Diaspora Judaism to the strong and proud religion and culture of "Jews in their land," they were onto something. One need not accept the Zionist evaluation of Diaspora Judaism as degenerate or doomed to concede to them that political power plays a critical role in religious formation. The Israeli Chief Rabbinate is perhaps as mystified by American Orthodoxy as the Vatican is baffled by the conduct of American Catholics. American Jews, many of whom see themselves as living in their own promised land, look nervously at the Israeli conflation of nationalism, politics, and religion, and the use of pure political power to suppress Jewish pluralism.

The differences between Western and Israeli Judaism are not confined to these big issues. While there is, of course, an overlapping set of religious practices between American and Israeli Jews, informed (or dictated) by the same texts, there are also significant differences. Israeli synagogue services often do not have a sermon, usually an important part of all Shabbat and holiday services in America. American Jews of all movements often formally, even lavishly, celebrate the coming to bar and bat mitzvah status of their youth, whereas Israelis rarely mark this event in the same way. Without minimizing the shared presence of several central acts (e.g., the use of a *ketubbah* or the ritual washing of the corpse) American Jewish wedding and funeral customs are more similar to many American Christian customs than they are to Israeli Jewish ones, which in turn find closer analogues throughout the Near East. The presence of rice and *kitnyot*, legumes and their derivatives, is so pervasive in Israel during Passover that it is sometimes difficult for visiting Jews who adhere to Ashkenazic customs to find appropriate food. Observant Americans visiting Israel might also find themselves further isolated during the holidays—Israelis observe most of the major holidays for only a single day, whereas "traditional" Jews from outside Israel most often adhere to two days. As much divides as unites the Jews of West and East.

The Jewish communities of the United States and Israel offer rich case studies of how living Jewish communities continuously recreate their Judaism. Even with the shared conditions of modernity—with their largely shared faith in reason, the opportunity to engage in Judaism on a voluntary basis, and their participation in societies heavily shaped by the same technological advances—these two largest Jewish communities of our day fundamentally differ in their reading of their texts and traditions. The texts and traditions are frequently identical, but their actualization, the ways in which their receivers understand and draw meaning from them, differ enormously. American Jews refract this legacy through the conditions of modern America, Israelis through their own unique social conditions. Power and land, the issues that so pervade the conception of Judaism in Israel, simply do not resonate in an American context.

According to most grand narratives of Judaism, the Enlightenment and the process of Jewish emancipation during the eighteenth and nineteenth centuries ruptured Jewish continuity. Before the eighteenth century, the "premodern" period, Judaism was thought to be relatively monolithic, led by the rabbis who also served as the communal leaders. Modernity brought diversity—best represented by the variety of the Jewish ideological movements—and individualism, the notion that individual Jews could become independent religious actors outside the constraints of the community. It is undeniable that Jewish life and practice did change in the Western communities that emancipated their Jewish populations. The notion of a historical break, though, should not be pushed too far. Jews from antiquity to the present have turned to their traditional texts and practices for answers to profoundly human problems, shaping these answers in ways that would be meaningful to *them*. The remainder of this book unpacks this assertion, charting the development of these traditional texts and practices and the manifold ways in which Jews, as communities and individuals, interpreted and added to them.

2

CREATING JUDAISM

SOMETIMES AT THE beginning of a semester I cruelly ask my undergraduate students to name three things that they know to be true about Judaism. Almost without fail, several, and not infrequently a majority, will include the assertion that Judaism is the "religion of the book" or, even more specifically, the "religion of the Bible." Unlike some other assertions, this one rarely raises any dissent; the idea that Judaism is in some way close to the Bible is an ingrained part of their outlook, whether or not they are Jews.

The intellectual history of this idea is not difficult to trace. Augustine of Hippo (St. Augustine; 354–430) was perhaps the first writer to fully articulate it in the fifth century CE. According to Augustine, Christians, who at this time had recently gained political power in the Roman Empire, should not harm the Jews because they served a critical role in the salvation history of the Church. The Old Testament had been superseded by Christ but was still to play an important role in the Church, in part as a witness that prophesied Christ's coming. The Jews, stuck in useless antiquity through their slavish adherence to the Old Testament, preserve and guard this prophecy (even if they themselves obstinately refuse to heed it) and will ultimately witness Christ's glory. Augustine, who probably had only a slight acquaintance with real Jews, defines Judaism as the continuing but unchanging religion of the Old Testament and on this basis alone recommends political toleration of the Jews.

About two centuries later, the new Muslim overlords of the Near East developed a similar justification for their grudging political toleration of the Jews in their empire. The Hebrew Bible was seen, in fact, as the record of a real divine revelation to the Jews. Muslim thinkers differed over whether the text is authentic, though later superseded, or whether the Jews had corrupted God's message through faulty transmission of the text of the Bible. In either case, however, Jews and Christians alike were to be considered "people of the book," who unlike pagans were to be tolerated within a Muslim polity.

Much later, in the nineteenth and twentieth centuries, Western Jews began to apply this phrase to themselves. As used by Jews in the modern period, the phrase is emptied of much of its theological baggage. Wanting to present themselves as intellectual or scholarly, they found the phrase "people of the book" useful. When pressed, they might identify that book as the Hebrew Bible (or, for a few, the Talmud), but the point is not the particular book but the studious attention to books generally.

These three strands converge in modern understandings of Judaism as the religion of the Bible. But is it really accurate or useful to call Judaism the religion of the Bible?

As should be clear from the last chapter, a great chasm stands between modern Judaism and the religion of the Hebrew Bible. To illustrate just a few of these differences: The religion of the Bible centers on sacrifice, to be performed (at least according to some passages) at a single, holy location, yet few Jewish groups have offered sacrifices since the destruction of the Jerusalem Temple in 70 CE. The Bible is completely unfamiliar with the modern Jewish practice of not eating milk and meat products together or indeed even cooking them in the same pots at different times. The families of the Bible were, by and large, polygamous, yet among Ashkenazim (Jews from European descent) polygamy has been officially banned for a millennium. The Bible does not know of synagogues, regular prayer, or the obligation of Torah study—all central components of modern rabbinic Judaism.

This distance between biblical religion and that of Judaism has been long noticed, and in fact generated one of the most bizarre moments in the long and torturous history of Jewish-Christian relations, the trial of the Talmud in thirteenth-century France. Prior to the thirteenth century, Christians subscribed to Augustine's notion of the Jews—they were to be politically tolerated because as the keepers of the Old Testament they serve as witnesses to the truth of the New. Their understanding of Judaism was derived completely from their own sacred texts, both the New Testament and the writings of the later Church fathers. In the intellectual ferment of the twelfth and thirteenth centuries (which gave rise to the modern university), Christian friars turned their attention to learning Hebrew and Jewish

sacred writings. And, to their horror, they discovered that the Jev
rich literature and tradition that diverged from the Bible. Far froi
stuck in "useless antiquity," the Jews maintained a vibrant and dynar
gion that was shaped in many respects by the Babylonian Talmud and a long
tradition of commentary on it. The Judaism that the friars discovered was
not the one they had expected. Their response was to put the Talmud on
trial, charging that it was a heresy against *Judaism*.[1] These Christian monks
thus positioned themselves as the guardians of "pure" Judaism (i.e., the religion of the Old Testament) against the Jews, who had perverted their own
religion with their Talmud.

The Bible has always played a central role in Judaism. That role, however,
is fluid, shifting, and highly complex. *The Bible* is itself an ambiguous term,
and the text that it signifies points both backward and forward. On the one
hand, the Bible points back to the religion(s) of its authors, groups of Israelites living over the course of centuries whose texts appear to have been
edited, combined, and canonized in the sixth century BCE. On the other
hand, it became the first link of a distinctively Jewish textual tradition, a text
to which most Jewish groups since antiquity have ascribed authority while
at the same time practicing a religion that would have been unrecognizable
to its authors. So, given this Janus-like nature of the Bible, what exactly is it
and how do we explain it?

Despite the easy and unselfconscious way that most popular media uses the
term *The Bible*, not all Bibles are alike. *Bible* is itself a Christian appropriation of a Greek word that means "book"; the Bible is "*the* book." For Christians, the Bible has (at least) two major parts, the Old Testament and the
New Testament. Originally written in Hebrew, the Old Testament records
God's covenant with His people Israel. According to early Christian writers
(including Paul), the arrival of the Christ (the "anointed one") occasioned a
new covenant that superseded the old. Hence, *Old Testament* is a theologically laden term, implying its status vis-à-vis the New Testament.

It is no surprise, then, that Jews never used or liked the term *Old Testament*. Early on, Jews began to term this collection of books the *Tanak*.
Tanak is actually an acronym (TNK) standing for the book's three major divisions. Torah ("Teaching") denotes the first five books (Genesis to Deuteronomy), which is why it is sometimes referred to in Hebrew as the *humash*
(the Hebrew root means "five") and in English as the Pentateuch (deriving

TABLE 2.1 Books of the Tanak

TORAH (PENTATEUCH)	NEVI'IM (PROPHETS)	KETUVIM (WRITINGS)
Genesis	Joshua	Psalms
Exodus	Judges	Proverbs
Leviticus	1 Samuel	Job
Numbers	2 Samuel	Song of Songs
Deuteronomy	1 Kings	Ruth
	2 Kings	Lamentations
	Isaiah	Ecclesiastes
	Jeremiah	Esther
	Ezekiel	Daniel
	Hosea	Ezra
	Joel	Nehemiah
	Amos	1 Chronicles
	Obadiah	2 Chronicles
	Jonah	
	Micah	
	Nahum	
	Habakkuk	
	Zephaniah	
	Haggai	
	Zechariah	
	Malachi	

from the Greek root for "five"). The second division, *Nevi'im* ("Prophets"), refers to the prophetic books, and *Ketuvim* ("Writings") includes the remaining books (e.g., Psalms, Proverbs, Job).

The terms *Old Testament* and *Tanak* thus indicate largely the same text while at the same time placing an implicit value on the theological importance and authority of that text. The Torah is no more "the Teaching" for a non-Jew than is the Old Testament "old" for a Jew. For this reason scholars use the value-neutral term *Hebrew Bible* to denote those parts of the Bible originally written in Hebrew.

Not only terminology divides Bibles. While mostly similar, the books and their order sometimes differs between Jewish and Christian Bibles (or indeed, among Christian Bibles themselves). The Revised English Bible, for example, puts 1 and 2 Chronicles after 2 Kings, whereas the Tanak places these books at the very end of Writings. The Tanak contains twenty-four books.

Perhaps the most significant difference between Bibles is their original language. In the third century BCE the Hebrew Torah was translated into Greek. A legend that probably postdates the translation tells of the Egyptian king Ptolemy summoning seventy Jewish elders to Alexandria to translate the Torah into Greek; isolated from each other, each emerged with precisely the same Greek translation of the Hebrew text. The legend of the seventy elders gave this Greek translation its name, the Septuagint (or LXX). Scholars today debate whether this translation was initiated by the non-Jewish king for administrative and legal reasons or whether it was a product of the Jewish community itself, which was losing linguistic access to the original Hebrew. Whatever the motivation, the Septuagint gained wide acceptance among Jews through antiquity. When Paul and the Gospel writers quoted the Hebrew Bible, they used the Septuagint. The Jewish philosopher Philo, writing in the first century BCE to the first century CE, also appears to have used the Septuagint.

Eventually, some Jews rejected the Septuagint in favor of another Greek translation before, ultimately, rejecting any Greek translation as authoritative. The Hebrew text of the Hebrew Bible would not be fully stabilized until the work of a group of Jewish scribes, the Masoretes, in the early Middle Ages; this became known as the Masoretic Text. In addition to finally fixing the text, they added the vowels (Hebrew does not use separate letters to indicate vowels), divisions, punctuations, and musical notations that govern the liturgical readings of the Torah.

For Jews today the Torah exists in two forms. For liturgical purposes it exists as a scroll. Torah scrolls are handwritten on parchment in a highly regulated fashion; a small or medium-sized scroll rarely costs less than ten thousand dollars. The scroll's text contains no vowels, punctuation, chapter

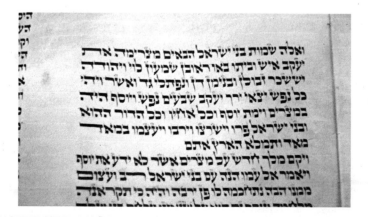

2.1 From a Torah scroll, the beginning of the book of Exodus.

Courtesy of Temple Emanu-El, Providence, Rhode Island

2.2 *Pentateuch, Haftarot, Megillot,* printed in Naples 1491 by Bnei Soncino. The commentary of Rabbi Shlomo ben Isaac (Rashi) runs along the outside margin in a different script. The Masoretic Text—the same text as shown in the Torah scroll above—runs down the center of the page.

Courtesy of the Library of the Jewish Theological Seminary of America

or verse markers, or cantillation notes—these must be memorized by the scroll's readers. Most commonly, then, Jews today read the Hebrew Bible from its Masoretic Text, which is printed as a codex (i.e., book form) and is much more accessible.

Many early Christians, however, adopted the Septuagint as the authoritative version of the Hebrew Bible. In the fifth century CE St. Jerome (ca. 345–420) produced a new, Latin translation of the Hebrew Bible, the Vulgate. The Western Church accepted the Vulgate as its authoritative text, whereas the Eastern (Orthodox) Church continues to use the Septuagint. To further complicate matters, the Protestant movements rejected the authority of the Vulgate, asserting that the Hebrew version of the Bible—or at least authorized translations of the Hebrew version (such as the King James Version, for the Anglican Church and its offshoots)—was authoritative.

The matter of language is important because all translations are also interpretations. The Hebrew of the Bible is not always clear, and Greek and Latin (and modern English) translators had to make interpretive decisions. By ascribing divine inspiration to the King James Version of the Bible in

1611, the Anglican Church sought to produce an authoritative English version eclectically drawn from previous English translations and the Hebrew, Greek, and Latin versions.[2]

By erasing the differences between versions and languages, the term *The Bible* in fact promotes a skewed picture. Although similar, the Jewish, Catholic, Orthodox, and Protestant Bibles are not the same. And, for traditions that understand every word of a text to be the living word of God, those differences have significant implications. Isaiah 7:14, for example, states: "Assuredly, my Lord will give you a sign of His own accord! Look, the *betulah* is with child and about to give birth to a son." The Hebrew word *betulah* most commonly means "young woman." Christians, however, relying on the Septuagint's translation (*parthenos*), have always read this word as "virgin" and used it as an important proof of the virgin birth and the fulfillment of the prophecy in Jesus. As demonstrated by the history of contentious, sometimes bloody, disputations through antiquity and the Middle Ages that swirled around the "correct" translation of this word, such differences are not a small matter.

Among Jews, however, the Tanak has remained remarkably stable since the production of the Masoretic Text. Through the ages Jews have fought heatedly about the meaning and authority of the biblical text, but they have largely agreed to base these fights on a common Hebrew text. No major Jewish group today ascribes divine authority to any particular translation of the Bible into a modern language; ultimately only the Hebrew version is seen as authoritative. In contrast to *The Bible,* today the *Tanak* does have a stable meaning.

The Tanak contains many different kinds of literature. It contains laws, often but not always gathered into codelike compositions. It is replete with poetry, prophecies, genealogies, and advice and aphorisms that scholars identify as "wisdom literature." It is often unclear if the biblical descriptions of religious beliefs and practices are meant prescriptively or descriptively; the utopian and mundane are difficult to untangle. Above all, though, the Tanak is a narrative. It is a narrative that sometimes loses its way, but as we have it the Tanak has a discernable narrative frame.

The Torah begins the historical narrative very much at the beginning, with the creation of the world, and ends with the Israelites about to enter into and conquer the land of Canaan. After quickly dealing with the formative events that would largely account for the universal features of the human condition and society, the first book of the Torah, Genesis, turns to its real interest, the beginning of Israelite history. According to the book of Genesis, God made a covenant with Abram (later changing his name to Abraham) and his heirs: If they would do what God demanded, God would make them numerous and cause them to inherit the land of Israel. The story of their children, Ishmael and Isaac, and Isaac's children, Jacob and Esau, is one punctuated by fertility problems and high family drama. God, though, affirms the covenant with Jacob, changing his name to Israel. Jacob's twelve sons (and one daughter, who disappears quickly from the story), who become the eponymous ancestors of the twelve tribes, are the "children of Israel." Jacob and his sons move to Egypt to escape famine, and soon their descendents find themselves enslaved by the Egyptians. God chooses Moses to lead the Israelites out of Egypt, into the desert of Sinai, where God contracts another, more detailed covenant with them; most of the Torah's narrative, including the details of this covenant, takes place in Sinai. The Torah ends with the children of these freed slaves poised to enter Canaan, and the book of Joshua (the first book in the section of the Tanak the Prophets) seamlessly tells of their conquest of the promised land. The book of Joshua picks up with the conquest of the land of Canaan by the Israelites, beginning with the famous siege of Jericho.

If the Torah's historical account appears at times to be almost mythical, the first books of the Prophets settles down to more recognizable historiography. The books of Judges and Kings, supplemented by many references in the other prophetic books, tell the story of the rise, consolidation, and fall of the Israelite monarchy (ca. 1000 BCE–586 BCE). After the conquest of Canaan, the Israelites, according to the biblical account, created a loose tribal alliance. With the divinely sanctioned rise of one powerful tribal leader, Saul, the loose alliance began to give way to a monarchy. Saul's successor, David, was an even stronger king who through a brilliant mix of brute power, persuasion, and realpolitik united the monarchy; a gain upon which his son Solomon was able to build through the conquest of neighboring non-Israelite tribes. After Solomon's death this kingdom divided into a Northern and Southern kingdom, each with its own Israelite king and each with its own temple—Shiloh in the North and Jerusalem in the South. The Hebrew Bible directly correlates the fortunes of the kingdoms to the behavior of their leaders; God punishes the wicked and rewards the righteous. The North fell in 722 BCE to the Assyrians, while the South lasted until 587–586 BCE before falling to the Babylonians.

Not long after conquering the southern kingdom of Judah and transferring some of her leaders to Babylonia, Babylonia fell to Persia. Allowed to return to their homeland, most of the Judeans exiled to Babylonia appeared to have stayed where they were, fulfilling perhaps too eagerly Jeremiah's exhortation to "build houses and live in them, plant gardens and eat their fruit. Take wives and beget sons and daughters. . . . Multiply there, do not decrease. And seek the welfare of the city to which I have exiled you" (Jeremiah 29:5–7). Shards of ancient contracts, if at all representative, indicate that these Judeans quickly established themselves in commerce and took Babylonian names.

Around 515 BCE, some of these Judeans, however, took the Persians up on their offer. The prophets Haggai and Zechariah testify to the high ambitions of this community. Both prophets celebrate the rebuilding of the Temple in Jerusalem as heralding a new age. "I am going to shake the heavens and the earth," God commands Haggai to relate to the civil governor, Zerubbabel, "And I will overturn the thrones of kingdoms and destroy the might of the kingdoms of the nations. I will overturn chariots and their drivers. Horses and their riders shall fall, each by the sword of his fellow. On that day . . . I will take you, O My servant Zerubbabel son of Shealtiel . . . and make you as a signet; for I have chosen you" (Haggai 2:21–23).

And then, just as suddenly as Zerubbabel appears in the historical record, he disappears, leaving little more than the foundations of the Temple. According to the biblical book of Ezra, "the adversaries of Judah and Benjamin" (4:1) thwarted Zerubbabel and his cohort. Who were these adversaries? The Judeans who were never deported to Babylonia! "Let us build with you, since we too worship your God, having offered sacrifices to Him since the time of King Esarhaddon of Assyria, who brought us here" (4:2). Only when Zerubbabel rudely rebuffed them did they begin to undermine him.

The same conflict awaited the missions, about fifty years later, of Ezra and Nehemiah. Both led groups of Judeans back to Jerusalem and both had Persian backing. Both also complain about the resistance they encountered not from those who want to block the rebuilding of the Temple but from those who want to join in rebuilding it. The community led by Zerubbabel, Ezra, and Nehemiah clearly saw itself as the true carrier of the Israelite tradition, authorized by God and backed by temporal might. The Tanak ends with King Cyrus's edict granting permission to anyone who wishes "to ascend" from Persia to Jerusalem in order to help rebuild God's house.[3]

As an accurate account of the past, parts of this narrative have been extraordinarily difficult to verify. None of the contemporary but meager evidence from period that the Torah covers corroborates this narrative, and

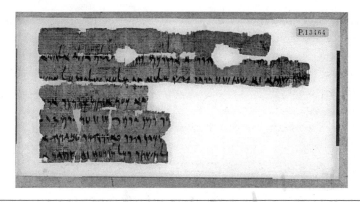

2.3 The "Passover Papyrus" from Elephantine, Egypt, 419 BCE. A letter to the Jewish garrison instructing them not to eat leaven during the holiday of Passover. Photo by Bruce and Kenneth Zuckerman West Semitic Research.

Courtesy Aegyptisches Museum, Berlin

some seems to contradict it. There is no Egyptian record, for example, of the massive enslavement of the Israelites recorded in the book of Exodus. The archaeological remains of the ancient cities of Canaan clearly indicate that they were not overrun in the time of Joshua; even the walls of Jericho did not fall. On the other hand, some internal biblical evidence and some shards of external evidence testify to some version of the united monarchy under David and its later division. The precise contours of the exiles return in the late sixth century are also impossible to verify, but given our knowledge of the Persian King Cyrus's decrees allowing others exiled peoples to return to their land, the biblical story, in some general way, seems plausible.[4]

Yet whatever this narrative lacks in historical accuracy it more than makes up for in the power of its imagination. Like Homer's *Iliad* was for ancient Greek identity, the Tanak's story was so attractive and vivid as to create Israel's formative myth. As portrayed through the Torah, Israel is not like any other nation. Israel is, quite literally, a family, connected by blood. Within the Torah itself there in fact seems to be no provision for "conversion," for becoming a full member of this extended family. The resident alien, the *ger*, might live within the Israelite community, but can never fully cross over. Israel, though, is not merely a family but also a people forged in the shared traumatic historical experience of enslavement and liberation, exile and ingathering. To top it off, Israel has a unique relationship, a covenant with her God YHWH, who takes an inordinate interest in His sometimes stubborn people. The Torah creates "Israel" and does so on multiple levels.[5]

Stories help to create "imagined communities"; they articulate a compelling link between people whose actual connections might be tenuous. The Tanak's story testifies to the formation of a distinctive Israelite identity from among the many peoples of the Ancient Near East. While we do not always know what actually happened, it is clear that at some point, probably slightly before or during the monarchic period, a distinctive Israelite identity emerged. Despite the many similarities these Israelites shared with their neighbors, they also attempted to distinguish themselves through their stories, language, beliefs, and practices. On the testimony of the Tanak itself, this was an identity in flux, contested by the Northern and Southern kingdoms, each of which staked its claim to be the real Israel.

If in the pre-exilic period the Tanak testifies to the formation of Israelite identity, in the exilic and postexilic periods a distinctive identity is taken for granted. Nehemiah and Ezra seem to have had no doubt as to what constitutes an authentic heir to the covenant and worshipper of the God of Israel: genealogical purity along with adherence to the law of Moses as articulated in the Torah. Here a distinctive identity is deployed as much to distinguish themselves from real outsiders as it is to distinguish them from their kin in Judea who never went into exile. The very formation of this new text, the Torah, from ancient and traditional stories, simultaneously asserts both continuity and discontinuity. Ezra and Nehemiah exclude those Judeans who were never exiled from their community and the newly built Temple. These exiles left the land of Israel as Israelites, the "Children of Israel," or "Hebrews," as the Tanak consistently refers to them, but they returned as Jews, the practitioners of a religion that despite its continuity with Israelite religion differs from it markedly.

What, then, was the shape of Israelite religion? Reconstructing Israelite religious history is as difficult as reconstructing its political and social history because the concepts and rituals of the Tanak do not quite add up to a coherent whole. Many later religious thinkers (of all kinds) would try to smooth out the Tanak's inconsistencies—that they are so occupied with these apparent contradictions in fact highlights them.

The very beginning of the Torah illustrates the problem. Genesis 1:1–2:4 tells the wonderfully neat story of the world's creation. God creates the world in a systematic, ordered way, using nothing more than language: "God said . . . and it was so." Every type of creation has its own day. Birds and fish, for example, not only are not created by the same word of God, they are not even created on the same day. God culminates creation with the antiseptic creation of humanity "in our image, after our likeness." Then God ceases work on the seventh day and declares it holy.

Not so in what scholars generally refer to as the second creation account (Genesis 2:4–3:24). Here God creates humans closer to the beginning of the story, introducing a less structured and more organic narrative of creation. Nor does God sit up on high and command with language alone; God gets His hands dirty. God "forms" and "blows"; He performs surgery to bring forth woman, who in the first creation account is created at precisely the same time as the man. This is not the God of Genesis 1. This is an immanent God whose presence is here and now. This God walks in the Garden of Eden seemingly unaware of what His creation is doing (Genesis 3:8–9). Unlike the God of Genesis 1, this is a God described in anthropomorphic language—this God is less majestic, more like us.

The tension between these two images of the divine plays out through the rest of the Tanak. The Ten Commandments famously forbid the representation of God, but the Hebrew Bible constantly, but not consistently, uses anthropomorphic language to describe God. Sometimes God seems to get angry, an emotion utterly unbefitting a supreme transcendent being. Similarly, the Hebrew Bible appears conflicted about whether God is omnipresent—the universal, unbounded God of the whole world—or whether this God—whom the Hebrew Bible calls YHWH (sometimes translated as "Jehovah")—is a national God who "lives" in a single tabernacle or Temple.

Is God even One? Isaiah declares a radical monotheism: "Only among you is God, there is no other God at all!" (Isaiah 45:14). This single God is responsible for all creation: "I form light and create darkness, I make weal and create woe—I the Lord do all these things" (Isaiah 45:7). But the Torah is not so sure. "Who is like you, O Lord, among the gods?" (Exodus 15:11) the Israelites sing after being delivered by the Egyptians. The verse is so potentially troubling that later translators tend to translate *gods* with "celestial beings" or "mighty ones." Even Deuteronomy 6:4, called the Shema by later generations and still seen by many Jews as the quintessential statement of faith, declares, "Hear O Israel, YHWH is our god, YHWH alone," which appears to acknowledge the existence of other gods.

The Tanak is no more successful articulating a coherent theology of covenant. The several covenants in the Torah are largely modeled on contemporary sovereign-vassal treaties of the Ancient Near East: Israel pledges its loyalty to God and God defends Israel. Yet there is an important and critical question about the conditionality of these covenants. In Genesis 15 God appears to make an unconditional covenant with Abram in which He pledges the land of Canaan to Abram's heirs. In return, it appears that Abram's heirs need do nothing; God's promise is independent of their behavior. However, in Genesis 17 God demands that Abram's male heirs be circumcised; this does appear to be a condition. The Torah's treatments of the covenants on Sinai are no clearer. On the one hand, they seem to assert that Israel's adherence to the laws is a condition for the covenant. On the other hand, they suggest that God's covenant is unconditional and that its violation by Israel will result in punishment, though not an end to the covenant.[6]

The Tanak contains an equally confusing set of answers to the issue of theodicy, God's justice. That God is just is a central idea of the Tanak. Yet how is this basic tenet to be reconciled with a reality that appears to fly in its face? Then as now there were bad people who prospered and good people who suffered. One possible theological solution is simply to disregard the empirical evidence: God rewards and punishes justly. One who is suffering must by definition deserve it. Writ on a national scale, defeat only comes to Israel as a result of sin. The terrible human and theological catastrophe of the fall of the First Temple in 586 BCE must have reinforced this idea. How, after all, could God have allowed the destruction of His own house? That God was not powerful enough to prevent it, or that God allowed it for no reason, or that God was uninvolved in human history to the point of allowing the Temple to be destroyed were not theological options. God's punishment was de facto proof of Israel's sins.[7]

Other voices within the Bible, though, recognize other answers. Children, one passage asserts, pay for the sins of their ancestors. A righteous individual or generation might be crushed because of misdeeds of long-dead great-grandparents. Ecclesiastes seems to assert that God is uninvolved in history, a transcendent God detached from humanity. Job offers a far darker portrayal of God's ways, concluding with the assertion that they are unfathomable.

Jews later develop an elaborate scenario of redemption and afterlife to explain how the world really is just. That, however, came later. The religion of the Hebrew Bible is lived in the present. Death is the end of life, forever. Some of the prophetic books maintain that there will be a redemptive age, heralded by an anointed messiah (perhaps a descendent of King David). Even they leave the details quite fuzzy. The ideas of a heaven in which disembodied souls are judged and of a future universal judgment day are absent from the Tanak. Reward and punishment have to occur in this world.

In the redemptive age God's promise to Abraham—that his seed will be multiplied and inherit the land—will be fulfilled. In some scenarios, it will be marked by apocalyptic violence, in others by extraordinary and unnatural peace. Not a lot seems to be at stake in these descriptions of the unknowable future.

This points to the tenuous role of belief—and theology generally—in biblical religion. Nowhere does the Hebrew Bible directly command belief in anything, even in God. At the same time, the Hebrew Bible seems to go to great lengths to convince its readers that YHWH really is the God of Israel and deserves obedience. This obedience, though, takes the form of acts rather than of declarations of faith. The acts assume and reinforce belief but not in any easily transparent correspondence. Just as the Torah develops a complex, sometimes contradictory theology, so too it articulates a complex set of practices to which it ascribes many, sometimes contradictory, reasons.

Among all the practices and rites commanded by the Torah, none is as prominent as the sacrifice. Much of the Torah simply assumes that Israel's primary obligation to God is to offer regular and prescribed sacrifices at the Temple. These sacrifices, as the book of Deuteronomy repeatedly emphasizes, were to take place exclusively within the precincts of the Temple that would eventually be established in Jerusalem. The Temple was seen as holy space par excellence, a spot on the earth that is closer to God than any other place. Sitting on the navel of the earth, the Temple was seen as located directly under an open portal to heaven through which would waft the savory smell of the burning sacrifice. Administered by a hereditary priesthood, the sacrificial service had to be performed at the right time, in the right way. A missed or botched sacrifice potentially heralded a national calamity. An individual who failed to offer the appropriate sacrifices and gifts to God through the sanctioned institutions of temple and priests could not expect continued divine favor.

The Temple thus authorized a very specific kind of religious authority. The Hebrew Bible repeatedly emphasizes that only priests, the genealogical descendents of Aaron, had authority to enter into the most sacred precincts of the Temple and to offer and consume (most) sacrifices there. Access to the divine passed through the priests; when regular Israelites required religious guidance about even mundane matters they were to inquire of the priest. Priests, for example, are portrayed as the experts at determining which splotches were to be considered "leprous" (the common translation of a word that almost certainly refers to some other skin disease or blight); their declaration, even if factually incorrect, is considered binding. When a man suspects his wife of adultery, he is to go to the priest so that he might perform an ordeal to either confirm or refute his suspicion (Numbers 5). "Every lawsuit and case of assault is subject to their ruling," Deuteronomy 21:5 declares of the priests.

But priestly authority is not the only kind of religious authority that the Hebrew Bible knows. Moses is a prophet who gains his authority from direct communication with God. Moses, of course, is exceptional, but the type of authority that he authorizes is ultimately institutionalized. Biblical prophets are not roving lunatics with visions; they are functionaries of the Temple. Deuteronomy even contains a test for separating "true" prophets from imposters. If priests are the functionaries that carry out the will of God, and kings are secular figures charged with maintaining civil order, prophets are the vehicles through which flows the divine will for both. They are most frequently portrayed as having no or little will of their own. God appropriates their bodies, and especially their voices, to convey the divine message. When the prophet Samuel anoints Saul as king, hacks the captive enemy king Agag to death, and replaces Saul with David, he is merely a divine instrument. Samuel, like Nathan (King David's prophet), Elisha, and Elijah perform important political functions. Later in the Hebrew Bible the prophet's political role is transformed to an exhortatory one. The prophets of the later kings of Judah do not personally slaughter the prophets of Baal as Elijah did; they exhort (rather ineffectually, it seems) the Israelites and their leaders to behave differently and bring news of approaching doom or consolation. Ezekiel offers a somewhat bizarre and idiosyncratic vision of both the divine and the Temple. After the destruction of the Temple, Jeremiah attempts to comfort his fellow exiles with visions of the defeat of their enemies and their own return to Zion.[8]

There is yet a third type of religious authority in the Hebrew Bible. The Hebrew Bible refers to the authority of the scribe more obliquely than that of priest or prophet. Not mentioned in the Torah, the scribe appears and seems to gain authority in the later books of the Hebrew Bible. Scribal authority comes from a combination of technical competence, office (especially as the drafter and keeper of royal decrees), and mastery of the Ancient Near Eastern wisdom tradition. Of these three types of authority, scribal authority is the only one that is attained—unlike the priest, one need not be born a scribe, and unlike a prophet its authority does not rely on God's ad hoc, even arbitrary, decision to make him His instrument. The biblical books of Proverbs and Job most likely derive from scribal circles; they gain their authority from a well-studied mastery of the secrets of nature itself.

These models of authority are types. While they illustrate distinct claims of authority, an individual might in fact make more than one claim simultaneously. Priests can also be prophets or scribes or even both. Outlining schematically these claims to authority puts into relief the claims that Jews would later make, eliminating prophetic authority, minimizing priestly authority, and utterly transforming the authority of the scribe.

Sacrifices and the official religious institutions constitute the most important but not the only path to the divine. Individuals could also curry divine favor through adherence to God's commandments. If one pole of biblical theology is Zion, the holy space of the Temple, the other, as Jon Levenson, a professor of Bible at Harvard, has helpfully noted, is Sinai, the elaboration of the terms of the covenant. The Torah (and prophets) expects individuals to engage in a wide range of personal behaviors. The Bible itself does not categorize these behaviors and rarely justifies them. Thus the Hebrew Bible seems to treat equally and put equal weight on the commandments to honor one's father and mother, to shoo away the mother bird before taking the eggs from her nest, to return stolen goods with a penalty, to avoid murder, and not to wear linen and wool together, although fulfillment of the first two is explicitly linked to the attainment of a long life. Israelites are to avoid consuming certain animals (for reasons that are never specified), to live according to a specific code of civil law and a curiously incomplete code of family law, and to maintain an economic structure that was utterly unworkable, canceling all debts and returning all land to their original owners every fifty years. Individuals could seek God's will from the prophet or establish a direct relationship with God through the giving of gifts to His house. When distressed, people were always free to petition God directly with spontaneous prayer.

The food laws are intriguing in this respect. The first humans, Adam and Eve, were apparently vegetarian. After humanity corrupted itself and God "repented" of his creation and destroyed all but Noah and his family, God seems to make a concession to Noah. Noah and his descendents were permitted to eat all flesh; there were to avoid only the blood (Genesis 9:3–4). The Torah later hedges this wide-ranging permission. Actually, only animals that are slaughtered at the altar in the central Temple, according to some passages—or at local cultic places, according to other passages—can be eaten; carrion is also forbidden. Nor can the Israelites eat "all" types of flesh. Among "beasts" only those that chew their cud and have split hooves are permitted. Fish require fins and scales. Insects require legs that "leap" on the earth. Many types of birds are prohibited, but no guiding principle behind the selection of these species (Leviticus 11) is apparent. The Torah nowhere explains why some animals are permitted while others are forbidden. To compound the mystery, the Torah contains the enigmatic command "not to boil a kid in its mother's milk" three times and offers an account of why "until this day" the children of Israel do not eat a nerve in the thigh (Genesis 32:33). This adds up to an odd mishmash of dietary restrictions through which an Israelite might do the will of his God.

The Psalms offer a different kind of example of the tension between institutional and personal service to God. Many, but apparently not all, of the Psalms were written for and performed within a cultic setting. That is, although the priests would silently perform the sacrifices, the Levites might have composed psalms to sing during parts of the sacrificial service. Seen in this way, the Psalms are like supplemental notes that accompany the gift to God. But it is not impossible that there was also a noncultic use for them. Individuals might have recited the moving poetry of the Psalms as part of their own personal effort to connect with the divine or perhaps even just the snippets of it that they remembered from listening to the levitical performances.

"One thing I ask of the Lord," the Psalmist sings, "only that do I seek: to live in the house of the Lord all the days of my life, to gaze upon the beauty of the Lord, to frequent His Temple" (Psalms 27:4). The Psalmist here captures a tension inherent in the religion of ancient Israel or indeed, nearly all religions. The Jerusalem Temple is not only the house of the Lord but also the institutional and communal center of religious life. Within it, though, the Psalmist seeks to engage in an essentially individual, almost anticommunal, act—to see God. The Psalmist, in fact, attempts to tame the ultimately anarchic individual drive to experience God by confining it to the Temple. God is to be found within the material confines and the institutional boundaries of the Temple. No idea here of the lone mystic pursuing his or her individual "spirituality" disconnected from a community.

Mystical experience generates not only a tension between the community and the individual but also a theological one. How can humans actually approach, experience, or understand the great and awesome God? What does it mean to "gaze" upon God? The Tanak does not provide any kind of systematic or reasoned answer to this problem, but it is clearly aware of it. On the one hand, it repeatedly asserts the impassable divide that separates humanity from divinity. God is totally, ontologically, other. God's awesomeness is so great as to be fatal: "you cannot see My face, for man may not see Me and live" (Exodus 33:20), God tells Moses.

This, however, does not stop Moses or the biblical writers from pursuing their quest to see God. Moses repeatedly nags God to see Him; the best he appears to get is a sight of God's receding "back." Elsewhere in the biblical narrative that surrounds the revelation on Mount Sinai the biblical author appears to forget this: "Then Moses and Aaron, Nadab and Abihu, and seventy elders of Israel ascended; and they saw the God of Israel: under His feet there was the likeness of a pavement of sapphire, like the very sky for purity. Yet He did not raise His hand against the leaders of the Israelites; they beheld God, and they ate and drank" (Exodus 24:9–11). This is not the only vision of God recorded in the Tanak. The first chapter of Ezekiel describes in extraordinary but entirely incomprehensible detail a vision of God. These passages, rupturing the biblical suppositions of God's utter otherness, testify to the essential problem of reconciling this idea with the desire to draw close to God.

Individuals would also experience the divine through their observance of the Sabbath and festivals. Here again the Hebrew Bible does not offer a complete or coherent account of these observances or the meanings behind them. Even the festal calendar of the Hebrew Bible is somewhat elusive: the existence of a seven-day week is portrayed as a fact of nature and result of the divine process of creation (although, of course, it is entirely arbitrary) and the sighting of the new moon is to be celebrated, but it is surprisingly unclear whether the biblical calendar was a lunar or a solar one. The year begins with the first day of Aviv (today called Nisan, which occurs in the spring and during which Passover is celebrated), but there is little indication how the years are to be numbered—presumably according to a seven- or fifty-year (Jubilee) cycle.

Of all the biblical festivals, the Sabbath (Shabbat) is clearly the most important. It is the only holiday naturalized as part of the first creation story: "And God blessed the seventh day and declared it holy, because on it God ceased from all the work of creation that He had done" (Genesis 2:3). We have to wait some time, however, to find out the implications of these blessings, and when we do the Sabbath takes on a different hue. Instructing the Israelites, recently freed from slavery and starting out into the desert, about the manna, the food that God daily rained down upon them, Moses tells them to gather a double portion on Friday so that they might eat it through Saturday: "Tomorrow," Moses says, "is a day of rest, a holy Sabbath of the Lord. Bake what you would bake and boil what you would boil; and all that is left put aside to be kept until morning" (Exodus 16:23). He then continues, to the disbelief of the Israelites, saying that no manna would fall on the seventh day, for God "has given you the Sabbath." There are no explanations for why or when God gave the Shabbat or how exactly to rest on it, and in the narrative the Israelites appear to be just as baffled as modern readers.

Nor is the Hebrew Bible much help at clearing up this confusion. The first rendition of the Ten Commandments commands Israel to "remember" and to "sanctify" the Sabbath, working six days and resting on the seventh as a kind of *imitatio dei*, hearkening back to God's rest from creation (Exodus 20:8–11). The repetition of the Ten Commandments in Deuteronomy, though, contains the word "remember" rather than "guard" and, more significantly, states a different rationale: "Remember that you were a slave in the land of Egypt and the Lord your God freed you from there with a mighty hand and an outstretched arm; therefore the Lord your God has commanded you to observe the Sabbath day" (Deuteronomy 5:15). Nor does the Hebrew Bible clearly specify what it means by "rest" or "guarding" the Sabbath, a lacuna, again, not lost on the ancient Israelites. In one story nobody seems to know what to do with a man gathering sticks on the Sabbath until God Himself intervenes and condemns him to death. Moses clearly forbids moving from one's habitation and "kindling a fire" (Exodus 35:3), but not until Isaiah do we hear of a prohibition against conducting business.

Both the conflicted accounts of meaning and ambiguity about what constitutes proper observance pervade the descriptions of other biblical festivals. The three pilgrimage festivals, Passover (*Pesach*), Tabernacles (*Sukkot*), and Pentecost (*Shavuot*), form the backbone of the Israelite festal calendar. All are portrayed in some passages of the Tanak as agricultural festivals, generally the celebrations of various harvests. The first two of these festivals, however, acquired historical associations early on. Pesach, for example, appears to conflate two different holidays, one that features the paschal sacrifice and one that foregrounds unleavened bread (*matzah*). Although the latter holiday almost certainly had agricultural origins, it was easily combined with the former to create a single festival that commemorated the exodus from Egypt (cf. Exodus 12:43–13:10). The biblical Passover is above all observed with food, the eating of the paschal sacrifice in a prescribed place and time as well as the avoidance of leavened bread for a week. There was almost certainly no fixed liturgy connected to the sacrifice; the Torah suggests that, more informally, the Passover meal sparked discussion about the history it symbolized.

Even on as central a rite as the paschal sacrifice the Torah leaves us confused. According to Exodus 12, each family is to slaughter an unblemished lamb: "They shall eat the flesh that same night; they shall eat it roasted over the fire, with unleavened bread and bitter herbs. Do not eat any of it raw, or cooked in any way with water, but roasted—head, legs, and entrails—over the fire" (Exodus 12:8–9). Compare Deuteronomy 16:5–7:

> You are not permitted to slaughter the Passover sacrifice in any of the settlements that the Lord your God is giving you; but at the place where the Lord your God will choose to establish His name, there alone shall you slaughter the Passover sacrifice, in the evening, at sundown, the time of day when you departed from Egypt. You shall boil and eat it at the place that the Lord your God will choose; and in the morning you may start back on your journey home.

No longer is this a local family custom. Deuteronomy, as it frequently does, centralizes the sacrificial rituals in the Temple in (what would be) Jerusalem. The method of cooking is also in direct contradiction to the prescription of Exodus. This contradiction was not lost on early readers of the Torah. Describing a Passover ceremony that is identical neither to the one in Exodus or Deuteronomy, 2 Chronicles says that they "boiled the Passover sacrifice in fire" (35:13), thus preferring nonsense to a contradiction.

Sukkot was transformed to commemorate the next stage of the journey, the wandering in the desert. The Israelites are to dwell in booths for seven days "so that your generations might know that I made the children of Israel dwell in booths in my bringing them out of Egypt" (Leviticus 23:43). Later Sukkot would acquire other historical overlays, as it became the holiday during which Solomon dedicated the First Temple—an association that might stand behind Zechariah's assertion (14:16–19) that in the messianic age all the nations will observe Sukkot. In addition to dwelling in booths, the Israelites are also to take fruit of the hadar tree and some branches from other trees, "and rejoice before the Lord your God seven days" (Leviticus 23:40). The verse, of course, is puzzling: How do you rejoice with vegetation? One remarkable scene portrays Ezra, reading this passage after returning to Jerusalem, using these branches to construct tabernacles (Nehemiah 8:14–15). Only much later would this biblical commandment be read to signify the practice of waving the *lulav*.

Oddly, Shavuot is left without any historical associations. Jews would later connect this holiday to the giving of the Torah on Mount Sinai, but the Torah itself does not specify this. It is also different from the other two festivals in that it is celebrated for only one day rather than seven (or eight, if one counts the "eighth day of assembly" that immediately follows

Sukkot). Yet another curiosity is that the Torah does not give a set date for its celebration; it is to occur fifty days after the omer offering that is to be made on the "day after Shabbat" after Passover. The ambiguity of this language—taken by the Rabbis and most later Jews to mean fifty days after the first day of Passover—generated a heated controversy in antiquity.

Two other festivals round out the biblical calendar. The first day of the seventh month is to be a "memorial of trumpeting." There is no hint in this description of what this festival, today known as Rosh Hashanah, is meant to remember or why one trumpets on it. Ten days later is Yom Kippur, the Day of Atonement, which has both a public and a personal aspect. On it the reigning high priest is to transfer the communal sins of Israel onto a goat (the "scapegoat"), which he then sends out into the wilderness. Individuals are to "afflict yourselves" and not work for the day. Neither of these holidays is associated with either agriculture or specific historical events.

In contrast to the Hebrew Bible's interest in annual time, it hardly ritualizes life cycle events. A male Israelite should be circumcised on the eighth day (although we are never informed how that circumcision should be done); there are regulations governing the choice of marital partners but no details about how one is to legally contract a marriage or celebrate a wedding; the rules about divorce are condensed into an allusion about a "divorce document"; and certain funerary practices (e.g., gashing oneself) are forbidden. The marking of adolescence, bar mitzvah, never appears in the Hebrew Bible, and in fact does not become a common Jewish practice until the Middle Ages

By almost any modern standard, the Tanak is a peculiar book. It is a historical narrative, law code, and collection of poems and proverbs all rolled into one. Its narratives are generally sparse, suggestive, and powerful, except where they are contradictory, repetitive, and in the case of the extended genealogies, simply tedious. By modern sensibilities, the laws are an odd agglomeration of ethical ideals, irrational and unexplained practices, and barbaric prescriptions. The Tanak's "beliefs" are frequently in tension, sometimes with mutually exclusive ideas presented together in the same story. The Tanak seems to advocate many views at the same time and with equal authority.

The earliest religious readers of the Tanak assumed its divine authorship. Nevertheless, they were sensitive to and struggled to explain these interpretive gaps, inconsistencies, and redundancies. Typically, as will be further discussed below, they acknowledged textual problems but attributed intentionality to them; God created a problem with the intention of teaching us something new. Flaws in the text are thus only apparent.

Modern scholars do not have the luxury of assuming a perfect text. Clearly, when the Tanak is presumed to be a human literary work, other explanations for these textual "problems" must be found; this is the view to which I alluded above when I mentioned the authorship of the Torah. The many theological, ritual, and other contradictions within the Torah alone have led scholars to propose the documentary hypothesis. According to this hypothesis, the Torah began as a collection of discrete sources. An editor, or group or groups of editors, spliced these sources together to create the Torah as it now survives. While there is no definitive proof for the veracity of this hypothesis (none of the suspected original sources have survived as independent texts), it does a remarkably good job of explaining many of the puzzling inconsistencies and redundancies in the biblical text. Scholars continue to debate, sometimes heatedly, which passage in the Torah derives from which source or when precisely the Torah was redacted and by whom (with most biblical scholars agreeing to date at least the final redaction to the time of the Babylonian exile, ca. 586–515 BCE), but scholars generally accept the hypothesis.

Where, though, did these earlier materials come from? Who wrote them, and why did the final redactor(s) include them? What interests do these earlier sources represent?

Most biblical scholars today think that there were five primary sources of the Torah, conventionally labeled J, E, P, D, and H. The J source is so called because of it use of YHWH for the name of God (Y = J in German), whereas texts associated with E use a different name (Elohim) for God. P is the priestly document (parts of Exodus and much of Leviticus), and D is the book of Deuteronomy, in recognition of the coherence and integrity of Deuteronomy when compared with the other four books of the Torah. At some point during or after the redaction there was probably another priestly intervention; these contributions have been called H.

Even as a scholarly hypothesis, the documentary hypothesis is not perfect. Yet it does have the advantage of explaining the innate weirdness of the Torah. It provides, for example, a plausible explanation for the two creation stories at the beginning of Genesis. For ancient readers of the Bible, such as the Rabbis and early Church fathers, this redundancy was not a minor problem. They explained it in several different ways, suggesting, for example, that there were two creations or that the second is an expansion of the first. Even they, however, saw it as a problem that needed to be addressed.

According to the documentary hypothesis, these two stories stem from two (or, really, three) different sources. The first creation account, like the more identifiably priestly documents, emphasizes a transcendent God and strict and natural categories and divisions and is thus seen as deriving from the P source. The messier second creation story, with its immanent, sometimes angry God and human drama, shares its narrative concerns with other biblical texts identified as deriving from the J and E sources. At some point the J and E accounts were combined into the story that is now the second account of creation. The final redactor (who may or may not have been involved with this earlier redaction) apparently felt that neither the P nor the JE story could be omitted; they both must have been seen as authoritative within the redactor's community. Finding no easy way to combine these two accounts, the redactor placed them side by side, despite their seeming contradictions.

The documentary hypothesis can explain both contradictions and redundancies. The Torah was not "made up" during the period of exile but carefully compiled from preexistent, perhaps quite ancient, sources. Over millennia these sources became so revered that the redactor dared not exclude them, even when they contradict or repeat each other. Note that this model includes an implicit assumption about the way in which stories and texts acquire authority—rather than suddenly appearing to universal acceptance and acclaim, they gradually gain authority until they become (or do not become) canonical for a certain community. The process by which a text becomes authoritative for a community is known as canonization, and it is most likely that the Torah was composed from sources that were themselves canonical.

The same gradual process of canonization was probably also at work in the addition of other biblical books to the Torah. All the way through the end of antiquity there were many books in circulation that claimed divine authority. Why were some included in what would become the canonical Hebrew Bible and others not? The prophetic writings included in the Hebrew Bible must be only a fraction of the literature of this type produced during the period of the First Temple and immediately after its destruction. Why include the apocalypses of Daniel, some of which we can date to some certainty to the Hellenistic period, but exclude the contemporary apocalypses of 1 Enoch, a pseudepigraphical book ultimately preserved only by the Ethiopic Church? Why include the precociously existentialist book of

Ecclesiastes, but exclude the more pious book of Ecclesiasticus (Ben Sira), which some Rabbis were citing as scripture well into the third century CE? The answers to these questions are complex and not fully understood, but they indicate that canonization was a communal and unpredictable process, rather than a one-time imposition from the top down.

The process of canonization itself probably spanned many centuries. It is possible that the community that authored the Dead Sea scrolls (ca. 150 BCE—66 CE) did not accept the book of Esther into their Bible but did include other books such as the Temple Scroll, which appears to conflate portions of the Torah and is narrated in the first-person voice of God. And even when canonization more or less came to an end (rabbis in the second century CE were still debating the appropriateness of including Song of Songs, a collection of erotic poetry, in the canon), the precise text of the various books remained in flux until the Masoretes created a standard text that was accepted by the Jewish community.

Nor can the Tanak be seen as developing in some kind of splendid isolation from its milieu. Aramaic, a Semitic language similar to Hebrew and the legal lingua franca of the Persian Empire, was incorporated into the late biblical books; Ezra, Nehemiah, and Daniel all contain sections in Aramaic. Aramaic would, in fact, remain dominant in many regions of the land of Israel and the Near East well into the Hellenistic and Roman eras. Some biblical religious ideas, such as dualism and a belief in an angelic host, probably originated within this Persian environment. References to contemporaneous historical events can be found in parts of Daniel, and Ecclesiastes exhibits familiarity with some Greek philosophical concepts.

❖ ❖ ❖ ❖ ❖

For all its diversity the Hebrew Bible cannot in any way be seen as a transparent account of the actual religious life of the Israelites. Like all sacred texts, the Hebrew Bible is more intent on delineating the *ought* rather than the *is*; the *prescriptive* rather than the *descriptive*. The community that accepted as sacred the Torah and the other books that would comprise the Tanak was probably only a fraction of the total community of Israel, and even they would not have—indeed, given the many contradictions and lacunae, could not have—lived entirely according to these writings. In fact, the Tanak's frequent polemics against practices of which it disapproves provides some evidence for the gap between the ideal religion it prescribes and common practice. Many Israelites continued to worship cult objects, or at cult sites, despite the pointed monotheism and centralization of the Tanak. No Israelite community, even that of the united monarchy under David and Solomon, apparently paid much attention to the Jubilee year. Israelites no doubt took seriously their Temple and its regular sacrifices as keeping them in good account with their god, but actual Israelite religious belief and practice was predictably diverse and frequently detached from scriptural prescriptions. While Ezra and Nehemiah's communities were resettling Jerusalem, a group of Persian Jewish mercenaries garrisoned on the Nile island of Elephantine in Egypt took their Jewishness so seriously that it brought them into violent conflict with local residents, unaware that the Torah forbade them to offer the paschal sacrifice in their own local temple.[9]

The gap between scriptural prescriptions and actual practice most likely widens once one leaves the narrow class boundaries of the Hebrew Bible's intended audience. The voice of the Torah, and, for that matter, practically every biblical book, is that of the Israelite male property holder. "You" are told with which women you may and may not have sex, how to treat your slaves, and how to resolve business disputes. Other groups, although together constituting a majority of the Israelite community, are pushed to the margins. Women, for example, are not discriminated against so much as they are ignored. They play important roles in several biblical narratives, but biblical law hardly addresses them. The Torah's main concern with women is sexual. Women are deemed ritually impure (not to be confused with morally impure or "dirty") during their menstrual periods and after childbirth and are to avoid sexual relations and contact with "holy space" during these periods. Adultery, in the law of the Hebrew Bible, is defined as sex between a man and a woman who is married to another man; the man's marital status is irrelevant to this legal definition. While a married woman's sexuality technically "belongs" to her husband, her misuse of it is also construed as a crime against God, and both adulterer and adulteress are condemned to death. The gender assumptions in this literature are entirely conventional and shared by contemporary societies. Accordingly, the Hebrew Bible provides virtually no insight into the actual religious lives of Israelite women. The Hebrew Bible portrays some women as strong and active agents, manipulating their fathers (Lot's daughters), husbands (Rebecca), fathers-in-law (Tamar), and others ; slaying generals (Yael); singing love songs (Song of Songs); and piously praying (Hannah). Despite the vividness of these literary portraits, they reveal little historically about real Israelite women.[10]

The Israelites, even the ones that generated the Torah, did not live in a vacuum. Parallels to many biblical stories and nearly all the biblical concepts and rituals abound in other extant literature of the Ancient Near East. The authors of the sources of the Hebrew Bible, as well as its redactors, were fluent in the Canaanite and Mesopotamian cultures in which they lived, and the fingerprints of these cultures can be found scattered throughout. Yet the biblical authors transformed those cultural resources, at times subtly and at other times more substantially. The Hebrew Bible drew basic theological concepts about the nature of God, covenant, and redemption from the peoples around them, as well as its institutions, modes of authority, and many ritual practices, while at the same time modifying and combining these concepts into something new and distinctive. That the Hebrew Bible is so concerned with separation from the "peoples of the land" testifies indirectly to the process of identity formation that would come to characterize later Jewish groups as well.

To chart the development of the biblical text and its gradual acceptance by the people Israel as the word of God is in some sense to chart the very beginning of Judaism. The existence of a holy text that can serve as a stable source of divine authority—in contrast to the oral and unpredictable mediation of prophet and priest—separates the authors of the Hebrew Bible, the Israelites, from its first readers, the Jews. If the sources that make up the Tanak reflect Israelite religious beliefs and practices, their redaction and canonization, most notably in the Torah, points toward a new religious crystallization as something we can label Judaism.

From the late sixth century and the building of the Second Temple in Jerusalem, the Tanak—at that time still a fluid and developing body of sacred texts—has served as the foundation for a distinctly Jewish textual tradition. In this sense my students, along with early Christians and Muslims, were correct: Nearly every Jewish group has placed the Tanak at its center—as the authoritative starting point of conversation. But a heavy emphasis must be put on the phrase *starting point.* Along with the canon there developed a distinctively Jewish way of reading the Tanak, an extrascriptural set of assumptions about the text and the "correct" interpretative techniques to be applied to it. Despite the later Protestant understanding (still very much with us today) that Scripture's meaning is transparently and completely contained within the text itself, Jewish religious communities have always read the Tanak through an interpretive lens.

What, then, does it mean to say that the Hebrew Bible has fundamental importance in Judaism as a record of God's revelation? Its narratives are a source of enduring myths that have helped to shape the worldview of many different Jewish communities. Its laws, although often reinterpreted, are the basis for, or at least can be used to authorize, Jewish laws and ritual. Its devotional literature continues to reverberate in Jewish liturgy. It is seen as containing all truth, and its study is a religious obligation.

Throughout history Jews have regarded the Tanak as foundational while developing complex modes of reading and supplementing it. For the French friars of the thirteenth century this was a perversion of what they imagined to be the pure biblical religion of the Jews. Yet, for the last fifteen hundred years, "Judaism" has almost universally meant "rabbinic Judaism," a mix of texts, interpretive lenses, traditions, rituals, and concepts created or systematized by the Rabbis. But the Rabbis did not emerge from a vacuum when the Second Temple was destroyed in 70 CE. Throughout the Second Temple period, Jewish communities began to develop and work out, alongside the Temple and its rituals, what exactly a religion based on a set of canonical texts might mean. And, as we shall see, they discovered that it could mean many different things.

3

BETWEEN ATHENS
AND JERUSALEM

I MAGINE A WORLD in which both Torah and Temple peacefully coexisted, in which the sages and their progenitors ran the Temple service according to the exact will of God as they discerned it in the Torah, in which the people of the land of Israel followed these prerabbinic and rabbinic interpretations voluntarily—with the occasional sectarian dispute strictly for the sake of heaven, in which the Jews outside the land of Israel looked carefully to the sages of Israel for guidance and strictly followed their advice. Imagine, that is, a world that never was.

When the Rabbis looked back at the Second Temple period (ca. 515 BCE—70 CE), this is more or less the world that they saw. They portrayed themselves as living in a silver age, a pale copy of the golden age of yore. The Temple lay in ruins and direct divine communication, in their evaluation, had ceased. But when the Rabbis developed their own vision of Judaism, with Torah and study at its center, they saw it as continuous with the practices of an earlier period. Rabbinic historiography, unsurprisingly, helped them to authorize their own values and project.

The real history of the Second Temple period, however, was far less monochromatic than the Rabbis painted it. It is an uneven story of variety and tension, of Jews struggling to integrate—or divide—Torah, Temple, and their own "unofficial" religious practices and to reconcile the mix with a self-understanding as Jewish. The Rabbis did not arise in a vacuum, but neither did they seamlessly continue the traditions of a golden age.

❖ ❖ ❖ ❖ ❖

Alexander the Great roared through the Near East in 332 BCE. The Persians quickly fell back, and, by the time of Alexander's death in 323 BCE, most of the Near East was securely in Greek hands. Alexander's enormous empire was divided between his generals; among these new administrative districts were those assigned to Ptolemy (Egypt) and Seleucus (Syria) and their descendents. The sliver of land that the Jews knew as Zion or the land of Israel fell squarely in between these two dynasties, and over the next century they frequently battled for control of it. Although for most of this period it remained under the control of the Ptolemies, the Seleucid king Antiochus III decisively wrested control of the land in 200 BCE.

Greek rule brought linguistic, administrative, and cultural changes, which affected Jews of different times and places in widely diverse ways. Aramaic was replaced with Greek as the lingua franca, although many Jews, especially outside the cities, continued to use it for nearly another millennium; Jesus appeared to speak Aramaic and the Palestinian Talmud, redacted around 400 CE, uses an Aramaic dialect. The Greek world put more emphasis than the Persians on the corporate identities of individual cities, each called a *polis* and containing its own administrative structures. While members of the polis had to pay taxes to both their city and the king, their primary allegiance and source of identity was with the polis.

The Greek city brought with it a complex of religious and cultural ideas that would become known as Hellenism. The precise shape of this complex varied widely, but generally included an appreciation of classical Greek literature and philosophical ideas. Homer, Plato, and the classical Greek playwrights and sculptors were not only studied but also used as models for new cultural creations. Hellenism was characterized not so much by slavish imitation of classical Greek models (although some scholars, particularly art historians, do see it this way) as by a dynamic engagement with those models that led to the production of a new and distinctive culture.

This was a culture that was widely embraced. Hellenistic kings as a rule did not impose culture. They might financially support the artists and thinkers that they liked, but they were also content to allow the native, conquered peoples to remain the barbarians the Greeks thought them to be. As long as they continued to peacefully pay their taxes, they were free to practice their ancestral customs. Most people in the Greek world, though, found Hellenism attractive. Communities of "natives" agitated for the right to form a polis and many began slowly to see their own cultures and religious customs in Hellenistic categories.

The Jews were not exceptional in this respect. Prior to the second century BCE, Jews showed no conspicuous aversion to Hellenistic culture. Some Jews and Jewish communities were quicker than others to adopt it, but this was often the result of many factors other than conscious resistance. In the legal documents from Egypt, for example, Jews appear to participate in the new Hellenistic cultural and administrative institutions more fully and with more acceptance than the native Egyptians, whom the "Greeks" (as the descendents of the Macedonian conquerors called themselves) despised. In Jerusalem two Jewish authors experimented with new Greek ideas and literary forms, although in Hebrew. Neither appear to have seen any conflict between Hellenistic ideas and their tradition. Ben Sira (Ecclesiasticus), who was probably a Jewish scribe in Jerusalem, wrote a long Hebrew book around 200 BCE that imitated the biblical wisdom style while at the same time confidently incorporating more cosmopolitan ideas. Although it was ultimately not included in the Tanak (but is included in the Apocrypha, a collection of Jewish writings that the Catholic Church to this day preserves in its canon), as late as the fourth century CE some Rabbis were citing it approvingly. Ecclesiastes, which was included in the Tanak, was also written at this time. Attributed to King Solomon, the author of this Hellenistic book draws upon current Greek philosophical ideas to cynically portray a world adrift.

Among Greek-speaking Jews, however, the translation of the Torah (and, over the course of centuries, the other books of the Tanak) into Greek had far wider ramifications. According to the legend found in later Jewish writers, around the year 200 BCE King Ptolemy desired to translate the Torah into Greek and summoned seventy Jewish elders to do the work. Each worked alone and each emerged with precisely the same translation. This miraculous event was commemorated by an annual festival. More important, this legend authorizes the Septuagint, or LXX, as a divinely sanctioned text. Scholars today do not know how far this legend can be pushed: Is there a historical kernel at its core, namely, that Ptolemy did sponsor this translation, either in order to aid judges who were now sometimes called upon to render decisions according to Jewish law or to add to the growing Alexandrian library? Or was this a translation sponsored by the Jewish community, losing its facility with Hebrew? In either case, the Septuagint was widely accepted by the Jewish community.

Given this broad Jewish acceptance of Hellenism, what is one to make of the Maccabean uprising, commemorated each year in the Jewish liturgical calendar as Hannukah? According to the "traditional" story, in 168 BCE the Seleucid king, Antiochus IV, forced Hellenism on the Jews, forbade them their traditional practices, and desecrated the Temple. This ultimately resulted in a Jewish uprising under the leadership of the Maccabee family, who recaptured and rededicated the Temple, in the course of which a miracle allowed a day's worth of oil in the Temple to burn for eight days. By 162 BCE the direct Seleucid control of the land of Israel gave way to a semiautonomous Jewish nation led by the descendents of the Maccabees, the Hasmonean kings. In this version of the story, which derives primarily from the book 2 Maccabees, a Jewish history written around 100 BCE in Greek and preserved in the Apocrypha, Hannukah is really about the Jewish resistance to Hellenism. It is this author, in fact, who first coins both the words *Hellenism* and *Judaism,* seeing them as locked in mortal and eternal combat. This was a usage later appropriated by early Christians, and its basic assertion—that there is an identifiably essential "Judaism" or "Jewish culture" in conflict with a single, bounded Hellenistic culture—has survived, to some extent, even to the present day.

The real story is not as simple. Scholars widely dispute the causes of the Maccabean revolt. What does seem clear is that the revolt was not about a culture clash between "Judaism" and "Hellenism" or even "assimilation." By no means are the Maccabee brothers anti-Hellenistic; one of the first things they did after their success was to acclaim themselves kings in traditional Hellenistic style. According to one modern interpretation, disputes between Jews over the political status of Jerusalem (i.e., should it be transformed into a Greek polis?) mixed with old family feuds to create such a chaotic situation that the Seleucid (Greek) overlords felt it necessary to intervene. Their insensitive (and perhaps cruel) intervention merely fueled the conflict, leading to open revolt. But there seemed to have been little Jewish discomfort with Hellenistic language, ideas, political structures, and economic institutions.[1]

It was in this world that Jews, both within the semiautonomous land of Israel and in the Mediterranean diaspora, began to work out the *meaning* of the Torah and, to a lesser degree, the other books that would ultimately be incorporated into the Tanak. The Torah itself was a relatively stable text, perhaps even more so in its Greek translation than its Hebrew original (which seems to have existed in different versions), and Jews almost universally expressed their adherence to it. The meaning of that adherence and the ways that they understood the Torah, though, varied widely. Yet if anything linked these diverse readings of the Torah it was their shared commitment to a text, in much the same manner that Greeks used their own canonical texts to power their creative cultural and religious production. It is commonly known that many Jews from this period who wrote in Greek used Greek ideas and concepts; their references to them are frequently overt. Scholars have traditionally lumped these texts together into something they have called "Hellenistic Judaism," which stands against the "purer," or less "Hellenized," Judaism of the land of Israel. This scholarly model has been progressively weakening, and I would suggest that the cultural context of the Hellenistic world decisively shapes *all* Judaism of the period. This shaping occurs not only on the relatively superficial level of concepts and terms but also at the more fundamental level of the way that the Torah, like Homer and Plato, are placed at the canonical center of a culture. There was a basic fault line in the Judaism of the period, and that line does, roughly, run between Jews inside and outside the land of Israel. However, it is less about the quantity of Hellenism or amount of "Hellenistic influence" than it is about power. As in our own world, in which the issue of power decisively and distinctively shapes American and Israeli Judaism, so too during the late Second Temple period was the reading of Torah fundamentally shaped by the issue of Jewish power.

Outside the land of Israel, Jews primarily saw the Torah, typically in its Septuagint version, as a kind of legal constitution. Just as each polis had its constitution, so too did Jews, constituting something like a dispersed *metropolis*, had their Torah. In the few cases where the Jews had some actual legal autonomy within a Hellenistic polis (they were rarely able to attain full, "Greek" citizen status in these cities), they may have used the Torah, as they understood it, as a guide for adjudicating civil (and perhaps even criminal) law. Throughout the Greek world, however, Torah served a more basic function within Jewish communities as a site of identity. Jews drew on the Torah's stories to create their own imagined community, and on its distinctive practices, as read in through their historically embedded lens, to enact this identity socially.

Today it is often difficult to pin down the concept of Jewish literature—what, after all, makes a literature "Jewish"? Among the ancient Jewish Greek writers, however, this is hardly a problem: Virtually all their literature is based upon the Torah. Moses became the Jewish Homer, Plato, and Solon (the Greek lawgiver) all rolled into one, and Jewish writers endlessly retold his stories. One writer, Artapanus, rewrote the biblical story of the Exodus to make the Jews the source of everything good in Egyptian civilization, while "Ezekiel the Tragedian" recast the Exodus story into a Greek-style drama, told in good verse. The Torah's narratives were taken seriously as a history of a people; using contemporary historiographic tools, "Demetrius the Chronographer" set to work reconciling the inconsistent biblical chronologies. These stories all helped to reinforce a sense of Israel as a people with a shared history.

Philo offers a more complex account of Jewish identity. His life provides an intriguing example of Jewish identity and its negotiation in a Greek city. Born in the first century BCE to what appears to be a wealthy and distinguished Jewish family, Philo spent his life (to the best of our knowledge) in Alexandria, Egypt. His nephew, Tiberius Julius Alexander, achieved such prominence that the Romans appointed him procurator in Judea in 46–48 CE. Philo himself was devoted to the study and writing of philosophy. He laments the day that this life came to an end, when the Jewish community of Alexandria called on him to lead a delegation to Rome to protest their treatment. Before being called into public service, though, he was prolific. Among other things he wrote on the creation of the world, the interpretation of the Torah (in its Greek translation), the stories of Genesis, the lives of the great biblical figures, and the laws and their meaning. As varied as they are, each of these works exhibits the same unswervingly solid sense of his own Jewish identity together with a complete comfort in and facility with Hellenistic concepts and philosophy.

Philo is far from representative of his Jewish contemporaries, either in his personal history or his thought. Moreover, despite his best efforts to create a coherent set of ideas about the nature of Judaism, he frequently falls short; he often contradicts himself or simply does not follow through with the thread of his arguments. At the same time, his ideas do resonate with those found in contemporary Jewish writings.

Philo curiously distinguishes the communities "Israel" and the "Jews." The former he links to the experience indicated by his understanding of the term's etymology—*Israel* means "one who sees God." All who, following the model of the biblical Jacob, directly experience God qualify as members of Israel. The *Jews*, though, he sees as a social entity with no *necessary* equivalence with Israel. That said, he does posit an overlap, in which the Jews are fundamentally identified with Israel. At the same time, Israel remains a designation open to those non-Jews who directly experience God.

Philo's model of Israel is ambiguous and leaves many unanswered questions: Is one's membership in Israel stable depending on one's continuing experience? Would he have considered Plato a member of Israel, and, if so, would Philo say that he remained a non-Jew, or does acquiring status as "Israel" in some way translate into Jewishness? At the same time, this understanding of Israel broadens its potential membership. How this was to work on the ground remains unclear, but Israel is here divorced from ethnicity. This theological definition of Israel reappears with vigor in early Christian writings, and, as I will discuss in a later chapter, probably in the writings of Maimonides.

Philo's writings also provide a window into how at least some Jews theologically read the Torah. Above all, Philo is an exegete; his writing is thoroughly informed by his reading of the Torah. As we have seen, though, the Torah is a multivocal text, and Philo freely emphasized the parts that he found congenial. When reading the beginning of Genesis, for example, he was more taken with the transcendent God of Genesis 1 than with the less assured God of the next chapter. Using allegorical techniques of interpretation, Philo relentlessly stamps out biblical anthropomorphism. Philo's God is transcendent and perfect, barely conceivable by mere mortals:

> Just so anyone entering this world, as it were some vast house or city, and beholding the sky circling round and embracing within it all things, and planets and fixed stars without any variation moving in rhythmical harmony and with advantage to the whole, and the earth with the central space assigned to it . . . and over and above these, living creatures, mortal and immortal beings, plants and fruits in great variety, he will surely argue that these have not been wrought without consummate art, but that the Maker of this whole universe was and is God. Those, who thus base their reasoning on what is before their eyes, apprehend God by means of a shadow cast, discerning the Artificer by means of His works.[2]

Except by the purest of minds (exemplified by, and perhaps limited to, Moses), God cannot be apprehended directly. Like other ancient philosophers, Philo saw the world and the cosmos as the best witness to God's existence.

Philo was certainly not the first writer to emphasize God's absolute otherness. Aristobulus, sometimes called the first Jewish philosopher, also has a palpable discomfort of biblical anthropomorphism. He exhorts his reader "to receive the interpretations [i.e., biblical anthropomorphisms] according to the laws of nature and to grasp the fitting conception of God and not to fall into the mythical and human way of thinking about God."[3] God's descent on Sinai could not be local, "for God is everywhere"—the Torah only portrays God's descent on Sinai in order to show "that the power of fire, which is marvelous beyond all things because it consumes all things, blazes without substance and consumes nothing, unless the power from God (to consume) is added to it."[4] When Aristobulus read the Bible, he did so as a Greek-trained philosopher: He, like Philo, really believed that this was what the Bible meant. The Torah may have been at the center of their self-understanding as Jews, but it was the Torah as read through the lens of their own Hellenistic culture.

This same tendency is clear in Philo's other writing. As in the Hebrew Bible, Philo attributes free choice to human beings; his anthropology, however, is entirely more pessimistic. The Hebrew Bible makes no real distinction between a material body and an eternal soul, a binary anthropology widely accepted by ancient Greek philosophers. Philo does. Although his anthropology is not consistent, several times he insists that humans are eternal souls trapped in imperfect bodies. The human's—ultimately unachievable—task is to strive like Moses to elevate, or even free, the soul from its earthly constraints. Pure piety is pure mind. If the ordinary person, or even philosopher, cannot achieve purity, he (for Philo, women were constitutionally unable to do this) can at least work to subdue the body and elevate the soul. One way to develop the mind is through the study of philosophy. Philo, in fact, reads the Torah's value as containing philosophical truths, unlocked through allegorical interpretation. The Torah's account of creation, for example, is not really about the creation of the world and the drama of Adam and Eve: it is primarily an allegorical statement about the nature of human beings.

Good Jews not only study the Torah allegorically to unlock its philosophical treasures, thus helping to free the mind from its corporeal imprisonment; they also behave morally. In Philo's readings, the Torah's laws have different dimensions. They are, in a sense, an embodiment of the more abstract law of nature. To behave according to the Torah's laws is to behave according to this universal law of nature and thus—in a Stoic sense—to be at one with the world. Simultaneously, Philo holds the laws of the Torah up as being the best and most moral of any nation. Philo ingeniously groups all the laws under the rubric of the Ten Commandments. Each precept, no matter how seemingly random, thus points toward a higher morality. Using Pythagorean number theory, he reads the Sabbath prohibitions as concretely enacting the perfection of the number 7 and the cosmic harmony that it embodies.

Aristobulus and Philo were not the only Jews of this time who understood Judaism as a philosophy that was largely in accord with nature. The authors of the Letter of Aristeas and 4 Maccabees portray Judaism as founded on reason; even some of the seemingly odder customs (e.g., the food laws) are given a rational basis. Josephus, a Jewish aristocrat and priest from the first century CE who would go on to fight in the revolt against Rome before crossing over to the Roman side, refers to Judaism as a philosophy. The growing tendency among these authors—who, it must be admitted, almost certainly represent a small, male, and elite minority of Jews at this time—epitomizes the ways in which historical contexts fundamentally shaped Jewish self-understanding.

Whence did Jews derive the idea that Judaism was a philosophy? Most likely, from non-Jews. As early as the fourth century BCE Greek philosophers began to recognize the Jewish religion as philosophical, an idea that soon spread throughout the Greek and Roman worlds. Apparently struck by the absence of images ("idols") in their worship, and identifying Jews with the mythical "wise men" of the East (especially India), several Greek and Roman philosophers referred to Judaism as philosophical. Men like Aristobulus and Philo, raised and to some extent educated in this same cultural environment began to see themselves as others saw them. Philosophy thus became a filter through which to read the Torah; the Torah yielded a philosophical reading because it was thought to be philosophical.

Yet understanding Judaism as a philosophy never, in the eyes of these Jewish writers, decreased the need for Jews to subscribe to the actual physical behaviors that they saw as commanded by the Torah. Philo insists that allegorical interpretation of the Torah's laws (as he understood them) supplements rather than replaces their literal applicability. Indeed, he rails against those Jewish "allegorizers" who were advocating a strictly allegorical reading of the Torah. If Philo was true to his word, in his own life he was a follower of the commandments.

But which commandments? The Torah is frequently as obscure about ritual practice as it is about concepts. Philo's exposition of what he saw as "correct" Jewish behavior is uneven. Jews, he says, should not work on the Sabbath, but the only example that he gives about how to understand "work" is not lighting a fire. Like the Bible, he prescribes a paschal sacrifice, but he suggests that it need not be made at the Temple in Jerusalem. He follows the biblical prohibitions against eating certain kinds of animals, but he seems unaware of any special way of slaughtering the permitted animals or of separating milk from meat products. He nowhere mentions regular prayer (except on the Sabbath) or phylacteries. He interprets the "Festival of Trumpets," Rosh Hashanah, as having a twofold significance, symbolizing both the trumpets that sounded at the giving of the Torah on Mount Sinai as well as the trumpets of war—he shows no awareness of this holiday as a New Year festival. He might be reflecting the practice of his community when he states that Yom Kippur "is carefully observed not only by the zealous for piety and holiness but also by those who never act religiously in the rest of their life."[5] At times Philo can go beyond the letter of the law. He says that the law condemns a prostitute to death, which is nowhere stated in the Torah or the later rabbinic tradition. His treatments of pedophilia and child abandonment draw upon early Jewish extensions of biblical prohibitions.

Scholars debate the extent to which Philo accurately portrays the Jewish practices of his day. Clearly, most Alexandrian Jews at the turn of the millennium were not like Philo. But it is not unreasonable to suppose that they too read, or had read to them, the Septuagint and understood it as their divinely ordained constitution. Maybe some offered sacrifices to the God of Israel at the Temple of Onias in Leontopolis—apparently a rival to the Jerusalem Temple established in the second century BCE by the priest Onias III who fled Jerusalem during the unrest—but most probably did not offer sacrifices to other gods. There were synagogues in the diasporan Jewish communities in which Jews probably prayed, especially on the Sabbath. Non-Jews almost universally noted that Jews did not work on the Sabbath, that they circumcised their boys, and that they did not eat pork; most of these writers found these customs both distinctive and peculiar.

It is also true that, even if some Jewish communities had the legal right to administer their affairs semiautonomously, they did so very much in accord with the non-Jews around them. One of the most striking characteristics of the scores of papyri found in Egypt that pertain to Jews or things Jewish is the very lack of a striking characteristic. Jewish contracts, whether for the sale of a house or a marriage, look much like all other Greek contracts of the time. The range and application of Torah were limited; not every comment or even law in the Torah was converted into a respected social and civic norm.

Nor did valuing Torah as a foundational document translate into seeing study of Torah as a mode of piety. The few diasporan synagogue inscriptions that date to the Second Temple period rarely mention the Torah. Contemporary epitaphs, which in general memorialize the characteristics that a society values, never mention adherence to the Torah or knowledge of Torah as worthy of commemoration. Rather, they commemorated somewhat banal qualities that Jew and non-Jew would all have seen as indications of a pious life.

This is the Judaism that many have called *Hellenistic*. If by that term scholars have meant that this is a Judaism shaped by a Jewish reading of traditional texts (Torah) and practices (e.g., Sabbath observance) through the lens derived from their environment, then perhaps it can be seen as a useful designation. On the other hand, if it is meant to designate a Judaism that is in some way "more Greek" than its Palestinian cousin, then it is less useful. The Jews of the land of Israel were also part of the Greek cultural orbit. They too understood Torah to occupy a central place in the life of the people Israel. Their reading of their tradition, however, did differ, and the key to understanding that difference, again, is power.

Philo's Judaism might at first blush appear to differ markedly from that of the apocalyptic writers of the Second Temple period, but both created the filters through which they read Torah from a similar cultural complex. Jewish apocalypses from the Second Temple period were probably, for the most part, originally written in Aramaic or Hebrew in the land of Israel, although most survive only in translation through preservation by Christians; aside from a few fragments found in the Dead Sea scrolls, for example, the book of Jubilees survives only in Ge'ez, a language of the Ethiopic Church. These apocalypses generally do not conform to most modern notions of what an apocalypse should look like. They rarely, for example, describe the final conflagration and the end of history as we know it in gruesome and vivid detail. Rather, they most frequently take the form of "tours of heaven," descriptions of human beings brought to the heavens, shown divine secrets (usually including the course of history), and then returned to mundane existence.[6]

Most of these Jewish apocalypses appear to be in direct dialogue with the Tanak. The figures that ascend to heaven, for example, are all biblical characters. Many apocalypses centered on the ascent of Enoch. Enoch is only mentioned in passing in the Hebrew Bible: "Enoch walked with God 300 years. . . . All the days of Enoch came to 365 years. Enoch walked with God; then he was no more, for God took him" (Genesis 5:22–24). In its biblical context, the verses apparently mean that Enoch was righteous and died without having committed (significant) sin. Early readers, though, were puzzled by this wording; after all, it never says that Enoch died. "Walk with God" thus became the exegetical hook upon which an ascent narrative was built.[7] Apocalypses (some postdating the Second Temple period) similarly grew around the ascents of Abraham, Ezekiel, Ezra, and Baruch (Jeremiah's scribe), among others.

The relationship between apocalypses and sacred traditions went far deeper than the use of biblical figures. The beginning chapters of 1 Enoch, for example, create a much richer mythological image of creation than does the Torah. Genesis 6:1–4 records a cryptic story of "children of God" who were attracted to human women and wed them. This notice is followed immediately by, but not causally linked to, God limiting the human life span to 120 years and the appearance of giants on earth. 1 Enoch spins this account into an elaborate story of fallen angels who become the source of everything bad on the earth. Not only did the fallen angels teach the wicked arts (e.g., war and magic) to humans, but their offspring, the giants, are interpreted as evil spirits that continue to function in the world.[8] This then is not a mere academic exercise in understanding the historical creation of the world. It is an enduring account of theodicy. The Hebrew Bible never settles on a single account of the presence of evil in the world, but one option that it does not consider is that the world is populated by evil spirits. In 1 Enoch, despite the presence of these malignant spirits, human beings still maintain the capacity to choose between good and evil, and Enoch is shown the end of days, with the righteous souls resting among the angels and the wicked eternally tormented.

The Dead Sea scrolls give us a unique glimpse into an ancient Jewish community that actually walked the walk of this apocalyptic world. These scrolls were found in the caves around the ancient settlement of Qumran, in the harsh Judean desert on the western coast of the Dead Sea a short distance southeast of Jerusalem.[9] Qumran was settled around 150 BCE, at the beginning of the Hasmonean dynasty. The Maccabees and their descendents took on not only the role of king but also that of high priest—two offices that had traditionally been divided. Under the Hasmonean kings the land of Israel remained semiautonomous. Although the early Hasmoneans militarily expanded their borders, they also had to keep a wary eye on the real military powers in the region, frequently needing some fancy diplomatic footwork to stay afloat in a dangerous world of shifting alliances. By 63 BCE the Hasmoneans lost their touch, inviting the Roman general Pompey to bring his army to settle an internal dynastic dispute. Rome did that and then far more—they would not leave until the Islamic conquest of the seventh century CE. The Hasmonean dynasty lived out its reign under the watchful eyes of Rome, which in 30 BCE decided to install its own choice for monarch, Herod.

3.1 The view from the ancient settlement of Qumran of the caves where the largest cache of the Dead Sea scrolls was discovered. Photo by Michael L. Satlow.

The community that wrote the Dead Sea scrolls were but one of several Jewish groups to have arisen during this period. Most scholars understand the scrolls to have been written (or at least used) by the inhabitants of Qumran; some consider Qumran to have been populated by the Essenes, a Jewish sectarian group discussed in several Greek texts, including that of Josephus. Whether or not the authors of these scrolls were Essenes, they do explicitly (if not always clearly) discuss the reasons for their withdrawal from the Jerusalem Temple. One cause appears to have been their calendar. Unlike the Temple priests, who used some kind of lunar calendar, the scrolls' authors subscribed to a 364-day (compare the years of Enoch's life!) solar calendar. The causes for this disagreement are unknown, and it is not impossible that the sectarians preserved what they saw as the "traditional" calendar that had been changed to a lunar calendar by the Temple priests. The effect, however, was quite devastating. Their festival calendars, both biblically prescribed, were no long in sync. Much like the division between the Roman Catholic and Orthodox Churches today, which celebrate Easter on different days, the divergent festal calendars made communal celebration impossible, and always made one community sinners in the eyes of the other.

3.2 A step pool, perhaps a *mikveh* for a ritual purity, found at Qumran. Photo by Michael L. Satlow.

The more significant dispute involved the clash of Torah and Temple. According to the scrolls' authors, the practices of the Jerusalem Temple were incorrect. The Jerusalem priests neither kept the proper laws of ritual purity nor offered the sacrifices correctly. Both were severe charges. The holy space of the Jerusalem Temple was marked by its ritual purity; defilement of the Temple by occupying Syrian troops was probably the primary cause for popular support of the Maccabean uprising, which ultimately led to the establishment of an autonomous Jewish state. To offer an impure and improper sacrifice was to offer no sacrifice at all and thus to risk divine wrath. What might strike modern readers as trivial discussions of minutiae (e.g., if you pour water from a ritually pure pot into an impure one, does the impurity of the lower pot travel up the stream of water to make the upper pot impure?) had serious repercussions.

The sectarians knew that their legal positions were correct because the Torah told them. And they knew that the Torah told them because they had a special interpretive key revealed to them by God. Like the characters in the apocalypses, the sectarians received the "hidden mysteries" of the heavens through a kind of divine revelation. This revealed key allowed the sectarians to unlock the hidden meaning of the Torah, an interpretive move that unsurprisingly remained unconvincing to outsiders. Whereas Torah could, and most of the time probably did, supplement and authorize the Temple practices, in the second century BCE some Jewish sectarian groups begin also to use it to challenge specific priestly practices.

Cut off from the Temple, the sect began to develop a distinctive set of beliefs, practices, and communal organization. Their beliefs show clear affinities to those of the apocalyptic books, fragments of which were found among the scrolls. As time passed and it became increasingly clear that they would not sway the priestly authorities to change their errant ways, they became progressively more dualistic, eschatological, and deterministic. Several scrolls divide humanity into "sons of light" and "sons of dark," with God predetermining each person's assignment. The War Scroll (1QM), which might date close to the Roman destruction of the community in 66 CE, portrays the final apocalyptic battle between the sons of light and dark. The sons of dark are "destined for the pit," and the sons of light, with God's help, will emerge victorious. In the interim the community sought to stay pure, both ritually and morally. The scrolls prescribe communal meals and limit access to the "pure food" to full members in the state of purity. While some scrolls acknowledge and seek to regulate contact between sectarians and nonsectarians, many seem to scorn such interaction altogether. Sectarian liturgy tends to praise God, the angels, and the heavenly works rather than to ask for favors. The scrolls are particularly punctilious about Sabbath observance (even forbidding defecation on the Sabbath!) and communal behavior. Rigidly hierarchical (although with the possibility of mobility up and down the hierarchy), the community insisted on proper deportment all the time.

Underlying the community's organization and its practices is the apocalyptic belief in the permeability of heaven. The scrolls' authors seem to believe that if their community can remain pure, the angels *here and now* will join and worship with them. Their hope appears not to be, like the central characters in the apocalypses, for individual ascent to the heavens but for angelic descent to their community. A chasm remains between the natures of humans and God, but the line between humans and divine beings is a blurry one.

The Dead Sea community was but one of several contemporary Jewish sectarian communities. The three most famous Jewish sectarian communities from the Second Temple period were the Essenes, Pharisees, and Sadducees. All appear to have risen in the 150s BCE, shortly after the Maccabean uprising and the beginning of the Hasmonean dynasty. The ancient historical sources describe all of them (although the Essenes least of all) as politically active. Like the authors of the Dead Sea scrolls, at least the Pharisees and the Sadducees based their authority on their ability to correctly interpret the Torah. Like the authors of the early Dead Sea scrolls, each group sought control of the Temple service through their claim to possess the correct interpretations of the biblical text. We need not doubt the sincerity of their positions to note that these sects were also using Torah to exert control over the central Jewish institution of the land of Israel.

If Jewish sectarianism began to increase prior to Herod, from Herod on it explodes. As the king of Palestine, Herod appears not to have done a bad job. His magnificent building projects created the beautiful city of Caeserea, vastly expanded and enhanced Jerusalem and the Temple (the visible remains of the Western Wall are part of the Temple's retaining wall built by Herod), and kept legions of people employed in these and other public works projects. With Rome's support, no foreign power dared threaten his kingdom, and internal troublemakers were suppressed. He went to great pains to avoid offending the Jews (his own identity as a Jew was somewhat debated in antiquity). His family life did have problems, but these would have an impact on the lives of the ordinary citizens of his kingdom only after his death.

Indeed, Herod left a mess when he died. His four remaining sons, each incompetent, divided his kingdom in 4 BCE. That did not last long. Soon Rome took direct control, appointing first prefects and then procurators to administer Judea. As Josephus describes these Roman agents, one was worse than the other, harshly taxing the people (many of whom were still unemployed from the collapse of Herod's building program) while not keeping civil order.

If Josephus is to be believed, by the first century CE the Pharisees had gained a reputation as leading exponents of the law. Yet the Pharisees appear to be moving in different directions simultaneously. One group of Pharisees was revolutionary, promoting an uprising against Rome. Other Pharisees focused on purity and piety rather than politics—the New Testament, for example, portrays them as greatly concerned with issues of ritual and legal minutiae rather than politics. Similarly, while some Essenes were politically active, probably most were far more concerned with their service to God as they understood it. About the Sadducees we know little directly. According to Josephus, they did not believe in the immortality of the soul (unlike the Pharisaic belief in what appears to be transmigration of the soul after death). Curiously, nothing written by an active Pharisee or Sadducee is extant.

The three "major" Jewish sects in some way represent just the tip of the iceberg. Josephus alerts us to a Judaean countryside thick with Jewish prophets and their followers. One prophet from Egypt managed to collect thirty thousand followers (Josephus's number, which is almost certainly an exaggeration) in an attempt to rise against Rome; the Roman procurator disbanded them. Another prophet, Theudas, attempted to part the Jordan River. Rome broke up his group and beheaded him.

The followers of Jesus appear to have been part of the same phenomenon. Like these sectarians, Jesus claimed his authority in part from his reading of the Hebrew Bible and in part from some kind of direct divine inspiration or power. And like the Egyptian prophet and Theudas, he was seen by the Romans as a potential threat. Scholars have long tried to recover the teachings of the "real" Jesus, in contrast to the differing presentations and interpretations of those teachings in the Gospels, which were written at least a generation after his death. What does seem clear is that Jesus was a Jew who accepted the authority of the Hebrew Bible, although he disagreed about its interpretation with some of his contemporaries. His earliest followers appear to have been Jews who adhered to Jewish law, as they understood it, but saw Jesus as the promised messiah. The repercussions of this belief are not minor, and they speak to perhaps the primary difference between Judaism and Christianity (in all of both their many forms) today. If the messiah has come, the world has been redeemed; the very nature of history has changed with the coming of Christ ("anointed one," in Greek). This Christian belief that the world has been redeemed creates the space in which the Old Testament can become old, its covenant belonging to the former order of things. Jews who rejected the belief that Jesus was the Christ thus reinforced their understanding of a world that was still unredeemed. The early followers of Jesus would by no means be the last group of Jews who expressed a belief that the world was redeemed, or in the throes of the redemptive process, but they were certainly among the more famous and influential.[10]

What linked these diverse Jewish groups together was an understanding of the authority of Torah and the power (symbolic if not always real) of the Temple. Most fundamentally, they subscribed to the Torah's myth of common descent: They saw themselves linked to each other as the children of Israel with their own land. The boundaries of this self-understanding were no doubt fuzzy, for, at the same time that this myth was projecting a biological component to belonging to the people Israel, ancient Jews themselves recognized the need for more permeable boundaries that allowed non-Jews to "convert" or enter into the community. There may have been "good" Jews and "bad" Jews (the Dead Sea scrolls' "sons of dark" were Jews), but all were seen as linked by mythic ancestry.

Jews, inside and outside Palestine, in various ways saw themselves as linked into a single polity at whose heart was the Torah. Abraham and Moses play important roles in the Jewish literature of the Second Temple period: Abraham is the genealogical founder of the people, but Moses is its divinely sanctioned lawgiver. No literature from any extant Jewish group of the Second Temple period—even the early Jewish followers of Jesus—suggests that Jews should not view the Torah as prescribing divinely demanded behaviors. The sects might have fought over their understanding of the Torah, but none denied its ultimate authority.

Even nonsectarian Jews, probably comprising the vast majority of Jews throughout the Second Temple period, appear to have acknowledged the authority of Torah. By the first century CE it had become the custom to read the Torah in local synagogues on the Sabbath. Human representation is strikingly absent from art in the land of Israel during this time, which has plausibly been interpreted as reflecting a widespread Jewish adherence to one particularly strict understanding of the second commandment, which prohibits the making of idols. Jewish apologetic literature takes for granted the authority of the Torah.

The Jewish engagement with tradition during the period of the Second Temple was largely a one-way street. These Jews took their textual and ritual traditions seriously, but, for many complex and ultimately unknowable reasons, few of their contributions to this tradition survived. Ecclesiastes, parts of Daniel, and some psalms were probably authored during the Hellenistic period, and the Tanak as a whole became more stable. Yet little else—the scores of Jewish apocalypses, Philo's philosophical writings, Josephus's histories, even compendia of Torah law such as those found among the Dead Sea scrolls—were thought to be worth preserving by later living Jewish communities. Ironically, were it not for the preservation of the literary material by later Christians and the accidental finds of papyri, scrolls, and rocks, we would know almost nothing about Jewish life in the Second Temple period.

It might have been otherwise. Copies of Ecclesiasticus (Ben Sira) and one of the Dead Sea scrolls, known as the Damascus Document, survived long enough (or were somehow rediscovered and copied) to make it into the Cairo Genizah, a repository of texts that had decayed and were awaiting burial in the attic of Cairo's Ben Ezra synagogue. Medieval Jews rediscovered and "translated" (with copious changes) Josephus, now called *Yosiphon*; after having some impact on Jewish historiography, this too would fade away. Ultimately, though, whatever intrinsic merit these writings may have had, however interesting and significant their solutions to the problems of wrestling with the tradition in their distinct historical contexts, they were simply overwhelmed by the very different approach of the Rabbis. Before any of this Second Temple literature could pick up traction, the Rabbis shifted the ground from under them. And instead of entering the "Judaic tradition," these rich religious texts were consigned to the dust heap of history.

4

THE RABBIS

FOR ALL THEIR riotous diversity, almost all modern Jewish movements are heirs of the Rabbis. Prior to the destruction of the Temple by the Romans in 70 CE, Judaism was a diverse and loose family of religious communities that drew upon local understandings of Temple and Torah. By 640 CE most of the vast literary production of the Rabbis had reached closure, and their distinctive understanding of the tradition would transform Judaism utterly.

The Second Temple period came to an end with the destruction of the Jerusalem Temple. In 66 CE the Jews revolted against Rome for reasons that scholars still hotly dispute. The revolt probably sprang from a messy combination of Rome's untenable tax demands and policy gaffes concerning the Temple, social and economic instability, protonationalistic religious ideas, and a restless Jewish aristocracy. The Jews of Galilee and Judea caught the Roman authorities off guard. Quickly regrouping, however, the Roman legions soon put an end to the Galilean revolt, with many of its major Jewish cities quietly surrendering to Rome's clearly superior army. The revolt's leaders fled to Jerusalem and captured the city and Temple precincts.[1]

Had, perhaps, the Jewish leaders surrendered quickly to Rome or had they not been fighting each other with a focus and venom that sometimes eclipsed their united war against Rome, perhaps—perhaps—the Romans would not have destroyed the Temple. Whatever it was that went wrong, though, went drastically wrong. Rome's difficulty breaching the city walls and the Temple's fortifications was a testament to both the strength of the revolt as well as Herod's masons. Josephus, writing under Roman patronage, later attempts to exculpate the Romans from the charge that they destroyed the Temple: it was Jewish infighting, and God's will, that destroyed the Temple. At least as likely, Rome's response was unusually harsh because of its difficulty suppressing the revolt. And it still was not over—some of the rebels escaped to Herod's palace at Masada, where they continued to resist Rome until 72–73.

The Temple's destruction had profound practical and theological ramifications. The twice-daily sacrifices that assured God's protection for Israel ground to a halt. At least for most Jews of the land of Israel, the Temple was the central religious institution, and it was not at all clear in the immediate wake of its loss how to replace it. The Temple stood on the nexus of heaven and earth; how could humans now bridge that gap?

Even worse were the theological implications of the Temple's destruction. Like all of their contemporaries, the Jews saw their temple not just as a human institution in which the deity was worshipped but as an actual house of the deity. God, in one or another form or manifestation, was thought to have lived in the Temple. The destruction of the Second Temple reopened the sores of the destruction of the first: how could God allow aliens to destroy His house? One uncomfortable answer, to be quickly rejected, was that God lost; the gods of the conquerors were stronger. A second answer that had to be taken more seriously was that God had abandoned the Jews. Early Christian writers latched onto this answer, arguing that the destruction of the Temple demonstrated God's desertion of the Jews after they had shunned Him in the person of Jesus Christ. Even ignoring the Christian arguments, Jews themselves were troubled by the possibility of God's desertion. The consequences of such an answer opened into a theological abyss.

The problem, of course, was not new. The book of Deuteronomy had already developed a metahistorical narrative linking sin, punishment, and exile. Because Israel's covenant to God is an eternal unconditional one, God never deserts Israel, even when the people have been disobedient. This is clearly a mixed blessing. When Israel sins, then, God punishes, often with national calamities leading to exile. Ultimately, God promises to restore His people to their promised land, but in the interim they dwell as a dispersed and exiled people. When the First Temple was destroyed in 586 BCE, several prophetic writers turned to this explanation. In this narrative the Babylonian destroyer Nebuchadnezzar is seen as an instrument of God's wrath. Nebuchadnezzar's downfall was due to his inability to recognize himself as a humble servant of God, instead attributing his victory to his own prowess.

When the Second Temple was destroyed, most Jews probably fell back on some version of this narrative. God's house could be destroyed only with

God's own consent. Yet instead of portraying Rome, like Nebuchadnezzar, as an instrument of God's anger, Jewish writers prefer to understand God as voluntary vacating His house, leaving it as simple stone and mortar and thus susceptible to Rome's assault. Although conventional, this answer did not satisfy everybody. In a Jewish apocalyptic (and pseudepigraphic) work entitled 4 Ezra that was probably written in the late first century CE, "Ezra" rejects this argument:

> Are the deeds of Babylon better than those of Zion? Or has another nation known you besides Israel? Or what tribes have so believed your covenants as these tribes of Jacob? Yet their reward has not appeared and their labor has borne no fruit. For I have traveled widely among the nations and have seen that they abound in wealth, though they are unmindful of your commandments. Now therefore weigh in a balance our iniquities and those of the inhabitants of the world; and so it will be found which way the turn of the scale will incline. When have the inhabitants of the earth not sinned in your sight? Or what nation has kept your commandments so well? You may indeed find individual men who have kept your commandments, but nations you will not find.[2]

The angel Uriel at first rejects the very notion that Ezra could understand God's ways. When you, like God, can weigh the weight of fire, come back and ask and maybe you'll understand, he responds. But then he relents and provides a more direct answer:

> If you are alive, you will see, and if you live long, you will often marvel, because the age is hastening swiftly to its end. For it will not be able to bring the things that have been promised to the righteous in their appointed times, because this age is full of sadness and infirmities. For the evil about which you ask me has been sown, but the harvest of it has not yet come. If therefore that which has been sown is not reaped, and if the place where the evil has been sown does not pass away, the field where the good has been sown will not come. For a grain of evil seed was sown in Adam's heart from the beginning, and how much ungodliness it has produced until now, and will produce until the time of threshing comes![3]

The destruction of the Temple is a sign of the approaching end of the world. At that time, the time of "threshing," God will settle all accounts.

4 Ezra represents one contemporary Jewish response to the destruction of the Temple, the Rabbis another. The rabbinic "foundation story," probably

written over three centuries after 70 CE, portrays the destruction as an opportunity rather than a catastrophe. This long and complex story attributes
the war with Rome to petty jealousies and portrays the Rabbis, led by the
great Rabban Yohanan ben Zakkai, as active in Jerusalem. Although desiring
peace, they are cowed by the powerful brigands leading the revolt. R. Yohanan finally decides to escape Jerusalem and is smuggled out in a coffin. After a
fateful encounter with Vespasian, during which his premonition that Vespasian would be acclaimed emperor is fulfilled, he gains Vespasian's favor:

> [Vespasian] said to [R. Yohanan]: "I am going [back to Rome] and will send
> someone else [to continue the siege]. Ask something of me and I will give
> it to you."
>   [R. Yohanan] said, "Give me Yavneh and its sages and the line of Rabban
> Gamaliel and doctors to heal Rabbi Zadoq."

And thus was born the myth of Yavneh, the great rabbinic academy that
arose out of the ashes of the Temple.

The true value of this story is as myth rather than history. It reflects a later
rabbinic self-perception as peaceful inhabitants of a non-Jewish empire,
perpetuators of a hoary tradition, experts in the interpretation of Torah,
and, implicitly, as Israel's new spiritual leaders. In other writings of the
Rabbis, Yavneh appears a bustling, vibrant rabbinic community and institution, a new Jerusalem centered around Torah and its study rather than the
Temple and its sacrifices, with Rabbis firmly in charge and priests hardly to
be found.

Historically, though, this picture does not add up. There appear to have
been no Rabbis in the Second Temple period. *Rabbi* literally means "my
teacher," and it is likely that some Jews used this honorific—as some Jews
apparently called Jesus. But it did not become a formal title until after the
Temple's destruction. Nor is the rabbinic portrayal of Yavneh historically
accurate. Some scholars, led by Yohanan ben Zakkai, may indeed have
gathered at Yavneh in the aftermath of the Temple's destruction to begin
something new, but if so it would have been a small study circle rather
than the institution portrayed in rabbinic literature, or even a small school.
Rather than continuing a grand tradition, complete with its own source of
temporal authority in the person of the patriarch (Rabban Gamaliel), these
few early scholars—with few followers—would have been cautiously feeling their way toward a new conception of their tradition.[4]

The Rabbis may not have been the carriers of a continuous historical tradition, but neither did they rise out of a vacuum. The Rabbis may have had some connection to the Pharisees, who seem to disappear (along with the other Jewish sects) in 70 CE, although the precise nature and strength of this connection remains obscure. Both groups interpreted the law, maintained a set of distinctive traditions outside the Torah, believed that the beliefs of divine omniscience and human free will could coexist, and adhered to certain purity restrictions outside the Temple. At the same time, these similarities are rather vague and the Rabbis themselves never explicitly claim descent from the Pharisees. Clearly, however, the Rabbis emerged from the same cultural and religious matrix. Their precise traditions and modes of interpretation might not have the hoary antiquity they sometimes claim for them, but their attempt to turn to Torah as a source of authority for discerning the living will of God did.

The earliest stage of the rabbinic movement most likely involved both scriptural interpretation and the explication of Torah law. Their concerns appear to have been quite practical: What does God want from Israel? How are Jews to fulfill, quite precisely, God's will? They must have had some followers who consulted them primarily about issues of purity and other limited ritual matters. But these followers were relatively few. The Rabbis began as a sectarian community making universal claims; they saw their claims not as targeted merely at their small group of followers, but at all of Israel.

The Bar Kokhba revolt of 132–35 CE changed the rabbinic movement, as it did most everything else in the land of Israel. A shadowy historical figure, Bar Kosiba (the name he used when signing the official documents that survived in the dry caves of the Judean Desert) led what appears to be a widespread revolt against Rome. The causes of this revolt are even more obscure than those of the revolt of 66 CE. Some of the rebels' coins are stamped "for the freedom of Jerusalem," suggesting a nationalistic impulse.[5] Some of his supporters referred to him as Bar Kokhba, "son of a star," and probably saw him as a messianic figure. His detractors called him Bar Koziba, "son of a lie." Starting in the region of the Dead Sea, the revolt appears to have spilled over into Arabia (present-day Jordan) and perhaps further north. Rome took it quite seriously. While and after vanquishing the rebels, the Romans embarked on an almost unprecedented program of pacification that involved the slaughter and eviction of Jews from Judea, the consecration of the Temple Mount (the site of the destroyed Temple) as a holy place for Jupiter, and (temporary) edicts against some Jewish practices (e.g., circumcision). Demographically, the revolt and its aftermath caused a shift of the Jewish population into the lower Galilee and Jordan Valley. The edicts, although short-lived, left a lasting historical trauma.

Although the later writings of the Rabbis generally do not make good historical sources, they do indicate that the Romans martyred some of their most prominent leaders. The gruesome rabbinic account of their martyrs was ultimately incorporated into the liturgy for the Day of Atonement (Yom Kippur); the medieval liturgy transfers the atoning power of the sacrificial service that took place on Yom Kippur during the biblical and Second Temple periods to the rabbinic martyrs and continued recitation of their tale. In any case, the Rabbis emerged after 135 CE more self-confident and entered a period of consolidation. From the mid-second century to the start of the third, the Rabbis not only continued to develop their program of interpretation and explication but also began to collect these diffuse, oral discussions.

The beginning of the third century was a second critical moment for the rabbinic movement. By assuming a newly created Roman office, Rabbi Judah the Prince (Romans and Christians called this office the patriarch) brought prestige, power, and resources to the rabbinic movement. In truth, not much is known about Rabbi Judah or the role of the patriarchate. He was some kind of liaison between Jews (whether of the land of Israel or outside it is unclear) and Roman authorities and collected various taxes from Jews—although we do not know what he did with the money. Whatever his role was, it fell far short of a national leader of any significance.

To the Rabbis, though, marginalized as they had been from their origins, the ascension of one of their own to a prestigious office was significant. The Rabbis used this event to claim national leadership, eventually retrojecting their self-image as national leaders back to the "line of Rabban Gamaliel." Despite these rabbinic assertions of leadership, Rabbi Judah played a more prominent role as a patron within the rabbinic movement than outside it; virtually no contemporary Roman or Christian source noticed him.

The rabbinic claim to authority rested more on the scribal tradition than the priestly one, although it also contained elements of the latter. As, perhaps, spiritual heirs of the Pharisees, they claimed to possess the "truest" interpretations of the will of God as revealed in the sacred texts. Unlike the priests, they asserted, anyone, by dint of effort and study, could achieve the ability to participate in this process; entrance was not limited by genealogy. Nor did it require any kind of divine inspiration of the type that can be found in the scriptural interpretations of the Dead Sea scrolls. "Service" to God, the *avodah* that used to refer almost exclusively to the Temple sacrifices, was transformed in rabbinic hands into participation in distinctively rabbinic types of piety including prayer and, primarily, talmud Torah.

The rabbinic emphasis on talmud Torah, the "study" of the entire Tanak that was broadly defined to include not just memorization but also painstaking interpretation, was a new development. Previously, Jews of course had revered the Torah and turned to it as a guide for proper behaviors, whether for daily religious life in Hellenistic Egypt or for the proper conduct of purity in the Temple. Study of the Torah was intended specifically to reveal its practical teachings. The Rabbis elevated the very act of study to the status of divine service. When the Hebrew Bible states, in the passage after the declaration of the Shema, "and you will repeat them (*veshinnantam*) to your children" (Deuteronomy 6:7), it means that quite literally—one must teach one's children the literal words. The Rabbis understand the verb to denote the continual study of the Torah. The elevation of study within the rabbinic movement culminates the trend begun during the earlier period of vesting Scripture with an authority that can be used to challenge that of priests and prophets.

It would be mistaken, though, to evaluate the rise of Torah study and the rabbinic movement generally as historically predetermined. There was no necessary, or even logical, line from the Jewish sectarian use of Torah to its rabbinic transformation. The Rabbis were profoundly shaped not only by their past, but, perhaps more important, by their present. The conceptual world inhabited by the Rabbis was not some essentially or intrinsically "Jewish" one, but one uniquely shaped at the intersection of pervasive Hellenistic contact, Ancient Near Eastern traditions, Roman political intervention, and the local customs of Galilee. The Rabbis were far from being Greek philosophers, but they were well aware of the outlines of the major and popular Greek philosophies, such as Stoicism, Cynicism, and Epicureanism. They probably had little acquaintance with Roman law—the Romans seemed to have largely let the Jews of Galilee handle their own affairs without interference—but they certainly knew of basic Roman legal concepts and categories as well as the institution of the jurist. They may not have known Homer, but they knew who he was and had some kind of understanding of how their non-Jewish contemporaries were reading him. Their frame of reference was similar to that of other literate Roman provincials throughout the

Near East, with whom, no doubt, they would have had more in common than they would have with, say, their revered progenitor Ezra.

Seen not as a diachronic development within Jewish history but as a Greco-Roman phenomenon, talmud Torah looks suspiciously and surprisingly like philosophy as it was understood at that time. The Rabbis saw the study of texts, accompanied by rigorous training of both mind and body, as a path to personal development and perfection. And if talmud Torah is a kind of Jewish equivalent to Greco-Roman philosophy, then Rabbis are its philosophers. This analogy should not be pushed too far—the Rabbis also look quite different from Greco-Roman philosophers, engaging in many activities (e.g., detailed discussions of inapplicable purity laws) that would have seemed downright weird to their contemporaries. But this structural similarity helps to illustrate how the Rabbis worked within their own unique and historically contingent conditions to make sense of their tradition.

If the Rabbis sometimes, at least on a structural level, look like Greco-Roman philosophers, they also at times appear in the guise of Roman jurists. It is perhaps no accident that Rabbi Judah the Patriarch was the framer of the earliest extant rabbinic document, the Mishnah. Standing between Rome and the Jews, Rabbi Judah may have developed a particular interest in the codification of rabbinic legal discussions. Literally the "repetition" (sharing the same Hebrew root as *veshinnantam*), the Mishnah is a signally audacious text. Organized by legal topic rather than the order of the biblical text and containing few justifications for its legal opinions, the Mishnah asserts an authority independent of Scripture.[6] Implicitly it makes a theological claim that the Rabbis would make explicit a few decades later: God gave two Torahs on Mount Sinai.

In these later rabbinic legends this "theology of the dual Torah" crystallizes. Its premise is that on Mount Sinai Moses actually received *two* Torahs. One is the well-known written Torah, the Pentateuch. The other was not written down; it was given orally to Moses, who passed it down orally through a chain of transmission that continues with the Rabbis. Because it too comes from God on Mount Sinai, this Oral Torah has (virtually) equal authority to the Written Torah.

A rabbinic story captures at least one understanding of the relationship between the Oral and the Written Torahs:

> Our sages taught: Once a Gentile came before Shammai. He said to him, "How many Torahs do you have?" He said to him, "Two, the Written Torah and the Oral Torah." He said to him, "I believe you about the Written

but not about the Oral. I will convert on the condition that you teach me the Written Torah [alone]." He rebuked him and dismissed him with a reproach.

He [the Gentile] came before Hillel. The first day he [Hillel] said to him, "*Aleph, beit, gimmel, dalet.*" The next day he reversed it. He [the Gentile] said to him, "Yesterday you did not tell it to me this way." He said to him, "Did you not rely on me [for that]? As regards the Oral [Torah], you should rely on me too."

(Babylonian Talmud, Shabbat 31a)

This story doubly retrojects the concept of Oral Torah. First, it sets the story in the days of Hillel and Shammai, who were said to live around the turn of the millennium and to be the most important immediate progenitors of the Rabbis. The story itself is marked, by the words *our sages taught* to the second or early third centuries CE. In truth, it is neither. The story is almost certainly a later (perhaps fourth-century) attempt to legitimize the concept of Oral Torah.

The story also indicates the relationship between the Written and Oral Torah. The latter becomes the lens through which the former is seen. Oral Torah not only substantively supplements the lacunae-laden Written Torah but also helps to determine how the Torah is to be read. And unlike the Written Torah, which by definition is seen as a static text, Oral Torah evolves and unfolds, continuing to reveal the will of God as latently disclosed to Moses and Israel at the primal moment at Sinai.

"Torah," for the Rabbis, thus became a concept as well as a text, including all God's past and continuing revelation. Conceptually Oral Torah might be compared to the role of the Holy Spirit in Catholic theology. Like the Oral Torah, the Holy Spirit is a conceptual mechanism for allowing the divine to act in a changing world; it guides one's understanding of the unchanging text. Unlike the Holy Spirit, though, the Oral Torah works as a human process rather than as a series of discrete moments of revelation. The Rabbis confidently arrogate to themselves the role of arbiters of God's revelation. Revelation is now in the hands of humans.

The Mishnah is a snapshot of the Oral Torah frozen at one moment in time. Rabbi Judah's Mishnah is a carefully edited and organized collection of a wide range of rabbinic positions. Rabbi Judah (or, probably better, his school or court) most likely had access to the oral "class notes" of many different rabbinic teachers from which he pieced together his own text, sometimes adding, anonymously, his own positions. It is written in a clear and succinct Hebrew. Containing too many unresolved disagreements to be a true code of law, the Mishnah appears to have been intended as some kind of legal guide or textbook, a starting rather than ending point for discussion.

The Mishnah contains six orders, each divided into tractates, and leaves few issues untouched. "Seeds" opens anomalously with a tractate on blessings and then continues with discussions of agricultural laws. "Festivals" devotes tractates to proper conduct and ritual on most of the holidays. "Women" primarily addresses the legal relationships between men and women, particularly marriage, divorce, and the ability of a father or husband to annul the vows of his daughter or wife. "Damages" discusses both civil and criminal law. "Purities" deals with matters of ritual purity, and "Holy Things" with matters connected to the Temple and the sacrificial system.

The Oral Torah attempts to clarify how a Jew should live his or her life according to the will of God. To add to the stakes, the Rabbis took seriously (even if they did not implement) the biblical penalties, whether sacrificial or penal, for the violation of God's word. This required them to make painstaking distinctions. The Hebrew Bible, for example, prohibits work on the Sabbath, but it hardly defines what it means by the term *work*. This is not an insignificant lacuna when the penalty for the violation of the Sabbath's work restrictions was death. Hence, most of the twenty-four chapters of the tractate "Sabbath" in the Mishnah attempt to define work as a legal category. Here is an almost random example taken from the middle of that discussion:

> One who writes two letters, whether with his right [hand] or his left, whether the same letter [written twice] or two different letters, whether two signs in any language—is guilty [of violating the prohibition against writing on the Sabbath].
>
> Rabbi Yosi said: They make accountable [one who writes] two letters only because [he makes] a mark, for they used to write on the boards of the Tabernacle to know which is joined to which.
>
> Rabbi said: We find a little name [or word] from a big name. *Shem* from *Shimon* or *Shemuel*; *Noah* from *Nahor*; *Dan* from *Daniel*; *Gad* from *Gadiel*.
>
> (*Mishnah Shabbat 12:3*)

The Mishnah attempts to clarify the precise boundaries of the prohibition against writing on the Sabbath. Two letters define "writing"; one letter appears not to count, although two symbols do. Rabbi Yosi's comment attempts to clarify the curious grouping of letters with signs: Both are marks.

The problem with marks is that they were used in the building of the Tabernacle in the wilderness of Sinai, and the Rabbis see activities associated with the building of the Tabernacle as paradigmatic of work. So, Rabbi Yosi seems to argue, the problem with the letters is not that they are letters but that they are marks.

Rabbi Judah the Patriarch (referred to simply as Rabbi in the Mishnah) disagrees. His cryptic statement appears to mean that if one intended to write a name (probably exemplary of any word) and wrote only the first two letters and then stopped, if those two letters constitute an independent name then one is culpable, but if not then one is exempt from punishment. Whereas Rabbi Yosi bases the prohibition against writing on the problem with marking, Rabbi's argument is semantic, based on whether the word has a meaning.

This short passage exemplifies many of the properties of the Mishnah. Written in linguistic and conceptual shorthand, it constantly refers to ideas outside of it: To understand a part requires understanding the whole. I added the words in brackets so the passage would make a modicum of sense to the uninitiated English reader. It leaves positions unresolved: who is right, Rabbi Yosi or Rabbi? And it carries within its precision the very seeds of its own deconstruction. How would Rabbi deal with the clause about signs? How would Rabbi Yosi deal with a case of temporary writing (e.g., writing in the sand or on a computer) that is not applicable to marking boards for building? What role does the intention of the writer play for all these positions? The Mishnah spends no time on these questions, and in general rarely does more than state the positions, occasionally with very short justifications. It leaves the questions that it generates hanging in the air.

At the same time that the Oral Torah was being composed, the Rabbis also turned their attention to the Written Torah. Understanding the Written Torah not as a transparent text but as one pregnant with depths of meaning, they developed a new interpretive technique to unlock its secrets. They call this new interpretive technique *midrash*. The word itself is suggestive. The Hebrew Bible uses the verb *d-r-sh* to refer to seeking the divine will through consultation with the prophet. Midrash literally means the "seeking," but it is applied to the biblical text: God's will is to be found in the text rather than through a human intermediary.

Biblical interpretation, of course, was not the invention of the Rabbis. Throughout the Second Temple period Jews interpreted the Hebrew Bible. Some, like the author of Enoch, spun elaborate stories to bridge narrative difficulties. Others made the biblical stories and laws more accessible and coherent by rewriting them. Philo systematically subjected the Bible to his own brand of allegorical interpretation. The Dead Sea scrolls record an inspired interpretation: the biblical text x means y because God revealed this meaning directly to the interpreter.

Midrash differs from all these interpretive strategies. Midrash is a rule-driven form of interpretation, or genre, that emerges from some basic rabbinic assumptions about the nature of the biblical text.[7] These assumptions about the nature of the text are critical to understanding midrash; they are premises without which midrash makes little sense.

The Rabbis assume the entire Tanak is perfect. This means that all those problems in the Hebrew Bible noted by biblical scholars—for example, repetitions, inconsistencies, redundancies, spelling mistakes—are really divinely sanctioned. The language of the Hebrew Bible is precise and succinct; every letter has its purpose. It is this detail-oriented assumption that drives most midrash. The Rabbis are far less concerned, at least on the surface, with reconciling a biblical verse with its context than they are with explaining smaller, textual irritants. The larger questions that grab the attention of modern readers, such as Abraham's state of mind as he went to sacrifice his son Isaac at God's command, get at most secondary attention in midrash; midrash is an interpretation of letters, words, and phrases. Linguistic anomalies are divine clues waiting to be unlocked. This assumption accounts for the historic emphasis that Jews have placed on the Hebrew text of the Bible, even when its readers and listeners do not know Hebrew. A vernacular translation can never fully replace the Hebrew text because only the Hebrew text is God's true word, latent with meaning. Muslims regard the Quran similarly: only the Arabic is truly God's word.

But how is one to unlock the latent meaning, for example, of a spelling mistake? The answer follows from a second rabbinic assumption about the nature of the biblical text. Because the entire text is the word of God, it is all equal and can therefore equally illuminate any other part of it. This assumption leads to a noncontextual way of reading the Hebrew Bible that many modern Western readers have difficulty grasping. (Incidentally, poststructuralist and deconstructive literary critics were delighted to find in midrash a kind of anticipation of their own way of reading.) The Rabbis understand the Hebrew Bible as a self-enclosed system that contains the keys to its own interpretive problems. Those keys, however, might be found in un-likely places. A problematic word or verse in Exodus, for example, might be "solved" by contrasting it to a word from Proverbs. To those trained to read texts for the thesis, theme, or narrative thread, the rabbinic atomization of biblical texts—the way that they read a word in the context of another word or verse in another place rather than in the sentence in which it is actually located—can appear utterly bizarre and random.

Whether or not it is really bizarre I leave to the reader's taste, but mid-rash is rarely random. Usually there is some kind of link between contrasted words or verses. The more uncommon the link, the "better" the midrash; the Rabbis recognize the futility of illuminating two disparate verses on the basis of their sharing a common word or concept. Two examples can illus-trate this approach.

According to Deuteronomy 21:18–21:

If a man has a wayward and defiant son, who does not heed his father or mother and does not obey them even after they discipline him, his father and mother shall take hold of him and bring him out to the elders of his town at the public place of his community. They shall say to the elders of his town, "This son of ours is disloyal and defiant; he does not heed us. He is a glutton and a drunkard." Thereupon the men of his town shall stone him to death. Thus you will sweep out evil from your midst; all Israel will hear and be afraid.

This passage seems clear enough. It begins with a (not uncommon) scenario and prescribes a remedy. For centuries of Jewish readers, though, the true meaning of this passage has hardly been obvious. Exegetically, the passage raises problems: Why "wayward" *and* "defiant"? Why include the line about being a "glutton and a drunkard"? Does it apply also to daughters? What happens if the community does not have the ability to stone? Just as promi-nent is the moral problem: Does the just and good God really command the execution of a child?

The rabbinic answer to this last question is no. Line by line, word by word, the Rabbis cleverly reread the passage:

" . . . who does not heed his father or mother": Is it possible that even if his father and mother say to him to light the candle and he doesn't light it [that he is called "wayward and defiant" and liable to death]? [No. That is why] Scripture [repeats] "who does not heed" "he does not heed us." Just as "he does not heed us" [later in the passage] refers to a "glutton and a drunkard" so too "who does not heed [his father or mother]" refers to a glutton and drunkard. And just as "he does not heed us" [later in the passage] refers to one who steals from his father and his mother so too [the verse] "who does not heed his father or mother" [does not apply] until he steals from his father and mother.

(Sifre Deuteronomy, section 218)

By repeating the term "does not heed" this passage is providing, according to this interpretation, a key for its own understanding. A "wayward and defiant son" is thus interpreted not as any ordinary teenage disobedience, but as the commission of a much more severe offense. The Rabbis go on to limit the applicability of this rule until it is nearly inapplicable.

A second, more complex example appears in a rabbinic commentary on Exodus 19, the story of God's revelation to Moses and Israel at Mount Sinai. After Moses and the Israelites prepared themselves, the Bible says, "Now Mount Sinai was all in smoke, for the Lord had come down upon it in fire; the smoke rose like the smoke of a kiln, and the whole mountain trembled violently" (Exodus 19:18). On this a midrash comments:

"Now Mount Sinai was all in smoke": Is it possible only the place of the Glory? [No, thus] Scripture says "all."

"for the Lord had come down upon it in fire": This says that the Torah is fire, from fire it was given and to fire it is compared. What is the nature of fire? If one draws near to it he is burned; if one is far from it he is cold. The only thing for one to do is to be warmed against its flame.

"the smoke rose like the smoke of a kiln": Is it possible that [this smoke was] only like [ordinary] smoke? [No, thus] Scripture says "of a kiln." But if "of a kiln," is it possible [that the smoke was] only like that of an [ordinary] kiln? [No, thus] Scripture says "The mountain was ablaze with flames to the heart of the skies" (Deuteronomy 4:11). Why then does Scripture say "of a kiln"? To break the ear with what it is capable of hearing. Similarly: "A lion has roared, who can but fear?" (Amos 3:8). And who gave strength and might to the lion? Was it not He? Rather, we describe Him with terms from His creations to break the ear, etc. Similarly, "And there, coming from the east with a roar like the roar of mighty waters, was the Presence of the God of Israel" (Ezekiel 43:2). And who gave strength and might to the waters? Was it not He? Rather, we describe Him with terms from His creations to break the ear, etc.[8]

Why does the biblical text include the word *all* in the first part of the verse? And what does it mean to teach by using the words *fire* and *smoke*?

Note the answer that the Rabbis do *not* give. They do not say that it says that because that is how it actually happened. Their interest in this verse is not on the event that it purports to describe, but on its language. The verse includes the word *all* lest you think that only the place of God's presence was encased in smoke. The midrash certainly is making a claim here about what happened, but the real concern is why the verse includes the word *all*.

Similarly, *fire* is specified to make a comparison. The verse says *fire* in order to show the similarity of Torah to fire. Once the Rabbis make this comparison they can exploit it. As the word of God, Torah is potentially dangerous; to get close to Torah is to get close to God, and the closer one gets to God the more dangerous the going for mere mortals. But distance from God is equally dangerous. The verse includes the word *fire* then to teach a lesson about a person's proper stance toward the Torah, close yet not too close. Note how different this interpretation is from that of Aristobulus (discussed in the last chapter), who understood the message of this passage as concerning the nature of fire.

Smoke troubles the Rabbis more. Surely the smoke that accompanied God could not have been any ordinary smoke. Indeed, the Rabbis expect the inclusion of *of a kiln* to teach something about the nature of the smoke. But they cannot figure out what. So instead they say that *of a kiln* is just a figure of speech, a human simile to make comprehensible the incomprehensible nature of God. Their use of the verb *to break* is unusual but deliberate. Using it to mean something more like *accustom*, they also signal with its use the power of the divine word. Humans can bear only so much of the divine before they are scorched or shattered by its power.

As this example shows, midrash is not simply an academic exercise. It is also the way that the Rabbis "do" theology. This particular set of biblical interpretations does double duty. On the one hand, it is resolving discrete textual problems. But, at the same time, it is working through a profound theological problem about the nature of God. Given God's overwhelming power, is it possible to conceive of an immanent God? How close can one really get to the divine? Subjected to this kind of searching, the Rabbis transform the biblical text from a dead historical book or a dry guide to living into a fundamentally contemporary and relevant text. Midrash bridges the gap between today and the yesterday of the Tanak. The story of God's revelation on Mount Sinai, a one-time historical event, becomes a commentary on the continuing nature of God's presence in Torah and the world.

Hinted at here, but much clearer in other midrashic texts and compilations, is its inherent multivocality. Because the Rabbis saw the Written Torah as latent with divine meaning, they never restricted themselves to single, dogmatic understandings of the biblical text. They might thus interpret a particular verse or word in a half-dozen different ways, several of which are mutually exclusive. They thus do not aim to arrive at *the* correct interpretation of Torah, but at the plurality of divine revelation in the text.

Medieval Christians were as puzzled by this approach to Scripture as they were at the Jewish neglect of biblical law. At a disputation in Barcelona in 1263, the Christian friars confronted the Jewish representative, Rabbi Moshe ben Nahman (Nahmanides), with a number of midrashic traditions that, they claimed, showed that the Talmudic sages also prophesied that Jesus was the messiah. Nahmanides first rejects their interpretation of the passages, but then continues:

> We have a third book which is called the Midrash, which means "Sermons". This is just as if the bishop were to stand up and make a sermon, and one of his hearers liked it so much that he wrote it down. And as for this book, the Midrash, if anyone wants to believe in it, well and good, but if someone does not believe in it, there is no harm.[9]

This response encapsulates two important characteristics of midrash, even as understood one thousand years before Nahmanides. Nonlegal midrash were "just" interpretations; they had no binding authority. Nor do they offer exclusive interpretations. The friars found these assumptions utterly baffling, for they denied the fundamental goal of Christian biblical interpretation to find the one, pure, divine message.

Midrash, as a literary genre, appears in many different rabbinic texts. Probably shortly after the redaction of the Mishnah around 220 CE several collections of midrash, organized by biblical book, were also redacted. The Rabbis maintain a somewhat odd epistemological dichotomy. For them, everything that deals with Torah is either halakhic or aggadic. Halakhah is anything that deals with legal issues; aggadah is everything else. These early collections, on Exodus, Leviticus, Numbers, and Deuteronomy, generally are halakhic—they proceed in order through the biblical book and draw out laws from the texts. As with the Mishnah, the individual midrashic traditions had undergone a process of selection and careful editing.

The Rabbis themselves thought that there was a historical break around the time of Rabbi Judah. They termed the Rabbis who lived before around

250 CE the *tannaim*, an Aramaic word that means "repeater" or "teacher." The name probably derives from their role as memorizers and repeaters of the oral traditions of their teachers; it soon more generally applied to their ability to add to and wrestle with these traditions. Later Rabbis attribute to the tannaim and their sayings a high degree of authority, especially when they seem to be in conflict with later rabbinic opinions.[10]

From a rabbinic perspective, the period of the *amoraim* began in the mid-third century CE and extended to around the fifth or early sixth century. What most distinguished this new group of Rabbis was not only their sense of inferiority relative to their teachers, but, more significantly, their self-perceived role as commentators on the tannaitic traditions. The amoraim acknowledged the authority of many of these earlier tannaitic traditions and they sought to explain, clarify, and interpret them. Otherwise there was more continuity than discontinuity between the tannaim and early Palestinian amoraim. From a political and social perspective, little had changed. Palestinian amoraim still lived in (probably urban) Jewish communities in and around the Galilee, and Roman authorities let these communities function semiautonomously. Rabbis continued to study in small, uninstitutionalized disciple circles around a major teacher. The "rabbinic movement" was thus a loose network of these circles and their followers. Only in the late fourth or fifth centuries do they appear to have created institutional structures such as an academy in Tiberias.

From the mid-fourth century on, Palestinian Rabbis were living in an increasingly Christianized environment. The Roman emperor Constantine had converted to Christianity and he and many of his successors were active patrons of Christian institutions. Churches were built throughout the land of Israel, and streams of Christian pilgrims made their way each year to Jerusalem. By the fifth century, imperial legislation had effectively marginalized the Jews, abolishing the office of the patriarchate (for unknown reasons) and limiting some Jewish civic rights.

While the Palestinian Rabbis from this period must have been aware of these developments, their writings hardly reflect it explicitly. Rabbinic literature rarely engages in polemical disputes with Christians or Christian teachings. In at least one respect, however, the Rabbis did appear to notice the growing strength of Christianity.

The problem, in short, was the Hebrew Bible. Beginning with Paul, Christians declared themselves to be the true Israel and heir of the divine promise. The Old Testament might thus have been superseded by the New Testament, but for Christians it remained profoundly relevant as a record of the covenant and a divine witness to the coming of Christ. God, in the Old Testament, prophesied the coming of Christ; the Jews were, in fact, faulted for not being able to see this in their own Scripture. Needless to say, the Rabbis disagreed with this reading of the Hebrew Bible. The battle for the meaning of the Hebrew Bible/Old Testament was engaged.

Palestinian Rabbis responded to this Christian appropriation of the Hebrew Bible. One response was to create more collections of midrash.[11] These new collections, on the biblical books of Genesis, Leviticus (again), Song of Songs, Ruth, and Ecclesiastes, were primarily aggadic. Implicitly, they assert a distinctively Jewish Bible, a range of interpretations that despite their multivocality share assumptions about the nature of the biblical text and correct ways of interpreting it.[12] They gave Jews resources to counter the Scriptural claims of Christians.

Early Christians, for example, made much of Genesis 49:10, part of Jacob's blessing to his son: "The scepter shall not depart from Judah, nor the ruler's staff from between his feet until Shiloh comes and the homage of peoples be his." On its own, the verse is notoriously difficult; some scholars translate the obscure phrase "until Shiloh comes" as "tribute will come to him." Christians read the verse as a prophecy for the supersession of the Jews. With the destruction of the Temple in 70 CE, the consequent destruction of Jerusalem, and the defeat of the Jews in 135 CE, the scepter did indeed pass from Judah. Thus Shiloh—read here as the new, redeemed age— must have come. An amoraic commentary on this same verse is succinct and insistent:

> "The scepter shall not depart from Judah"—this is the throne of the kingdom, "Your divine throne is everlasting; your royal scepter is a scepter of equity" (Psalms 45:7). Why "nor the ruler's staff from between his feet"? When he comes about whom Scripture says, "Trampled underfoot will be the proud crowns of the drunkards of Ephraim" (Isaiah 28:3).
> "until Shiloh comes"—he whose kingdom [really is] his.
>
> (*Genesis Rabba* 99:8)

For the Rabbis, this refers to the coming of the true messiah, whose approach will be known by the trampling of the "drunkards of Ephraim"— most likely a reference to those who claim that Jesus was the messiah!

More bothersome to the Rabbis than the Christians, though, were the majority of Jews who did not fully accept rabbinic authority. Disdainfully called the "people of the land" (*am ha-aretz*) by the Rabbis, these Jews were hardly country bumpkins; throughout late antiquity they took seriously the traditions of their ancestors, building elaborate and expensive synagogues and perhaps turning to local (now Temple-less) priests for authority. Because they have left us little in the way of literary or legal texts, we can reconstruct only fragments of their religious lives. Their synagogues sometimes contained elaborate mosaic floors, replete with pictorial representations (often of biblical scenes) and a zodiac, which itself sometimes contained a human figure in the middle (a representation of Helios?). These remains, together with the rabbinic diatribes against both the depictions and the people who made them, remind us that a claim to authority is precisely that, only a claim. The Rabbis, especially of Palestine, were no doubt deeply embedded in their larger Jewish societies, maintaining a full network of social relationships and participating in the larger Greco-Roman culture that permeated their environments. So, while they did not appear to isolate themselves, neither were they entirely successful in getting other Jews to accept their universal claims. The Rabbis claim to be speaking for and to "Israel," although it is doubtful through the end of late antiquity whether Israel seriously heeded them.

Mishnah and midrash, representing the distinctively rabbinic approaches to Oral Torah and the interpretation of the Written Torah, began a process of the radical transformation of the written tradition of Israel. The publication (which might have meant the memorization and oral recitation rather than the production of actual written manuscripts in late antiquity, none of which survive) of the Mishnah shifted the nature of Oral Torah. Amoraim turned Oral Torah into a *textual* practice based on the study and interpretation of the Mishnah. They thus began to apply many of the assumptions and techniques they had used for the study of the Tanak to the Mishnah. While the Rabbis had more tolerance for contradictions in the Mishnah than they did for those in the Tanak, they nevertheless ascribed to the tannaim a high degree of intentionality; like the Torah, the Mishnah carried latent meanings.

The result was *talmud*, which is as much a practice and process as it would become a text in its own right. The Mishnah has a direct, declarative style and rarely justifies its pronouncements. The amoraim set to work complicating this simple style; they grab the questions hanging in the air and attempt to nail them down to earth. Why does the Mishnah say it in precisely this way and not another? Doesn't a particular rabbi's opinion in the Mishnah contradict what he said elsewhere in the Mishnah? What is the justification for this legal opinion? Rabbinic study circles attempted to address these, among many other, "problems" in the Mishnah.

Palestinian amoraim were joined by their Babylonian counterparts. We know surprisingly little about the Jews of Babylonia from the sixth century BCE until the third century CE. Clearly, there was a continuous Jewish community there, but little if any of their own literature survives. The tannaim were entirely Palestinian. During the amoraic period, though, there was an explosion of Babylonian rabbinic activity.[13] These rabbis lived in a very different political and cultural environment from their Palestinian brethren. Under Persian rule they knew Zoroastrianism rather than Christianity. Perhaps the absence of Christianity helps to explain their relative disregard of midrash; Babylonian Rabbis did not produce a single midrashic collection. In any case, Babylonian amoraim did actively produce Talmud, and they did so with a markedly different flavor than their Palestinian counterparts. They too studied and discussed the Mishnah in small disciple circles, but interpreted it within the context of their own culture.

In the fifth century CE the Palestinians bring together these amoraic discussions into a single text. The Palestinian Talmud (sometimes called the Jerusalem Talmud or Yerushalmi) hints at a new style that would flower about a century later with the redaction of the Babylonian Talmud (Bavli). This style is argumentative.

Rather than just providing an answer to the complex problems of the Mishnah, the Rabbis constructed complex arguments and counterarguments. The Palestinian Talmud puts into conversation amoraic traditions that were produced in different times and places in isolation from each other. Each section opens with a small section of the Mishnah (in order) and then proceeds to debate its meaning or to move out tangentially from there. Despite its basic argumentative structure, the actual text of the Palestinian Talmud is rather spartan and its logic of moving from one amoraic tradition to the next is not always obvious.

Scholars do not know why the Rabbis redacted the Jerusalem Talmud in the late fourth century, thus freezing the process of Oral Torah in the same way that the redaction of the Mishnah did. One theory conjectures that under the pressure of Christianity the Rabbis were afraid their teachings would be lost. Contrarily, one might suggest that the production of the Talmud was an act of confidence and assertion in an economically booming Jewish Galilee. Whatever the reason, the Palestinian Talmud was not the last word.

Babylonian amoraim continued their discussions about the Mishnah, and with each other, for another century. Around 500 CE the Babylonian Talmud underwent a process of redaction that left it more or less in the form that survives to this day.[14] Although following the same arrangement as the Palestinian Talmud, the Babylonian Talmud is far larger and more intricate. The reason for the Babylonian Talmud's redaction is also not fully understood, but at least in part must be related to the growing institutionalization of the rabbinic movement in Babylonia. As the Rabbis themselves consolidated, perhaps they felt a need to consolidate their past teachings. In fact, the Babylonian rabbinic academies developed such institutional prestige that they would eventually so heavy-handedly assert the superiority of the Babylonian over the Palestinian Talmud that, for all practical purposes, the latter was dropped from the rabbinic curriculum. Later rabbis adopted the principle that when the two Talmuds diverged the Babylonian Talmud's opinion or version was always preferable. The "victory" of the Babylonian over the Jerusalem Talmud was to some extent due to politics, but even so it would never have succeeded unless the text was itself rich and complex enough to sustain interest.

There is nothing quite like the Babylonian Talmud. It is written in both Hebrew and Aramaic, often shuttling between the two Semitic dialects. It is a book of law that often refuses to make a decision about the law; an interpretation that frequently succeeds only in complicating the Mishnah; a set of rigorous arguments punctuated with light stories, jokes, and bizarre tangents; and an insular system in which to understand any single part one must be familiar with the whole. It is a quintessentially dialogical text, at once in conversation within itself and encouraging dialogue with its readers and among them. It is very much a product of its age and place, exhibiting many similarities and parallels to Persian and Zoroastrian cultures and traditions, but as a literary work it is unique.

This dialogical nature of the text accounts for the typography of the modern page of Talmud. The earliest Talmudic manuscripts date from the Middle Ages and contain no commentary. Throughout this time, however, Jews produced a large number of commentaries on the Babylonian Talmud. Beginning as commentaries on the text of the Talmud alone, they quickly expanded to commenting on other commentators as well. The Babylonian Talmud, itself largely a commentary, became the foundation of an ongoing dialogue that we might call the rabbinic, or even Jewish, tradition. Traditionally, studying the Talmud with the commentators was a multimanuscript affair.

TABLE 4.1 Orders and Tractates of the Mishnah and Talmuds

ZERA'IM (SEEDS)	MO'ED (FESTIVALS)	NASHIM (WOMEN)	NEZIKIN (DAMAGES)	KODASHIM (HOLY THINGS)	TOHOROT (PURIFICATIONS)
Berakot* + (Blessings)	Shabbat * + (Sabbath)	Yebamot*+ (levirate marriages)	Baba Kamma*+ (First Gate; damages)	Zebahim*+ (Animal Offerings)	Niddah*+ (Menstruant)
Pe'ah+ (Corners of the field)	Erubin*+ (Combinations; Sabbath boundaries)	Ketubot*+ (Marriage Settlements)	Baba Mezi'a*+ (Middle Gate; found property)	Menahot* (Meal Offerings)	Kelim (Vessels)
Demai+ (Doubtfully tithed produce)	Pesahim*+ (Passover)	Nedarim*+ (Vows)	Baba Batra*+ (Last Gate; real estate, inheritance)	Hullin* (Profane things)	Oholot (Tents)
Kil'ayim+ (Agricultural Mixtures)	Shekalim+ (Shekels)	Nazir*+ (Nazirite)	Sanhedrin*+ (Court)	Bekorot* (Firstlings)	Nega'im (Leprosy)
Shebi'it+ (Sabbatical Year)	Yoma*+ (Yom Kippur)	Sotah*+ (Suspected adultress)	Abodah Zarah*+ (Strange Worship)	Arakin* (Evaluations)	Parah (Heifer)
Terumot+ (Heave Offerings)	Sukkah*+ (Booth; Tabernacles)	Gittin*+ (Bills of divorce)	Horayot*+ (Rulings)	Temurah* (Substitutions)	Tohorot (Purity)
Ma'aserot+ (Tithes)	Bezah*+ (Egg; laws of festivals)	Kiddushin*+ (Betrothal)	Shebuot*+ (Oaths)	Keritot* (Excisions)	Mikvaot (Pools of Immersion)
Hallah+ (Dough)	Rosh Hashanah*+ (New Year)		Makkot*+ (Floggings)	Me'ilah* (Trespass)	Makshirim (Preparations; liquids that cause impurity)
Orlah+ (Uncircumcision of trees)	Ta'anit*+ (Fast)		Eduyot (Testimony)	Tamid* (Continual offering)	Zabim (Genital flux)
Bikkurim+ (First Fruits)	Megillah*+ (Scroll; Purim)		Abot (Ethics of Fathers)	Middot (Dimensions)	Tebul Yom (Immersed during the day)
	Mo'ed Katan*+ (Minor festival)			Kinnim (Bird Nests)	Yadayim (Hands)
	Hagigah*+ (Festival Offering)				Ukzin (Stalks)

An asterisk (*) beside the name means that the Babylonian Talmud contains commentary on it; a plus (+) signifies that the Palestinian Talmud contains commentary on it.

The printing of the Talmud changed that. An Italian printer, Joshua Soncino, began publishing assorted tractates of the Babylonian Talmud in the 1480s. Modeling the Talmudic page after those of Latin Christian biblical commentaries, Soncino placed the main text of the Talmud in the middle of the page and surrounded it with commentaries. When Daniel Bomberg printed the first full edition around 1520, he standardized the commentaries to appear on each page of Talmud. Bomberg's format has remained remarkably stable; the Vilna edition of the Babylonian Talmud, printed by the Romm family in the 1880s, maintained Bomberg's format, squeezing some more recent commentaries into the margins.

The retention of this format into the present day markedly contrasts with its abandonment by Christians. Whereas Christian commentaries were printed in a more "univocal" style, the typography of the Babylonian Talmud captures multivocality. It is as if the conversations of the ancient Rabbis spilled outside their margins into and across future generations.

While encouraging an intergenerational conversation, the typography of a page of the Babylonian Talmud also respects the integrity of its component parts. Only in the heat of conversation can the comments of the famed medieval commentator Rashi be read directly into the ancient dialogues; Rashi's commentary is clearly marked in a dedicated space on the page and in a different typescript. The insistence on preserving the integrity of each individual text is part of the process that we have already seen in midrash. As later texts cite and build upon the authority of earlier ones, they engage in a process of "back-canonization." Commentaries thus accrete over a text in a way that solidifies the authority of the lower levels—to question the authority of these earlier texts risks knocking over the entire edifice. Just as the commentaries to the Talmud help to cement the authority of the Talmud, so too the commentaries on the commentaries enhance the authority of these earlier commentators. Most vulnerable are those with whom the conversation ceases.

Bomberg's edition of the Babylonian Talmud also standardized its pagination. The use of a standard pagination—in which each page (or folio) has an "a" and "b" side—points to the Babylonian Talmud's social setting. In one sense by the sixteenth century the Babylonian Talmud had become a reference book. Many authors, whether commentators, poets, jurists, or philosophers, had turned to it for authority. Yet these authors could only reference the Talmud according to vague indicators that were of little help to the noninitiate (for example, "in the section that begins with the following words"). A standard pagination allowed future editors of these later texts to indicate these references more precisely.

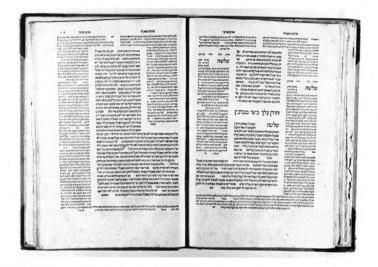

4.1 Folio from an early printed edition of the Babylonian Talmud. The text of the Talmud runs down the center of the page with commentary in the margins around it.
Courtesy of the Library of the Jewish Theological Seminary of America

But the Babylonian Talmud was, and is, not just a reference book. Jews have always seen the text as embedded in its own performance. Prior to its wider dissemination allowed by standardized printing and increasing literacy, scholars would study the Babylonian Talmud within an institutionalized framework. Within the context of the academy, or yeshiva, the Talmud was not meant to serve as the private and silent reading of an individual scholar. Its study was a communal activity. Whether read, explained, and discussed in pairs or in larger groups with a teacher, the social context of the Babylonian Talmud's reading reinforced its argumentative nature. Many Jews today, even those not formally part of a yeshiva, continue this traditional way of studying the Babylonian Talmud. They may study informally in pairs or in synagogue groups led by a rabbi, whether in the original Hebrew and Aramaic or in translation.

Thus the text of the Babylonian Talmud together with its traditional typography, commentaries, and mode of study all drive to emphasize process over product. As the many later texts that draw upon specific traditions in the Talmud make clear, product is not unimportant. To enter into the study of the Talmud for its own sake is seen as entering into the exciting and dynamic unfolding of God's continuing revelation. It is also to internalize a distinctively rabbinic way of thinking. Rabbinic thinking, like all epistemologies, organizes knowledge into a set of discrete categories. Thinking like the Rabbis means thinking in their categories while remaining sensitive to the tensions that these categories create within and between each other.

The Babylonian Talmud relentlessly juxtaposes its categories and principles. One extended passage, for example, dwells on the legal problem of honoring one's parents. The Torah clearly states that it is imperative to honor one's parents, but it does not state how. Does "honor" mean "do not shame," "support financially," or "obey"? If a parent shames you in public, what is the proper response? What about the case when an elderly parent demands financial assistance but you have only enough money to educate your children, another rabbinic imperative? If your father and mother give you conflicting instructions, to which should you listen? Does honoring your parents extend to cases where they tell you to dishonor your teacher or God? What are the ramifications of all these answers on related applications of the same principles?

This has brought us far from the religion of any Jewish community from the Second Temple period. In one sense the Rabbis are very much a product of their historical contexts—Palestinian and Babylonian rabbis, living in very different cultural milieus, often diverge at precisely the points where their surrounding cultures do. They trace their own history back into the Second Temple and even biblical period, and, as we have seen, the claim might be exaggerated but it is not a pure fiction; there are historical continuities. At the same time, they radically transformed these continuities. They started with the Torah but ended with Mishnah, midrash, and Talmud, which would constitute the foundation of rabbinic Judaism. The redaction of the Babylonian Talmud marks as sharp a break with the Judaism that preceded it as did the Torah for the religion of Israel. From the end of late antiquity to the present, Jewish communities have marked themselves by their participation in the "conversation" that begins with the Babylonian Talmud. It is to the shape of this conversation that we now turn.

5

RABBINIC CONCEPTS

T HEOLOGY, FOR MOST of us, can mean two different things. More formally it refers to a systematic and relatively rigorous explanation of the divine and the world. Like some types of philosophy, it begins with certain premises and logically builds upon them a coherent system of thought. In this sense the goal of theology is to tame and systematize potentially contradictory beliefs about the divine. It would be the job of theology, for example, to reconcile a belief in only one God, who is good, with the enduring presence of evil in the world.

A second, more colloquial use of the term *theology* denotes simply the foundational beliefs or dogma of a religion with little regard to their systematization or coherence. As heirs of the Western Christian tradition, we tend to privilege these religious beliefs as essential to true religiosity. A person's theology thus means one's personal beliefs, which are then seen as constituting the core of religious expression. When institutionalized, these beliefs often become a dogma, a set of assertions that one *must* believe to be considered "orthodox" ("right-thinking") by that religious tradition.

By either of these definitions, the Rabbis were poor theologians. For all their rigor and attention to detail, the Talmuds almost never systematically work out what we would call theological positions; their analyses focus on matters of law and their justifications. When the Rabbis do discuss theological matters, they usually do so in midrash and in an ad hoc manner. Given the rabbinic emphasis on multivocality, it should also come as no surprise that the Rabbis make little effort to enforce particular beliefs. While some Rabbis do draw a few lines in the sand when it comes to belief, these are relatively marginal to the entire thrust of rabbinic Judaism.

But the rabbinic inattention to *theology*, as we understand the term, does not mean that the Rabbis were uninterested in theological matters. In fact, the Rabbis were intrigued by the same questions that theologians have been struggling with for millennia. What is the nature of God? Why did God create the world and everything in it, including evil, this particular way? What does it mean to be human, created in God's image? Why did God make a covenant with Abraham and his descendents, and what is the meaning of that covenant, and the one on Sinai? What will happen at the end of time?

Rather than addressing these issues in any systematic or even explicit way, the Rabbis consider them organically, growing out of other discussions or biblical verses. Their theological reflections are sharp flashes or illuminations that pass as surprisingly as they appear. When seen together, these flashes do not quite add up to a coherent theology, but they do create a kind of theological collage in which different answers blend into others in a variety of different directions. Or, to use a different metaphor, they define a map in which the topography varies greatly depending on the perspective.

One distinctive characteristic of rabbinic theology is its ability to maintain creative tensions. As with their legal discussions, the Rabbis like to toy with the boundaries. Instead of deciding, for example, whether they prefer to see God as distant and uninvolved in human affairs (transcendent) or as nurturing and deeply involved, they opt for both. This is why the answer to the question "What do the Rabbis think about x?" can routinely produce frustration; the answer often includes its opposite—and most every shade in between. Yet despite the elasticity of rabbinic concepts, there are clear limits. Some answers, or even questions, never make it onto the map. The Rabbis might wonder about questions of divine plurality and the nature of divine beings other than God, but never would they find acceptable an answer that posits the existence of a second god.

This creative tension extends to the Rabbis' relationship to biblical theology. The Rabbis continually seek to link their concepts and beliefs to the Hebrew Bible. In many cases this is not a stretch; the contours of rabbinic thinking, on a very basic level, follow the options found in the Hebrew Bible. Other times, though, the Rabbis creatively rework or even subvert biblical ideas while claiming to remain true to the text.

This chapter, then, is an attempt to sketch out the terrain of the major rabbinic concepts and to show the range of theological options they provide. The assortment of topics that occupy the Rabbis more or less follows the contours of the Tanak: God, covenant, Torah, sin, repentance, theodicy, Israel, and redemption. The Rabbis do not have a single straightforward position for any of these topics, and my goal is to highlight the creative tensions that they form and the relationships between theological concepts rather than to insist on any single "dominant" understanding. The very fact of theological multivocality is critically important. By creating a range of theological options rather than dogmatically insisting on one, rabbinic literature provides a collection of theological possibilities upon which later Jews will draw. One Jewish community might find an immanent God more to its liking than another, but both communities can find authority for their positions in this diverse literature.

Is God near or far? Is the "real" God the transcendent one of the first creation account or the immanent, caring, and excitable one of the second? The Torah's juxtaposition of the two radically different ideas of God in the first chapters of Genesis was to some extent a historical accident, the work of a redactor unable to exclude either of these two sacred stories. For the Rabbis, though, these seemingly different ideas represent two different aspects of the one God. Even God's two names (the J and E names), in this reading, indicate the poles of God's nature.

From Genesis 1 the Rabbis drew the idea of God's utter transcendence. Whereas the Second Temple authors of the apocalyptic works reconciled the idea of majestic and transcendent God with a permeable heaven into which human beings could pass for quick guided tours, the Rabbis draw a sharper separation between God and creation. This is a God so awesome that humans cannot abide anywhere near God's presence. In one midrash God (accidentally?) kills all the Israelites at Mount Sinai when uttering the first letter of the Ten Commandments—the silent *aleph*! (In His mercy, He then resurrects them.) Noting the consistent use of God's name as *elohim* throughout Genesis 1, the Rabbis identify it with God's attribute of justice. The transcendent God is also the ultimate infallible judge, unswayed by "mitigating circumstances," who metes out precise penalties and rewards to human beings.

Yet whereas Genesis 1 portrays God as majestically aloof and alone, the rabbinic reading of this account tends to soften God's transcendence. One very clever midrash that echoes throughout other rabbinic traditions plays off the first Hebrew word of the Torah, *b'reshit*, normally translated "*In the beginning*, God created the heavens and the earth." The term *reshit*, they note, occurs also at Proverbs 8:22, in which Wisdom says, "The Lord made me the beginning (*reshit*) of his work, the first of his acts of old." Reading the Hebrew preposition *b'* as "with" rather than "in" (a justified construal of this prefix), they transform the first sentence of the Torah to read: "With the Torah, *elohim* created the heavens and the earth." The repercussions of this reading are profound, for they now suggest that the Torah is the primordial blueprint for creation. God now has a partner (albeit one of a very different nature). God's word, the agent of creation throughout Genesis 1, is no longer a fleeting sound but the Torah itself. The word, which occupies the space between the unapproachable God and creation, becomes accessible. By way of comparison, the Gospel of John has a different reading of Genesis 1: "In the beginning the Word already was. . . . He was with God at the beginning, and through him all things came to be" (John 1:1–3). John interprets God's word (the logos) as His incarnation; Jesus, not Torah, is the accessible intermediary between God and His creation.

Actually, the rabbinic reading of Genesis 1 populates the heavens. Genesis 1:26, "Let us make man," troubles the Rabbis: To whom is God speaking? Immediately ruling out the possibility of another god (and, on the principle of the divine nature of the language of the Torah, rejecting the "us" as a figure of speech), the Rabbis suggest that He was speaking to the angels. From this interpretation they weave a complicated argument between God and the angels, who are portrayed as opposing the creation of humankind. There may be only one God, and this God might be inaccessible to humans, but He is neither alone in the heavens nor even firmly in control of the heavenly host.

If the Rabbis mute the transcendence of the God of Genesis 1, they also transform the immanence of the God of Genesis 2. The God of Genesis 2 gets His hands dirty: He creates not by word but by molding and surgery, "walks" in the garden, does not seem omniscient, and gets unexpectedly angry when things do not go His way. Partly in continuation with traditions that date back to the Second Temple period, and partly, perhaps, in response to Christian ideas of incarnation, the Rabbis are careful never to go as far as Genesis 2 in their portrayal of God. God never comes to earth. But God, for the Rabbis, really is immanent. If the God of Genesis 1 represents the aspect of God's justice, the God indicated by His four-letter name, YHWH, indicates His mercy. This is the God who tempers justice with mercy so that He does not, as He should by all right, destroy fragile and fallible humanity. This is the God who weeps at Israel's exile (which He caused), comforts the mourners and escorts the bride to the wedding canopy, and listens to the communal and personal supplications of His people.

It is in the rabbinic treatment of mysticism that this tension emerges most clearly. Rabbinic literature cryptically alludes to those who explicate the "work of creation" and the "work of the chariot." They are uneasy about both groups. The former, apparently, referred to those who used the texts at the very beginning of Genesis as a basis for cosmological (and probably eschatological) speculation. They may have sought an experience of the divine through some kind of understanding of the mysteries of creation. The second group, more clearly, used the first chapter of Ezekiel as their base text for mystical speculation. They may have sought to "gaze" upon God, to ascend to heaven in the fashion of the earlier Jewish apocalyptic authors.

We still know relatively little about these groups, although what we do know raises three issues that would continue through later Jewish mysticism. First, they are based in a traditional text. Just as the Psalmist sought to domesticate the mystical experience by confining it to the Temple, the Rabbis understand the divine revelation as transmitted through tradition to be the basis of mystical speculation. They too had no concept of individual spirituality cut loose from tradition. Second, mysticism is esoteric. This is not stuff for the masses; it is both difficult and dangerous to master. The Rabbis forbid the explication of both the "works of creation" and the "works of the chariot" in public. Finally, the goal, as in most classical understandings of mysticism, never appears to be unification with the divine. Those who seek to master the cosmological mysteries did so for reasons that remain obscure, although it is unlikely they thought that by doing so they would become one with God. Those who contemplated the "works of the chariot" sought a vision of God; they too appear to have preserved the line between human and divine.

One of the few rabbinic texts that refer to mystical experience is illustrative:

Four entered into Pardes, Ben Azzai, Ben Zoma, "Other," and Rabbi Akiva. One gazed and died, one gazed and was wounded, one gazed and cut the shoots, and one ascended in peace and descended in peace. Ben Azzai gazed and died—about him Scripture says, "The death of His faithful ones is grievous in the Lord's sight" [Psalms 116:15]. Ben Zoma gazed and was wounded—about him Scripture says, "If you find honey, eat only what you need, lest, surfeiting yourself, you throw it up" [Proverbs 25:16]. Elisha [= "Other"] gazed and cut the shoots—about him Scripture says, "Don't let your mouth bring you into disfavor, and don't plead before the messenger that it was an error . . . " [Ecclesiastes 5:5]. Rabbi Akiva ascended in peace and descended in peace—about him Scripture says, "Draw me after you, let us run! The king has brought me to his chambers. Let us delight and rejoice in your love, savoring it more than wine . . . " [Song of Songs 1:4].

(*Tosefta Hagiga* 2:3–4)

If you do not fully understand this passage you would hardly be alone. The Talmuds both struggle with it, as do scores of later interpreters. Is Pardes heaven or the divine abode or an earthly paradise ("paradise" derives from the Persian word *pardes*, which literally refers to a royal garden or orchard)? Did Rabbi Akiva and the others actually "ascend," and upon what or whom did the others gaze? What does "cut the shoots" mean, and how does the Scriptural verse relate to it? Why did Rabbi Akiva survive the encounter unscathed? This passage is esoteric to its core.

As understood by its earliest rabbinic interpreters, it refers to a mystical ascent, perhaps triggered by explication of the "works of the chariot." The object of the gaze is the divine presence, portrayed as so awesome that it destroyed three out of four of these great rabbinic figures. Sight of the divine might be fraught with danger, but, this passage asserts, it is nevertheless possible. The text leaves the door to heaven open, even if heavily guarded.

Jews produced another kind of mystical literature alongside these early descriptions of the divine. This literature, best represented by *Sefer HaRazim* (The Book of Mysteries), combines visions of God with prescriptions for winning divine favor. That is, *Sefer HaRazim* is a book of magic, and it joins other Hebrew and Aramaic "magical" texts from late antiquity, which include amulets, curse tablets, and bowls inscribed with love spells.

The use of the term *magic* calls for another definitional pause. Magic is hardly an objective or a value-neutral term. Traditionally, it has been and continues to be used as a term of opprobrium; it denotes "bad" religious practices. "We" have religion; "they" have magic. "Magical" practices are generally seen as those that encroach upon divine power. The idea, for example, that a magical spell, if done correctly, will mechanistically compel divine power to do something, constrains the divine will: God no longer has the absolute power of choice. In practice, however, this somewhat logical division between acts of prayer and supplication that preserve divine power and acts that have a mechanistic effect on the cosmos quickly blurs. The Torah condemns some, but not all, practices that we might label as *magical* (the others, later commentators were quick to assert, are *miraculous*). The Rabbis find some amulets deplorable ("idolatrous" practices) but others kosher. When a woman attempts to compel angels, who are often seen as not having any free will to begin with, to make her husband love her, is this magic?

Once the barrier between heaven and earth is punctured, the lines between what might be called purely "mystical" and purely "magical" disintegrate. To gaze upon the divine or to receive instruction from the mouth of divine beings is to learn the mysteries of the cosmos. And to learn is also to gain the ability to control. As early as the third century BCE, the author of 1 Enoch recognized the connection between angelic revelation and magic, asserting that human knowledge of magic in fact came from the angels. For the author of *Sefer HaRazim* there is no contradiction, indeed no significant difference, between visions of the divine and spells to harness and use divine power.

The issue of divine immanence is linked with the problem of how God can or should be represented. The Rabbis follow the biblical idea that God cannot be visually represented—a prohibition that Jews in Palestine actually observed during the Second Temple period. On the other hand, they have no problem with *verbal* anthropomorphic descriptions. God may not actually "walk" on earth, but God can be described as walking. One striking passage that illustrates this theme is found in the Babylonian Talmud (Berakhot 6a):

> From where do we learn that the Holy One, blessed be He, puts on *tefillin*? As it is written, "The Lord has sworn by His right hand, by His mighty arm," [Isaiah 62:8]. "His right hand"—this is Torah, as it is written, " . . . Lightening flashing at them from His right" [Deut. 33:2].
>
> "by His mighty arm"—this is *tefillin*, as it is written, "God is strength to his people" [Psalms 28:8]. How do we know that *tefillin* is "strength"? As it is written, "All the peoples of the earth will see that the Lord's name is proclaimed over you, and they shall stand in fear of you" [Deut. 28:10].

Whatever the original intent of the biblical verses, this rabbinic reading of them tames God's awesomeness. The phylacteries contain portions of the Torah, and suddenly God is transformed from the fearful lightening hurler into something much more accessible, a man wearing two leather boxes. Incidentally, here is another excellent example of rabbinic midrash, which juxtaposes biblical verses to create an entirely different understanding of Isaiah 62:8.

The Talmud continues (Berakhot 7a):

Rabbi Yohanan said in the name of Rabbi Yosi: How do we know that that Holy One, blessed be He, prays? As it is written, "I will bring them to My sacred mount and let them rejoice in my house of prayer [literally, the "house of my prayer"]" (Isaiah 56:7). "Their prayer" is not written, but "*My* prayer"!

What does He pray? Rav Zutra bar Tuviah said in the name of Rav: "May it be My will that my compassion will conquer my anger and my compassion prevail over My attribute [of justice], and may I conduct Myself with My children with My attribute of compassion and may I stop short before the strict measure of justice.

This extraordinary passage describes God's prayer to Himself. The Rabbis portray God as wishing (!) that His compassion will outweigh his sense of absolute justice. Hardly the perfect, unified God of the later Deists, this God battles himself in order to suppress His desire for justice.

Following convention, I have described God with male pronouns. To the extent that the Rabbis ascribe a gender to their anthropomorphic descriptions of the divine, it is in fact male. The Rabbis have a rich metaphoric vocabulary for describing God. Some of these terms and concepts are gender neutral, such as the Place, Name, Rock, and Merciful One. Many, though, are male: God is a king, judge, warrior, shepherd, father, and, perhaps most commonly, "The Holy One, blessed be He." Even more than the authors of the Hebrew Bible, the Rabbis avoid using feminine imagery for God. The only feminine descriptor of God that they use with any frequency is the *Shechinah*, or Presence, and even then they avoid giving the Shechinah any attributes that they mark as feminine.

Had the Rabbis been rigorous theological thinkers (in our sense), they would have then asked the next natural question: what does it mean to call God a "king" or to use masculine images to describe Him? In what precise sense do these terms "describe" God? They never do explicitly ask or answer these questions. It is likely that some Rabbis really did understand God as possessing some kind of body, albeit one that humans could not approach or necessarily comprehend. Others might have had a more abstract understanding.

The richness and variety of rabbinic descriptions of God might best be understood, however, within the wider context of the Greek, Roman, and Zoroastrian worlds. Most practitioners of Greco-Roman religions did not see the material representations of the gods ("idols," as they were polemically called) as the actual god; they understood them as symbolic of one aspect of the divine. A single god might have several names, pictorial depictions and myths, but all pointed to different aspects of the same divine reality. When the Rabbis use anthropomorphic language to describe their one God, then, they are participating in the wider cultural practice of representing different aspects of the same divinity. They are violently opposed to representing God in painting or sculpture, but they nevertheless do believe it possible to represent God verbally and anthropomorphically. In addition to serving as symbols of God's attributes, these representations foster a sense of divine immanence in their listeners.

The tension between these depictions of God as immanent and transcendent, especially as embodied in descriptions of His attributes of "compassion" and "justice," spill over into rabbinic discussions of theodicy. Theodicy is a problem of particular importance for monotheistic religions, as they must reconcile the idea of a single and good God with the presence of evil and (seemingly) random unfairness in the world. To the Rabbis, God's role as supreme judge is not negotiable. As one midrash says, "Rabbi Akiba said: Concerning whom is it written, 'Why should the wicked man scorn God, thinking You do not call to account?' This is one who says that there is no judgment and that there is no judge. But there is judgment, and there is a judge" (*Genesis Rabba* 26:4, on Genesis 6:3). Despite all appearances to the contrary, the world is a just place.

In reconciling the apparent injustice of the world with their theological conviction that God is just, the Rabbis rely primarily on the biblical answers. Good people prosper and bad people do not. Alternatively, they suggest that humans are incapable of understanding the way that God administers justice. One aggadic story tells of Moses being brought back to earth to watch the gruesome execution of Rabbi Akiba. "Master of the universe," Moses exclaims, "This is Torah and this is its reward?" "Silence," God replies, "thus I have decided" (Babylonian Talmud, Menahot, 29a). Even Moses, the man of God, cannot understand God's ways.

But the Rabbis are not fully satisfied with these traditional answers. The Rabbis had the luxury (which most of the biblical authors did not) of being able to use the concept of an afterlife in their discussions of theodicy. By deferring the punishments or rewards to the "next world," the Rabbis preserve the idea of a just cosmos. In fact, they go further: God actually punishes the righteous. Sometimes called "punishments of love," these afflictions of the righteous were seen as cleansing:

Rabbi Eleazar said in the name of R. Zadok: Why are the righteous compared to a tree? Because it stands in a pure place and its branches extend into an impure place—if one cuts its branches, it stands entirely in a pure place. Thus does the Holy One, blessed be He, bring sufferings on the righteous in this world so that they might inherit the world-to-come, as it is written, "Though your beginning be small, in the end you will grow very great" [Job 8:7].

And why are the wicked similar in this world to a tree? Because the whole thing stands in an impure place, and its branches extend into a pure place. Thus the Holy One, blessed be He, brings good to the wicked in this world in order to torment them in the world-to-come and in order to cause them to inherit the lowest level, as it is written, "A road may seem right to a man, but in the end it is a road to death" [Proverbs 14:12].

(Babylonian Talmud, Kiddushin 40b)

This explanation curiously portrays God as both compassionate and strict. By meting out the punishment of the righteous here on earth, God allows them to prosper in the next world. Suffering should thus be embraced as a divine opportunity for purification; the Rabbis themselves seem somewhat uncomfortable with this solution. On the other hand, in this passage God is careful not to punish the wicked in this world in order to cause them even greater suffering in the next. One might question how just this really is, but it allowed the Rabbis to explain the world's apparent injustice.

Another explanation for misfortune is the existence of demons. This explanation shares a similar cosmology to that of 1 Enoch: the world is full of evil and mischievous forces that malevolently play with human beings. As in 1 Enoch, this explanation distances God from evil, but at the cost of compromising the idea of an absolute monotheism; there may not be another god, but there are these other divine spirits with independent wills. With this explanation Torah becomes a magical shield against the forces of evil. Thus, for the Rabbis who accept this cosmology, the study of Torah is the first line of defense against the evil forces, not because it will bring divine favor on the scholar or instruct him (and her?) in the correct path, but because it will magically ward them off. Babylonian rabbis appear more taken with this explanation than their Palestinian counterparts. This is almost certainly attributable to their cultural environments; Zoroastrian cosmology has a much stronger notion of the active presence of supernatural malevolent forces than does Greek or Roman cosmology.

Obviously related to the theological problem of individual theodicy is that of free will. For God to be able to punish human beings justly, humans must have free will. It would not be just to punish those who are not responsible for their actions. But can humans really have free will if God is omniscient? If God knows what each person is going to do, does that person really have free will? The Rabbis would compromise neither their belief in God's omniscience nor their conviction that humans had absolute free will. Their position is unhelpfully summarized by Rabbi Akiba, "All is foreseen but permission is given" (*Mishnah Avot* 3:15). They were content to leave this as a paradox.

About the nature of human free will, however, they had much more to say. The Rabbis complicate the monistic anthropology of the Hebrew Bible. According to the Hebrew Bible, the human being is a single whole; there is no division between body and soul. Many Rabbis continued to subscribe to this monistic idea. You are you, not a "real" you (the soul) trapped in a transient container (the body). But this monistic entity nevertheless is divided. God instilled in humankind two desires or inclinations, one good and the other "bad." The good desire motivates individuals to study Torah, do God's will, and do meritorious deeds; the bad desire drives people to covet, steal, commit sexual transgressions, and worship idols.

This understanding of the split human self allows the Rabbis to solve several thorny problems. It is a dynamic model of the process of free will. The self becomes a battleground in which the individual is charged with helping the good desire defeat the bad. Because we have the capacity to defeat the bad desire, we are ultimately fully responsible for our behavior. There is no notion here of "original sin." Humans are born morally neutral, and when they reach an age at which they are capable of exercising control over their behavior they become legally culpable for their sins. At the same time, this model helps to explain why we have "bad" desires; it is an inherent part of being human. And why would God create the "evil inclination"? "Were it not for the evil inclination, a man would not build a house, take a wife, or beget children" (*Genesis Rabba* 9:7).

Being merciful, though, God did not simply leave humans to wrestle with their evil inclination. He gave Torah. A midrashic parable captures the relationship between the inclination and Torah:

> "Therefore impress these My words upon your very heart: bind them as a sign on your hand and let them serve as a symbol on your forehead . . . " (Deuteronomy 11:8). It is said that the words of Torah are compared to a

life-saving remedy. A parable: A king becomes angry at his son and strikes him, giving him a bad wound. He then puts a bandage on the wound, and says to him, "My son, as long as you keep this bandage on, you can eat what you want, drink what you want, draw a bath any way you want it, and you will not be hurt. But if you take it off, immediately a sore will arise." Thus did the Holy One, blessed by He, say to Israel: "My children, I created in you an evil desire . . . as long as you engage in the study of Torah, it will not rule over you. But if you cease studying Torah, it will surely rule over you."

Just as Torah can be seen as a magical shield against malevolent forces, so too it is imagined as a fortification against the evil inclination. Like many such parables, this one raises uncomfortable questions about God's justice: Why, precisely, did the king strike his son? At the same time, it understands Torah as the cure for the wound of the human condition.

While the Rabbis see Torah as conferring benefits to the individual, its real importance is on the communal level. At its most essential level, the Torah is one of several covenants that God made with Israel and the world. For the most part, the Rabbis adopt the covenantal theology of the Hebrew Bible. God, they believe, made a succession of contracts with the people Israel. These contracts both demand things from them as well as offering rewards. The contractual nature of the relationship between God and Israel is a fundamental biblical and rabbinic concept.

Fundamental, however, does not mean unproblematic. The Rabbis are particularly bothered by the possibility of an "opt out" in the contract. That is, did God make a covenant that conditions the fulfillment of God's promises on Israel's performance of its stipulations, or will God fulfill His promises regardless of Israel's behavior? The question is explosive, particularly after the claims of the early Christians that Israel has lost its covenant as the result of its actions (either the incident of the golden calf or the rejection of Jesus as messiah). It is not at all clear, for example, whether the circumcision that God demands of Abraham and His descendents is a mere sign of God's promise to multiply them and settle them in the Land of Israel or a condition for it.

The Rabbis unambiguously (and unsurprisingly) reject the possibility that the covenant was conditional. God's promise is firm and eternal, no matter how Israel behaves. This might be why they like metaphors such as king or father to describe God. A king cannot abandon his people to find a new people to rule, and a father's link to his children is durable. Other metaphors, such as husband, are more theologically problematic and thus the Rabbis do not use them nearly as often: Husbands can divorce wives unilaterally.

The Rabbis are fully aware of the theological problem that follows from their belief in an unconditional covenant. With an unconditional covenant, God's response to Israel's misbehavior is not annulment of His promises but punishment. By accepting the covenant Israel obligated itself, both "now" and in the future, to fulfill God's will or face His wrath—neither side has an opt out. But could Israel's original acceptance of the Torah have been truly voluntary? When God made the offer of Torah to Israel, did Israel really have a choice? Does not the creator make the ultimate offer that you cannot refuse? This, then, brings us back up against the problem of free will. If Israel was compelled to enter the covenant on Mount Sinai, a just God would be unable to punish them for their lack of adherence to it, just as in our own legal system a contract entered into under duress is void.

On the one hand, the Rabbis want to emphasize that Israel entered into the covenant voluntarily:

Therefore, the nations of the world were offered the Torah so that they would not have an opportunity to say before the Shechinah, "Had we been offered the Torah, we would have accepted it." Behold, they were offered it and they did not accept it, as it is written, "The Lord came from Sinai; He shone upon them from Seir; He appeared from Mount Para, and approached from Ribeboth-kodesh, lightning flashing at them from His right" [Deuteronomy 33:2].

It was revealed to the children of Esau. He said to them, "Do you accept the Torah?" They said to Him, "What is written in it?" He said to them, "Do not murder." They said to him, "This is what our father bequeathed to us. . . ."

It was revealed to the children of Amon and Moab. He said to them, "Do you accept the Torah?" They said to Him, "What is written in it?" He said to them, "Do not commit adultery." They said to him, "But we are all from adultery. . . . How shall we accept it?"

It was revealed to the children of Ishmael. He said to them, "Do you accept the Torah?" They said to Him, "What is written in it?" He said to them, "Do not steal." They said to him, "But this is the blessing with which our father blessed us. . . . "

When [God] came to Israel—" . . . lightning flashing at them from His right"—everyone opened their mouths and said: "Everything that the Lord has said we will do and we will hear," and it says, "When He stands, he makes the earth shake; when He glances He makes the nations tremble" [Habakkuk 3:6].

Rabbi Shimon ben Eleazar said: If the children of Noah cannot even fulfill the seven commandments that they took upon themselves, all the more so the mitzvot of the Torah!

commandments,   (*Mekilta d'Rabbi Ishmael*, on Exodus 20:2)

The midrash neatly contrasts Israel's willing acceptance of the Torah—before even hearing its contents—to the behavior of the nations of the world. This passage does double duty, asserting the voluntary nature of Israel's acceptance of the covenant and justifying God's withholding of the rewards of the covenant from the other nations ("the children of Noah").

On the other hand, some Rabbis were not satisfied with this triumphalist explanation. They saw a more nuanced negotiation between God and Israel:

"And they stood at the foot of the mountain" [Exodus 19:17]. Rabbi Abdimi bar Hama bar Hasa said: It teaches that the Holy One blessed be He, overturned the mountain over them as a tank and said to them, "If you accept the Torah it is good, but if not, there will be your graves."

Said R. Aha bar Yaakov: This is a great indictment of the Torah!

Rabba said: Despite this, the generation accepted it in the days of King Ahasuerus. . . .

Reish Lakish said: "And there was evening and there was morning, *the sixth day*" (Genesis 1:31). Why is there is an extra [letter] *hey* ["the"]? It teaches that the Holy One blessed be He made a condition with the works of creation. He said to them: If Israel accepts the Torah you will remain, but if not, I will return you to primordial chaos.

(Babylonian Talmud, Shabbat 88a)

This passage reflects the rabbinic awareness of the precarious nature of their free will. Both their lives and creation itself depends on their acceptance of the Torah—hardly a free choice! Indeed, even the Rabbis recognize that this lack of freedom "indicts" the Torah; its prescribed punishments for violations of God commandments are unfair if Israel did not enter the covenant willingly. Hence Rabba is forced to posit another moment when the Jews did freely "confirm" the forced choice of their ancestors.

The covenant was seen as applying to, and binding, all of Israel in all future generations. Its force is on the communal rather than individual level. "Israel" is a corporate body to be punished or rewarded as a whole. This understanding of Israel goes back to the Hebrew Bible, but Jews living in the Hellenistic world appear to have read the biblical concept through their own lens. For Greeks the world was divided into two groups, "Greeks" and "barbarians." The barbarians, in turn, were subdivided into ethnicities (*ethnoi*), each of which had its own customs, gods, etc. The Jews adapted an inverted model of this schema. For the Rabbis the world was divided into "Jews" and others, usually designated as "worshippers of the stars," or idolaters. As with every other ethnic group, they created a semipermeable boundary. "Jewishness," like being Greek, was determined primarily through genealogy. As the notion of Jewishness as a kind of citizenship solidified, more formal ways of conferring this citizenship—conversion—were developed.[1]

This understanding of Jewishness involves basic inseparability of ethnic identity and religion; to be Jewish is an ethnic designation, but that ethnic group has a unique set of what we would call "religious" practices. By extracting religion from ethnic identity, Christianity changed the way that both were understood. To Christians, ethnic identity and religion became completely separable. Even by late antiquity the refusal of Jews to unlink religion from ethnicity began to look archaic.

The Rabbis, however, clung to an ethnic conception of Jewishness. For many of them, either a Jewish mother or a formal conversion was required to enter Israel. But, while it is assumed that Jewish practice and subscription to fundamental Jewish concepts are part of what it means to be Jewish, they are not determinative. Being a Jew does not mean believing or doing anything, only being part of an ethnic group (as we today consider Irish Americans, Chinese Americans, etc.). The modern result of this conception is that we can talk of a "Jew with no religion," as the recent National Jewish Population Survey does. "Christians with no religion" makes no sense.

Understanding Jewishness as ethnicity has ramifications on the other side as well. Just as one cannot leave Irishness, one cannot leave Jewishness. The Rabbis consider a Jew who worships idols or "converts" to Christianity to be a sinner but still a Jew. Thus a Jew who converted to Christianity might see herself as a Christian, while Jews continued to see her as a Jew.

Identity is a matter of perspective. Like the people Israel itself, each of its members is inescapably bound to the covenant.

In rabbinic hands "Israel" thus becomes a kind of porous ethnicity. This notion of Israel might itself reflect a rabbinic understanding of the Jewish condition as both embedded within as well as distinctive from their surrounding culture. Such a rabbinic understanding of Israel thus hangs suspended between both the biblical notion of Israel (tied to a much less porous notion of ethnicity) and the experiential notions of Israel espoused by Philo and, in a very different way, early Christians who thought that the real children of God's promise—the true Israel—are those who accept Jesus as Christ. This is a flexible notion of Israel that can create difference in the midst of sameness, used today to strengthen group identity by both secular humanist Jews (who emphasize ethnicity) and classical Reform Jews (who emphasize a religious community).

Although the formal partners of the covenant are God and Israel, as a corporate entity, the obligations of the covenant rest on the individuals who comprise the people Israel. The concept of Torah as containing the whole of God's revelation is one of the distinctive characteristics of rabbinic Judaism; the concept of mitzvot is the other. The Hebrew Bible, of course, is full of laws that are applicable to individuals. Jews during the Second Temple period read these laws as components of an ethnic constitution. The Rabbis, however, developed and placed them at the center of what it means to be a pious Jew.

Mitzvah (plural, *mitzvot*) literally means "commandment." The Rabbis saw the mitzvot literally as God's commandments, the way in which God wants the people Israel to live.[2] Indeed, the extraordinary care with which the Rabbis draw out and detail the mitzvot indicates the core question to which much of rabbinic Judaism is the answer: *What does God want from us?* Following the commandments for them is not just about living "correctly" or identifying with the people Israel or accruing individual or communal merit for the world-to-come, although it is also all of those things. Primarily it is about living according to the will of God, and thus living in God's presence.

When Paul set out to explain what had changed with the coming of Christ, he focused on the dichotomy of law and spirit. The law, he argued, served as a mere pedagogue that prepared humanity for the spirit. This dichotomy between law and spirit has had a remarkable staying power and even today is frequently taken for granted. Modern discussion of "spirituality," for example, has little place for the structure and institutions of "law."

The Rabbis would have found such a dichotomy incomprehensible. Far from shackling the spirit and individual, the mitzvot were seen as bringing one closer to the real freedom of living in God's presence. Just as Greek philosophers distinguished between the fleeting, spurious happiness of material pleasures and the real happiness of truth, so too the Rabbis identified real happiness as living according to God's will. To follow God's commandments is to live according to the halakhah. Literally meaning "path" or "way," *halakhah* comes to denote the entirety of Jewish law.

But how is one to know what God demands? Ultimately this is the function of Oral Torah. Containing not just content but also a method, Oral Torah creates an interpretive structure that allows for the dynamic evolution of halakhah. Rabbinic legal reasoning is just as rich, complex, and occasionally obtuse as that practiced in any modern legal system. It is the practice of Oral Torah, the ongoing debates according to the principles of this legal reasoning, through which halakhah is determined. In fact, the Rabbis themselves seemed more determined to develop and bequeath legal institutions than they do an actual code of halakhah.

The Rabbis created a Judaism in which they stood in the center. Most Jews in antiquity (indeed, until modernity) were not even literate; all the more did they lack knowledge of the sophisticated traditions and interpretive techniques necessary (in rabbinic eyes) for determining the halakhah. Following the halakhah meant following the Rabbis themselves. Moreover, because there was no uniform code of halakhah, the authority for determining it rested with each individual rabbi. The Rabbis, then, envisioned a Jewish society in which individuals would turn to their local rabbi for a determination of halakhic questions. Each rabbi was legally sovereign in his own locale. Thus, despite the shared traditions and interpretive techniques among the Rabbis, this system naturally led to variations of halakhic practice. The Rabbis envision a kind of "high court," the Sanhedrin (the historical question of whether it actually existed, and if so, in what form, is still unsettled), but its jurisdiction is limited to capital cases and the disciplining of rabbis who strayed too far out of the wide halakhic boundaries.

Rabbinic Judaism is itself something of a simplification. Not only did different groups of Rabbis, whether Palestinian or Babylonian, early or late, differ about halakhic practice and techniques of determination. Even individual rabbis within a given cohort were given the freedom, within some boundaries, to create and relax legal institutions.

Observance of the mitzvot is accessible in a way that Torah study is not. Even the Rabbis admit that few have the intellectual and material resources that would allow them to participate in a life devoted to Torah study. All, however, have the obligation—as articulated by the Rabbis—to observe the mitzvot. For the Rabbis, Jewish-born, unblemished men are fully obligated; all others (e.g., children, women, slaves, those with disabilities) have lesser but specified obligations.

Rabbinic assumptions about the nature of women and their social roles began a logical cascade that ultimately led to limiting their halakhic obligations and thus also their opportunities for participation in public rituals. Most Rabbis, very much like their Greek, Roman, and Christian contemporaries, believed that women were constrained by both constitution and social roles (which were themselves seen as part of the natural order). Imposing an obligation on one who was incapable of doing it was unfair. If women neither had the internal discipline nor the opportunity, for example, to fulfill a commandment that was limited to a specific period of time, it would be unfair to demand this of them. On the other hand, according to a rabbinic legal principle, if they were not obligated to fulfill a commandment then they could not serve as an agent for one who is obligated. More concretely: a woman cannot lead a prayer service, according to the Rabbis, because she is not herself obligated to pray and therefore cannot help men to fulfill their obligation.

Other rabbinic limitations on women's participation in public rituals were based on other principles. The Rabbis, like all elite men in antiquity, expected women to behave modestly. An immodest woman committed no sin per se against God, but rather risked embarrassing her father or husband. Also, keenly aware of gender boundaries and expectations, the Rabbis were afraid of being shown up by a woman: They developed a principle of "honor of the public" to exclude women from public activities that they saw as the domain of men, with the assumption that her performance would be interpreted as shaming the men who were present. Today, in Orthodox circles especially, these assumptions and principles have generated renewed and heated discussion.

Whatever the concrete benefits of the observance of the mitzvot, they were also seen by the Rabbis as legal obligations. Jews have free will and thus the ability to decide whether to follow the commandments. Not following them, though, is equivalent to living against the divine will; it is to sin. Sin not only moves the sinner outside God's presence but also leads to legal culpability. According to the Torah, the "solution" to this legal culpability was to bring a sacrifice to the Temple. The kind of sacrifice to be brought was dependent on the kind of sin committed, and the sacrifice itself was thought to absolve the sin. Throughout the period of the Rabbis, though, that was no longer an option. How, then, could sin be absolved?

Repentance thus became the solution to the legal culpability of sin. The Hebrew word for repentance, *teshuvah*, literally means "turning," or a re-orientation of the self. It means both to atone for the sins of the past and to reform oneself in order not to repeat them. Theoretically, God's forgiveness can only follow the individual's sincere regret and pledge to do better.

Structurally and psychologically, the problem with teshuvah is that it is an entirely internal and subjective experience. Comparing teshuvah to Catholic confession highlights this problem. For Catholics confession can only be efficacious within the institution of the Church: a priest has the ultimate and sole right to grant atonement on behalf of God. A priest hears the confession, prescribes practical tasks that must be performed, and then grants atonement. This process clears the penitent to take communion and, psychologically, to "start over." Ancient Jewish sacrifice worked in a similar way, marking absolution with a concrete act. By contrast, teshuvah does not involve anyone else. The penitent has full responsibility for initiating it and determining both how it is to be done and whether it was effective.

Excluding an external authority from this process has theological advantages and psychological disadvantages. By putting full responsibility on the penitent, it reinforces the notions of human responsibility and free will. By excluding human intermediaries, it affirms that God alone has the power to judge and forgive. On the other hand, how is one to know if God has truly forgiven? It leaves open the very real possibility that the penitent will feel always unforgiven and insecure, ultimately to be crushed by the ever increasing weight of guilt.

The Day of Atonement, Yom Kippur, structurally solves this problem. Both the rituals and the liturgy for this day are meant not only to spur the individual to genuine atonement and teshuvah, but, just as important, to assure the individual that God really has forgiven. Repentance is an ongoing process rather than a single event, but Yom Kippur assures that it is not in vain.

❖ ❖ ❖ ❖ ❖

The rabbinic emphasis on living *now* according to God's will leads them to downplay eschatology. Their goal is to bring the individual to the good life rather than eternal salvation. So while the Rabbis do discuss the world-to-come—in their typically scattered and incoherent way—they never elevate individual salvation as the primary goal of performing the mitzvot or repenting.

Their notion of a world-to-come does, however, play a particularly important role for their theodicy. Positing a final Day of Judgment (rarely mentioned in the Hebrew Bible), as seen above, allows the Rabbis to reconcile their notion of a just and involved God with their observations of the patent injustice of society. At the end of time, perfect justice will be restored.

When God metes out justice at the end of time, He will do so to resurrected human bodies. The Rabbis, despite their disagreements about whether human beings have a soul, are insistent on this point. At the end of days, God will revive the corpses and then judge them. These bodies will never die again, but will live out God's judgment. On what exactly happens to the individual after the Day of Judgment the Rabbis are very sketchy; they have no fully developed notions of "heaven," "hell," or "limbo." They disagree about the status of the mitzvot at the end of time but generally assert that the mitzvot will still be binding and practiced. The doctrine that bodies would come back to life, though, was so important to them that the Mishnah declares that a Jew who does not believe that it is actually found in the Torah is a heretic and will not share in the afterlife. That is, they label as a heretic even a Jew who might believe in the doctrine but doubt its origin in the Torah. Recognizing the tendentiousness of this assertion, the Rabbis in the Talmud go to great lengths to find biblical verses that they claim demonstrate its truth.

One set of rabbinic traditions identify the Land of Israel as the site at which resurrection will take place:

> R. Shimon ben Lakish said in the name of Bar Kappara: Those who die in the land [i.e., Israel] are revived first in the days of the Messiah. What is the reason? Because he gives the soul to the people for its sake.
>
> But from this it follows that our Rabbis who die in the Exile lose out!
>
> Rabbi Simi said: The Holy One bores out the earth and they roll like bottles and when they arrive at the Land of Israel their souls are restored.
>
> (Palestinian Talmud, Kilayim 9:4)

When the Day of Judgment at the end of time arrives, God will vivify the corpses buried in the land of Israel. The Talmud then creates a problem. Whereas R. Shimon ben Lakish merely suggests that they would be resurrected first (followed, presumably, by everyone else), the (Palestinian!) Talmud reads him as limiting resurrection to the corpse buried in the land, thus excluding people (especially Rabbis) buried elsewhere. God's compassion solves the problem: Their corpses are allowed to get to the land, where they pop out.

From antiquity to the present, some Jews desired to be buried in the land of Israel precisely because of this belief that resurrection would occur there first. In fact, the common Jewish burial practice outside the land of Israel of adding some soil from Israel to the casket or grave also derives from this belief—perhaps God will "count" the grave as part of the Holy Land.

Although the land of Israel plays a role in the rabbinic eschatology of the individual, this role is much more pronounced in their communal eschatology. God's covenant is with the people Israel, and it is to the people as a whole that He promised a land. The land of Israel is thus the promised land, the land the Torah says God promised to Abraham and his descendents. At the time of the Rabbis, of course, this was a promise unfulfilled; for the contemporary Christians the very loss of Jewish sovereignty over the land was a sign of God's disfavor. The Rabbis instead understood the loss of Jewish sovereignty over the land as a deferment of the promise. God will keep His promise at the end of time. At that time, the Jews will regain control of the land and will stream into the land from all the other nations, thus fulfilling God's covenantal promise.

The land of Israel (*Eretz Israel*) occupies an important place in rabbinic thought less for its present sanctity than for the promise it represents. Many later of readers of the Bible were so struck by this conceptual or mythological quality of the land of Israel that they would unlink it completely from the entire geographical region, as, for example, when the Puritans and Mormons termed America the "Promised Land." The Rabbis too understand the land in highly symbolic and mythological terms, but never to the point of disconnecting it from a specific geographic location. To mourn the destruction of the Temple and loss of control over the land is to hope for the future redemption; they are sides of the same coin. One rabbinic story captures some of the complexity of this understanding of the land:

> Once Rabbi Yehdah ben Beterah and Rabbi Mattya ben Harash and Rabbin Hanina son of Rabbi Yehoshua and Rabbi Yonatan were all traveling outside of the land of Israel. When they arrived at Puteoli [an Italian coast-

al city] they remembered the land of Israel. They cast their eyes down and wept. They then ripped their garments and recited the verse, "For you are about to cross the Jordan to enter and possess the land that the Lord your God is assigning to you. When you have occupied it and are settled in it, take care to observe all the laws and rules that I have set before you this day" [Deuteronomy 11:31–32]. And they said: Dwelling in the land of Israel is equivalent to all the mitzvot of the Torah.

(Sifre Deuteronomy, Section 80)

The Rabbis of this story mourn both the historical destruction of the Temple and their own present distance from the land. They look forward not only to their own eventual return home but also to the end of days. Their last line is clearly hyperbolic; they would never assert that living in the land exempted a Jew from observing the other commandments. Rather, they seem to understand dwelling in the land as meritorious because its residents in a sense anticipate the final ingathering.

Thus, for the most part the Rabbis subscribe to a restorative rather than utopian eschatology. Their eschatology is imaginative, to be sure, but it involves returning to a state they believe once existed, not to some new,

5.1 The crowded graveyard on the Mount of Olives in Jerusalem. Some Jews believe that in the world-to-come those buried close to the site of the Jerusalem Temple will be resurrected first. Photo by Michael L. Satlow.

previously unlived utopia. Generally, they take the moments of life in the Garden of Eden, revelation on Mount Sinai, and life in Solomon's Temple to be paradigmatic. In the world-to-come real (but now immortal) human bodies will live as humans (perhaps even with the same bodily functions), but in a world with perfect justice and no strife. They will, according to many Rabbis, rebuild the Temple in Jerusalem, offer sacrifices there, and live according to the mitzvot, with all the nations of the world acknowledging the God of Israel as the sole God. God will announce the advent of this age by means of a human agent, the "anointed" (messiah). The Rabbis of course differ about their views of the messiah (i.e., when the messiah will come; the relation of Elijah to the messiah), they more or less share an understanding that the world "today" remains unredeemed, waiting for a human messiah to herald its redemption. Obviously, these ideas constitute a fundamental disagreement with those at the root of Christianity.

As the Rabbis imagine it, the redeemed world sits right on the cusp of human achievability; it is almost, but not quite, as if human beings themselves could create such a world. This position on the cusp results in a deep tension between reading rabbinic eschatology as passive or active. A passive eschatology puts all responsibility for the world-to-come in God's hands. God works on God's own schedule, completely oblivious to what occurs on earth. Humans might try to predict what this schedule is—assuming, for example, that God left clues in prophetic texts—but these predictions do nothing to influence the actual end of time. We are but pawns in God's unfathomable plan.

On the other side of this theological spectrum an active eschatology asserts that human beings can bring the end of days. Humans can create a totally just society and live according to God's will, or they can act in a manner that will hasten God's initiation of the world-to-come. A form of this active eschatology has informed modern liberal political thought, which is fundamentally optimistic about the human ability to create a just society.

Both notions, often in open contradiction, are found in rabbinic literature. The danger of passive eschatology is that it devalues human initiatives. Many Rabbis insist that humans must take an active role in the redemptive process; only when Israel prepares itself will God act. Others, however, not only believe that humans cannot influence redemption but also that humans are forbidden even from speculating about when redemption will arrive. An active eschatology has other dangers. The notion that humans can "force God's hand" can be seen as presumptuous and assumes a God who can be influenced. Practically, it is inherently unstable and can easily lead to revolt and violence. Some Rabbis apparently were comfortable with these dangers (for example, the supporters of Bar Kokhba), but most probably were not.

What these eschatological views do *not* boil down to is the clear modern idea of progress. Following a largely Christian idea, most modern Westerners understand time to progress in a way that is both linear and teleological. One thing builds upon or follows another in a more or less straight line to a final goal. We march, in a Christian or modern secular understanding, toward salvation (or ultimate conflagration). For the Rabbis, though, time was neither linear nor teleological. We move around rather than forward, ultimately to come to rest at the spot where we began, like the earth's rotation around the sun. But, also like the earth rotating on its axis each day, rabbinic time makes an annual circle, continually revisiting the paradigmatic moments of Israel's history. This understanding of time as circling back on itself even as it hurtles back toward an originary moment helps to account for the rhythm of a life led in the presence of God and the rituals that structure it.

6

MITZVOT

BIBLICAL RELIGION IS one of big gestures. There is little that is small or banal about it. The Torah's plotline moves from the height of paradise in Eden to the depths of the slave-pits in Egypt, from God's fiery appearance at Mount Sinai to premonitions of His residence in the Temple in Jerusalem. Encounters with God are exceptional and dangerous, usually occurring in the highly scripted, bloody sacrifices, Moses's cautious entrance into the Tent of Meeting, or (the often unwelcome) divine visitation upon the prophet. The rituals of the First and Second Temple were spectacular and awesome spectacles performed and mediated by the priesthood in tightly controlled sacred spaces.

Despite its assertions of God's omnipresence, the Tanak emphasizes sacred space. Some spaces are simply more charged than others; God's presence is either stronger or more acutely felt there. Just as a sense of place and movement between places—all leading to the final place, the promised land—drives the biblical narrative, so too does biblical theology lay suspended between Sinai and Zion, the two central places of God's presence. This emphasis on place, and especially the place of the single Temple in Jerusalem, is so deeply ingrained in this tradition (and shared by contemporary nonbiblical religions) that as late as the fourth century CE, 300 years after the destruction of the Second Temple, about 230 years after the disastrous uprising of Bar Kokhba, and at the height of the rabbinic movement, Jews continued to pine for the restoration of the Temple and actively worked to restore it.

The Rabbis, however, went in a different direction. To paraphrase the modern Jewish theologian Abraham Joshua Heschel, instead of building temples in space they built temples in time.[1] Time, rather than space, became for them the central location of holiness. Eschewing the big gesture, the Rabbis understand devotion to God to be the gradual accumulation of quotidian activities. Holiness is to be enacted in time rather than space, with rituals shaping the rhythm and texture of daily, weekly, and annual life.

These rituals make up the stuff of the mitzvot, or commandments, which together comprise the halakhah, loosely translated as "path" or "way." The halakhah is an embodied answer to the questions, How do I live according to God's will? How do I suffuse my life with holiness? Halakhah is the response to God's covenantal demands.

But how do we know what God demands? Unlike the prophet Haggai ("seek a ruling from the priests," 2:11), the Rabbis give the authority for determining the halakhah to the rabbinic sage. The local rabbi, ideally, has the knowledge to answer these halakhic questions. Combining knowledge of traditional answers and a familiarity with authoritative texts and accepted methods of interpretation, the sage can craft justified answers to daily problems. Although ideally in dialogue with other rabbis, the local rabbi is autonomous, and his halakhic opinions are seen (by the rabbis) as binding only in his own locale. Thus, even theoretically, rabbinic halakhic opinions can be quite diverse.

The Rabbis did not invent halakhah. In addition to inheriting a textual tradition (most important, of course, the Torah), they also lived in a Jewish world in which many religious practices were simply taken for granted. Many Jews did circumcise their children, abstain from certain meats, and observe the Sabbath and other holidays. Jews did not need the Rabbis to tell them that the God of Israel likes prayer, and at least some Jews remained punctilious about issues of ritual purity even in a world without a Temple. The Rabbis appear to have drawn on these isolated traditional practices, systematizing, clarifying, and expanding them. There is much about traditional Jewish practices that we do not know, but it is likely that they did not have anything approaching the scope and legal precision the Rabbis assigned to them. Jews did not work on the Sabbath, but they may or may not have considered writing to be work, and they almost certainly did not try to define precisely what "writing" meant. The biblical prohibitions on eating certain meats are clear, but most Jews probably did not extend the food laws to specific ways of slaughter or separating dairy and meat products. Jews probably prayed together on the Sabbath and festivals, at other times individually and spontaneously; the Rabbis work this into an obligation with a fixed liturgy. Even in this period, despite our relative paucity of knowledge, there was a fluid dynamic between rabbinic halakhah, traditional practices, and the texts used to authorize both.

The major accomplishment of rabbinic halakhah thus appears not to be the determination of halakhic norms, but the integration of several discrete and traditional practices into the master narrative of Israel's history and the concept of Torah as God's continuing revelation. Rabbinic literature both turns traditional practices into precisely scripted rituals and textualizes them, linking them to each other, the Tanak, and rabbinic modes of thinking. Only from the period of the Rabbis can one talk of *the* halakhah as an independent category; norms are put into an interdependent system. At the same time, the textualization of these traditional and underdetermined practices preserves a record for future generations, providing resources for practicing and making sense of these rituals.

A less lofty but equally important consequence of rabbinic halakhah is its inscription of Jewish difference. There is nothing particularly new about this; the Tanak itself prescribes distinctive rituals and Jews in the Second Temple period were noted for the rituals that were seen as separating them from the rest of the world. In many cases, however, the Rabbis took this further. Jewish distinction in the halakhah extends into the very rhythms of life, rippling up from daily routines to life cycle events. No set of rituals inscribe difference as much as kashrut, the Jewish food laws that sharply limit what can be consumed. Here, though, it is also important to note that the difference is not just between Jews and non-Jews, it is also *among* Jews. Rabbinic halakhah, then, does not just separate Jews from non-Jews, it can socially separate Jews from each other.

The halakhah is fundamentally grounded in the assumption of humanity's overwhelming dependence on God. The world and all life in it belong to God. God gives the gift of life and takes it back at His choosing; He grants use, but not ownership, of the world and its pleasures to His creations. One Talmudic passage develops this idea:

> The Rabbis taught: It is not permitted for a person to enjoy anything of this world without a benediction, and whoever partakes of this world without offering a benediction has committed an act of sacrilege.
>
> How can this be redressed?
>
> Let him go to a wise man who will teach him to offer a benediction.

He is to go to a wise man? What will he do for him? He has already performed a forbidden act!

But Rava said, "It means that he is to go to a wise man initially, and he will teach him the practice of offering benedictions, and he will not commit acts of sacrilege."

Said Rabbi Judah in the name of Samuel, "Whoever enjoys anything of this world without offering benedictions, it is as if he had partaken of what belongs to the heavenly realm, as it is written: 'The earth is the Lord's and the fullness thereof' (Psalms 24:1)."

Rabbi Levi pointed to a contradiction. It is written: "The earth is the Lord's and the fullness thereof" and it is also written "The heavens are the heavens of the Lord, but the earth has He given to the children of men" (Psalms 115:16)!

But there is no contradiction. The one statement applies before one has pronounced a benediction, the other, after one has pronounced the benediction.

Said Hanina b. Papa: "Whoever enjoys anything in this world without offering a benediction, it is as though he has robbed the Holy One, praised be He, and the community of Israel. It is thus that we interpret what is written: 'one who robs his father and his mother and says, "It is no transgression," is a companion of one who is a destroyer' (Proverbs 28:24). 'Father' we interpret as applying to the Holy One, praised be He, as it is written, 'Is He not your Father, who created you?' (Deuteronomy 32:6); and mother we interpret as applying to the community of Israel, as it is written, 'Hear my son, the instruction of your father, and do not abandon the teaching of your mother' (Proverbs 1:8)."

(Babylonian Talmud, Berakhot 35a–b)

As is typical in midrash, the real starting point for this discussion is a textual problem: Psalms 24:1 and 115:15 appear to contradict each other! The former asserts that the earth is God's, the latter that God gave it to humans. The solution to this problem, presaged in the opening paragraph, is that human blessings change the status of the earth and its pleasures. All belongs to God, but God permits humans to enjoy the pleasures of the earth—provided they ask first.

There are some human pleasures, however, of which humans can never partake. Working from the biblical stories of the aftermath of the flood and God's charge to Noah, the Rabbis develop the idea that God limits all human freedom to some degree. Because the blood is the life and all life belongs to God, no human is free to take it. Nor is sexuality a "free" domain in which all are free to play with whomever they want; God limits permissible sexual partners. Like the original moment of human creation in the Garden of Eden, humans are given great, but nevertheless limited, authority to enjoy that which truly belongs to God.

One of the implications of God's covenant with Israel, with its promise to make the children of Israel God's special people holy unto God, is to further limit Israel's ability to partake of God's pleasures. At Sinai, according to the Rabbis, God gave the mitzvot to Israel. Observance of the mitzvot set Israel apart as a separate holy people. The mitzvot internally and externally signal obedience to God. Their strictures go well beyond those given to the rest of humanity. They infuse, both positively (things that one must do) and negatively (things that one must not do), the very fabric of daily life.

By strictly regulating dietary consumption, for example, kashrut tightly structures the life of the rabbinic Jew. The Rabbis first follow the Tanak in declaring certain animals permissible (kosher) or not. The Torah limits permissible mammals to those that both have cloven hoofs and chew their cud—this is the reason the pig is excluded. It lists kosher and nonkosher birds, which is generally understood (although the Torah gives no general reason) as prohibiting birds of prey. And it permits only fish that have both fins and scales, excluding shellfish. There are, in addition, a number of insects (mainly locusts) that are permitted.

While they stick closely to this biblical list of kosher and nonkosher animals, the Rabbis go well beyond it when they declare how permitted animals are to be made "fit" (the literal meaning of *kosher*) for consumption. Keying off the biblical injunction of not consuming an animal's blood (Genesis 9:4), the Rabbis prescribe an elaborate procedure for the slaughter of kosher animals. They largely took this operation from their understanding of the steps involved in sacrificial slaughter. In order to drain out the maximum amount of blood, the slaughterer must quickly draw a sharp blade across the throat of a mammal or bird (fish and insects do not, in the rabbinic understanding, have "blood"). The requirement of slaughtering uninjured animals in this way largely excludes from consumption animals that were hunted (unless they were trapped by a net) or that died naturally. The blood is then "returned" to God by being covered with dirt. In order to fully drain the flesh of its blood, the meat must then be salted and let to sit. Once properly soaked and salted, the flesh is considered kosher. Most kosher meat today sold in stores has already been prepared in this way.

If the preparation of meat is one of the most distinctive features of rabbinic kashrut, the separation of meat and dairy products must closely rival it. Justifying this previously unattested distinction on the Torah's thrice repeated injunction against boiling a kid in its mother's milk, the Rabbis divide all foods as "meat," "dairy," or "parve." Meat and dairy cannot be mixed, while parve foods—fish, fruits, vegetables, grains, etc.—can be eaten with either.

Forbidding the mixing of meat and dairy products goes beyond prohibiting the eating of cheeseburgers or having a cup of milk with a steak meal or an ice cream immediately after it. It extends to a complicated separation of dishes too. The Rabbis understood many materials, such as wood and ceramics, to take on the "taste" of the foods with which they come into contact. So a pottery plate used for a piece of hot kosher meat can, in the future, never be used for dairy. One result of this stricture is the need for a kosher household to own two complete sets of dishes, silverware, pots, and utensils, one meat and the other dairy. A second result is to virtually prohibit a kosher Jew from eating most (or all) foods prepared in a nonkosher environment. Even ordinarily kosher foods would have been cooked in and served on nonkosher utensils, thus rendering them nonkosher.[2]

In addition to these three systemic characteristics, the Rabbis add a few disconnected dietary restrictions. Following an isolated story in the Torah, they prohibit the sciatic nerve of an animal, which has the practical affect of declaring nonkosher meat from the hindquarters of mammals (e.g., filet mignon). They prohibit the drinking of any wine that has come into contact with a non-Jew, partly out of fear that the non-Jew would have made a libation offering from it to a pagan deity and partly to prevent social interaction. They also prefer that bread, oil, and milk come only from Jewish sources.

One obvious ramification of these laws is social segregation. The rabbinic Jew will have a difficult time eating or drinking with non-Jews or even non-rabbinic Jews. Like circumcision or the wearing of the four-fringed garment (the *tallit katan*), the laws of kashrut distinguish the rabbinic Jew. They also help to create an isolated economic community in which observant Jews restrict their commercial interactions in certain critical areas to other Jews.

To understand kashrut solely as a means of social segregation, however, is to miss their pervasive impact on individual Jews. Mary Douglas, a structural anthropologist from Cambridge University, suggested that the Torah's laws of permitted and forbidden animals embeds a deep concern for natural categories: The forbidden animals, she notes, are primarily "betwixt and between," animals that hover between paradigms, such as the lobster, a "walking fish."[3] By extension, the rabbinic insistence on separation of meat and dairy can also be seen as reflecting, and thus inculcating through concrete practice, a belief in different organizing categories. One, for example, is not to mix life (i.e., blood or milk) with death. Seen in this way, eating practices nonlinguistically reinforce basic conceptual ideas.

Perhaps. The truth is that neither the Tanak nor the Rabbis are very clear about what this system *means*. While Douglas's suggestion (which she has since reconsidered) helps to make sense of a morass of otherwise bewildering laws, like many structural anthropological explanations it assumes an inherent and universal meaning for the ritual. Yet, like most Jewish rituals, kashrut is underdetermined; it does not come with an inherent meaning that all Jewish communities realize. From the first century BCE on, Jews have struggled to understand kashrut, considering it, among other things, to be reflective of irrational devotion to God, superior Jewish morals or hygiene, or a Jewish love of animals and the environment. But this struggle almost always moves from the inside out, from a prior commitment to kashrut to the justification for it.

Whereas kashrut structures the rabbinic Jew's daily life negatively, prayer structures it positively. The Rabbis mandated two daily prayer services, following the model of the twice-daily sacrifices performed at the Jerusalem Temple. These morning and afternoon services—to which a third "additional" (*musaf*) service is added immediately after the morning service on Sabbath and festival mornings—serve as a mode in a postsacrificial age of showing obedience to God, emphasize central rabbinic concepts, and create a space in which the individual can formulate personal requests and hopes. The Rabbis never standardize the precise texts of these prayers, although they do prescribe the topics. They also understand these two prayer services, like the daily sacrifices of old, as just a starting point. Prayer was to infuse the day. Blessings should precede and follow every act of consumption; it should mark virtually every visual and aural pleasure. One of the goals of both kashrut and prayer—along with a myriad of other assorted activities—is to suffuse daily living with holiness.

Contemporaneous non-Jews lived in what the historian Keith Hopkins calls a "world full of gods."[4] The early fathers of the Church would deride these non-Jews as "pagans"; the Rabbis call them "worshippers of the stars." In fact, on a basic, structural level, rabbinic Jews lived in precisely the same world and shared quite similar assumptions. "Pagans" understood the world to be suffused with divinity and piously called for regular daily recognition of and obeisance to it. Gestures of acknowledgement were made to the statues of the gods ("idols") that studded the ancient city and most meals were preceded by some kind of sacrifice or libation offering to the gods. Rabbis vehemently disagreed with the "idolaters" about their explicit belief in several gods; their myths; and the way they represented their gods, but both agreed that piety took place in daily action.

Whereas "idolaters" focus holiness in an image or at an altar (although they acknowledge divine omnipresence), the Rabbis release holiness from all confines of space. The Rabbis ascribe some degree of elevated sanctity to a Torah scroll, and even less to a synagogue building. God resides wherever a prayer quorum (defined as ten men, a minyan) or even an individual pray or study Torah. Whatever a given space might do psychologically to an individual (for example, one might *feel* closer to God at the Western Wall), God is in no way more attuned to a prayer uttered in Jerusalem than one in Des Moines. The Rabbis spatially decenter holiness, pushing to its logical conclusion, the assumption of God's omnipresence.

Many—probably most—Jews in antiquity did not subscribe to this rather diffuse and abstract notion of holiness. They built synagogues decorated with ornate mosaics, many of which contain a large zodiac around some personification of the sun, as noted earlier. While scholars debate the precise interpretation of these mosaics, the Jews who made them (presumably not followers of the Rabbis) note on their donation inscriptions that they considered the synagogue to be a "holy place," not just a simple pile of stones like any other.

The tension between the rabbinic notion of diffuse and transient holiness and the idea that holiness concentrates in a particular space remains with us today. Observant Jews still flock to the Western Wall to pray because on some level they believe that their prayers will be better heard there. Men who normally do not wear a head covering (*kippah* or yarmulke—a practice only instituted in a later period) frequently don one when they enter a synagogue, even if it is only to participate in a completely secular event far from the sanctuary. Here the logical answer to God's omnipresence collides with some deep human need for making holiness tangible.

Whereas most days contain a diffuse and transient holiness activated by human activity, the Sabbath is innately holy, a "Temple in Time," as Heschel calls it. In the Torah, observance of the Sabbath (Shabbat) is a form of *imitatio dei*, an imitation of God's cessation from labor after six days of creation. But the biblical meaning of Shabbat is far from clear. It is also God's day; like the Temple (God's house), Shabbat "belongs" to God. And while it

6.1 Rebbe Menachem Mendel Schneerson, leader of the Lubavitch Hasidim, in 1992. He is wearing a prayer shawl (*tallit*) and phylacteries (*tefillin*) on his forehead and arm. Jewish men traditionally have worn phylacteries during most daily morning services. Today some women also wear them.

Copyright © AP/Wide World Photos, used with permission

marks creation, Shabbat also embodies the historical memory of the exodus from Egypt.

Prior to the Rabbis, Jews observed Shabbat with enough frequency that non-Jews noted the Jewish predilection for "laziness." Some of these communities, such as the authors of the Dead Sea scrolls, did attempt to grapple with the legal gaps left by Scripture: What does God precisely want from us on Shabbat? None, however, approached the problem with the same intensity and rigor as did the Rabbis.

The Rabbis use ritual to fuse the biblical concepts of Shabbat. Drawing on an implied link between the biblical description of the building of the Tabernacle and Shabbat, the Rabbis claim that the definition of "work" can be derived from those activities necessary for the construction of the Tabernacle. They thus identify thirty-nine general categories of work that range from spinning the fabrics used in the Tabernacle to writing, which was used to mark the beams. The Rabbis then expand these general categories into a comprehensive definition of forbidden activities.

The rabbinic laws of Shabbat simultaneously point both toward its universal (creation of the cosmos) and nationalistic (the formation of the people Israel and God's covenant with them) aspects. In one sense they have made both the Tabernacle itself as a microcosm and the original moment of creation as incomplete without it. To participate in the rituals and laws of Shabbat is to participate not only in the inherent holiness of the day but also in God's cosmic plan.

This, of course, is but one way of casting and understanding the large and enormously complex body of physical activities that comprise, for the Rabbis, Shabbat observance. To live as a rabbinic Jew meant, and for many continues to mean, fundamentally altering one's life on Shabbat. Their definition of work goes far beyond ours, including many creative and destructive activities. The Rabbis focus on objective acts rather than subjective feelings; *work* has a formal legal definition in which how one feels about the activities are at best secondary (although one's intentions are made relevant for the determination of legal culpability). They prohibit, for example, writing poetry or engaging in some artistic hobby, but permit moving a heavy piece of furniture up the stairs if it is to be used on Shabbat. All activities that involve money, whether earning or spending it, even for "recreational" activities, are also prohibited.

Following the Torah, the Rabbis prohibit all forms of fire making and cooking. Fires that are kindled before the Shabbat might be enjoyed during that Friday night and the next day, but they may not be stoked or tended. So an oil lamp, for example, can be kindled prior to the beginning of Shabbat on Friday night and one may read by its light until it burns down. Foods may be warmed over an existing fire but not cooked; this is a fine line with its own set of complex distinctions. Boiling water is considered "cooking," but water can be boiled prior to Shabbat and left warm on a fire throughout the day.

The prohibition on traveling and carrying also has widespread implications. Rabbinic law prohibits all forms of "carrying" between a public and private space or within a public space. Under this law, for example, one could carry a book between rooms in a house, but not from one house to another. This blanket prohibition raises its own intricate set of problems: What is "carrying"? Does it include clothes or ornaments that one wears? Carrying a baby? What defines public and private domains?

These problems were, in fact, so complex and potentially burdensome that the Rabbis devised a legal fiction to eliminate them altogether. The *eruv* is a boundary that transforms, in a narrow legal and technical sense, a "public" space into a "private" space, usually by encircling it. This boundary marker might be as simple as a string, or it might be a patchwork of walls, poles, fences, etc. By making a public space into a private one, however, the eruv allows for all forms of carrying within that space. The classic example of such a space is a walled city (e.g., the Old City of Jerusalem), but an eruv could be constructed almost anywhere.

These prohibitions create an empty space that the Rabbis attempt to fill with positive rituals. Physical "rest" is not merely defined by the prohibition of different activities—the Rabbis prescribe the consumption of three (in contrast to regular days, on which there were only two) meals on Shabbat, at which, ideally, special foods are served. Special and clean clothes should be donned. In addition to prayer, Torah study was seen as an especially appropriate activity. Two loaves are used for the meals to commemorate the double portion of manna that the Torah says that God gave to the Israelites every Friday. The end of Shabbat is marked by a short ritual (*havdalah*) that involves drinking wine, looking at a fire, and smelling spices—thus marking the break between Shabbat and the rest of the "profane" week.

The rabbinic system of Shabbat observance is so elaborate and complex, and so many aspects of it are unattested in any other contemporary sources, that it raises the question of how widespread it was. Did ordinary Jews observe Shabbat "rabbinically"? While it is impossible to answer this question definitively (or quantitatively), it is likely that most did not. Jews continued to observe Shabbat according to their local traditions, but only the few rabbinic communities and circles would have preferred the structured rabbinic scheme to their own traditional mores. If the townspeople had been cooking their food for Shabbat and warming it in a certain way for generations, why would they listen to rabbis telling them that it was now suddenly wrong? How fine a distinction would most Jews have made between public and private domains? It is possible that many Jews did attempt to follow rabbinic prescriptions, or (more likely) that in forming their laws the Rabbis attempted to standardize already common local practices. But it is also possible that there was a wide gap between rabbinic and nonrabbinic Shabbat practices.

If Shabbat sets a rhythm to the week, the festivals set one for the year. The rabbinic calendar is primarily lunar, although it has a few solar elements to it. Each day begins in the evening, and each month begins with the new moon. Because the lunar cycle can be 29–30 days, over twelve months this leads to a 354-day year. Very quickly such a calendar would lead to the months rotating through the seasons—which in fact is precisely what happens today in the Islamic calendar, which is also lunar. The Rabbis, however, prefer to intercalate a full month every few years to keep the months in their traditional seasons. During the rabbinic period the turn of the months and intercalation were done by decree of a rabbinic court: in theory it was not a mechanistic act automatically triggered by astronomical phenomena. Also, because word had to spread by the court, there was always a chance it would not make it in a timely fashion to far-flung communities. This is the (stated) origin of the observance of a festival for two days outside the land of Israel: an extra day just in case word did not make it in time. Given the general gap between rabbinic and nonrabbinic Jewish practice, this of course raises the intriguing question of whether all Jews were on the same calendar at this time. In any case, later Jewish communities more closely linked the calendar to astronomical tables.

The earliest role of the biblical holidays provides the most likely explanation of why keeping the months in their season was so important to the Rabbis. The Torah discusses the three major festivals—Passover (Pesach), Pentecost (Shavuot), and Tabernacles (Sukkot)—as agricultural celebrations linked to the harvest cycle of the land of Israel. Even in the Torah, however, these probably original reasons for the festivals are overlaid with historical ones. Passover becomes not only the celebration of the spring harvest, commemorated with the eating of unleavened bread, but also the national holiday par excellence, marking Israel's exodus from Egypt and forging into a nation. The tabernacles of Sukkot are not only temporary booths put up to facilitate harvest but also an embodied historical memory of Israel's march through the Sinai. Only Shavuot is left relatively underdetermined historically, although a link to the giving of the Torah on Mount Sinai is perhaps implied.

Without obliterating the agricultural underlayer of these festivals, the Rabbis nevertheless hone in on and deepen their historical overtones. This can most clearly be seen in their treatment of Passover. In the Torah the two core rituals for Passover are the eating of unleavened bread (matzah) with its avoidance of leavened products for a week, and the family sacrifice and consumption of a lamb. Throughout the periods of the First and Second Temple, Pesach, like Shavuot and Sukkot, was a pilgrimage festival in which Jews should go to Jerusalem. With the destruction of the Second Temple, however, the Rabbis recast the festival. Eliminating the paschal sacrifice, they focused on the matzah; for them it replaced the lamb as the primary symbol of the holiday. They replaced the messy family barbecue of the lamb with the ordered, highly ritualized seder—a pedagogical meal for which a highly formalized liturgy (the Haggadah) would eventually be created.[5]

At least as important as the seder, though, is the avoidance of leaven during the seven (eight outside the land of Israel) days of the festival. The Rabbis define leaven as any grain that has been moistened for more than eighteen minutes. Matzah is a mix of flour and water cooked within eighteen minutes of mixing. Avoidance, for them, means not simply refraining from eating these products but ridding one's residence of them totally. Even utensils and dishes that have been used for leavened products are not to be used during Pesach. To their two complete sets of ordinary pots and dishes (meat and dairy) rabbinic Jews must add another two sets for use only on Pesach.

Rabbinic explanations for these practices are incomplete and, the truth be told, not very compelling. But there is a way in which these elaborate rituals, so rich in allusion but opaque in easy meanings, float free of explanation. Later Jewish communities will accept and reject various aspects of these rituals, explaining them according to their own unique sensibilities. Their very curiosity and explanatory malleability might in fact be an important factor of their survival.

Of the three pilgrimage holidays, Shavuot stands out. Unlike the other two, it is only a single day (two outside the land of Israel) rather than seven. Nor, like Pesach and Sukkot, does it receive a Talmudic tractate devoted to explicating its laws and customs; the Rabbis mention it only incidentally. In fact, the Rabbis appear not quite to know what to do with this festival. They continue to see it, more than the other two festivals, as an agricultural holiday. Because, according to the Torah, Pentecost concludes a fifty-day period from Passover, they link it to Passover and, to a lesser extent, to the giving of the Torah. But they do not develop distinctive customs and rituals for it—to the extent that these exist, they only develop in the postrabbinic period.

Sukkot, which always begins in September or October, is as rich in imagery and ritual as Pesach. Conceptually, the Rabbis push the tabernacle in many simultaneous directions. In addition to being an agricultural symbol and a remembrance of the desert trek, it becomes the Temple holiday par excellence and a premonition of the eschatological tabernacle that God will establish. No longer is the tabernacle a simple booth, it is now a highly regulated structure in which Jews are commanded to eat (and preferably sleep) for the entire festival. It must be temporary, have at least three walls of a certain height, have a roof made of natural material thick enough to offer protection but thin enough to allow one to see the stars—a kosher booth (sukkah) follows a comprehensive building code.

The Rabbis also formally ritualize the biblical admonition to rejoice with various flora during Sukkot. This becomes the *lulav* and *etrog*. The lulav is a collection of branches (the number, kind, and condition are specified) of three different trees, and the etrog is a fragrant, lemonlike citrus fruit, the citron. These "four species" are to be taken up and waved in a prescribed manner daily during the holiday (except for Shabbat) and at various points during the morning service. The seven-day festival ends with an eighth, semi-attached day, "the eighth day of assembly," or *Shemini Atzeret*. (Thus outside the land of Israel the entire festival lasts nine days.) Shemini Atzeret has little of its own identity; it is subsumed to Sukkot, and the liturgy connected with it emphasizes the start of the rainy season in the land of Israel.

Sukkot ends a busy festival season that begins with what would be known as the High Holy Days. Rosh Hashanah, the biblical "festival of trumpeting," is for the Rabbis one of four annual "new year" days. Like our own calendar, in which our "new year" does not correspond with the federal government's fiscal year or the academic year, the rabbinic calendar noted different new year's days for different functions. The fifteenth day in the month of Shevat (*Tu b'Shevat*, usually falling in February), for example, marks the new year for the application of agricultural laws relating to trees.

Rosh Hashanah, the Torah's "festival of trumpeting," marks for the Rabbis the change of years as used for most legal documents. Onto this technical function they then overlaid themes of God's sovereignty and judgment. Now the biblical trumpeting—which in the Torah is given no reason—becomes associated with God's overwhelming power and an intimation of the final Day of Judgment. Indeed, whereas the Torah makes no connection between the Festival of Trumpeting and the Day of Atonement (Yom Kippur), which falls ten days later, the Rabbis begin to interpret Rosh Hashanah in light of Yom Kippur, understanding it as beginning a ten-day period of penitence that culminates on Yom Kippur.

The trumpet, or *shofar*, is the core symbol of Rosh Hashanah. Rabbinic discussions of this holiday deal predominantly with its declaration by the

6.2 Ultra-Orthodox Jews at the covered area of the Western Wall, holding the *lulav* and *etrog*.   *Copyright © AP/Wide World Photos, used with permission*

court and with the rules regarding the production and blowing of the sho-far. Made from a hollowed ram's horn, the shofar is blown in a prescribed way at specified points during worship. While the Rabbis also associate Rosh Hashanah with the "birthday of the world," this theme is incidental at best: God's role as king and judge are on display here.

Rosh Hashanah, which lasts two days even inside the land of Israel, does not end as much as segue into the ten days of repentance. While not for-mally a holiday, the next ten days were seen as the period of judgment. God is imagined as spending these ten days deciding the fates of all creation for the coming year; humans can, at this last moment, influence the judgment.

This judgment is finally made and sealed on the Day of Atonement. As they do with Passover, the Rabbis radically rework the Torah's version of Yom Kippur. Without a Temple there is no scapegoat; sins cannot be meta-phorically cast off into the wilderness. They thus shift the Torah's focus on this ritual, highly hierarchical event to the requirements of personal stock taking and penitence. The personal fast takes center stage in the rabbinic Yom Kippur. The Rabbis preserve the communal aspect of the holiday, in which God is imagined as judging not only individual Jews but Israel as a community, but the emphasis is more on the personal. Fasting from all food and drink for twenty-five hours (the fast begins one hour before dark), avoiding washing, sex, and the wearing of leather shoes, the individual is to make atonement for his or her sins in order to obtain a judgment of life for the coming year.

One of the functions of the high drama of the biblical atonement ceremony was to provide an appropriately awesome and objective moment that would "assure" its onlookers that the atonement was effective. The challenge of the rabbinic Yom Kippur ceremony is to convey this same conviction while taking into account the subjective acts at the core of teshuvah. On the one hand, the rituals of Yom Kippur must be seen as succeeding in order to give people the hope of a clean slate; on the other hand, the Rabbis recognize that true repentance occurs only within the individual. The Rabbis never fully reconcile this tension, but it is significant enough that it led to the further drawing out of the penitential period. Echoes of this theme extend well into Sukkot, when later the last full day of Sukkot, *Hoshanna Rabba*, is seen as marking the *real* end of the annual period of judgment.

Following the Torah, the Rabbis prohibit work also on the festivals and the High Holy Days, or Days of Awe. The work restrictions are almost identical to Shabbat; for Yom Kippur they are in fact identical. On the other major festivals, though, and unlike Shabbat, one is allowed to cook and to transfer a preexistent flame in order to cook on the other festivals. Carrying within a public domain is also permitted.

In contrast to these holidays, there are no work restrictions on the minor holidays. These holidays commemorate real or imagined historical events, usually transformed by the Rabbis. Hannukah, for example, began as a commemoration of the victory of Judah Maccabee and his family, the Hasmoneans, over the Seleucids in the 160s BCE. After purifying and rededicating the Temple in Jerusalem, according to the books of the Maccabees, the Maccabees declared a festival in Kislev (November or December) modeled on Sukkot. Apparently uncomfortable with this festival's origin as a commemoration of a military victory and the celebration of the ascension of a specific family to the throne, the Rabbis transformed it into a celebration of God's miraculous power. The menorah is to be lit to commemorate God's stretching of the limited pure oil for eight days until more pure oil for the Temple service could be found. The Hasmoneans at best play a supporting role in their rendition of the holiday.

Tisha b'Av, the ninth day of the Hebrew month of Av (July or August), commemorates the destruction of the First and Second Temple. It is the only other twenty-five-hour fast day in addition to Yom Kippur. Just one of a historically expansive and shifting list of commemorations of national tragedies, Tisha b'Av became a magnet, a kind of grand commemoration of all of Israel's national tragedies. Although the Rabbis prescribe the same regimen of abstinence for Tisha b'Av as they do for Yom Kippur, it remains a minor holiday on which work is permitted. Traditionally the biblical book of Lamentations is recited on it. There are a number of minor fasts (no food or drink only during daylight hours) scattered through the calendar, almost all of which commemorate ancient historical catastrophes.

Purim is the polar opposite of Tisha b'Av. It is a minor festival of historical victory. The biblical book of Esther is read on it, an almost farcical story about the unlikely salvation of the Jews from an evil plot to destroy them—whether there is any historical basis to it is a matter of debate. The primary rabbinic concern is with the ways in which Esther is written and read; the legal technicalities. Because Purim falls one month before Passover, it also tends to get pulled into its orbit, beginning a time of preparation.

Aside from the High Holy Days, the Jewish liturgical calendar is strikingly historical. Each holiday, with its accompanying rituals, relives a historical paradigm. This need not be the case: Some societies celebrate mythological events (that is, things that happen in the supernatural world), and the American holiday calendar contains several ahistorical commemorations (e.g., Labor Day, Veterans Day, Memorial Day). To live through the Jewish year is to live through, even enact, Israel's mythic past. The historical drama of creation, redemption from Egypt, revelation (to a limited degree), and exile from the destroyed Temple is condensed into a single year, or even a single day each week. While each holiday has a predominant theme, elements of all these themes inhere in each holiday—and all point toward a redemptive future.

Whereas the Rabbis carefully structure and regulate the rhythms of annual time, they are much looser about life cycle events. As Arnold van Gennep argued long ago, life cycle rituals are almost always marked with rituals of separation, transition, and incorporation. A person is separated from his or her previous status, marks the movement to the new status with rituals that emphasize that one is "betwixt and between," and is then incorporated into the community of those who share this new status.[6] Seen against this nearly universal pattern, the rabbinic life cycle rituals are surprisingly thin and incoherent. Their interest in these events is limited to areas in which they intersect with other areas of law. Their focus on circumcision, for example, relates directly to the commandment to circumcise as a sign of the covenant rather than to its function as a birth or initiation ritual. Correspondingly, the birth of girls, for whom there are no distinctive legal issues, receive no rabbinic notice at all.

As in the Torah, rabbinic circumcision (*brit milah*) ideally takes place for Jewish boys when they are eight days old. As expected, whereas the Torah merely specifies that such children are to be circumcised, without providing the technical details, the Rabbis focus their attention precisely on these technical details. They discuss how much of the foreskin must be removed, in what fashion, and the need to draw at least a drop of blood from the wound. The Rabbis demand this final requirement not only from Jewish boys but also from previously circumcised male converts to Judaism. Yet although circumcision does mark a movement, especially for the convert, into the community of the covenant, the Rabbis regulate none of the other rituals that may accompany it.

Puberty, which we mark today with a wide variety of religious and secular rituals (e.g., a bar/bat mitzvah, confirmation, sweet sixteen, or prom) is not signaled at all by the Rabbis. The ages of twelve for a girl and thirteen for a boy are legally important: At those ages they bear full responsibility for observance of the commandments and are equally subject to the full force of its penalties. For the Rabbis, however, the movement to this new status is a technical, legal event. Although they discuss a few rituals related to the start of formal schooling, they generally ignore childhood rituals.[7]

Similarly, their interest in marriage is generally legal and technical. Marriage is a legal state with legal repercussions and thus demands objective standards to constitute it. For the Rabbis the (primary) defining act is the transfer of an object of value from a man to a woman with proper intention and in front of witnesses. Today frequently the object is a ring, but it could just as well be a coin or a jug of beer. Intention is usually indicated with the recital of a short formula: "With this [object], you are betrothed to me according to the law of Moses and Israel." From that moment on, the couple is legally married. The Rabbis then require the recitation of a set of blessings and the signing of a prenuptial economic agreement (the *ketubba*) before cohabitation and sexual relations.[8]

Perhaps the most important ramification of marriage is adultery. The Rabbis follow the Torah in defining adultery as sex between a man and a woman married to another man. That is, a man commits adultery only if he has sex with another man's wife; his own marital status is irrelevant. But a married woman commits adultery whenever she has sex outside her marriage, and the Torah makes the adulterous couple liable for death. Precisely defining when a marriage begins and ends takes on capital importance.

While the formation of marriage requires mutual consent in rabbinic law, divorce does not. As a legal act, rabbinic divorce is unilateral: A man delivers a document of divorce (*get*) to his wife. A woman cannot legally divorce without her husband's consent. One of the results of this asymmetry is the problem of the *agunah*, or "anchored woman."[9] If a woman wants a divorce but her husband, for whatever reason (e.g., spite or demands of a more advantageous divorce settlement), refuses to give it to her, she is forbidden to remarry (or have sex with any other man) until he relents. Or, if he disappears or becomes mentally incompetent and is thus unable to initiate the divorce, she is similarly anchored. On the other hand, because the Rabbis, like the Torah, assume a polygamous society, a husband is free to take another wife whether or not he divorces.

The Rabbis extensively discuss and expand the Torah's prohibition of sex with a menstruant (*niddah*). They transform what appears to be a simple purity regulation into a sexual one, in which purity per se is secondary: sexual relations during menstruation are prohibited simply because the Torah says so, not because such relations convey impurity. The Rabbis extensively discuss what defines a "menstruating" woman (i.e., whence the blood needs to flow and how to know), with whom they prohibit all forms of sexual contact. They also expand the Torah's prohibition to include seven "white days" following the end of menstruation. After a woman's period has ceased she is to wait for one week without the emission of any blood before immersing in a ritual bath, the mikveh. The mikveh, according to the Rabbis, must contain a specified quantity of "living water," usually drawn from naturally collected rainwater and then mixed with previously stored (or, today, tap) water. Also used to complete a conversion to Judaism, immersion in the mikveh marks a change of status. Only then is the couple free to resume sexual relations.

The Rabbis, as well as many later Jews and modern scholars, have offered a plethora of explanations for this set of regulations. One rabbinic explanation is that it is beneficial precisely because it limits sexual relations, which they generally viewed positively, if with some ambivalence. Later commentators point to the fact that a couple resumes sexual relations close to the time of a woman's ovulation as evidence for the rabbinic emphasis on procreation. In fact, the Rabbis believed that a woman was most fertile immediately before her period. Again, there is an underdetermined element in these practices that can, and have, lent themselves to a wide variety of explanations.

Whether or not the timing of the resumption of sexual activities was in any way linked to procreation, the Rabbis (like their counterparts throughout the Roman world) did indeed emphasize the importance of procreation.[10] The ancient schools of Hillel and Shammai disagree about whether a man is obligated to produce two boys or one boy and one girl, but agree that there is a minimum requirement of two children. Some later Rabbis suggest that a man is obligated to keep producing children; the legal obligation is centered on the man. The issue of procreation is of course linked to birth control, on which the Rabbis leave a conflicting legacy. Some Rabbis assume that couples will practice birth control, while others forbid the "wasteful emission of semen." They never explicitly extend this prohibition, stated in the context of male masturbation, to marital sexual relations, but it is easy to see how later rabbis inferred from it a prohibition on most forms of barrier birth control.

While the Rabbis see marriage as the only conceivable context for the production and rearing of children, perhaps surprisingly, marriage has no actual legal bearing on the status of a child. There is no category of illegitimate or bastard child in rabbinic law in the way that we frame this status. Illegitimate children have exactly the same legal status, rights, and responsibilities as children produced in marriage. According to the Rabbis, the child of a Jewish mother, from any father and in (almost) any relationship, is Jewish.

The exception to this general statement, the *mamzer*, is worth a side discussion. The word *mamzer* occurs twice in the Tanak, and neither occurrence much illuminates its meaning. According to Deuteronomy 23:3, "No *mamzer* shall be admitted into the congregation of the Lord; none of his descendants, even in the tenth generation, shall be admitted into the congregation of the Lord." Not only is the term *mamzer* obscure, but the restriction is as well. What does it mean to be excluded from the congregation of the Lord? Throughout the Second Temple period both the definition of a *mamzer* and the meaning of the restriction were debated. The Rabbis too debate the meaning of a *mamzer*, but ultimately settle on defining it as a child of an adulterous or incestuous relationship. A full Jew in every other way, a *mamzer* (male or female) was forbidden from marrying another Jew who was not a *mamzer*.

It is possible that the Rabbis derived this understanding of the term *mamzer* from popular Jewish understandings. Such children, like slaves, may have been seen as having "bad blood." The Rabbis would here have added legal precision and ramifications to a popular usage. They may even have been trying to mitigate the social effects of the usage, both by limiting it to a very narrow class of people as well as by affirming the mamzer's Jewishness, restricting the liability just to the domain of marriage.

While the impact (if any) of this rabbinic legal definition on their own social environments can no longer be recovered, it has had later ramifications that the Rabbis could not have foreseen. According to rabbinic law, any woman who is not divorced through a proper document of divorce (the get) remains married. If she receives a civil divorce but not a get, or a get that some rabbis see as not valid according to Jewish law, and she then remarries and has children, those children are accounted as *mamzerim*.

The problem of the mamzer is a more serious one than that of marriage to a non-Jew, because while the latter (and her children) can always convert the mamzer bears a permanent disability. Due to the serious nature of this disability and the frequency with which exactly such scenarios take place in modern-day America, contemporary rabbis have gone to great lengths to "eliminate" the category of the mamzer. One of the easiest legal ways to do this is to annul the original marriage; since there never was a marriage there could be no adultery. Hence, when a prominent Orthodox rabbi declared that weddings conducted under Reform and Conservative rabbinic supervision were not valid under Jewish law, his motivation was less to disparage these rabbis (although I am sure that he did not mind doing this) than to deal with the problem of the mamzer.

Outside technical legal discussions that define such categories as the mamzer, the Rabbis do not concern themselves with the Jewish wedding. Clearly there were popular wedding customs, but these never gain the authority of law in rabbinic texts. This, in part, accounts for the enormous diversity of Jewish wedding customs throughout history, all of which could (at least in theory) punctiliously follow rabbinic law. The rituals that turn a wedding from a legal act into a life cycle event are left relatively unregulated. Even the breaking of the glass at the end of many modern Jewish weddings was unknown to the Rabbis.

Death too receives scant and incidental rabbinic notice. The most extensive rabbinic treatment of death and its rituals arises incidentally from a discussion of proper mourning practices on the intermediate days of festivals. This treatment is a potpourri of assorted mourning practices (e.g., the ripping of a garment at the death of a close relative or communal leader) and periods and the impact of Shabbat and holidays on them. They have little to say about the treatment of the body and its burial; these are elaborated in the early Middle Ages. Instead they focus on the mourning periods. For most close relatives they prescribe a seven-day intensive mourning period (the *shiva*), to which many of the fast abstentions apply. This is then folded into a thirty-day period (*sheloshim*), which (after the shiva) requires a lower level of abstention. For all except a parent, the formal and ritualized mourning period ends at the end of the sheloshim. For parents, it continues for eleven months.

Of all of these rabbinic life cycle events, van Gennep's schema can be applied usefully only to death, and then only to the mourner rather than the deceased. The mourner is separated, goes through a transition period, and is then reintegrated back into society.

Here it is important to distinguish the rabbinic prescriptions of these events from their actual practice and understanding in their society. Rabbinic literature hints at many popular practices that indicate that most people did treat these events as part of the life cycle, not just as legal technicalities. Marriage was accompanied by rituals, including the singing of bawdy songs that in some areas emphasized the bride's transition to womanhood. We get a faint glimpse of birth rituals that acknowledge the birth of a child and his (but not her) integration into the community of Israel. Although they occasionally appear in the pages of the Talmud and other rabbinic literature, these rituals rarely gain the status of law.

In their literature, ways of discussing things, concepts, and rituals the Rabbis set the parameters of a conversation that continues to this day. The Judaism of the Rabbis was neither neat nor incoherent, and both of these conditions contributed to its success.

It is precisely the riot of voices that emerge from rabbinic literature, the contradictions in their concepts and the underdetermined quality of much of their ritual that will later allow for such broad Jewish diversity. Rather than laying out a unified dogma, the Rabbis created a dense web of ideas, texts, and rituals that can be combined, broken, and recombined in ways limited only by human imagination. Or, to use another metaphor, the rabbinic legacy is an enormous toolbox, a set of resources for future Jews.

The Judaism of the Rabbis, in all its messiness, was normative in only one specific sense: the Rabbis themselves declared it so. Prescription is not description, though, and both the rabbinic concepts and rituals were always in tension with what Jews actually did or did not do. Most Jews at that time probably paid little attention to the Rabbis, their ideas and their rituals, although they might well have engaged in some general way in the practices that the Rabbis discussed.

So if rabbinic Judaism was extraordinarily diverse (or, one might say, diffuse), created in response to specific historical needs that have long since passed and virtually ignored by Jews at that time, why did it not only survive but in fact shape nearly all future Jewish religious life? The genius of the Rabbis was their ability to simultaneously articulate a normative vision of Judaism while vastly expanding the bounds of what can count as normative. The Rabbis make a general claim to authority from Mount Sinai, where both the textual traditions and the modes of interpreting them were revealed by God. But this claim is *general*, not a claim of divine origin for each specific rabbinic statement. The resources they created are so rich that they can—within some important limits—be used to authorize many diverse religious ideas and practices and combinations thereof. That is precisely what began to happen during the period of the geonim.

7

THE RISE OF REASON

I N 640 THE light of Byzantium flickered and went out.

This, in any case, was how at least one Jewish liturgical poet in Palestine saw the Arab invasion, and the prospect delighted him. Jewish life under the Christian emperors had grown increasingly difficult. From their origins Christians had had a problem with the Jews and their religion, all the more so because the first Christians were in fact Jews. Not only was Jesus a Jew but his story—the meaning of his life, as understood by his followers—made no sense without the Hebrew Bible. The Christian story *requires* an Israel with whom God has, or had, a covenanted relationship. Jesus fulfills the ancient prophecies of the Hebrew Bible even as he supersedes the old covenant. Neither the Gospels nor Paul are comprehensible without the background of what they called the Old Testament.

Real Jews posed a puzzle for early Christian thinkers. If Jesus was the messiah of Israel foretold in Jewish Holy Scriptures, why did the Jews not only reject him but even collude in his execution? And if God had severed His covenant with the Jews and transferred His grace to His new people, those who accepted Jesus as His messiah, why did the Jews persist, seemingly oblivious to this ontological change?

This was a major intellectual problem whose solution had serious social ramifications. In the first two centuries of the Common Era, Christian self-definition was at stake. Did one need to be a good Jew in order to be a good Christian? Could one even be a "Christian" without being a Jew? The nature of the Christian mission hinged on these answers. Ultimately, of course, many early adherents rejected the idea that one needed to be a Jew to be a

Christian and sought converts among non-Jews. By the late second and early third centuries CE, Gentile Christians outnumbered Jewish Christians.

In the best of circumstances the establishment of a self-identity is a tricky business, and in the case of Christians in the second and third centuries it was complicated by increasing Roman hostility to Christianity. The Romans legally recognized the Jews; they may not all or always have liked them, but they grudgingly acknowledged their antiquity and their rights to follow their ancestral traditions. Typically the Romans exempted the Jews from acts that went against their ancient practices: for example, sacrificing or swearing an oath of loyalty to the emperor. As a people now covenanted, through Christ, to God, Christians too could not participate in these activities. But as Christians, *not* Jews, they received no legal accommodation from the Romans. Quite the reverse: the Romans, for whom "new" equaled "bad," were naturally suspicious of Christians as adherents of a new religion. Christians could thus find firm ground on either side, but it meant either becoming "Jewish" or participating in activities and sacrifices that they labeled "pagan"—in the middle, though, they dangled.

By the mid-fourth century the situation had changed completely. Now Christianity was not only licit but the religion of the emperors. This led into further uncharted territory: What did it mean to build a Christian society, a "city of God" here on earth? And what role could Jews have in such a society?[1]

For Augustine, who lived in the fifth century in North Africa, Jews were an indispensable part of Christian society. Jews, he argued, served two important roles. First, they preserved and testified to the truth of the Old Testament and its prophecies (in Augustine's reading) about Jesus. Second, by remaining stubbornly stuck in "useless antiquity," they will be living witnesses to the ultimate truth and splendor of Christ. Their refusal to acknowledge Christ will, ironically, serve to testify for Him. Because they play these crucial theological roles, Augustine argues, Jews should not be harmed. Their societal roles might be limited, but they should not be physically assaulted or killed.

Indeed, the Christian emperors (no doubt for their own reasons, which were very different from Augustine's) consistently condemned assaults on Jews. This, however, meant neither that Jews maintained the status they had previously nor that they were physically secure. Within early Byzantine law Jew became a distinct legal category, one whose rights were increasingly circumscribed. Jews were prohibited from owning Christian slaves, from marrying Christians, and from discriminating against Jewish converts to Christianity. The patriarchate was stripped of its ability to collect taxes, demoted in status, and by the fifth century abolished. In the sixth century Jews officially gained inferior status in courts of law when one party was (an "Orthodox") Christian.

Jews may have rarely been subjected to "official" violence, but it is clear that the officials could be lax about protecting them from the mob. "It seems right that in the future," an imperial legislation from 423 states,

> None of the synagogues of the Jews should be indiscriminately seized or put on fire. If there are some synagogues that were seized or vindicated to churches or indeed consecrated to the venerable mysteries in a recent undertaking and after the law was passed, they shall be given in exchange new places, on which they could build.[2]

Fifteen years later the emperors reiterated their permission to Jews to repair their synagogues, but "they shall not dare to construct anew any synagogue."[3] Despite its tendentiousness, a letter that describes Christian mob violence against Jewish synagogues on the island of Minorca in 418 most likely minimizes, if anything, the damage inflicted upon the Jewish community there.[4]

Legally, Jews were no better off under Muslim rule. They remained a protected legal minority. According to Muslim political theory, both Jews and Christians at some earlier point received authentic revelations from God, which they recorded in their sacred texts. Although these sacred texts, some Muslims asserted, were hopelessly corrupted in transmission (others argued that they are faithful records but had since been superseded)—thus necessitating God's revelations to the prophet Muhammad—they and their readers retained some degree of sanctity. These early Muslims were the first to characterize Jews (and Christians) as "People of the Book," which combined with their monotheism earned them the right to live unmolested in Muslim society. These *dhimmi*, legally protected religious minorities, had to pay taxes to the Muslim authorities and adhere to other legal and economic restrictions, but, unlike other the adherents of non-Abrahamic religious traditions, they were allowed to continue their religious practices.

Jews are not portrayed much better in the Quran than they are in the New Testament. Jews are opponents of Muhammad and frequently scheme against him. Among the *hadith*—the non-Quranic Islamic traditions about the prophet Muhammad—Jews frequently appear as plotters against Islam. These texts and traditions never necessarily led to the persecution of Jews, but they supply, just like the New Testament, incendiary "prooftexts" for those inclined to engage in them.

Despite these similarities between Christian and Muslim evaluations of Jews and Judaism, the Jewish relationship with their Muslim overlords appears to have been less strained and adversarial than it was under the Christians. Through the Middle Ages there is little evidence of Muslims attacking Jews and their synagogues. Jews tended to have more legal freedom under Muslim rule, which led to increased economic, social, and intellectual contact between Jews and Muslims.

The impact of these contacts was immense, but they did not happen quickly. It took time to translate the rapid military conquest of North Africa and the Middle East into effective political rule; all the more so into cultural and intellectual shifts. The classical Greek and Roman cities long kept much of their character; only gradually did they lose their square layout and open communal spaces. It took over a century to move from Greek to Arabic as the official language.

Perhaps the most dramatic example of early Muslim impact on the Jews is the development of Karaism. Traditional Karaite historiography traces their origin back to a mid-eighth-century Persian Jew named Anan ben David who was alarmed by the growing divergence between the Hebrew Bible and the traditions of the Rabbis, as he understood both. His response was to reject the literature and interpretations of the Rabbis in order to return to Scripture. Over the next three centuries there developed a lively and bitter polemic between the Karaite and the Rabbanite Jews, as the followers of rabbinic Judaism were called. One Karaite writer summarizes the argument with the Rabbanites:

> We say that these (people) whose way is blameless belong to the Karaite sect who hold fast to the Lord's Torah, who abandon the "commandment of the men learned by rote," and who do not rely upon the Mishnah and the Talmud, the laws and legends, which are full of erroneous statements contrary to the Lord's Torah.[5]

The "commandment of the men learned by rote" stands, of course, for the Rabbanites. Japheth b. Eli echoes a familiar Karaite refrain in rejecting the traditions of the Rabbis. Other Karaite writers emphasize the importance of individual grappling with Scripture.

Pure scripturalism, of course, is impossible; the Hebrew Bible is simply too cryptic and contradictory to respond to the more mundane issues that arise while attempting to live according to its dictates. Recognizing the need to flesh out and resolve the tensions within the biblical text, in 770 Anan ben David authored a guide for living, entitled *Sefer HaMitzvot* (The Book of Commandments). In it he draws out his own set of mitzvot from Scripture alone. Predictably, his mitzvot are often at odds with those of the Rabbis. About the use of fire on Shabbat, for example, he writes:

> One might perhaps say that it is only the kindling of fire on the Sabbath which is forbidden, and that if the fire had been kindled on the preceding weekday it is to be considered lawful to let it remain over the Sabbath. Now the Merciful One has written here: "Ye shall not kindle fire" (Exodus 35:3), and elsewhere: "thou shalt not perform any work" (Exodus 20:10), and both prohibitions begin with the letter *taw*. In the case of labor, of which it is written, "thou shalt not perform any work," it is evident that even if the work was begun on a weekday, before the arrival of the Sabbath, it is necessary to desist from it with the arrival of the Sabbath. The same rule must therefore apply also to the kindling of fire, of which it is written: "Ye shall not kindle," meaning that even if fire has been kindled on a weekday, prior to the arrival of the Sabbath, it must be extinguished.[6]

Anan's interpretative technique looks suspiciously like Rabbanite halakhic midrash. He has related two biblical verses and drawn a logical analogy, using the clearer legal conclusions that derive from one verse (Exodus 20:10) to inform the other. Anan offered such an extended justification for this mitzvah precisely because it goes against the halakhah of the Rabbis, which allows for the use of fires that had been kindled before Shabbat on the Sabbath itself.

Sabbath laws were but one area in which Karaite halakhah diverged from its rabbinic counterpart. Their different understanding of the laws regarding incest made marriage difficult between Karaites and Rabbanites; perhaps that was one of the goals behind the different formulation of these laws. The Karaite halakhic books allow the eating together of fowl and dairy products, but Anan forbids the consumption of all birds other than the pigeon and turtledove, the only two ritually pure birds that were sacrificed on the Temple's altar. They have no mikveh, and their rules regarding purity (especially menstrual purity) are far stricter than those of the Rabbis.

In their eyes, Anan ben David and his followers were reclaiming the sacred core of Judaism. It would be another century or so after Anan until they would call themselves "Karaites," drawing on a Hebrew root used for Scripture. The Judaism of their rabbinic contemporaries was just as heretical in their eyes as their Judaism was to the rabbis. Seen through rabbinic eyes, they were a dangerous and deviant sect. Their challenge to rabbinic authority was real, and their following deep. Strong and probably large Karaite communities existed throughout the Middle Ages; many documents from a Karaite community in Cairo that ended up in a local synagogue (and were found in the Cairo Genizah collection) testify to the community's continuing vitality. Today there are still several thousand Karaites, living mainly in Israel.

Karaism was very much a product of its time. Its social and cultural location in Iraq and Iran in the early Middle Ages accounts for both its unique characteristics and its popularity. Throughout the early Middle Ages Muslim theologians were wrestling with the authority of the hadith vis-à-vis the Quran. Islamic scripturalists rejected the hadith as a source of independent authority; all authority was invested in the Quran alone. Karaism's insistence on the authority of the Hebrew Bible and the lack of authority of rabbinic tradition is analogous.[7] The traditionalists in both camps emerged victorious, but the two faced a similar challenge.

In a more general way, however, Karaism also refracts its understanding of Judaism through a wider cultural lens. For Muslims Jews were distinctive because they, like Muslims, possessed a written account of a genuine revelation. The difference, according to some Muslims, was that the Jewish account was corrupted and inaccurate. To ascertain and preserve the authenticity of their own traditions, Muslim theologians and writers were greatly concerned with keeping track of their own chains of transmissions. Thus every classical hadith is accompanied by a list that details who heard the hadith from whom, going all the way back to its origin.

For the Karaites the Rabbis and their traditions implicitly subverted the authority of Scripture and threatened the authenticity of living according to God's will. Karaism is an almost natural outgrowth from a society that emphasizes the authority and authenticity of scriptural records of revelation. Jews should read the Bible just as Muslims read the Quran. Many Jews in Islamic lands would have instinctively understood and been sympathetic to the Karaite approach to the Tanak, even if they were unaware of the theological battles between Islamic scripturalists and traditionalists.

7.1 A Karaite betrothal document from around 1030 CE, found at the Cairo Geniza.
Courtesy of the Library of the Jewish Theological Seminary of America

The battle between the Karaites and the Rabbanites was on one level a struggle for power. Both claimed the authority to serve as Israel's spiritual leaders, with its official recognition by the Muslim overlords and the perks that go with this recognition. On another level, though, it was also a battle for the shape of Israel's textual tradition. Well into the Muslim period the Rabbis and their legacy had still not "won." Perhaps ironically, it was precisely the Karaite challenge to the Rabbanites that may have led to the latter's victory. Forced to consolidate their political power as well as to thoughtfully work out and clarify their positions in order to respond creatively to the Karaites, the Rabbanites assured the place of the messy legacy of the Rabbis in Israel's textual tradition.

◈ ◈ ◈ ◈ ◈

Although perhaps a little less obviously, the rabbis and their followers no less than the Karaites refracted their textual traditions and rituals through the prism of the developing cultural norms and values of Islamic society. While there are clear lines of continuity between the classical Rabbis and the later rabbis who worked in Islamic lands, the latter profoundly transformed their organizational, textual, and conceptual inheritance.

Throughout late antiquity the Rabbis appear to have worked primarily in small study circles, both in the land of Israel and in Babylonia. Toward the end of this period larger rabbinic academies may have begun to develop in both locales: Tiberias in Palestine and, in Babylonia, in the two nearby cities on the Euphrates, Pumbedita and Sura. Whatever the origins and scope of these academies, they achieved prominence only after 640 CE.

The organization and activities of the rabbinic academy in Tiberias remain obscure. It had an active group of scholars that sought to promote their halakhic opinions to a wider Jewish community but was fatally outmaneuvered by the Babylonian competition. The greatest legacy of this community is the Masoretic Text: the Masoretes were a group of scholars who produced a canonical version of the Hebrew Bible with vowels and cantillation. This canonization of the vowels of the text and systematization of the cantillation—articulated in a tenth-century tract by Aaron Ben Asher—was consistent with the general trend toward canonization that became characteristic of the Babylonian academies.

Whatever its pre-Islamic structure and organization, the geonic academies in Babylonia must be seen as developing in tandem with the emerging Islamic religious academies. These Babylonian academies were rigidly hierarchical. Rabbis were ranked according to their knowledge (at least in theory); at the head of each academy stood the geon. The two (sometimes there were one or two others at more minor academies) geons (geonim) stood in a complex and sometimes tense relationship with each other, the Palestinian academy, and the exilarch, the political appointee who officially represented the Jews before the Islamic ruler.

The geonic academies were quite different from modern yeshivas or universities. Most of the rabbis attached to each academy would spend the greater part of the year at their homes, studying a designated tractate of the Talmud. Once or twice yearly they would gather for a week or two, reviewing their learning and listening to the geon lecture. They would also be tested, their stipends adjusted accordingly.

This geonic emphasis on the study of the Babylonian Talmud was the first step toward its inclusion among the sacred books of the Jews. When,

why, and how the Talmud was redacted is yet another subject of continuing scholarly debate. It is clear, though, that the geonim received a version
of the Talmud that more or less resembles the form and wording of the one
used today. They then set to work solidifying and explicating it, carefully
separating what they increasingly saw as the sacred text of the Talmud itself from their own use of and additions to that text. The process, in other
words, is similar to that of earlier sacred texts that "back-canonize" the texts
upon which they comment and rely.

Why, though, did the geonim treat the Talmud like this? In part, it is
because they inherited this text from the amoraim and the anonymous
rabbis who followed them. The Babylonian Talmud represents the sole
surviving legacy of the Babylonian amoraim; unlike the Palestinian amoraim, they never produced independent collections of midrash. While
the Babylonian Talmud never presents itself as a canonical or authoritative text (although the Rabbis in it do sometimes claim this authority for
their own views), it was a substantial body of hoary material that could
not be ignored.

But the geonic treatment of the Talmud was not predetermined either.
It is possible that despite the many differences between the two literatures,
the geonim saw the Talmud as the functional equivalent of the hadith. Just
as Islam had a set of extrascriptural traditions that they treated textually
and to which they gave independent authority, so too the geonim began to
see the Talmud as a text with its own integrity and authority.

The analogy between Islamic views of the hadith and the geonic understanding of the Talmud in fact runs deeper. Muslims used the hadith as a
source of religious law; they read them not for simple edification but to
learn how God, through the prophet, wanted them to live. Similarly, the
geonim read the Talmud not as the odd literary work that it is, but as a legal
guide. This would be the Jewish hadith, the authoritative extracanonical
text that helps to guide a life lived according to the will of God.

The problem is that despite its size and complexity the Talmud is not a
legal guide and does not have the directness of the hadith. It is no easier to
live according to the Talmud than it is to live according to the Tanak. In fact,
it might be a good deal harder.

To respond to this problem, the geonim institutionalized a new legal
genre, the responsum (*teshuvah*, "answer," the same word used for "turning
back, repentence"). Earlier rabbinic literature records the practice of Jews
asking local rabbis for legal rulings that were to be—at least in the eyes of
the Rabbis—legally binding on the individual. There is no evidence, though,

that there was a more formal procedure in which a rabbi was asked to deliver a written legal opinion that justifies its legal reasoning.

Muslim scholars, the *ulama*, were developing precisely this legal institution during the geonic period. The *fatwa* is a justified ruling, sometimes written, that usually responds to a legal question. Usually the procedure would be for an individual or local cleric (*imam*) to submit a question to a more recognized scholar. The scholar would then issue a written response justified with citations from authoritative texts (e.g., the Quran and hadith). Muslims were then free to accept this opinion or not depending on its persuasiveness, the status of its author, or any number of other factors.

If the organization of the geonic academies can be seen as roughly analogous to the academies of the ulama, so too can the development of their primary activity, the production of responsa. In what most likely began as a local activity, individuals would submit questions to the academies. These questions—or at least the harder ones—would be taken up when the academies were in session, discussed and debated before the geon who would ultimately issue his opinion, which would be recorded. Unlike the fatwa, the geonic responsa were understood (at least by the rabbis who issued them) to be binding upon the individual who submitted the question, although this authority did not automatically extend to others.

Due to a combination of political factors, this activity quickly spread from its local origins, in and around Baghdad, throughout the wide-ranging 'Abbasid Empire. In 750 CE power over the Islamic empire moved from the Umayyads in Damascus to the 'Abbasid dynasty in Iraq. Suddenly, the exilarch and geonic activities found themselves at the center of a vast empire. They thus became the beneficiaries not only of the cultural and intellectual explosion occurring around them but also of easier access to the centers of power. To use an anachronistic phrase, they were on the radar screen.

Although a few surviving responsa predate the rise of the 'Abbasids, the vast majority of geonic responsa were produced after 750 CE. Communities, mainly from North Africa (which was part of the 'Abbasid Empire), would send their questions to the geonim. There can be little doubt that their location near Baghdad gave them an advantage in their competition with the rabbis of Palestine. Rabbis in both communities apparently keenly felt this competition. As early as 760 CE Babylonian rabbis were actively promoting themselves over their Palestinian peers. One open letter by a Babylonian named Pirqoy ben Baboy states:

Even in the days of the Messiah, they (the Babylonian academies) will not experience the travail of the Messiah, for it is written (Zechariah 2:11) "O Zion, escape, you who dwell in Babylonia," . . . and Zion is nothing but the academy, which is distinguished in Torah and precepts, as it is written (Micah 4:10), "Writhe and cry out, daughter of Zion, like a woman in childbirth, for now you shall depart the city and dwell in the field and go to Babylonia; there you will be saved, and thence will God redeem you from the hand of your enemies." And redemption will come first to the academy of Babylonia; for, as Israel is redeemed by their (the academies') virtue, redemption comes first to them.[8]

This thoroughly polemical passage completely degrades the contemporary rabbis of Palestine. "Zion," the privileged and promised land of the Tanak, no longer refers to a concrete and unchanging geographical location but instead to the place of greatest Torah learning, that is, Babylonia. This assertion, which builds upon a sentiment found also in the Babylonian Talmud, boldly transfers the biblical promises and blessings from Palestine to Babylonia.[9] Not only was this thought to be effective propaganda, but it no doubt also reflected what the geonim really believed: They were living in the real promised land.

The responsa cover a wide variety of issues. North African communities had copies of the Babylonian Talmud, and they turned to the geonim for clarifications of both its text and meaning. Occasionally they asked theological questions. It is precisely in the questions, rather than answers, that we can begin to develop a sense of contemporary Jewish concerns. One such concern was the formalization of prayer.

The Talmud and other classical rabbinic literature formalize prayer in a general fashion. It dictates mandatory times for prayer, lists some mandatory prayers, and gives guidelines concerning their language. However, the precise language of prayer was left to the community and/or individual. This early fluidity led even rabbinic Jews to develop innovative prayers, as shown by the rich variety of the surviving liturgical poetry, or *piyyut*. These *piyyutim* were composed for specific, sometimes one-time performances, and are characterized by their allusiveness and frequently deep knowledge of rabbinic traditions. Even the weekly liturgical readings from the Torah were fluid, with Palestinian Jews generally preferring a triennial cycle—completing the entire Torah once every three years—and Babylonians an annual cycle. These decisions too, though, must have varied locally.

Both local Jews and the geonim apparently were growing uncomfortable with this fluidity. A request from a Spanish Jew sometime between 857 and 875 gave a renegade geon, Amram ben Sheshna, an opportunity to promulgate "an order of prayers and benedictions for the entire year." To the extent that we can reconstruct his answer to this request (the manuscripts are badly corrupted), it appears that he attempted to produce a canonical prayer book, one that not only provided basic prayer rubrics but also the precise language itself. Clearly Amram did not create this full liturgy on the spot; it almost certainly culminated an ongoing attempt on the part of the geonim to standardize prayer.[10] Such an attempt, perhaps not incidentally, would have brought Jewish worship in line with the detailed Islamic *salat*, or liturgy, which had also recently undergone a process of standardization.

Amram's *seder* ("order," from whose root comes the term *siddur*, later used to denote a Jewish prayer book) was soon eclipsed by that of arguably the greatest geon, Se'adyah ben Joseph. Born in Egypt, Se'adyah moved to Babylonia where he quickly rose to the position of the geon of Sura, serving from 928–942 CE. His relationship with the exilarch was exceptionally rocky, and he resisted efforts to depose him. Despite his political difficulties, Se'adyah was by far the most prolific of the geonim, not only advancing trends that were already in motion but also expanding geonic activities into new arenas.

Se'adyah's prayer book was a monograph produced at the author's own initiative rather than as a response to a request or question. The monograph is remarkable not only as our best extant witness to the early canonization of Jewish liturgy but also for its explicitly popular audience. Here Se'adyah self-consciously abandons his usual custom of providing prooftexts: "Rather, I will bring for all of this only undocumented, precisely formulated statements, because I composed this treatise not for (purposes of) proof, but for instruction."[11] This goal is also reflected in the instructions of the prayer book, which he writes in Judeo-Arabic, a dialect of Arabic written in Hebrew letters. By the tenth century, Jews in Islamic lands had turned to Arabic as their lingua franca, relegating Hebrew (which many probably did not understand) to liturgical functions.

As for all of the other geonim, the bulk of Se'adyah's time was most likely spent responding to requests for halakhic guidance. Ultimately, the proportion of questions addressed to the geonim that deal with academic or theological matters was small when compared to those that ask specific and applied questions of Jewish law. The geonim fielded questions of ritual, personal, and civil law. Some of these questions depended little on historical context and were part of the geonic attempt to standardize Jewish practice. Others, such as the permissibility of doing business on a specific non-Jewish holiday or how to treat apostate Jews, had very specific historical contexts.

Geonim were not shy about acting as legal innovators when they felt the times demanded it. They assumed that they had the authority to enact decrees that might even go against traditions in the Talmud. The first such decree was issued in 650/51 CE, and concerned the "rebellious wife." A later responsum, by Rav Sherira Geon (fl. 968–1004), refers to it:

As to your question, concerning a woman living with her husband, who says to him, "Divorce me! I do not wish to live with you!"—is he required to give her something from her *ketubah* or not? Is such a woman considered rebellious or not? We have seen that, by the letter of the law, we do not oblige the husband to divorce his wife when she sues for divorce, except in those cases where our Sages stated that it is incumbent on him to divorce her (*M. Ket.* 7:10). . . .

Later they enacted another *takkanah*, that the court should issue a proclamation concerning her for four consecutive weeks, and the court should admonish her: "Know that even if your *ketubah* amounts to one hundred *maneh*, you have forfeited it. . . . "

Finally, they enacted that the proclamation be issued for four weeks and she forfeits everything; nevertheless, the husband was not obliged to grant her a divorce. . . .

It was then enacted that she should be kept waiting for twelve months without a divorce, in the hope that she might be placated. But after twelve months, the husband is forced to grant her a divorce. Later, our Sages the *Saboraim* realized that the daughters of Israel were appealing to the gentile courts to obtain a coerced divorce from their husbands, and some were divorcing their wives under duress, resulting in doubts concerning the validity of such a divorce, creating a calamitous situation. Accordingly, in the time of Mar Rav Rabbah [and] Mar Rav Hunai, may they rest in peace, it was enacted that a rebellious wife suing for divorce should receive intact all the "property of iron sheep" that she had brought with her, and that the husband should make good all destroyed or lost property. But whatever he himself undertook to bestow upon her, whether yet extant or not, he need not pay her, and if she should seize any such assets [the court] will confiscate them and restore them to the husband. As to the husband, we force him to write her an immediate write of divorce, and she is entitled to the [statutory payment] of 100 or 200 *zuzim*. This has been our custom now for more than three hundred years, and you, too, should do so.[12]

This responsum, and the decree (*takkanah*) upon which it is based, tries to negotiate between a tricky legal problem and a concrete historical one. In Talmudic law a woman brings a dowry (which might contain "property of iron sheep," i.e., property of which the husband can enjoy use and profit but that he is not allowed to alter or alienate) into a marriage. Additionally, the groom pledges a monetary sum to be paid to his wife (or heirs) upon the dissolution of the marriage. This pledge is known as the *ketubbah*, and if its amount is not stipulated it is a statutory 100 or 200 *zuzim* (depending on the status of the bride). But should a wife acquire the legal status of a "rebellious wife" by consistently behaving in certain, specified ways (e.g., flirting with other men) her husband can penalize her by reducing the amount of her ketubbah.

The problem is the nature of Jewish divorce in classical rabbinic law. Divorce is unilateral: only a husband can instigate it—he cannot be compelled—and his wife's consent is not required, although upon divorce he must return his wife's dowry to her and pay her the amount of her ketubbah. The economic consequences, perhaps, are meant to serve as a brake on capricious divorces.

But this is a legal institution highly vulnerable to abuse. If a man cannot (e.g., he goes "missing in action") or does not want to divorce his wife out of spite, she is "anchored" (agunah, explained in the last chapter), unable to marry anyone else. There is little to stop a determined man from blackmailing her, insisting that she forfeit her dowry and ketubbah in exchange for his giving her a bill of divorce, the get. At the same time, should a woman try to force a divorce she risks being labeled a "rebellious wife," and having her marriage settlement reduced in vain, as the rabbis or courts would hesitate to compel her husband to divorce her.

It is thus not surprising that despite the potentially serious consequence of being shunned from the Jewish community, frustrated Jewish women would have turned to the Islamic courts for relief. From the perspective of the contemporary rabbis, this was a double disaster. First, it undermined the authority of the Jewish courts and the geonim. Second—as the responsum explicitly states—it resulted in compelled divorces, which by rabbinic law are no divorces at all! The consequence from a rabbinic legal perspective is that such a woman was unable to remarry; her sexual relations were technically adulterous and her future children would bear the legal stigma of being mamzerim.

Rav Sherira Geon invokes both the decree of 650/51 CE and the authority of custom to finesse the problem. The rabbinic court can indeed compel a husband to issue a divorce to his wife and the divorce "counts." Although in such a situation he must return the dowry to her, he need not make good on the amount of his pledge that exceeds the statutory ketubbah payment. By giving Jewish women legal recourse in Jewish courts, they would presumably be more hesitant to seek external intervention.

This responsum is not entirely typical but nevertheless illustrates how the geonim walked the line between theory and practice. This particular ruling, like many geonic decisions, was not accepted by later rabbis. But then, later rabbis worked with different conceptual frameworks, assumptions, and historical contingencies. Other geonic innovations, such as the institution of a third daily service in the evening (still leaving the Jews two short of the five daily services of Muslims) and the male wearing of a head covering as a religious obligation found wider acceptance.

The most vivid evidence of the geonic trend toward standardization is the incipient development of the law code. The first Jewish law code might best be attributed to the Karaite Anan ben David, but it was soon followed by rabbinic competitors. Two major law codes were compiled during the geonic period, the *Halakhot Pesukot* and the *Halakhot Gedolot*. The former was written in Hebrew and Aramaic, translated into Judeo-Arabic, and soon fell off the rabbinic curriculum; it survives only in fragments found mainly in ancient manuscript caches. On the other hand, the *Halakhot Gedolot*, probably composed in the mid-ninth century, became part of a living tradition of study that extends to the present. The *Halakhot Gedolot* follows the order of the Babylonian Talmud, adjudicating laws as they arise. Such a composition was more useful as an aid to the student of Talmud than as an actual guide for living.

The geonic drive toward standardization and codification, a tendency that paralleled what was happening in the Islamic academies, spilled over from law into scriptural interpretation and theology. Previously, of course, Jews had also engaged in the interpretation of Scripture and in theological and philosophical activities. These earlier efforts in fact highlight the geonic innovations in these areas.

Se'adyah was arguably the first systematic Jewish theologian and with-out doubt the first whose thought continued to play a role in later Jewish philosophy. He wrote his most well-known treatise, the *Book of Beliefs and Opinions,* in 933. The book implicitly and explicitly engages Muslim phi-losophy, called Kalam. The schools of Kalam were attempting to interpret Islam systematically, primarily by applying Greek philosophical ideas. One school, the Mu'tazilites, were particularly influential on Se'adyah and later Jewish philosophers. The Mu'tazilites took a radical position on the unity of God, rejecting all shades of anthropomorphism and even the ascription to God of attributes.

Se'adyah claims that the purpose of the *Book of Beliefs and Opinions* was to dispel the mistaken ideas that Jews have absorbed from this heady intel-lectual environment:

> When, now, I considered these fundamentals and the evil resulting there-from, my heart was grieved for my species, the species of rational beings, and my soul was stirred on account of our people, the children of Israel. For I saw in this age of mine many believers whose belief was not pure and whose convictions were not sound. . . . I saw, furthermore, men who were sunk, as it were, in seas of doubt and submerged in the waters of confusion, and there was no diver to bring them up from the depths, nor a swimmer who might take hold of their hands and carry them ashore.[13]

Se'adyah sought to bring order and a system to issues of belief. His project was little different from that of the many Islamic philosophers who were contesting similar issues. Se'adyah felt the need to *explain* Jewish beliefs to Jews, to offer a coherent system of thought that would allow Jews to make sense of their religion as it was being articulated and understood by Mus-lims. That is, Se'adyah was responding to the increasing Jewish understand-ing of their own religion as it was seen by Muslims, as having a distinctive and coherent theology.

The first part of the *Book of Beliefs and Opinions* deals with epistemo-logical issues: How do we know something? The burning question at the core of his discussion is the relationship of what would be known as "revela-tion" versus "reason." Humans have three intellectual faculties according to Se'adyah: sense perception, intellectual perception, and logical reasoning. "Authentic tradition" is the fourth, and independent, source of knowledge.

The belief in a single truth drives Se'adyah's epistemology. The knowledge derived through the human intellect ultimately is the same as that conveyed in tradition; tradition is a kind of shortcut to knowledge that humans could in any case achieve. Reason and revelation are two independent paths to the same truth. Note, however, that the tradition has to be "authentic." On the one hand, contemporary Islamic concern with the authenticity of the hadith no doubt played a role in Se'adyah's formulation. On the other hand, he was taking a swipe at the Karaites who, by implication, carried an inauthentic tradition.

Se'adyah's God was, for all practical reasons, the same as the Mu'tazilite Allah. Se'adyah's God was far more omnipotent and awesome than that of the Rabbis. Anthropomorphism was completely inappropriate. Se'adyah rejects not only simple and obvious anthropomorphism (e.g., talking of God as if God had a human body) but even the application to God of more abstract human characteristics, such as justice. We, as frail humans with limited cognitive abilities, might think that we "know" aspects of God, but we should not confuse our knowing with a belief that it is the reality of the thing: God is so indivisible that God is absent of "attributes."

The God of the Rabbis, like that of Philo, appears to have created the earth from some kind of primordial stuff. The biblical account itself seems to suggest such an idea. Se'adyah's God does not mess around with stuff; Se'adyah introduces the notion of *creatio ex nihilo* ("creation from nothing") into Jewish readings of the Hebrew Bible. For Se'adyah, God creates with will—God wills it and it is. God built the world and all in it from nothing at all.

Se'adyah is well aware of the familiar theological problems occasioned by a belief in God's absolute omnipotence. Despite God's foreknowledge of everything, he adheres strictly to the notion of human free will. God abhors certain human activities "for our own sakes in His way of mercy"; despite God's desire for our weal, we are free to act as we may.[14] Nor is God's foreknowledge of a human action its cause. As Se'adyah cleverly points out, if that was so then all would have existed from eternity—that is, the moment God first had knowledge of it.

He also deals head on with theodicy. Se'adyah is aware that the righteous sometimes suffer in ways we might regard as unjust. His answer is more subtle than Deuteronomy's, with its claim that all human suffering is deserved: "I find that suffering befalls the pious in this world in one of two ways: either as punishments for the relatively small number of their transgressions . . . or, alternatively, as a visitation from God in order to test them, provided He knows that they will be able to endure it."[15] It is the latter category, testing, that he applies to the suffering of innocent children: "I have no doubt that they will be compensated, and that the suffering which God in His wisdom inflicts on them is like the punishment which they receive at the hands of their father who may strike and confine them in order to protect them from some harm."[16] God's goodness is above suspicion.

The paternalistic metaphor (even Se'adyah is unable to find language that entirely avoids metaphors) also plays a role in Se'adyah's explanation of the commandments. God gave two types or classes of commandments. Rational commandments could have easily been derived through reason. One hardly needs the Torah to know that theft, murder, and adultery are bad. Such laws are revealed only to confirm our rational facilities. However, other commandments—such as the food laws or the laws governing the Sabbath and festivals—are, from a rational perspective, "neutral." Se'adyah tries hard to find that these commandments have some rational and comprehensible benefit for humans. Kashrut, for example, "makes it impossible to liken any of the animals to the Creator . . . also it prevents people from worshipping any of the animals, since it is unthinkable that one should worship either what one serves for food or what one declares as impure."[17] Where Se'adyah can find little or no rational basis, he ascribes their revelation more generally to God's goodness: God has given commandments to humans so that by doing them we might accrue reward. These seemingly arbitrary activities, that is, are "good" for the sole reason that they issue from God.

More heavily and systematically than the Rabbis, Se'adyah relies on the concept of the afterlife to keep the concept of God's justice plausible. Following contemporaneous philosophies, Se'adyah asserted that the human was composed of two parts, body and soul, thus breaking with biblical and rabbinic monistic views of the self. The soul is the eternal and intelligible part of the person; it contains the rational part of the self. Upon death the soul separates from the body to be stored until the final Day of Judgment. At that time God will resurrect the bodies (recomposing them, if necessary) and restore to them their souls. The Day of Judgment will usher in the messianic era.

Se'adyah strikes a brilliant compromise between an active and passive eschatology: "We believe that God has appointed two alternative periods for the duration of our servitude in exile, one extending until such a time as we do penitence, the other being terminated at a fixed time. Whichever of these times arrives first, it carries Redemption with it."[18] Humans can hasten redemption with our actions, but, even if we do not succeed, it will nevertheless arrive. Whether we want this is another matter. Se'adyah's end of days scenario is apocalyptic and harsh, with "terrible hardships" inflicted on the Jews to purify them of their sins. Only when these hardships are completed and the dead brought back to life will God's presence rest again on the Temple in Jerusalem and Israel slip into a sunnier, eternal future.

Se'adyah Geon's approach to the study of Torah was as revolutionary as his systematic theology. Midrash looked as odd to Se'adyah as it does to many modern Western readers. It interprets Scripture out of context, sometimes in a seemingly random fashion. Se'adyah had little patience for this way of reading. Midrash was unscientific; it was neither rational nor did it conform with contemporaneous approaches to sacred literature. Indeed, Se'adyah tried to bring the most modern scholarship—developed primarily for the study of the Quran—to the study of Torah.

Most prominently this modern scholarship involved grammar and lexicography. Alarmed that "many of the children of Israel do not know the basic eloquence of our language,"[19] Se'adyah dedicated several Judeo-Arabic tracts to Hebrew linguistics. His purpose in these works is both to elucidate the meanings of individual works and, more ambitiously, to begin a more scientific systematization of the Hebrew language. Although somewhat primitive by later standards, his work founded a tradition of the study of biblical Hebrew that climaxes with Ibn Janah's (also known as Rabbi Jonah) two-volume study of biblical Hebrew in eleventh-century Spain. Se'adyah also translated the Bible into Arabic in an edition that continues to be used by Arabic-speaking Jews.

Se'adyah applies those academic methods to his interpretation of Scripture, which in turn flows from his epistemology. As he states in his introduction to his commentary on the Torah:

> A reasonable person must always understand the Torah according to the outward meaning of the words, i.e., that which is well known and widespread among the speakers of the language—since the purpose of composing any book is to convey its meaning perfectly to the reader's heart—except for those places in which sense perception or intellectual perception contradicts the well-known understanding of an expression, or where the well-known understanding of an expression contradicts another, unequivocal verse or a tradition.[20]

He then goes on that should all else fail and the Torah really cannot be understood rationally (e.g., anthropomorphisms), it must be interpreted metaphorically so that "this Scripture will be brought into accord with the senses and the intellect, with other verses and with tradition." Scripture must be squared with reason.

This interpretive approach to Scripture becomes known as *peshat*, literally "simple" but usually translated as "contextual." Se'adyah Geon's own commentary tends to be sparse. He devotes most of it to clarifying the meaning of individual words. Occasionally these clarifications reflect larger theological or interpretive concerns, reconciling the biblical text with reason. On Genesis 3:20, for example, Se'adyah sensibly determines that when Eve is called "the mother of all the living" Scripture means to say "the mother of all life that speaks," that is, humankind. To Se'adyah Genesis 3:8 could not possibly mean, as it seems to say, that God was "moving about in the garden"; it is instead the voice of God passing through the garden. Following an older exegetical tradition, he explains the odd story of Genesis 6:1–4, which appears to describe the mating of divine beings with humans, as a story of mixed-class marriage: the sons of the nobility marry common women. Unlike midrash, peshat speaks in a single voice.

If there is a motif that runs through the Judaism of the geonim, it is the move toward closure and standardization. The geonim attempt to tame both the messiness of the Talmud and the riot of competing biblical interpretations. They created law codes, liturgies, and theologies. The geonic literary legacy is hardly uniform, but neither is it as cacophonous as that of the Hebrew Bible or the Talmud. Ambiguities and contradictions in their tradition bothered them; they were problems to be solved rather than opportunities to be exploited.

The geonim moved toward standardization because they could. They were part of an Islamic society that itself was concerned with and developing tools for the formation and consolidation of religious identity. Halakhah became the Jewish *shari'ah* (the Islamic way of living in accord with the divine will); the Tanak a Jewish Quran. The result was a Judaism that would have been as recognizable to Muslims was it was to Jews.

Then there is also the not insignificant issue of power. The geonim functioned within a relatively stable empire with reliable routes of trade and communication. They were also fortuitously located near its center of power. The schools of the land of Israel in their competition with the Babylonian geonim were surely hindered by their physical distance from Baghdad. Although the Babylonian geonim appear never to have gained any official recognition, they forged close (if sometimes tense) relationships with the exilarchs, who did have official authority over the Jewish community. When the geonim attempted to standardize and consolidate tradition, they were also consolidating their own power.

Jews in the Islamic world probably recognized the Judaism of the geonim, but the extent to which they accepted and participated in it is an entirely different question. Many Jews, such as the Karaites, had little sympathy for it. The range of questions submitted to the geonim demonstrates that even Jews within their orbit had different understandings of what it meant to practice the religion of Israel. And the extant, noncanonical mystical texts from this period remind us that there were large communities of contemporary Jews about whom we know practically nothing.

Were we to limit our reading to the "canonical" geonic texts—the law codes, responsa, theological writings, and biblical commentaries—we might conclude that geonic Judaism was nearly devoid of elements that we label mystical. This may actually be true; the geonim rarely mention mystical speculation or practices. The *Hekhalot* texts, however, suggest otherwise.

Beginning late in the rabbinic period (around the sixth century CE) and extending into the early Middle Ages, Jews produced a series of texts that report visions of the divine. One of the strangest of these texts, the *Shiur Qomah* (The Measure of the Stature), describes in precise, intricate, yet incomprehensible detail the measurements of God's body. Several texts, now called Hekhalot literature, purport to describe what the Rabbis actually saw in paradise. Envisioning the divine, heavenly abode as a series of chambers (the meaning of hekhalot), the texts trace the journey of Rabbi Akiva through heaven, led by his guide, the angelic Prince of Torah. Like the *Shiur Qomah*, the authorship, function, and social setting of the Hekhalot texts remain obscure. Whoever produced them did refer to and appear to have regarded as authoritative some previous rabbinic texts. The ideal end of such a journey, it appears, was the transformation of the individual into a kind of divine being.

Who wrote these texts and what is their purpose? On these questions there is no scholarly consensus at all. They are not quite instruction manuals for ascent, although they contain descriptions of many techniques that the protagonists use to ascend. They are full of references to the Hebrew Bible and, to a lesser extent, rabbinic literature, although they do not appear to be merely exegetical exercises. Famous rabbis (e.g., Rabbi Akiba and Rabbi Ishmael) stand at their center, but their behavior hardly comports with the image of the rabbis and their Judaism found in geonic rabbinic literature. Whatever the answers to these questions, these mystical texts did enter into a living tradition; their manuscripts circulated in Western Europe in the Middle Ages, although, again, we do not know who actually read and "used" them.

One of the most interesting features of these early Jewish mystical texts is the central role of text. Language plays a role in most mystical experiences of any kind, but this literature assigns to texts a central, mediating role. By structuring its stories around and frequently alluding to earlier texts, it makes mystical practice a textual practice, and vice versa. Even the mystic finds God through text. Indeed, it is hard to understand this mystical literature solely as a dry academic exercise, even if it is not really a how-to guide of ascent. At least some Jews who sought to experience the face of the living God directly would have turned to and studied these texts; they, rather than, for example, simple, unmediated inward meditation, were the key to mystical experience.

The geonim, by their own judgment, were living in a different and lesser era than those of the classical Rabbis. They understood themselves as the conservators, commentators, and codifiers of the great rabbinic tradition. Yet their achievement was not as modest as this self-conception might suggest. Unlike the Rabbis, the geonim had both power and influence, and they used both to transform the sprawling rabbinic tradition into a religion. Out of the stuff of the Rabbis, it was the geonim who created rabbinic Judaism.

The last geon of Pumbedita, Hayya b. Sherira, died in 1038 and was not replaced; the light of the geonim was soon extinguished. This was due in part to an internal struggle with the exilarch, but the demise of the geonim had more to with the changing times. The period of formation and consolidation was passing. The geonim stood at an hourglass point of Jewish history; they gathered and attempted (with admittedly limited success) to standardize and authorize the traditions that they received, but this consolidation led to a new explosion of creativity and diversity. Their center, as weak as it was, did not hold.

8

FROM MOSES TO MOSES

OWARD THE END of Moses Maimonides' opus, *The Guide of the Perplexed*,[1] after hundreds of pages of dense philosophical discussions, Maimonides abruptly switches tone to tell a parable:

The ruler is in his palace, and all his subjects are partly within the city and partly outside the city. Of those who are within the city, some have turned their backs upon the ruler's habitation, their faces being turned another way. Others seek to reach the ruler's habitation, turn toward it, and desire to enter it and to stand before him, but up to now they have not yet seen the wall of the habitation. Some of those who seek to reach it have come up to the habitation and walk around it searching for its gate. Some of them have entered the gate and walk about in the antechambers. Some of them have entered the inner course of the habitation and have come to be with the king, in one and the same place with him, namely, in the ruler's habitation. But their having come into the inner part of the habitation does not mean that they see the ruler or speak to him. For after their coming into the inner part of the habitation, it is indispensable that they should make another effort; then they will be in the presence of the ruler, see him from afar or from nearby, or hear he ruler's speech or speak to him.[2]

Maimonides then goes on to explain what he means. Those outside the city are those "who have no doctrinal belief." Those inside the city, but with their backs to the ruler's habitation, are those who "have adopted incorrect opinions," either due to error or following somebody else's incorrect opinions. Those who turn toward the ruler's habitation, seeking to enter it but still not seeing even its wall, are "the multitude of adherents of the Law . . . the ignoramuses who observe the commandments." The jurists concerned only with law and not philosophical speculation are those who walk around searching for the gate. Only those engaged in philosophical speculation enter further, with the beginner in the antechambers. The inner court is reserved for those who "have achieved perfection in the natural things and have understood divine science." Those of the perfect who then turn completely to God enter before Him, rising to the status of prophets.

On its surface this parable and its explanation could hardly be clearer. For Maimonides there is a hierarchy that extends from those who have little rational facility to those with increasing practice of and competence in legal matters (the mitzvot), finally culminating with philosophers, among whom the perfect become prophets. The best Jew is the philosophical Jew, and if he does not exactly declare adherence to the mitzvot to be useless, he does lessen its utility.

Yet, like most everything else in Maimonides' writing, the interpretation of this parable is more complex than it appears. Three chapters after this parable, at the very end of the *Guide*, Maimonides claims that perfection is knowing and *imitating* God. Perfection is not to be achieved through abstract philosophical speculation but by recognizing God's virtues of loving-kindness, righteousness, and justice and living our lives in accordance with these virtues. Earlier in the *Guide*, while discussing Moses, Maimonides states that "the utmost virtue of man is to become like unto Him, may He be exalted, as far as he is able; which means that we should make our actions like unto His."[3] Is perfection to be found in philosophical understanding or in righteous acts, an *imitatio dei*?

Maimonides' apparent denigration in this parable of the value of the mitzvot is even more puzzling. The parable appears after a long discussion of the commandments in which he sorts all of the commandments into fourteen categories. "The Law as a whole," he claims, "aims at two things: the welfare of the soul and the welfare of the body."[4] It thus brings perfection in two senses, both as a political guide that eliminates social wrongdoing and as an instrument through which individuals can perfect their characters. In this discussion the Law hardly appears as secondary to more abstract speculation.

Moreover, despite the parable's denigration of jurists, Maimonides was in his day, and remains in ours, one of the foremost jurists of rabbinic law. Although the geonim began the process of clarification and codification of rabbinic law, Maimonides created the first true code of Jewish law.

The *Mishneh Torah*, which with its comprehensiveness, new topical organization, and beautiful and clear Hebrew remains widely studied by modern Jews. Composed over a decade, the *Mishneh Torah* hardly seems the work of a man who understands himself to be walking around the habitation, "searching for the gate."

Maimonides' legacy is complex. One of the towering figures in Jewish history, he is still revered by many; some Jews even make pilgrimages to his supposed grave in Tiberias. "From Moses [of the Bible] to Moses [Maimonides], there was none like Moses," went a saying popular even in the Middle Ages. Yet during his life, and in the centuries after, his *Guide of the Perplexed* was condemned as heretical, with some Jewish communities actually burning copies of it. The star of the *Mishneh Torah* rose quickly but was soon eclipsed by subsequent law codes, most notably the sixteenth-century *Shulhan Arukh*. How do we make sense of him, his understanding of Judaism, and this legacy?

Moses ben Maimon was born during the twilight of what nineteenth-century German-Jewish historians would call the "Golden Age" of Jews on the Iberian peninsula. Maimonides (the "son of Maimon," in Arabic) was born in 1135 in Cordoba. Cordoba had a storied past. Abd al-Rahman, the Umayyad prince whose family the 'Abbasids slaughtered in Damascus, arrived in Cordoba in 755 and declared his emirate a year later. Here in al-Andalus, on the periphery of the enormous empire controlled by the 'Abbasids from their base in Baghdad, al-Rahman began to build a remarkably open and vibrant society. Although technically a mere provincial governor who served at the whim of the 'Abbasid caliph, al-Rahman in effect ruled al-Andalus as an independent political entity. As time passed, the rulers of Andalusia increasingly saw themselves as independent rulers, not subject to the authority of Baghdad. In 929 Abd al-Rahman III formally declared himself caliph and thus independent of Baghdad.

One of the defining characteristics of al-Rahman and his successors was the extent to which they took the Islamic concept of the dhimmi. The dhimmi, literally, were the "peoples of the book," Jews and Christians, monotheists who worshipped God. Not as right-minded as Muslims, but not as abominable as polytheists, they are given by the Quran a distinct and protected legal identity. As long as they were peaceful and paid their taxes, they were not to be harmed. The application of the concept of dhimmi, however, could be quite elastic. One Islamic society could tolerate but disadvantage its dhimmi, while another could develop a full-blown multiculturalism. The 'Abbasids tended toward the former, al-Andalus the latter. Among all the nations during the Middle Ages, only in al-Andalus could Jews rise to significant positions of political power: in the early eleventh century a Jew, Samuel ibn Nagrila (Samuel HaNagid), even became a vizier of Granada.

This is the age that famously led to a flowering of Arabic, Jewish, and, to a lesser extent, Christian literature. Muslim and Jewish poets produced secular and religious poetry that is virtually indistinguishable. Poets in Arabic and Hebrew lauded the good life, wine, women, and the love of boys. Samuel ibn Gabirol, a Jew born in the area of Cordoba around 1022, created devotional poetry in Arabic that was so infused with Neoplatonic ideas that he incurred the wrath of his coreligionists—he moved to Granada, where Samuel HaNagid served as his patron. He apparently continued to develop his Neoplatonic ideas into a tract, the *Fons Vitae*, a complete copy of which survived only in Latin. In this tract, read (but often rejected) by later Christian theologians and perhaps Jewish mystics, Ibn Gabirol claimed that all matter emanates from God, like the relationship between the sun and sunlight.

Ibn Gabirol's scholarship was but one type of contemporary Jewish academic activity. The rabbis of al-Andalus built upon their received textual tradition, in the process stamping it with the distinctive marks of their culture. Born in Fez, Rabbi Isaac ben Jacob Alfasi (sometimes known by his acronym, the Rif) moved to Lucena, near Cordoba, in 1088 and died there in 1103. By then he had already authored a kind of code of Jewish law, the *Sefer Halakhot*, an abridged version of the Babylonian Talmud that excluded the nonlegal sections. This epitome of the Talmud was probably based on the Arabic practice of abridging their classical texts, a form known as *mukhtasar*.

In Lucena the Rif assumed the post of head of the local yeshiva. The scope and activities of this yeshiva are not entirely clear. He was succeeded by Rabbi Joseph HaLevy ibn Migash (the Ry) who apparently made his mark writing Talmudic commentaries. Among his students was Rabbi Maimon, Maimonides' father.

The legal writings of the Spanish rabbis were not just simple academic exercises. The Rif was uninterested in sections of the Talmud that did not have direct practical relevance. Moreover, unlike the rabbis of the Talmud and the geonim, the Spanish rabbis had real judicial power. Granted judicial authority in varying degrees—sometimes even including the right to administer capital punishment—Spanish rabbis developed a strong ideology of communal legislation. Individual Jewish communities, their leaders and rabbis, claimed authority to determine and administer their own law. Their legal responsa, primarily written in Arabic, thus speak directly to local concerns, and the execution of their judgments could be backed with judicial force.[5]

Jewish biblical interpretation in Muslim Spain was even more tightly linked to the prevalent intellectual, communal, and cultural conditions. Abulwalid Merwan ibn Janah, Rabbi Jonah, was born in Cordoba around 990 and studied in the yeshiva at Lucena. A doctor by training who ultimately settled in Saragossa, Rabbi Jonah's crowning achievement was the production of an extensive grammar (*The Book of Embroidery*) and a thesaurus (*The Book of Roots*) of biblical Hebrew. Like Se'adyah, Rabbi Jonah brought the rigor and sophistication of contemporary Arabic linguistics to bear upon the Hebrew Bible; Rabbi Jonah is often credited as being the first to recognize that Hebrew words generally contain a three-letter consonantal root. Surviving only in the original Arabic and a later translation into Hebrew, these works remain fundamental to the study of Hebrew grammar.

Perhaps the greatest practitioner of this interpretive approach, however, was Rabbi Abraham ibn Ezra. Born in Toledo around 1092, Ibn Ezra spent his formative years in Cordoba; in 1140 he left Cordoba, wandering through Europe until his death in 1167. Although he wrote the bulk of his biblical commentaries during this period of wandering, they are thoroughly suffused with the rational and linguistic concerns that characterized Andalusia. On the other hand, his decision to write these commentaries in Hebrew rather than Arabic would have been more in line with European (Ashkenazic) rabbinic practice.

Ibn Ezra was a man of letters. He composed poetry (including one that laments the conversion of one of his sons to Islam) as well as philosophical, mathematical, astronomical, and grammatical tracts. He is best remembered, however, for his commentaries on the book of Job and the Pentateuch. He was deeply committed to the use of grammar and the importance of context (peshat) for understanding Scripture. The application of this scientific approach to the biblical text would become characteristic of peshat and its practitioners, commonly known as the *mepharshim* ("expositors"). Underneath the dryness of Ibn Ezra's philological commentaries lay a restless and daring mind. Ibn Ezra at times leaned toward a Neoplatonic pantheism, believing that the created cosmos is in fact composed of emanations of the divine. Preceding Baruch Spinoza by some five hundred years, he also doubted the divine authorship of some of the verses in the Torah.

Ibn Ezra and the Spanish rabbis, of course, were not the only rabbinic proponents of the peshat approach. Ashkenazic rabbis found their greatest and most influential proponent of this method in Rabbi Shlomo ben Isaac—Rashi. Rashi lived from 1040–1105, and made his living as a vintner in northern France. His commentary on the Tanak (not to mention much of the Babylonian Talmud), written in Hebrew, was and remains vastly influential. Ibn Ezra often disagreed with Rashi's interpretations, but he did not feel free to simply ignore them. The source of many of these disagreements can be easily attributed to their different cultural settings. Whereas Rashi was more comfortable using earlier rabbinic sources to interpret Scripture (even if he had to extract a single voice out of the multivocal midrash), Ibn Ezra put his faith more in reason and the human sciences.

One brief example can illustrate the different approaches of Rashi and Ibn Ezra. According to the second half of Exodus 23:19, "You shall not boil a kid in its mother's milk." In the Talmudic period the Rabbis had already noted that this injunction appears three times in the Torah and derived from this repetition a blanket prohibition against eating milk and dairy products together. On this verse Rashi comments:

> "You shall not boil a kid": "Kid" includes a calf or sheep, for the word "kid" signifies a tender young [animal, i.e., not a specific species]. And you find this in many places in the Torah where it is written "kid," it is necessary to specify after it "flock." For example: "I will send a kid of the flock" (Genesis 38:17) . . . "Go to the flock and fetch me two choice kids" (Genesis 27:9). [These verses] teach you that where it is written simply "kid," even a cow or sheep is to be understood. And in three places [this verse] is written in the Torah: One [teaches] the prohibition of eating [milk and meat products together], one the prohibition of deriving benefit [from the mixture], and one the prohibition of cooking [milk and meat products together, even if you do not eat them].

Rashi takes pains to clarify that the Torah does not simply prohibit eating goat with dairy products. A kid, he argues, is a word that includes other species. The Torah itself, he claims, supports this understanding. Just as in these other verses *kid* is paired with the word *flock* to specify livestock generally, so too even where *flock* does not appear it should be understood. The upshot is a defense of the rabbinic understanding of the verse and its legal consequences.

Here is Ibn Ezra on the same verse:

[Rabbi Shlomo, i.e., Rashi] says that *gedi* (a kid) means young and tender. He says it applies to young oxen and young lambs. He claims that the phrase *gedi izzim* (a kid of the goats) (Gen. 38:17) proves this, since there is no reason to connect them. However, this is not so. The term *gedi* applies only to a goat. Thus in Arabic the term *gedi* means a goat. It is never used for any other kind. However, there is a difference between a *gedi* and a *gedi izzim*. A *gedi* is larger than a *gedi izzim*. A *gedi izzim* still needs to be with other goats. . . . Our sages have received the tradition that an Israelite is not permitted to eat meat and milk.

I will now explain. Note that it is the Torah's custom to speak of that which is most prevalent. For example, the Torah refers to the ostrich as a *bat ha-ya'anah* (Lev. 11:16). Now why does the Torah do something here which it does not do in any other place? For in no other place does the Torah refer to an entire species by the term "daughter of" (*bat*). Note that the flesh of the *ya'anah* is as dry as wood. It is not the custom for people to eat it, as it contains no moisture. The only flesh of this species that is eaten is that of the "daughter" (*bat*), whose flesh has a little moisture in it because it is a young female. However, young ostrich males have no moisture in them.

Similarly, people do not eat meat and milk, for it is not pleasant to do so. Meat takes long to cook, but milk boils quickly. It is not the custom even today in the land of the Ishmaelites for a person to eat a lamb cooked in milk because the lamb is very moist and so is milk. It is thus harmful. . . .

There is no need for us to search for the reason it is prohibited. The reason is hidden from the eyes of the intelligent. It is possible that it is prohibited to seethe a kid in its mother's milk because to do so is very cruel.[6]

This remarkable passage rejects Rashi's understanding of the word *kid*: "Kid," Ibn Ezra claims, really does mean goat. But why only goat? Here Ibn Ezra supplements his linguistic argument with the empirical observation that goat, unlike other meats, actually tastes good (and, in a passage I did not include, he claims that it is healthy too) when cooked in milk. So *goat*, like the only edible kind of ostrich, has to be specified.

Ibn Ezra then squarely confronts the problem with that interpretation: if the Torah prohibits only cooking and eating goat with milk, whence comes the more general prohibition on mixing all meats with dairy? This he attributes to a tradition that the Rabbis received and whose true understanding is beyond human comprehension. Maybe there are health considerations, but maybe not.

Ibn Ezra is hardly a radical. He does not hesitate to affirm the validity of the prohibition of eating meat and dairy products together. But he is also intellectually courageous, willing not only to accept an interpretation that proves problematic but also to wrestle its consequences. Rashi piously bolsters the rabbinic interpretation of the verse with a "rigged" linguistic analysis, whereas Ibn Ezra follows a more intellectually consistent and honest path.

When Ibn Ezra started his wandering through Europe, Maimonides was only five years old, and Judah Halevi had only five (or perhaps one) more years to live. Although he was Ibn Ezra's contemporary, Halevi ended up taking a very different path. Born in Tudela in 1075 or 1086, Halevi gained fame as a poet and moved through Muslim Spain. He spent time in both Granada and Lucerne; while in Lucerne he got to know the Talmudist Isaac Alfasi. Eventually he settled for some time in Cordoba. In 1140, the same year Ibn Ezra left Cordoba, so did Halevi—sailing on to Egypt where, on his way to the Holy Land, he would die. His poetry was secular and religious, written in Hebrew and Arabic.

While best known in his time as a talented poet, today Halevi is best remembered as the author of the *Kuzari*. This prose tract, originally written in Arabic, was translated—probably shortly after Halevi's death—by Judah ben Saul ibn Tibbon, a Jew who also translated Se'adyah's philosophical writings and Rabbi Jonah's grammar into Hebrew. (His family would later translate Maimonides' *Guide of the Perplexed*.) The *Kuzari* purports to tell of a conversation between the king of the Khazars and a Christian, a Muslim, a rabbi, and a philosopher. In the middle of the story the king is convinced by the rabbi and becomes a Jew.

The *Kuzari* is a broadside against philosophy. In this narrative the Christian and Muslim fade into the background; the real battle is between the rabbi and the philosopher. Halevi here zeroed in on a problem that would soon receive increased attention by philosophers and theologians of all types: Are faith and reason compatible? Halevi draws a clear dichotomy between these two approaches to religion and just as clearly elevates faith over reason. Asked by the Khazar king about his belief, the rabbi responds with a dogmatic assertion: "I believe in the God of Abraham, Isaac and Israel, who led the Israelites out of Egypt with signs and miracles. . . . We believe in what is contained in the Torah."[7] The king is taken aback by this answer:

I had intended from the very beginning not to ask any Jew, because I am aware of the destruction of their books and of their narrow-minded views, their misfortunes having deprived them of all commendable qualities. Shouldst thou, O Jew, not have said that thou believest in the Creator of the world, its Governor and Guide?

The king, in other words, is expecting a philosophical response. The rabbi, however, goes on to argue that the proper way to approach the question is to mention "what is convincing for me and for the whole of Israel, who knew these things, first through personal experience, and afterward through an uninterrupted tradition, which is equal to experience."[8] Philosophers, who "inherited neither science nor religion," cannot achieve the truth afforded by personal experience and tradition.[9] Faith trumps reason.

Halevi does not shy away from the essentialism inherent in this formulation. "Any Gentile who joins us sincerely shares our good fortune, but he is not equal to us," the rabbi declares to the king's consternation.[10] Israel knew God first through personal experience and then through tradition; the Jews are inherently and essentially preeminent. For Halevi this personal, innate knowledge of God is to lead to service of God. The excellent or pious Jew is the one who fulfills all God's laws, which are "entirely beyond the sphere of our intellect; it does not reject them, but it must obey the order of God, just as a sick person must obey the physician in applying his medicines and diet."[11] Ritual commandments such as circumcision are inscrutable but nevertheless establish a connection to the divine. Observance of the commandments attunes the pious man's mind to the divine power.

For the poet Halevi there is something mystical and essential about Jews and Judaism. This is by no means a traditional or conservative stance, and it is one that is deeply informed by Islamic notions. Halevi's concern with tradition and its importance, found also in Seʻadyah, correlates with the value assigned to it by contemporary Muslim theologians. His insistence on the essential nature and superiority of the Jews, however, breaks with previous Jewish and Islamic thinkers. Moreover, his rejection of Seʻadyah's belief that faith and philosophical reason are ultimately reconcilable marks a new, anti-intellectualist strand in Jewish thought.

Halevi's rejection of the worth of philosophy stands in stark contrast to Ibn Ezra's faith in the human sciences. Their contrast, though, illustrates the complex and shifting intellectual currents of Cordoba. In 1086 the weak Muslim rulers of Andalusia, in the face of threatening Christian forces moving south, called on the Almoravids for military aid. Berbers from the area of Morocco, the Almoravids practiced a somewhat puritanical form of Islam quite different from that of Andalusia. They quickly defeated the Christian forces but then decided to stay on in Andalusia, soon annexing the local provinces, or *taifas*. By 1109 the Almoravids were burning the works of the tolerant Muslim theologian al-Ghazali in Cordoba, provoking an uprising. An intra-Muslim "culture war" had led to bloody civil disobedience.

Although it did not directly concern them, local Jews and Christians felt the repercussions of these upheavals. The relatively free and open intellectual climate of Cordoba had chilled as the Almoravids tried to impose their "orthodox" version of Islam. Politically, Jews and Christians were given far less latitude, as the Almoravids understood the concept of the dhimmi in narrower terms. Both trends were exacerbated under the Almohads, another conservative Muslim group from North Africa who overthrew the Almoravids in 1147 and consolidated their reach into Andalusia around 1172.

Ibn Ezra's, Judah Halevi's, and, a little later, Maimonides' own emigration from Cordoba must have stemmed in part from this unrest. At the same time, they took different things out of the Islamic "culture war." If Ibn Ezra can be seen to some extent as part of the "old guard," a man committed to the intellectual ideals of the old Cordoba, then the older Judah Halevi's devaluing of reason to faith and commitment to an essential Jewish separateness were more congenial to Almoravid values. Maimonides, though, had yet a third answer.

We do not know much about Maimonides' early years. His father, Maimon, was a prominent Jewish judge. Maimonides no doubt received what we might call both a religious and secular education, although it is unclear where or how he received it. Much of this education, however, was imparted on the run. In 1148, when Maimonides was about thirteen, the Almohads took Cordoba. Maimonides' family, like many other Jews, fled at the Almohad insistence that non-Muslims convert to Islam. Maimonides and his family wandered for the next decade through southern Spain and northern Africa, finally settling in 1159 in Fez, the seat of Almohad power.

And it was in Fez that Maimonides became a Muslim.

While we have no direct evidence of Maimonides' "conversion" to Islam, circumstantial evidence suggests it. The Almohads insisted that all who lived under their sovereignty make a public profession of the *shahada*, "There is no God but God [Allah] and Muhammad is God's messenger." This is the conversion formula for Islamic jurists; one who recited it in front of witnesses became a Muslim. The Almohads were apparently aware and tolerant of Jews who would make this public declaration but continue Jewish practices privately. Maimonides and his family were in Fez until 1165 and it is hard to imagine that they could have avoided "converting," while at the same time sharply segregating their public from private, Jewish, lives.

There is, then, perhaps as much defensiveness as there is sympathy in his defense of those Moroccan Jews who recited the shahada rather than face death. Around 1165 a rabbinic contemporary of Maimonides, in answer to an inquiry from a Jewish forced convert, ruled that it is better for a Jew to face death than to recite the shahada: "Whoever utters that confession is a gentile, though he fulfills the entire Law publicly and privately."[12] Calling this rabbinic ruling "weak," "senseless," "foul of content and form," "harmful," "tedious," "confused," and "long-winded foolish babbling and nonsense," Maimonides rules that the Almohad persecution is different than the ones that preceded it: "There has never yet been a persecution as remarkable as this one, where the only coercion is to say something."[13] Such a requirement, Maimonides insists, does not demand martyrdom; he should "confess and not choose death." At the same time, he must remain a Jew in private, setting it "as his objective to observe as much of the Law as he can."[14] Nor is it right to look down upon these converts; they, like all sinners, must be welcome in the synagogue. The best course of action of all, though, is to emigrate. Whether it was his response to the rabbi or the six stressful years of living as a Jew in private and Muslim in public that finally steeled his and his family's resolve, in 1165 they left Fez for the land of Israel. Not finding a good place to settle, they made their way south and settled in Cairo.

While still in Fez Maimonides began one of what would become his three primary literary legacies, an Arabic commentary to the Mishnah. He appears to have completed it around 1168, shortly after he arrived in Cairo. By then he had already authored a few brief treatises on logic, the calculation of the Jewish calendar, and some short legal compilations of the type that were characteristic of the Spanish halakhic schools. The *Commentary to the Mishnah*, however, was of an entirely different scope. This sprawling work already demonstrates the interests and themes that he would develop in his two more influential works, the *Mishneh Torah* and *The Guide of the Perplexed*.

In one sense Maimonides' *Commentary to the Mishnah* fits well into the commentaries produced by other Andalusian rabbis. Like the commentary of Ibn Ezra, Maimonides' commentary marshals and applies the philological and logical tools of the human sciences to the text. Maimonides carefully explicates the language and meaning of the Mishnah in its own context. That is, while he is clearly aware of the Talmudic and later rabbinic commentaries of the Mishnah, his primary goal is to explain the Mishnah on its own terms. So he offers a kind of peshat of the Mishnah, sometimes, as did Ibn Ezra's approach to the Torah, even going against traditional explanations.

The method was thus traditional, but the choice of the base text was radical. From close to its earliest years, the Mishnah was transmitted and studied almost exclusively in its Talmudic context. The very act of extracting the Mishnah from this context and treating it as worthy of commentary in its own right was subversive; it undermined the Babylonian Talmud's monopoly on its interpretation. At the same time, by applying exegetical techniques that were more commonly used in biblical interpretation to the Mishnah, he raised the Mishnah's status. The Oral Law deserved treatment equal to the Written Law.

One of the purposes of such an approach was to elevate and secure the notion of tradition. Maimonides begins his commentary with a long introduction, which itself starts by tracing the chain of tradition of the Oral Law. Maimonides and Judah Halevi shared the Muslim concerns of possessing an "authentic" tradition. Maimonides understands the Mishnah as functionally equivalent to the hadith, the Islamic traditions of the prophet. Like the hadith, the Mishnah was an independent source of authority with an authentic chain of transmission. Ashkenazic Jews living in a Christian world that did not have this kind of concern would not write independent commentaries on the Mishnah until the sixteenth century, and then it would be because of currents in the Renaissance.

It is in the most influential and well-known passage in the *Commentary*, though, that Maimonides shows the clearest affinities with contemporary Islamic thought. Departing from his typically pithy comments, he writes a long essay on the meaning of Mishnah Sanhedrin 10:1: "All Israel has a portion in the world-to-come. . . . But these have no share in the world-to-come: One who says, '[the doctrine of] resurrection of the dead is not from the Torah'; 'the Torah is not from heaven'; and the *apikoros*." Maimonides begins his comments with a general discussion of the world-to-come. "What everybody always wants to know, both the masses and the learned," Maimonides complains, "is how the dead will rise."[15] Then he goes on to suggest that the doctrine of the world-to-come is deplorable but unavoidable. Deplorable because it caters to our basest instincts, assuring us, like children, that if we do good we will be rewarded. Unavoidable because most humans are unlike the patriarch Abraham, who served God out of love rather than fear. Yet if the sages knew this, why did they develop such a seemingly irrational concept such as resurrection of the dead? It is to teach something through a paradox: "When you encounter a word of the sages which seems to conflict with reason, you will pause, consider it, and realize that this utterance must be a riddle or parable."[16] The sages, Maimonides claims, really mean to teach that the ultimate good is a state in which the "souls enjoy blissful delight in their attainment of knowledge of the truly essential nature of God the Creator."[17] One who serves God out of love should not do so with an eye toward resurrection.

Maimonides does not deny that there will be a world-to-come, but he does tone down its importance. The primary difference between the world-to-come and our own day is the ingathering of the Jews to the land of Israel and the diminution of oppression and toil. The righteous will be brought back to life to live in eternal fellowship.

This last assertion of Maimonides is no mistake. Maimonides deliberately transforms the Mishnah's inclusive statement about "all Israel" to one that includes only the righteous. This led him to formulate the thirteen principles of "our religion." These principles—a nice, relatively neat codification of the "essential" beliefs of Judaism—have been as controversial as they have been stunningly influential. A simplified, metrical version of these principles, the *Yigdal* hymn, was composed around 1404 and remains today in the standard liturgy of many Orthodox (and Conservative) prayer books.

It is at the end of his explanation of these thirteen principles that he returns to the issue that he raised previously with his assertion that only the righteous have a share in the world-to-come:

When a man believes in all these fundamental principles, and his faith is thus clarified, he is then part of that "Israel" whom we are to love, pity, and treat, as God commanded, with love and fellowship. Even if a Jew should commit every possible sin, out of lust or mastery by his lower nature, he will be punished for his sins but will still have a share in the world to come. He is one of the "sinners in Israel." But if a man gives up any one of these fundamental principles, he has removed himself from the Jewish community. He is an atheist, a heretic, an unbeliever.[18]

The scholar Menahem Kellner has argued that Maimonides here is making the radical claim that Judaism—the religion of Israel—is defined not by ethnicity or proper observance of the mitzvot but by a litmus test of belief.

Maimonides consistently asserts this, as when, for example, he mandates doctrinal indoctrination as part of the conversion process, a requirement unattested in previous halakhic literature. Maimonides never goes so far as to claim that a believing non-Jew was, without formal conversion, an actual Jew, but he seems to make ethnicity and formal conversion secondary to correct belief.

Maimonides' commitment to belief and cognition hearkens back to the parable from the *Guide of the Perplexed* with which this chapter began. God, for Maimonides, was beyond human comprehension. He devotes much of the *Guide* to defending this understanding of God, explaining biblical and rabbinic passages that appear to describe God. Primarily reading earlier anthropomorphisms as riddles, parables, and metaphors, Maimonides attempts to preserve his understanding of God as perfect, transcendent, and ultimately unknowable. Yet despite the chasm that separates humans from God, men (he explicitly denies this possibility to women because of his belief in the intrinsic lightness of their intellectual capabilities) can achieve perfection through knowledge. Perfection through cognition leads to perfect behavior, but observance of the mitzvot without proper cognition can never lead to perfection. The Jew who is fully observant of the mitzvot but who maintains "incorrect" beliefs stands "inside the city" but with his back to God; the Jew who denies the essential principles can hardly be called a Jew.

If this reading of Maimonides is correct (and it is a contested one among scholars of Maimonides), how did Maimonides develop this notion of "Judaism" as a doctrinal religion? Quite possibly from the Almohads. The Almohads, as noted above, insisted on a doctrinal declaration as defining Muslim identity. They were "Orthodox" Muslims who defined religious identity primarily in terms of creed and belief. It is not a little ironic that the same society that most likely forced Maimonides himself to declare belief that the prophet Muhammad was the messenger of God also decisively contributed to his understanding of "authentic Judaism." Maimonides' Judaism is structurally similar to the Almohad Islam; both emphasize belief in the unknowable God and His authentic revelation.

Maimonides' response to his religious environment in Fez was by no means the only possible one. As we have seen, and Maimonides' writings make abundantly clear, many of his contemporaries emphasized orthopraxy over orthodoxy; observance of the mitzvot mattered more than correct belief. Medieval Jews who lived among Christians who also emphasized the defining and essential qualities of faith and belief never went as far as Maimonides in elevating faith to the center of what they thought it meant to be Jewish.

Maimonides' codification of the principles of faith in this early work highlights two themes that would run through much of his later writings. The first is his penchant to codify. Maimonides liked systems and went to great lengths to put the messy textual legacies that he received into systematic form. This is not the case for only his Jewish writings; even his medical writings are far more compelling as systematic orderings of existing knowledge than they are as original contributions to medical science. He takes great pains in the *Guide* to differentiate philosophical ideas, frequently introducing his own ideas with a systematic survey of the current "state of the field" among contemporary thinkers, Islamic and Jewish. But his greatest effort at codification is directly connected to the second theme that emerges from his discussion of faith, the place of the mitzvot.

In 1178 Maimonides completed his codification of Jewish law, the *Mishneh Torah*. He apparently worked on the code from 1168 to 1178 in Cairo in his spare time; he had also learned medicine and had joined the sultan's court as a physician. Like his *Commentary to the Mishnah*, Maimonides' *Mishneh Torah* is at once traditional and radical. The *Mishneh Torah*, as we have seen, is not the first halakhic code. Both the geonim and the Spanish rabbis had produced codifications. In content Maimonides relied on these codes. Unlike them, however, the *Mishneh Torah* is not arranged by the scriptural or Talmudic order of the commandments, but by their topic. Also, unlike these earlier codes, the *Mishneh Torah* is written not in Arabic but in a Hebrew that clearly evokes the language of the Mishnah itself. In his choice of name, organization, and language Maimonides signaled his audacious understanding of the *Mishneh Torah* as the new Mishnah.

In the *Mishneh Torah* Maimonides is in a clear but complex dialogue with the Mishnah and Talmud. He accepts the Mishnah's insistence on topical organization but rejects the Mishnah's topics, replacing them with his own classification scheme. He insists that all aspects of law are worthy of codification, even those laws (e.g., purity) that have little or no contemporary practical relevance. He seems to reject forcefully the dialectical nature of Talmudic legal discussions, but peppers the *Mishneh Torah* with exegetical and philosophical clarifications. Although the *Mishneh Torah* resembles the Mishnah far more than it does the Talmud, it also virtually rejects the multivocality and preservation of divergent opinions that characterize the Mishnah. Maimonides fully and absolutely accepts the authority of the Talmud, whose laws he sees as binding upon all Israel, and yet sets out to write a code so that "a person who first reads the Written Law and then this compilation, will know from it the whole of the Oral Law, without having occasion to consult any other book between them."[19] Every Jew is required to study Gemara, but he defines Gemara not as the fixed text of the Talmud that comments upon the Mishnah but as a process of reflection, discernment, and reasoning.

As his parable in the *Guide* suggests, Maimonides had little patience for scholars of the Talmud whose sole goal was to elucidate the mitzvot. He saw *talmud torah* (study of Torah, both Written and Oral) as a kind of means toward the ultimate goal of human perfection. The *Mishneh Torah* is a shortcut, allowing its readers to determine easily and quickly what they must do to live in God's presence while freeing their time for the study of Gemara, by which he primarily means philosophy.

Today, in the *yeshivot* and traditional rabbinic seminaries, Maimonides and his *Guide* are as neglected as Rambam and his *Mishneh Torah* are revered. In these communities he is known not by the Arabic patronymic but by his acronym Rambam—Rabbi Moses ben Maimon. This veneration is all the more surprising because almost no Jewish community today considers Rambam's legal rulings to be authoritative. In fact, the *Mishneh Torah* was a little too audacious even for its own time. Rabbi Abraham ben David, Rabad (1125–1198), of Posquières in Provence strongly opposed Maimonides' code, both in principle and in many of its details. A code without its reasoning, Rabad held, was counterproductive. Perhaps Rabad won: the *Mishneh Torah* unleashed a flood of precisely the kind of commentary that Maimonides sought to suppress. How did he know this? Why did he rule this way and not that way? Like the Mishnah upon which it is based, the *Mishneh Torah* spawned its own "talmud," learned rabbinic commentaries that sought the reasoning behind the terse halakhic rulings.

Rabad's victory was hardly complete. The tension between the code and the commentary, between the definitive legal ruling and its more open and less easily standardized reasoning, continues down to the present day. Maimonides' code was soon supplanted by the *Arba'ah Turim* (the "four rows") by Rabbi Jacob ben Asher (Toledo, ca. 1270—ca. 1343). The *Tur*, as it is commonly known, steps back from the radical elements of Maimonides' code. The son of a well-known halakhic commentator on the Talmud, Rabbi Asher ben Yehiel (the Rosh), Rabbi Jacob includes only those areas of law that were practically relevant as well as divergent opinions. His organization is topical but different than that of the *Mishneh Torah*. Like the *Mishneh Torah*, it spawned its own commentaries.

Among the most important and learned commentators on both these codes was Rabbi Joseph Karo. Born in Spain in 1488, he eventually settled in Safed, in the Land of Israel, where he died in 1575. Karo's commentaries on both the *Mishneh Torah* and the *Tur* are notable for their long and intricate discussions of the legal issues that underlie the terse halakhic prescriptions. More than any other commentator, Karo appears to conform to Rabad's critique of the code. But appearances can be deceiving. Karo distilled these commentators not just into another code, but into what would become *the* authoritative halakhic code, the *Shulhan Arukh* (the "set table"). Predictably, the *Shulkan Arukh* attracted its own commentaries and supercommentaries. Today many (but not all) traditional Ashkenazic Jews turn to the *Shulkan Arukh*, with the additions of Rabbi Moses Isserles (1530–1572)—a Polish rabbi who incorporated Ashkenazic practices—and a commentary called the *Mishnah Berurah*, authored by Rabbi Israel Meir Kagen (also called the Hafetz Hayyim, 1838–1933), who lived in Poland. The standard edition of the *Mishnah Berurah* contains several supercommentaries on Rabbi Kagen's commentary. Although the code and its commentaries have come far from Maimonides' pioneering effort, the *Mishneh Torah* remains an important cornerstone of the rabbinic curriculum.

Maimonides' philosophical legacy is at least equally complex. His philosophical interests are, of course, evident in his earlier writings, but he does not turn his full attention to philosophy until his work on the *Guide of the Perplexed*. Written in Arabic between 1185 and 1190, the *Guide* is, first and foremost, intended for the reader whose study of reason has thrown his belief in the foundations of the law into question. "Hence he would remain in a state of perplexity and confusion as to whether he should follow his intellect, renounce what he knew concerning the terms in question, and consequently consider that he has renounced the foundations of the Law."[20] In more modern terms, it is meant to guide one through a crisis of faith by showing how reason and revelation are not in conflict. Secondarily, Maimonides aims to clarify the "very obscure parables" in Scripture so as to reveal their internal meaning. Here Maimonides pursues the plan of identifying parables by their apparent contradiction with reason and then explaining their deeper meaning.

The *Guide* is not for everyone. It is a complex, at times esoteric, and contradictory treatise written for a reader with an excellent background in classical rabbinic texts, Greek and Islamic philosophy, and the natural sciences (as they were then understood). Maimonides has little patience for the less learned reader of this tract. The *Guide* frequently launches into extended reviews of philosophical issues in which he systematically lays out the different positions from Aristotle to the Mutakallimun, a group of contemporary Islamic philosophers with whom he frequently disagreed. The path to God, the *Guide* suggests, runs through Aristotle and al-Farabi.

Even more literally, the *Guide* is not for everyone. Under all the daunting erudition of the *Guide* lies a fundamentally limited and historically contingent understanding of Judaism. Maimonides here creates a Judaism congenial to the learned Jew of his time, one who is knowledgeable of and fully committed to the mitzvot but whose intellectual outlook is shaped by the secular disciplines of philosophy and science. This is the Jew who gets uneasy at the thought that his religion might be focused more on behavior than on the "pure belief" valued by the best Islamic philosophers around him. No doubt this is the same Jew who does not know how to understand the Scriptural parables, those passages that seem rationally absurd. The *Guide* is for those Jews, like Maimonides, who wanted to live in the wider world and who needed an intellectual model through which they could understand what it meant to be Jewish.[21]

Maimonides readily admits that most Jews do not think as he does. Most Jews stop with the "external" meanings of things; they are, as he says in his parable, "the ignoramuses who observe the commandments." Maimonides was an elitist, and he scorned those Jews who did not share his ideas. In his *Epistle to Yemen*, written in 1172, Maimonides castigates those Jews who believed that the messiah had arrived. In the course of his argument, however, it becomes clear that the Islamic world was teeming with Jews claiming to be messiahs and their followers. Shortly before Maimonides was born, "some respectable people" in Cordoba itself rallied behind a messiah, who was later publicly flogged by "the influential and learned men of our community." Most Jews did not read Aristotle and would have had little sympathy with Maimonides' Judaism.

Nor is this a simple split between the elite and the masses. All later Jewish thinkers were influenced by Maimonides, but not all agreed with him.[22] In 1233 Rabbi Solomon of Montpellier had Maimonides' books burned as heretical. Levi ben Gershom (1288–1344), also called Gersonides or Ralbag, launched a more reasoned attack on Maimonides. The author of *The Wars of the Lord*, Gersonides faulted Maimonides not for taking Aristotle too far but for taking him not far enough.[23] Gersonides was particularly troubled by Maimonides' insistence on God's omniscience and the philosophical problems that that insistence raises for free will: For God to be just, humans must have free will, but, if God knows everything that will happen, how can humans truly have free will? Maimonides, Gersonides claims, never sufficiently answers this problem. His own answer is that God is not omniscient. God, he asserts, knows things *in general*, but not *in particular*. Before they happen, particular actions, like the moral choices that humans make and for which they are rewarded or punished, are unknown even to God. Hardly a religious radical, Ralbag also wrote a learned commentary on the Torah.

A slightly later Jewish philosopher attacked Maimonides from the other side. If Gersonides thought that there were points at which Maimonides flinched from reason, Hasdai ben Abraham Crescas (1340–1410) thought that he overvalued it. Crescas's odd philosophical—or, perhaps better, antiphilosophical—work, *Light of the Lord*, sought to show how reason, especially in the form of Aristotelian philosophy, fails. The truth of revelation is thus to be held even against the evidence of reason.

The true importance of the *Guide* was its ability to open up an alternative "Jewish" conversation. Just as Alfasi brought codification to the rabbinic practice of lawmaking, and Rashi and Ibn Ezra launched a new way of interpreting the Bible, so too did Maimonides jumpstart Jewish philosophy as a theological discourse. The *Guide* may have originated as a treatise intended for a tiny sliver of the Jewish population in the Islamic world, but its eventual influence was profound. It put the issue of "reason versus revelation" squarely on the table and demonstrated that Jews can use philosophy, Jewishly, to answer it. As with his *Commentary on the Mishnah*, which applied contemporary interpretive techniques to rabbinic literature, and his *Mishneh Torah*, which demonstrated the possibilities of the code, so too the *Guide* served as a fulcrum, synthesizing and systematizing previous efforts in a way that would generate an explosion of future reflection. Maimonides did not invent rabbinic commentary, halakhic codification, or Jewish philosophy, but it is possible that without his contributions in these fields none would have blossomed.

Maimonides died in 1204, in Egypt, and according to legend was buried in Tiberias, in Israel. An austere rationalist, he would have been horrified at the idea that Jews today visit his grave in the hope that their prayers will be answered. Rambam's understanding of Judaism differs considerably from those who today seek his supernal intercession or perhaps just a brush with his vestigial holiness. Yet the very irony of modern-day Jews praying at Rambam's grave highlights both his lasting influence and his complex legacy.

Maimonides lived on a cusp between the vibrant intellectual life that characterized old Cordoba and the more cautious retrenchment of the Almoravids and Almohads. He drew from the former, but his Judaism was ultimately of the latter, rigorous and dogmatic. His genius was his ability to bridge between the old and the new, to synthesize and codify in a way that linked past to future. Few Jews regard the *Mishneh Torah* as authoritative and even fewer read, no less subscribe, to the ideas in the *Guide of the Perplexed*, but both works have generated literature and ideas that have fundamentally shaped modern Jewish understandings.

Maimonides opened not only new ways of "conversing" with traditional texts but also a new path to God. Although for Maimonides God is essentially beyond human understanding, humans can approach knowledge of God through reasoned study. It is precisely this knowledge that brings one closer to God—for Maimonides the line between the wise man and the prophet is a thin one indeed. At the same time, Maimonides rejects the possibility that there are other paths to God. The unlettered, however pious, righteous, and observant, can never make it into the King's antechamber. Reason becomes a necessary element of faith.

Neither Judah Halevi nor Hasdai Crescas were comfortable with this idea. Neither Halevi nor Crescas fully reject philosophy, nor do they see it as relevant to the true service of God. For them the true path to God runs through faith and the embodied observance of the mitzvot.

Maimonides put the issue of faith versus reason on the table with such compelling force that it continues to reverberate. Especially since the Enlightenment, the question has been at the heart of the Jewish—as well as Christian—theological endeavor. What role should reason play in the interpretation of traditional texts, and what should one do when reason appears to contradict tradition? The issue deeply informs this book as it does the academic study of religion generally, which privileges reason. What role do faith claims play in "secular" discussions of religion? These questions are just as vibrant now as they were in Maimonides' own day.

Whereas for Maimonides the goal of authentic piety was to know God, for the pilgrims at his grave it is to experience God. Like the dichotomy between faith and reason, the one between knowledge and experience is hardly a clean one and does not line up easily with divisions of orthodox and popular religion. God can be experienced through simple, emotional acts of faith or through tremendously sophisticated intellectual means. Mysticism is a response to the desire to experience God, and few Jewish books can rival the complexity and sophistication of the central and most important book of Jewish mysticism, the Zohar.

9

SEEING GOD

R. ABBI JOSEPH BEN Ephraim Karo (1488–1575) was accustomed to visitations. Over the course of his writing the enormous (and enormously learned) commentary on the *Arba'ah Turim*, the code of Jewish law written by Rabbi Jacob ben Asher in the early fourteenth century, and then a digest of this commentary in the form of his own law code, the *Shulhan Arukh*, Karo received guidance from a heavenly mentor, which Karo identified with the soul of the Mishnah and frequently just called Mishnah. He carefully recorded these visitations in a book that would receive the title *Maggid Mesharim* (Teller of the Upright Matters). In one entry he records a not atypical encounter with Mishnah, who told him:

> Busy yourself constantly in the study of Torah, for when you casuistically examined the opinions of the Rambam [Rabbi Moses ben Maimon] yesterday, the two views you expressed are correct and the Rambam is pleased that you have succeeded in uncovering his full meaning and is pleased that you always quote his opinions and discuss his views casuistically. Your words are right except in the few instances I shall show you. When you die, the Rambam will come out to meet you because you have defended his decisions and, even now, he pleads on your behalf. And he is among the saints, not as those sages who say that he has been reincarnated, etc. For let it be that so it was decreed because of certain heretical views he expressed but the Torah he had studied protected him as well as his good deeds, so he was not reincarnated, etc., but he was reincarnated and then he died and he is now among the saints.[1]

Karo's heavenly mentor brings him not sublime visions of the Ultimate but confirmations and corrections of small points of law and legal reasoning. Mishnah calms Karo's doubts not only about his specific interpretations of Maimonides' *Mishneh Torah* but also more generally about his engagement with Maimonides. Scholars have suggested that "etc." is a euphemism for "as a worm," and that this passage testifies to the continued ambivalence with which Maimonides was held. If Maimonides really was punished for his "heretical" views by being reincarnated as a worm, then Karo's engagement with his legal opinions would be misguided. Don't worry, Mishnah assures him, for having first been reincarnated as a worm, and thus punished for his heretical views, Maimonides died again to live among the eternal holy ones.

Mishnah does not carry the lofty messages and insights that one might expect from a divine emissary. Mishnah, in fact, frequently comes across as a hypostasis of Karo's anxieties. Mishnah assures Karo that his son will become a great rabbi, during whose lifetime "no greater kabbalist will be found."[2] Mishnah exhorts Karo to avoid the "evil inclination" and provides him with a collection of maxims to live by. When Karo oversleeps, Mishnah wakes him up:

> The Lord is with you wherever you go and the Lord will prosper whatever you have done and will do, but you must cleave to Me and to My Torah and to My Mishnah at all times, not as you have done this night. For, although you did sanctify yourself in your food and drink, yet you slept like a sluggard, for the door revolves upon its hinges but the sluggard is on his bed, and you did not follow your good habit of rising to study the Mishnah. For this you deserve that I should leave and forsake you since you gave strength to Samael, the serpent and the evil inclination by sleeping until daybreak.[3]

Even when Mishnah reveals kabbalistic secrets to Karo, they frequently lead to practical, usually banal, moral or ethical suggestions. Not that Karo was a mere dilettante in Kabbalah; he was a member of a circle of kabbalistic scholars active in sixteenth-century Safed (a city in the northern Galilee), many of whom—including Isaac Luria—would write influential and revered mystical tracts.[4]

Karo's reliance on a heavenly messenger for clarifications of his legal reasoning had precedents. Jacob of Marvège (twelfth to thirteenth centuries) had gone so far as to submit legal questions to heaven and then collect the answers under the title *Responsa from Heaven*. Jacob's questions are relatively technical. "I asked: When women recite the benediction over the lulav or when someone recites the benediction over blowing the shofar on behalf of women is it or is it not wrong and is the benediction in such cases a vain benediction?"[5] At stake here is whether a woman has a positive obligation to wave the four species on Sukkot or to hear the shofar on Rosh Hashanah. Classical rabbinic sources assert that women do have this obligation, although they elsewhere exempt women from time-dependent, positive commandments—a class into which these two commandments fall. If women do not have these obligations, then the recitation of a blessing for these acts —which contains the words *who commanded us*—would be false, or vain, and thus prohibited. The divine answer, which quotes Scripture and casuistically reasons from Talmudic discussions, ultimately allows women to recite these blessings.

Jacob's and Karo's use of divine messengers in their legal reasoning ultimately differ significantly. Jacob submits questions; Karo appears to be a passive recipient of revelation. And whereas by publicizing their origin in the divine realm Jacob asserts divine authority to his answers, Karo's diary of his revelations appears to have been a private document; one would scarcely suspect his communication with an angel from his legal commentary or code. Yet, at the same time, Jacob and Karo struggled with the same problem: whether Jewish law was realist or nominalist. That is, are the mitzvot static divine commands that exist independently of the jurist or rabbi, with the job of the latter to uncover them (the realist position), or does law gain its authority by virtue of it being declared authoritative by the proper authorities (the nominalist position)? *Responsa from Heaven* was an articulation of the realist position so extreme that many medieval rabbis rejected Jacob's approach. In any case, both authors are indicative of the way in which Jews from the Middle Ages blurred concepts that to modern readers seem obviously distinct.

Law versus spirit, legal versus spiritual, legalistic versus mystical. To many of us, these terms are obvious and clear opposites. The understanding, however, that law and spirit are antithetical has a specific genealogy that goes back to the apostle Paul's attempt to contrast the Law (that is, the Torah) with the Spirit of God as revealed through Jesus Christ. There is nothing natural or obvious to the dichotomy; it is a culturally constructed one. The odd mix of spirit with law found in the writings of Jacob of Marvège and Rabbi Joseph Karo was hardly odd to them. For them, spirit and law were not even quite distinct entities, no less antithetical ones.

The simple fact that there is no word in ancient or medieval Hebrew or Aramaic for what we call mysticism deserves reflection. Kabbalists, the medieval purveyors and practitioners of what we today refer to as Jewish mysticism, did not have a word for mysticism. Like the dichotomy between law and spirit, the very category mysticism (which is aligned with spirit rather than law) has strong Christian roots.

This is not to say that the term *mysticism* is not useful when discussing some Jewish concepts, practices, or texts, only that it is important to be clear about both the limitations and use of the term. In what way, for example, were Karo's revelations mystical? When modern scholars use the term, they frequently attempt to signify a religious understanding in which 1. the individual 2. aspires to unite with 3. the all-encompassing One. Although both Jacob of Marvège and Joseph Karo communicated with divine beings, neither would be considered mystics by this definition. Karo communicated as an individual (although through the medium of communally produced texts), but his aspirations to unite were limited to "cleaving" to Mishnah, and whether he understood the universe to be a single, all-encompassing reality (as did some other kabbalists) is unclear. Despite his kabbalistic training, Karo's actual mystical experiences owe more to a classical form of what we might call Jewish mysticism, the desire to experience the fullness of God's presence.

The thirteenth-century kabbalists inherited an incoherent and messy set of Jewish mystical traditions. As we have seen, earlier Jewish texts—including those that entered the Jewish canon (like the Hebrew Bible, the Mishnah, and the Babylonian Talmud) and those that did not (e.g., 1 Enoch) or had a more marginal status (e.g., the Hekhalot texts)—contained scattered, sometimes ambivalent, reflections of the human desire to experience God directly through his or her senses. These accounts took various forms. Some of these older texts tell of a tour of heaven (and sometimes hell). Others hint at practices of mystical ascent achieved through meditation on an older text. One collection of mystical recipes (*Sefer HaRazim*) focuses on theurgy, the use of certain practices and verbal formulas to harness the divine power to do one's will. Outside of some amulets and bowls inscribed in Aramaic with "magical" formulae, we know little about the actual practice of mystical techniques among Jews in antiquity.

If the Jewish scholars of Christian Spain who developed the Kabbalah knew of these literary precedents, they did a good job hiding it. Asserting themselves as heirs of Tradition (the literal translation of Kabbalah), they nevertheless put forth mystical ideas and texts that despite some tenuous ties to this earlier Jewish mysticism were radically discontinuous with it. Rather than developing organically out of a long tradition of Jewish mysticism (the model advanced by the great scholar of Jewish mysticism, Gershom Scholem), the Kabbalah is best seen as a product of its own times, the result of reading and translating earlier traditions through the double lens of contemporary culture and a fertile and original imagination.

One of the earliest and most influential products of this new Jewish mystical movement was *Sefer haBahir*, the Book of Illumination. This book appears to have emerged at the end of the twelfth or beginning of the thirteenth century in Provence, although it is pseudepigraphically ascribed to Rabbi Nehunia ben Ha-Kanah, who appears in rabbinic mystical traditions. The *Bahir* is hardly illuminating—its poor organization and cryptic commentaries on a few scriptural passages from the beginning of Genesis are often difficult to decipher. The *Bahir*, though, is the first kabbalistic work to refer to an understanding of the *sefirot*, a concept that would become central to later kabbalistic texts. The *Bahir's* understanding God as the sum total of a number of semiautonomous divine emanations radically departs from previous Jewish understandings of both God and the world.

According to the *Bahir*, the world, like God, is eternal. The creation described in the Tanak was more an act of revelation than of actual creation, a making visible of that which had always existed. The moment of "creation," though, revealed more than the material world. It also was the moment of the divine emanation, in which the ten sefirot formed out of the "hidden light" of the divine. *Keter* ("crown") emanated first, and from it were formed the sibling sefirot of *hokhmah* (wisdom) and *binah* (discernment). Then, in a complicated interplay of divine power from these three sefirot, the seven lower sefirot came into existence. Together these ten constitute the inner life of the divine. Put a bit more simplistically, God is the interaction of these ten sefirot.

Scholars have long seen parallels between the *Bahir's* notion of the sefirot and Neoplatonic and Gnostic ideas that were popular in some contemporary Christian circles, most notably the heretical Cathars. Like the Cathars, the *Bahir* seems to posit a dualistic universe in which evil emerges from the improper flow of divine energy but takes on independence from the divine.

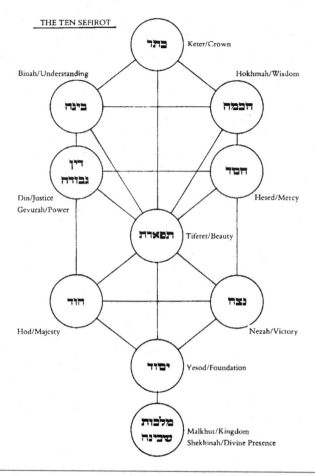

THE TEN SEFIROT

Keter/Crown

Binah/Understanding

Hokhmah/Wisdom

Din/Justice
Gevurah/Power

Hesed/Mercy

Tiferet/Beauty

Hod/Majesty

Nezah/Victory

Yesod/Foundation

Malkhut/Kingdom
Shekhinah/Divine Presence

9.1 The *sefirot*. From "Kabbalistic Texts" by Lawrence Fine. *Reprinted with permission of Simon & Schuster Adult Publishing Group from* Back to the Sources: Reading the Classic Jewish Texts, *edited by Barry W. Holtz, page 321.*

Copyright © 1984 by Barry W. Holtz

Scholars are less clear about what this and other parallels *mean*. Was the author of the *Bahir* directly familiar with and did he borrow from the ideas of the Cathars, or the reverse? More likely, both were working in the same general universe of ideas, and both shaped their texts to fit into this shared conceptual universe. Given our lack of knowledge about the provenance of the *Bahir*, though, this has to remain speculative.

Whatever the Cathars' influence on the *Bahir*, the line from the ideas expressed in the *Bahir* to the Zohar is direct. The Zohar seems to cite the *Bahir* and might allude to it with its name (Splendor, which in Hebrew also implies light). Like the *Bahir*, the Zohar has the form of a scriptural commentary. Written in an archaizing Aramaic and ascribed to Rabbi Shimon bar Yohai (an early rabbinic figure from the first century), the Zohar is much longer and richer than the *Bahir*.

The Zohar was not written in the first century but in the thirteenth. Sections of it were cited by kabbalistic authors around 1290 in Castile, and the first references to it as more or less complete appear about thirty years later. How seriously anyone took its ancient attribution is unclear, but at least some contemporary kabbalists were suspicious of it. At the beginning of the fourteenth century one kabbalist, Isaac of Acre, claims that the widow of a man named Moses de Leon told him that he had authored the Zohar himself and attributed it to an earlier figure in order to increase it monetary value. Today most scholars recognize de Leon as the primary shaper, if not necessarily sole author, of the Zohar. The claim that the Zohar was pseudepigraphical (i.e., falsely attributed) set off a lively controversy in kabbalistic circles, but the controversy did little to dampen enthusiasm for the text. Over the next three centuries scores of kabbalistic manuscripts appeared, most indebted to the Zohar. These manuscripts probably circulated only within small groups of kabbalists, although kabbalistic ideas were already creeping into the public domain. Rabbi Moses ben Nahman (Ramban, or Nahmanides, 1194–ca. 1270) was a member of a more conservative kabbalistic circle in Catalonia, and around the time the Zohar was taking shape he explicitly incorporated kabbalistic interpretations into his popular commentary on the Torah. The later Torah commentary (1320) of the Italian rabbi Menahem Recanati quoted from the Zohar; his work was one of the first kabbalistic works to be printed. The Zohar itself was published 1558–60, but by that time Jewish mystics had long seen it as the foundational and canonical text.

At the heart of the Zohar is a myth. This myth, firmly rooted in the idea of the sefirot found in the *Bahir*, has both a historical and continuing component. The Zohar is a myth in an almost literal sense: it is a story about God, telling of His revelation, from the Infinite—the *Eyn Sof*—to the lower levels of the sefirot. The story is a frankly sexual one, with matings between existing sefirot that led to the birth of lower ones. The Zohar thus puts forth a conception of God that breaks almost completely from that of the Rabbis, philosophers, and earlier Jewish mystical texts.

This conception of God is not static. The Infinite did not simply emanate into ten sefirot at some past time, to exist from then to now in perfect repose. The Godhead is eternally dynamic, comprised not just of the sefirot but also of the energy that flows between them. And sometimes, like an elaborate plumbing system with a clog, the energy does not flow as it should.

In all respects, for a thinker like Maimonides the Zohar is a theological nightmare. Rather than subscribing to the idea of an eternal God, it posits One who emerged or developed in time. Rather than understanding God as "perfect," an "unmoved mover," the Zohar has a vision of a dynamic God, always in the process of change. Even worse, sometimes God goes awry. But these obvious theological problems with the Zohar—all of which were recognized by later kabbalists, who attempted to piece together solutions to them—really are only the tip of the iceberg.

The real theological problem within the Zohar is that it lays suspended between polytheism and pantheism. Again, the contrast with Maimonides sharpens the problem with the sefirot. For Maimonides, God's indivisibility extends to God's attributes. A single, indivisible God is one that does not have separable attributes. To Maimonides the idea that God could be divided not only by attribute but also by essence would be heretical, for it throws into question God's oneness. It opens the Zohar to the charge of polytheism. In response to this charge, the Zohar's defenders vigorously asserted that God was indeed one, ultimately indivisible in the Eyn Sof. The Eyn Sof and the overflowing of divine power constitute a single and unified whole that engulfs all.

This moves the argument from the pot into the fire; from polytheism to pantheism. If the divine engulfs all, that means the divine is found in nature—the created world is but a part of the whole. It means that evil is part of God, and that humans are not just made in the divine image but that they (like animals too) in fact contain part of the divine within them. The Zohar and its later readers wrestle, without resolution, with both problems.

On the issue of evil the Zohar leans toward the *Bahir's* reliance on some form of Gnosticism. The Zohar is not systematic about anything, but in general seems to regard evil as a set of interlocking "shells" that surround a side of the sefirotic Godhead. This is the "other side," *sitra ahara*, that exists outside the divine and rages against it. Variously conceived as the dross produced when sefirah gevurah (power) emerged, the result of tension between gevurah and hesed (compassion), or the exiled negative energy of the Eyn Sof, the sitra ahara has frightful powers. The world is riven in this cosmic battle between good and evil.

One passage from the Zohar attempts to describe the origin of evil:

> God said, "Let there be an expanse in the midst of the waters . . . (Genesis 1:6)—Here is the mystery in detail, separating upper waters from lower

through mystery of the left. Here conflict was created through the left side. For until here was mystery of the right, and here is mystery of the left, so conflict raged between this and the right. Right is consummate of all, so all is written by the right, for upon it depends all consummation. When the left aroused, conflict aroused, and through that conflict blazed the fire of wrath. Out of that conflict aroused by the left, emerged Hell. Hell aroused on the left and clung.

The wisdom of Moses: he contemplated this, gazing into the act of Creation. In the act of Creation a conflict arose between left and right, and in that conflict aroused by the left, Hell emerged, clinging there. The central pillar, who is the third day, entered between them, mediating the conflict, reconciling the two sides. Hell descended, left merged in right, and peace prevailed over all.[6]

This passage uses one code to break another. Genesis 1:6, the passage asserts, is really about the emergence of evil from the Godhead. But to understand that, the reader needs to know both the sefirotic system itself as well as the key to it. The "right" refers to the right side of the sefirotic "body," that is, the sefirot of wisdom, love, and endurance. The "left" refers to the sefirot understanding, power, and splendor. According to the first paragraph, hell was the result of the left side becoming "aroused," and hell continues to cling to its original source.

The second paragraph describes a temporal development in the Godhead. During creation, power and love were locked in conflict. The "central pillar," the sefirah of beauty, then mediated between them, allowing hell to separate from the left side and descend. The passage continues with interpretations of other scriptural conflicts (e.g., between Korah and Moses, as described in Numbers 16) and their "real" meanings, which always refer to the relationships between the sefirot. This brings the author to contemplate one practical implication:

Havdalah. Separation, as Sabbath departs, separates those who rule the weekdays from Sabbath. As soon as Sabbath departs, a specter, an evil officer, ascends from Hell, intent on seizing power the moment Israel recites: *Let the work of our hands prosper* (Psalms 90:17). Emerging from the rung known as Sheol, he desires to mingle in the seed of Israel and dominate them. But Israel takes action with myrtle and wine, reciting *havdalah*, so he departs from them. As soon as they recite the blessing of separation over the cup, that specter sinks into his place in Sheol, site of Korah and his gang.[7]

This passage now links the ritual called havdalah, which marks the end of the Sabbath, with the cosmic mysteries. Separation hearkens back to the creation of the expanse, and thus evil, and in fact seems to evoke the specter from hell. Only the ritual activities of havdalah, specifically the smelling of myrtle and blessings over a cup of wine, ward off the specter for another week.

This passage is in many ways representative of the Zohar. It is thoroughly esoteric. In this passage the reader needs to know the meaning of "left," "right," and "central pillar." But elsewhere the sefirot go by a rich variety of other names as well. Colors, patriarchs, and parts of the body, when mentioned in Scripture, all become veiled references to the sefirot. When the Torah reports, for example, that "Jacob left Beer-sheba and set out for Haran" (Genesis 28:10), one rabbi comments that "he left the sphere of the land of Israel . . . and went to an alien domain."[8] Translated, this means that "beauty" (Jacob) left the sefirah of kingdom (Israel) for the "other side," the place of demonic forces. What in the Torah is a simple declarative statement that moves the plot along becomes in the Zohar a coded reference to a divine drama that has cosmic consequences. The Zohar, incidentally, does not here spell out the ramifications of this statement that beauty went into exile.

The assumption that the Torah encodes the inner life of the divine gives a new meaning to the idea of revelation. The Torah becomes an act of God's self-disclosure, at once a manifestation of this disclosure as well as its coded description. Torah has an inner and outer life. Those who cannot see beyond the Torah's "garments" see only the stories and legal prescriptions. However, the soul of the Torah is the access that it provides to the complex dynamic that constitutes God. Torah, moreover, has its own continuing dynamic. For the kabbalists there is a direct line from the written Torah to the oral one; rabbinic tradition is complicit in God's self-disclosure. The Zohar alludes to rabbinic interpretations on nearly every page, suggesting that the Talmud itself can be read as describing the divine mysteries. Nor did the Talmud end this process. Any initiate continues the dynamic process of revelation through the informed study of the static, canonical texts. Mystical access to God is still possible, but one can obtain it only through a set of fixed texts.

For the Zohar and its kabbalists, though, what exactly is a mystic? What is the importance of learning the divine mysteries? Unlike earlier mystical texts, the Zohar does not attempt to describe visions of the divine; the purpose here does not appear to be ascent to the heavens. Instead, the Zohar points toward knowledge of the divine mysteries as being important on two levels, human and cosmic. The former we have already seen in the passage about havdalah. Havdalah keeps the evil officers at bay, protecting against the "other side." This discussion blends, as mentioned earlier, elements that we might call mystical and magical. While warding off an evil specter smacks of magic, as traditionally understood, clearly the Zohar does not differentiate it from any other part of its mysticism. All involve tapping into divine power, which can result in personal benefit. "How intensely human beings should contemplate the glory of the blessed Holy One, praising His glory," Rabbi Eleazar exclaims in the Zohar, "For if one knows how to praise his Lord fittingly, the blessed Holy Ones fulfills his desire. Further, he multiplies blessings above and below."[9] Fittingly, of course, means according to the qualities of the sefirot. Proper worship brings divine blessings to earth.

The "blessings above," though, refers to the cosmic consequences of this mystical practice. Sometimes called "theosophic Kabbalah," this form of mystical practice centers on contemplation of the divine nature. The goal of such contemplation is less the attainment of individual reward than it is the actual redirection of the flow of divine energy. Unlocking the key to God's inner life provides to the mystic the power to transform it. Israel's adherence to the mitzvot, *when done with the proper understanding and intention*, helps to reunite the lowest sefirah, Shechinah, with the upper sefirot and thus promote divine wholeness. Theosophic Kabbalah, then, is not a disinterested intellectual exercise but a theurgic practice that alters God's nature.

The Shechinah's current estrangement from the upper sefirot mirrors the people Israel's estrangement from the land and God. The Zohar's notion of redemption has two parallel movements, above and below. Just as the Shechinah will reunite in loving embrace (actually, the Zohar prefers the image of sexual intercourse) with foundation (the divine phallus), so too Israel will reunite with the land and God. To perform the mitzvot is to help to reunite the Shechinah to its lover, with the result of speeding the time of redemption. God has entrusted Israel with the task of making God whole again, at which final point time will end.

Despite the teleological dimension of the Zohar's understanding of a life of piety as it drives toward redemption and the end of time, by and large the Zohar's eschatology is passive rather than active. Humans can hope to bring about flashes of divine unification, but God remains dynamic, not frozen in harmony. The main body of the Zohar assumes a continuing annual cycle and ebb and flow of divine worship, practice, and God's internal power. The

Zohar, in general, neither points toward a cataclysmic apocalypse nor does it counsel humans to become messianic activists. Its theurgy seeks to halt the further degeneration of the universe rather than transform it positively.

Theosophic Kabbalah, with its emphasis on cosmic theurgy achieved through contemplation, was ultimately the most influential form of Jewish mysticism, but it was not the only one available in the thirteenth century. Another form of Jewish mysticism, often called prophetic or ecstatic, was best represented by Abraham Abulafia.[10] Born in Christian Spain in the mid-thirteenth century, Abulafia traveled across Europe to Palestine and then back again, living in 1270 around Catalonia before moving to Sicily around 1280. He was familiar with theosophic Kabbalah and bitterly critiqued its idea of the sefirot: if Christianity was mistaken for dividing God into three, he argued, all the more contemptible is the idea that God can be divided into ten! Abulafia, that is, found the conception of the sefirot to be polytheistic. Instead of focusing on contemplation of the nature of God, Abulafia believed that humans could in fact achieve a form of mystical union with the divine.

Abulafia's understanding of mystical union owed much to Maimonides and other philosophical conceptions of the divine. Following philosophical ideas current among Jewish and non-Jewish thinkers, Abulafia believed that there was a cosmic force called an agent intellect. This is the last and lowest of ten emanations of the divine intellect; it is the force that illuminates the human intellect and enables it to reach perfection. Abulafia's mysticism focused on the possibility of humans uniting with this divine agent intellect. Such a person becomes, at that moment, not only a prophet but the messiah himself. The agent intellect is itself a supernal messiah that carries the power of salvation. To unite with it is to tap into this saving force.

Abulafia saw himself as the messiah. Having experienced union with the agent intellect, Abulafia began to apply to himself the scriptural and rabbinic references to the messiah. Believing, for example, that the messiah will be recognized on Rosh Hashanah in Rome, he (unsuccessfully) sought an audience with the pope at that time. Abulafia saw himself engaged not only in a deeply personal journey but also in a public and redemptive one. Unlike most kabbalists of his time, he sought to spread his kabbalistic insights outside small esoteric circles and in so doing to affirm his own role in the approaching redemption.

Abulafia's legacy is not confined to his role as a "failed messiah." He introduced a range of mystical practices to facilitate union with the agent intellect. In the tradition of some of the Hekhalot texts, he was fascinated with the name of God and divine beings and attributed power to the manipulation of the letters of the divine name. The power that he saw in language extended to his use of *gematria*, an interpretive technique of translating letters into numerical values and then back into other words that have the same value. For example, the first letter of the Hebrew alphabet (*aleph*) has the value of 1, the second of 2, through the ninth letter, at which point the letters stand for tens and then hundreds. So Abulafia equates a phrase that traditionally refers to David, "David the son of Yishai, messiah [or anointed]," with "Messiah the son of David, [the] youth." Equivalent in numerical value (both add up to 742 according to this code), this gematria allows Abulafia to identify the messiah with the agent intellect, which he asserts is the "youth." Gematria was but one of several decoding techniques that Abulafia brought to his study of the Tanak.

Ecstasy, for Abulafia, also required physical training. Like the theosophic kabbalists, Abulafia demanded a relatively ascetic lifestyle. Only by controlling the body and its messy urges could one hope for unification with the divine. For Abulafia the goal of such unification was human perfection, to have one's potential fully illuminated by God in the form of the agent intellect.

As we have seen, medieval Jewish mysticism, Kabbalah (in both its theosophic and ecstatic forms), builds upon the biblical and rabbinic textual traditions. These Jewish mystics saw the language of divine revelation as the path to God. The Tanak was seen as an act of God's self-disclosure. The Zohar sees the Torah's text as a symbolic code whereas Abulafia works more on the level of individual letters, words, and phrases, but both share an assumption about the nature of the language of divine revelation. They, like rabbinic midrash, understand the language of Scripture as perfect. Unlike midrash, they see within the text an actual description of perfection, unlocking the mysteries of the cosmos.

Despite the gap between the rabbinic and kabbalistic readings of Scripture, the kabbalists depend heavily on these earlier rabbinic readings as well as on the rest of the rabbinic tradition. The kabbalists did not approach Scripture in a personal and unmediated fashion. Rather, they saw Scripture through the lens of the Rabbis. When the Zohar, for example, discusses the story of the serpent in the Garden of Eden, it assumes that the serpent copulated with Eve—a reading clearly derived from an older midrash. Before all else, the kabbalists were good Talmudists, and they implicitly and explicitly saw their own endeavor as the authentic continuation of the rabbinic tradition. They styled themselves, after all, as *kabbalists*, preservers of the tradition.

Yet there is no straight line either from the Rabbis and their writings or from earlier manifestations of Jewish mysticism to the kabbalists. Like the philosophy of Maimonides, the emergence of Kabbalah was in no way predictable; it did not result from some teleological and organic unfolding of Judaism. Rather, the kabbalists of medieval Spain engaged their past, as transmitted to them through their traditional texts and rituals (e.g., havdalah), as a means of renewal and recreation. Kabbalah is yet another unanticipated crystallization of collective Jewish identity, interpretation, and practice emerging from the intersection of tradition and real life.

Medieval Jewish mysticism thus did not develop out of some pure and disconnected contemplation of tradition. The mystics were themselves historically embedded within a Christian society. The precise relationship between the Kabbalah, particularly the Zohar, and historical conditions remains murky. Many scholars argue that the Zohar is a product of its cultural context—thirteenth-century Christian Spain. The kabbalists are in dialogue not only with their tradition but also with current philosophical and even Christian theological ideas.

Abulafia's critique of theosophic Kabbalah (as now seen in the Zohar, which probably was not available to him) is telling in this respect. In part it is a philosophical critique. Abulafia's mysticism draws on the philosophical ideas and language that were current in learned philosophical circles. He implicitly argues that the theosophic kabbalists in fact go out of their way to avoid using this well-known philosophical cant. Theosophic Kabbalah, this critique suggests, is shaped by its opposition to philosophy; it is a response to Maimonides. Maimonides, that is, shaped the theosophic kabbalists *negatively*. Their image of a dynamic, imperfect God developed only against Maimonides' Aristotelian notion of a perfect God at rest.

If on the one hand theosophic Kabbalah was a reaction against Maimonides, on the other it has affinities with some Christian theological ideas.[11] Abulafia saw these affinities immediately in the notion of the sefirot, which is so central to theosophic Kabbalah. For Abulafia, these sefirot come dangerously close to hypostases of the divine—that is, the idea that divine aspects or characteristics can be embodied, much in the way that Christians saw God as trinitarian, comprised of three bodies sharing a single essence. Abulafia preferred a more philosophical system of emanations. Despite his attack on the theosophist kabbalists for their doctrine of the sefirot, Abulafia himself would ultimately develop a trinitarian schema that looks remarkably similar to the Christian one. Scholars have also recently argued that the theosophist understanding of the lowest sefirah, the Shechinah, is remarkably similar to the Christian understanding of the Virgin Mary as a divine female figure that intercedes with God.

This is not the only similarity between the theological ideas of the kabbalists and those of contemporary Christians. Christian mysticism was itself developing at that time, also in part as a reaction against philosophical reasoning.[12] Like the kabbalists, the Christian mystics insisted on strict ascetic regimens. The development of Kabbalah took place in a much broader cultural environment.

Kabbalah had a profound influence throughout the circum-Mediterranean. Although primarily confined to esoteric circles (perhaps giving it a certain cachet?), occasionally thinkers such as Abulafia would write for a wider audience. Study of Kabbalah engaged some of the best Jewish minds of the high Middle Ages (such as Maimonides' son), and kabbalistic texts were noted and studied even by Christian Hebraists, upon whom they made a strong impact. The expulsion of the Jews from Spain in 1492 only strengthened the influence of the Zohar and other kabbalistic texts. Kabbalah—now made more accessible through the dispersion of its many Spanish students and scholars—offered an image of an imperfect world beset by the forces of evil that many Jews found compelling in the face of the traumatic expulsion.

For a brief time in the sixteenth century the center of kabbalistic study and creativity came to rest in Safed, in the northern Galilee in (modern-day) Israel. This was the community of Rabbi Joseph ben Ephraim Karo, with whom this chapter opened. This circle of kabbalists has been widely studied. They began the practice of saying a collection of hymns, now known as *Kabbalat Shabbat*, during the Friday evening prayer services. Anchored by the hymn *Lekha Dodi* ("Come, my beloved"), an original composition by Solomon Alkabez, this prayer service was decidedly theurgic; it was intended to help reunite the Shechinah to the higher sefirot. *Lekha Dodi* is itself a kabbalistic hymn, dense with allusions to God's inner life.

The Kabbalat Shabbat service exemplifies the distinctive contribution of the mystics of Safed. Dampening the Zohar's passive eschatology, these

Jewish mystics emphasized the human ability to change God and bring about redemption. The emphasis on human participation in the redemptive process was in part tied to their heightened sense of messianic expectation: They were living, so they thought, in the Final Drama, as shown by the great trauma of the expulsion from Spain. Exile, in fact, became a prominent theme for the Safed kabbalists, an idea that they projected onto the Shechinah living in exile from the upper sefirot. Much more so than in the Zohar, the Safed kabbalists asserted the human ability to bring the Shechinah—and therefore Israel—out of exile *permanently.* A hymn like *Lekha Dodi* was charged with this express purpose. Said with the proper understanding and intention, it was thought to work theurgically on God and move the world one step closer to ultimate redemption. Kabbalat Shabbat is just one of several rites developed by these mystics that would ultimately enter the "mainstream" of Jewish traditional practices, albeit emptied of its theurgic core.

Another well-known invention that probably originated with the kabbalists from Safed was the Tu b'Shevat seder. The Mishnah mentions the fifteenth day of the Hebrew month of Shevat (usually falling in January or February on our calendar) as a "new year" for the trees. For the Mishnah and the Talmud this is entirely a technical matter that helps to compute the "age" of the tree for purposes of tithing; there was no ritual or rite to mark the date. Tu b'Shevat receives almost no attention in post-talmudic rabbinic literature either. With its emphasis on trees, though, Tu b'Shevat began to acquire a richer symbolic texture. Given the tree imagery used by these kabbalists, Tu b'Shevat became a ripe target for ritual activity. The ritual of a special, theurgic meal, the seder, that was held on the fifteenth of Shevat is known only from a somewhat later text, the *Peri Etz Hadar*, whose first printed edition was in the early eighteenth century and that was known only in Eastern and Sephardic Jewish communities. This work describes a meal in four parts. The core of the ritual is the eating of ten types of fruit (corresponding to each of the sefirot) for each of the three lower worlds, Creation, Formation, and Making. The characteristics of the fruits correspond to these groups; for example, the fruits to be eaten in the Creation part of the seder have no shell because they need not be protected from evil.

The Tu b'Shevat seder is a *tikkun*, a "fixing" of, in this case, the sefirah of foundation (*yesod*). The assumption is that male sexual transgressions damage the divine phallus, yesod. The rites of the Tu b'Shevat seder, connected as they are to the image of natural fecundity, heals foundation. "By virtue of performing this *tiqqun* for the fruit tree, he will heal his part in the flawing of *Zaddiq* [the sefirah yesod] who makes fruit," the rite reads.[13] That is, the seder is essentially a penitential rite for masturbation and other forms of illicit (male) sexual activity. It is little surprise that the rite never caught on in more rationally minded Jewish communities, and it remained relatively marginal even in Sephardic communities until the Jewish National Fund resurrected it (in vastly altered form!) in the mid-twentieth century to promote fund-raising for its planting efforts.

The Tu b'Shevat seder drew upon the particular strain of Kabbalah from Safed developed by Isaac Luria. Luria (1534–1572) died young and left no writings of his own. His visions and creative ideas were collected and systematized (to a degree) by his foremost disciple, Hayim Vital. Luria's "system" builds upon earlier kabbalistic ideas but fashions them into new cosmological myth.

Lurianic Kabbalah, as it came to be known, develops two extraordinary ideas, that of "contraction" (*tsimtsum*) and of "breaking the vessels." Tsimtsum is a response to the pantheism inherent in earlier kabbalistic ideas. Luria claimed that the Eyn Sof is so awesome that nothing can stand in its presence. Rather than encompassing all, then, in order to allow for creation it must contract, leaving a void outside itself in which creation can occur. God voluntarily renounces power in order to allow for creation. God, in one formulation of this idea, puts Himself into exile, banishing Himself to His inner chambers. (This, some have argued, might be a continuing response to the expulsion of the Jews from Spain and the feeling of homelessness and exile that followed from it.) God's divine light, however, does not remain entirely confined to these chambers. For Luria, God pulsed, and these pulses alternatively wash up traces of divine judgment in the cosmos and then send back the divine power that orders it to allow the world to subsist. Gershom Scholem calls this "a gigantic process of divine inhalation and exhalation."[14] Tsimtsum, of course, is not without its theological problems. Luria's idea of breaking the vessels was in part a response to one of these problems, the seemingly unbridgeable gap between humans and God, and in part to another, the problem of evil.

Luria's theory of the breaking of the vessels has many variations, and is in any case too complex to relate in detail. Essentially, however, it involves the idea that the divine light, itself a mixture of the residue of the tsimtsum and the dross of evil thrown off by the sefirah of judgment, exploded from its shelter of the upper three sefirot into special vessels that had been emanated in order to catch it. The light, though, proved too strong for the vessels and they shattered. In a highly ordered process, this shattering then unleashed the cosmological drama. The process of the shattering allowed evil to coalesce as an independent, external force at the same time that it released aspects of the divine, sparks, into the cosmos from which the Eyn Sof had contracted. Some later formulations transferred evil to the shattered vessels themselves, imagining them to now encircle and contain the divine sparks.

For Luria, his colleagues, and his followers, God is imperfect. Not only are there inherent and continuing defects in the Godhead, exacerbated by the sins of humans, but also pieces of God are exiled from the Godhead, trapped in the material creation. It is at this point that Luria's myth acquires practical consequences. As in other kabbalistic systems, Luria believes that humans are capable of transforming, or restoring, the Godhead. This process of "fixing" he calls tikkun; when the Godhead is fixed redemption will occur. The worshipper participates in tikkun through observance of the commandments with the correct mystical intent. This idea gave rise to a number of short declarations that precede the performance of various mitzvot. Enacting tikkun, though, involves more than a verbal declaration and the proper intent (kavanah). Successfully done, a tikkun lifts the worshipper up into the very sefirot he is attempting to fix. (As far as we know, in Luria's time there were no female practitioners of Kabbalah.) The individual soul is given ample chance to perform tikkun, on both the Godhead and itself; souls were thought to transmigrate, or be reborn, until they have achieved perfection. To return to the terminology used above, Lurianic Kabbalah blended theosophic and ecstatic strains.

Lurianic Kabbalah was widely accepted and prepared the ground for Sabbatai Zvi. The "failed messiahship" of Sabbatai Zvi (1625–1676)—his declaration in 1665, with the assistance of his "prophet," Nathan of Gaza, that he was the messiah followed soon after by his apostasy to Islam and the sudden collapse of the movement that crystallized around him—is one of the most interesting and dramatic stories in Jewish history.[15] Although too complex to detain us here, it is worth noting how the Sabbatean movement, flourishing at a time of heightened Christian and Jewish messianic expectations, drew quite naturally upon Luria's doctrines. As articulated by Nathan of Gaza, the soul of the messiah was mingled with the divine light that fell into the abyss and was entrapped by the evil fragments of the shattered vessels. The "serpents" torment the soul of the messiah, and when tikkun is completed the messiah will be released from his prison and torments and will reveal himself. This doctrine had the added advantage of explaining

Sabbatai Zvi's erratic behavior—was he not being tormented by the serpents? Today we would undoubtedly opt for a different diagnosis.

The Sabbatean movement spread quickly and was not confined to the uneducated. Many traditional rabbis enthusiastically declared that Sabbatai Zvi was the true messiah; they saw little contradiction between Nathan of Gaza's doctrines and their own understanding of Jewish messianism. It was precisely this wide (although certainly not universal) acceptance of Sabbatai Zvi as the messiah that made his apostasy so painful. Confronted by the sultan with a choice between conversion to Islam and death, Sabbatai Zvi chose conversion. Some of his followers, like Nathan of Gaza, reevaluated the kabbalistic doctrines to account for this unexpected turn of events. For some it was a sign of his descent into the vale of the serpents for the final battle, from which he would emerge victorious. For others his antinomian behavior signaled the achievement of tikkun and the dawning of a new age—even if they were themselves not quite convinced enough to abandon their own observance of the mitzvot. For many of his former followers, though, his apostasy was proof of the mistakenness of their belief in him. The scandal provoked by Sabbatai Zvi's apostasy spread widely, tarnishing rabbinic reputations as it also pushed his "true" believers deep underground.

There is a fair amount of debate over the lasting "positive" influence of the Sabbatai Zvi affair. Did the developing antinomian trends among these underground conventicles of followers, for example, play a role in the development of later Jewish groups that deemphasized the role of halakhah? There is far less debate over its enduring negative impact. Until the recent phenomenon following the death of the Lubavitcher rebbe, Sabbatai Zvi was the last Jewish messiah to have gained a wide following. That Jewish communities are today far less likely to accept a messianic claim is in part the legacy of his apostasy.

The affair of Sabbatai Zvi also tarnished the reputation and influence of Lurianic Kabbalah. When, in the eighteenth century, Hasidism arose in Poland and the Ukraine, its reception was colored by the events of the previous century. Hasidism was a religious revivalist movement that drew on Lurianic Kabbalah, especially the notion of tikkun. The movement, which quickly splintered into different branches and dynasties, met resistance along two fronts. First, Hasidic groups typically assigned greater spiritual power to a guide whom they termed a rebbe. Each Hasidic group had a single rebbe, who was seen, in some groups, as a kind of intermediary between earth and heaven. The ascription of an almost semidivine status to a human made contemporary Jewish religious leaders apprehensive. Similarly, although Lurianic Kabbalah did not lead directly to Sabbatai Zvi's apostasy, the apostasy nevertheless demonstrated problems latent within Kabbalah. It did not help that, around the same time that Hasidism was developing, a Polish Jew, Jacob Frank (1726–1791), drew upon kabbalistic traditions (explicitly rejecting, in fact, the rabbinic traditions upon which they were founded) to justify the rejection of halakhah and the promotion of sexual license; Frankists were known for their ritual orgies. Hasidism's use of Lurianic ideas, and its emphasis on the joyful worship of God over (but never excluding) punctilious observance of the mitzvot, were enough to stoke in contemporary Jewish rabbis the fear of a latent antinomianism.

Apostasy is in the eye of the beholder, and such labels are invariably applied by victors of a religious conflict. Sabbateans were, in their day, just Jews, drawing on their tradition in the same creative ways as do all others. They were not a social movement and lacked a distinctive religious ideology; an understanding of Judaism as broken into movements and ideologies would not arise until the nineteenth century. Like the cases of the early Christians, today's Messianic Jews, and perhaps even the messianic followers of the deceased Lubavitcher rebbe, the affair of Sabbatai Zvi also illustrates the boundaries set by Jewish communities. Despite the wide tolerance for diverse understandings of Judaism, Jewish communities have also drawn lines, rejecting some claims to Judaism. These rejections are in part historically contingent; almost two millennia of conflict between Jews and Christians has most likely led to a lower degree of tolerance today for Messianic Jews than the early followers of Jesus might have found in their Jewish communities. In part, though, they can be understood by the degree of their rupture with tradition. The explicit rejection of the textual tradition and the conceptual boundaries that it creates makes Jewish communities uneasy. Thus, although belief today that the Lubavitcher rebbe was (is) the messiah is structurally similar to that found in these other Jewish messianic movements, few Jewish communities would consider declaring these Hasidic believers heretics; despite their belief, these Jews continue to engage and ascribe authority to tradition. Messianic Jews, on the other hand, are marginalized on the basis of their rejection of rabbinic traditions and texts. The followers of Sabbatai Zvi fell somewhere between these poles, with those groups that were able to conform to community norms able to maintain a place (however uneasily) within their communities, while those, like the followers of Jacob Frank, who rejected these norms were in turn excluded.

Jewish mysticism was a complex phenomenon. Early on, as practiced by small esoteric groups working from a fixed textual tradition, it was an attempt to supplement the love of God (as performed through the observance of the mitzvot) with the experience of God. As found in the earliest kabbalistic writings and the Zohar, Jewish mysticism had become something entirely different. Forged in the specific historical context of Medieval Christian Spain, Kabbalah promoted a new myth for new purposes. Medieval Jewish mystics drew deeply on earlier Jewish texts and ideas, actively reshaping them into something original. It is just as important to acknowledge the traditions and ideas the kabbalists ignored or minimized as it is to see the lines that connect them to the tradition. Emphasizing the power of human beings to transform the divine, the kabbalists downplay the idea found in biblical, rabbinic, and philosophical texts of a transcendent, perfect God. Moreover, different kabbalistic communities drew upon their heritage differently, forming, shaping, and discarding as they saw fit. In the hands of Nathan of Gaza, Lurianic Kabbalah takes one form; in the hands of the later Hasidim, it takes quite another. Inheriting the legacies of Maimonides and the Zohar, with their opposed visions, Hasidim in the eighteenth and nineteenth centuries drew on the latter. The great nineteenth-century German Jewish historian, Heinrich Graetz, made a very different choice.

10

EAST AND WEST

EINRICH GRAETZ (1817–1891) could not have been clearer about his view of the Zohar.[1] "Through its constant use of coarse expressions," he writes in his monumental *History of the Jews*, "often verging on the sensual, in contradistinction to the chaste, pure spirit pervading Jewish literature, the Zohar sowed the seeds of unclean desires, and later on produced a sect that laid aside all regard for decency." The Zohar was a Jewish aberration, and its author, Moses de Leon, a forger, ignoramus, and profligate; a victim of "Messianic enthusiasm." The Zohar did violence to the meaning of the Bible, "perverted the verses and words of the Holy Book, and made the Bible the wrestling-ground of the most curious, insane notions."[2]

Graetz's virulent antipathy toward the Zohar and Kabbalah was not a mere personal peccadillo. Beginning his *History of the Jews* in Germany in 1853, Graetz inserted himself squarely in the middle of two heated conflicts. German Jews were still embroiled in the argument over Jewish emancipation. Although in several areas of Germany they had, with difficulty, acquired the right to citizenship, this right remained tenuous. Many Germans continued to oppose the integration of Jews into civic society. This opposition was complex and stemmed to a great degree from economic and social considerations. Many Germans opposing Jewish emancipation, however, also argued on the basis of religion: Judaism was in some way superstitious and primitive, a religion of "pots and pans" in contrast to the pure, spiritual, and ethical dictates of Christianity. They thus linked their understanding of the religious "essence" of Judaism to the character of its practitioners, with calamitous ramifications. The Zohar was no help to those Jews who wished to respond to the charge that Judaism was irrational and primitive; by the standards of the day, those would not be unfair characterizations of the Zohar. So in attacking the Zohar as aberrant, Graetz was also building a positive case for a Judaism whose "essence" was "high-minded" and rational and, thus, for the civic rights of German Jews.

At the same time, Graetz was an active participant in the internal struggles of the Jewish community. The principles of the Enlightenment, with its focus on the value of the individual and its weakening of the force of tradition, had as much impact on Jews in Germany as it did on non-Jews. Modern Jews had to confront not only the heady possibility of their civic integration into the body politic but also the meaning of their traditions and texts as seen through these values. Although their responses to modernity varied widely, all Jewish communities in the West confronted the same set of problems. One German response that would later crystallize into the Reform movement started in the early nineteenth century by insisting on some small, cosmetic changes to Jewish worship services. Sermons, for example, should be delivered in German rather than Yiddish. By the 1840s, however, some "Reformers" were advocating a more sweeping overhaul of Jewish ritual practices. Samson Raphael Hirsch responded to these demands by defending Jewish tradition but declaring it compatible with modernity, a stance that would develop into Modern Orthodoxy. Originally an advocate of this position, Graetz soon joined yet another emerging movement under the leadership of Zacharias Frankel. For Frankel, the Reformers went too far in rejecting traditional practices but Hirsch not far enough in acknowledging the value of secular truth. Graetz opposed the Reformers. His attacks on the Zohar's allegorizing of Scripture, on what he saw as its tendency to denude the biblical verses of their natural meanings in favor of spiritual ones, is also a not so veiled attack on the reforms that were then current. The Tanak should be read, in his view, in a "historical-positive" sense, as a source of norms. The Zohar's more symbolic method of reading Scripture just provided support for the Reformer's reading.

Graetz's attack on the Zohar thus highlights the crossroads to which nineteenth-century German Jews had come. German Jews did not have a stark choice between "tradition" and "modernity"; the traditional way of life, itself a product of the historical condition of Jews in medieval Germany, had become unsustainable. Medieval Ashkenazic Jews—so-called after the Hebrew term for Germany, Ashkenaz—had lived in semiautonomous communal organizations, each called a kehillah. The rise of Enlightenment values and consequent collapse of many (but not all) of the social and civic

barriers that separated Jews from Gentiles thus posed two distinct but in-
terrelated dilemmas. The medieval, feudal model was based on the idea that
the Jews were a single, undifferentiated ethnic, social, and religious group
whose place in society was clearly dictated by Christian understandings
of the Jews and their meaning within the Christian story. On a communal
level its demise left the Jews in terrain that was unfamiliar to both them and
their Gentile neighbors. Was a German Jew just like every other German?
Enlightenment values would seem to imply that they were. This, however,
immediately raised the second problem. It implied that the single factor
separating German Jews and German non-Jews was religion, or "Judaism."
German Jews now had to articulate and justify, to themselves and non-Jews,
what Judaism was. And there were many possible answers.

Typically, we see the nineteenth-century lives of German Jews through
the lens of the Holocaust. Their pact with modernity was quixotic, their
end tragic; they were never in the end successful in integrating. Yet in their
choice to confront modernity head-on, German Jews had little choice. Eastern European Jews had an encounter with modernity that was no less trans-
formative, even if their response was different. Judaism as we understand
the term today was, by and large, the product of this encounter with modernity. The textual traditions, concepts, and ritual practices, as we have
seen, of course have long and convoluted histories. But the way that we
understand them to be bundled together in a nice, neat package that we call
Judaism is distinctly modern, and the place that understanding gives to *ideology* differentiates it from previous understandings of Jewish life and practice. What ideology gains in terms of coherence and rational justification,
though, it also loses in terms of elasticity; it prepares the ground not for a
single but diverse Judaism but for multiple Jewish movements, each distinguishing and defining itself against the others. Nineteenth-century Europe thus gave birth not only to *Judaism* but to the different movements of
Judaism as well. Now each Western Jewish movement—whether neo-Orthodox, Haredi (Ultra-Orthodox), Conservative, Hasidic, Reform, or (later)
Reconstructionist—would orient and justify itself according to a particular
ideology, a legacy that is still very much alive.

By the time of Heinrich (Hirsch) Graetz, Jews had been wrestling with
Enlightenment ideas for about two centuries. Benedict (Baruch) Spinoza
usually gets the credit for being the first Jewish Enlightenment thinker.[3]

Spinoza was born in 1632 in the Spanish-Portuguese Jewish community of Amsterdam. The community had been founded about a century earlier by Jewish refugees from Spain and Portugal, many of whom had been forcibly converted to Catholicism. The Jews found themselves grudgingly tolerated in Amsterdam as long as they kept a low profile. Many became merchants, and while as a community they never achieved great wealth they were able to support basic communal institutions. The community had established a Talmud Torah (Jewish primary school) and, by 1675, had built a huge synagogue. Organized along a traditional Sephardic model, the community appointed a board of lay leaders (the *maamad*) to administer its affairs. The maamad had strong administrative but only weak coercive powers; its main weapon was the power of excommunication, whose threat the board occasionally wielded even against its own rabbis when they dared to question its authority.

Amsterdam's Jews neither would nor could simply reproduce Jewish life as it existed in fifteenth- and sixteenth-century Spain and Portugal. The community and the maamad were deeply concerned with policing religious

10.1 Sounding of the shofar on Rosh Hashanah, from Bernard Picart, *Cérémonies et coutumes religieuses de tous les peuples du monde* (Amsterdam: J.F. Bernard, 1728).
Courtesy of the Library of the Jewish Theological Seminary of America

boundaries that remained in flux. The internal cause of this flux was the unique situation of the Marranos, those Jews who in Spain and Portugal converted to Christianity but continued to "be" Jewish in secret. Allowed in Amsterdam to become Jewish publicly as well as privately, they now began a process of discovering what it was that Jews actually do and think. Combined with their understandable anxiety about the "correctness" of what they were learning, they were also particularly eager to create and protect the boundaries of authentic Jewish life. For the Amsterdam community the issue of the Marranos did not end in the sixteenth century. Well into the seventeenth century, the Jews of Amsterdam and the Iberian peninsula continued to travel to each other's communities, for reasons both familial and economic. Some Jews from Amsterdam went to Spain to bring Marranos back to Judaism, a proselytizing activity the Church punished with death. Marranos, simultaneously, continued to flee the Iberian peninsula, often ending up in Amsterdam.

This internal anxiety was compounded by the ever present need to stay on the right side of Amsterdam's ruling and warring factions. The Christians in Amsterdam were embroiled through the seventeenth century in their own religious conflicts, pitting Reformed and orthodox Calvinists against each other. Neither of the two major Christian factions was fond of the Jews, but both were willing to tolerate a Jewish presence in Amsterdam. One of the conditions for this toleration was that they cause no trouble. For the maamad this expectation extended from communal institutions (e.g., the Jewish community must provide for its own education and welfare for the destitute) to religious beliefs—they wanted to appear as good, orthodox God fearers with the same basic ethical and theological values as, for example, the orthodox Calvinists.

In 1656 the maamad excommunicated Baruch Spinoza. He was only twenty-three years old and, to our knowledge, had not written a word. The text of the excommunication—which was publicly read in Hebrew in the synagogue—is remarkably pointed; the most virulent of the maamad's many notices of excommunication. Making reference to Spinoza's "abominable heresies" and "monstrous deeds," the long notice of excommunication remains frustratingly vague about what it is that Spinoza actually did to warrant such an extraordinary condemnation. If, however, he was beginning to articulate the philosophical ideas that he would later write, the reasons for the excommunication begin to come into focus.

Spinoza created a naturalistic philosophy. He did not exactly deny the existence of God, but he instead understood the deity to be located in the active (creative) force of nature. In this sense Spinoza was a pantheist. God was in nature rather than some supernatural force that worked in history. This denial of a supernatural God would open the door to more forceful ideas during the Enlightenment of God's distancing from human affairs. While this idea alone would have upset the Jewish community of Amsterdam, there is evidence to suggest that they would have taken its ramifications a good deal more seriously.

The denial of a supernatural God that acts in history logically leads to an unraveling of most of the conceptual threads that had run through previous Jewish theological and philosophical understandings. Without a supernatural God there can be no covenant and no divine involvement with the people Israel. The notion of a revelation becomes absurd. Spinoza explicitly addresses this issue in the *Theological-Political Treatise*, which he published in 1670, well after his excommunication and seven years before his death. The *Theological-Political Treatise* argues that the Bible, far from containing the word of God, was written by a particular community of people who benefited politically from it. The Bible is, above all, a political document couched as a theological one, using the idea of a punishing God to enforce social norms. At the same time, Spinoza recognizes that Scripture can have a good effect, serving as the word of God only to the degree that it inspires humans to ethical action. Two centuries later, Karl Marx would adopt a version of this idea, calling religion an "opiate for the masses" intended to disguise social inequalities by justifying them in the natural order.

According to the historian Steven Nadler, it was less these ideas than another consequence of Spinoza's denial of a supernatural God that hit the nerve of Amsterdam's Jewish community: the denial of an immortal soul. Spinoza's philosophy, as it survives in his posthumously published *Ethics*, is notoriously slippery about the human soul. Is there a personal soul, separable from the body, that survives after death? Although Spinoza's direct answer is unclear, he might reasonably be construed to reject the idea of a personal soul. In fact, the idea of a personal, separable soul runs against the grain of his other arguments. Spinoza appears to think that the idea of a separable soul then rewarded or punished is one invented for political power, like the idea of a just God promulgated in the Bible. To Spinoza the world ultimately is neither just nor unjust; the question of justice in nature is moot.

According to Nadler, this was a particularly sensitive issue for Amsterdam's Jewish community. In addition to their skittishness and insecurity about their own orthodoxy, the Jews of Amsterdam also had to contend with the ramifications of their Marrano past. Would those Jews who were forced to convert to Christianity merit eternal life? Were they part of the "all Israel" who would gain a share of the world-to-come? This was not a simple academic exercise. The issue had embroiled the community. All four of the city's rabbinic leaders in the mid-seventeenth century had weighed in with tracts or polemics that argued for the immortality of the soul. They differed about the ultimate fate of those Jews who had converted, but they agreed that the soul was immortal and that it was the object of God's reward or punishment. Spinoza must have known in those circumstances that denying the existence of an immortal soul would bring down upon him the ire of the Amsterdam Jewish community.

There is also an external aspect to Spinoza's excommunication. When the Calvinists allowed the Jews to settle in Amsterdam, they did so on the assumption that they would be as rigidly orthodox as the Calvinists themselves. They conceived a model of the Jewish community as a religious community much like their own and went so far as to legislate the basic theological propositions to which they expected the Jews would adhere. The law of 1619 promulgated by the provincial assembly of Holland stated that the Jewish community must subscribe to a number of beliefs, among which is the belief that "there is life after death in which good people will receive their recompense and wicked people their punishment."[4] Whether or not the Calvinist leaders in Amsterdam in 1656 were really ready to punish the Jewish community for the views of a renegade twenty-three-year old who had published nothing, the Jewish community took seriously the policing of its theological borders.

The impact of Calvinist understandings of "proper" Jewish behavior goes beyond the issue of Jews merely trying to maintain their civic rights. Spinoza's significance (for our purposes) is that he was the first serious Jewish thinker to claim that the Bible is not the word of God and that God remained uninvolved in the history of Israel. These ideas had a marked but indirect effect on later Jewish thinkers; Jews did not read Spinoza as in any way part of their textual tradition, but his ideas would become increasingly influential over the next two centuries. The significance of the Amsterdam community with which he broke, though, is that it ascribed a powerful role to proper theological belief; it demanded an ideological commitment. Torn with questions of identity and religious boundaries, the Spanish and Portuguese Jews of Amsterdam increasingly began to understand themselves as members of a distinctly *religious* (rather than ethnic) community defined by proper belief. In this we see a harbinger of what would become in Germany the flourishing of Jewish ideology and, in one sense, the birth of Judaism itself.

The impact of the Enlightenment on the Jews, and the process of Jewish emancipation through which they gained civic rights, occurred slowly and unevenly throughout Europe. France was among the first countries to grant civic rights to its Jews, only to rescind some of these rights before restoring them again. Some parts of Germany were far quicker than others to grant rights to Jews, and Eastern European Jews as a rule lagged far behind their Central European cousins. The unevenness of this process can be seen, for example, in Piedmont, in northern Italy, where during Spinoza's time the Jews lived in strong and dynamic communities yet were denied civic rights until 1848.

In the late eighteenth century Jews needed a special dispensation to live in Berlin, the capital of Prussia. So it is perhaps ironic that it was in Berlin that the Jewish Enlightenment movement, the Haskalah, would find its roots. The Haskalah developed as one eighteenth- and nineteenth-century Jewish response to the Enlightenment, a Jewish attempt to transform Jewish life and culture along modern values. In the traditional historiography of the Haskalah, Moses Mendelssohn looms large.[5] Mendelssohn was born in 1729 in Dessau and received an education that was probably more or less typical of Jewish boys at that time, consisting primarily of Talmud and codes. When he was fourteen he left Dessau for Berlin—although he claimed to be following his rabbinic teacher, who took a pulpit there, the presence of some early German Jewish intellectuals may also have attracted him. These Jewish thinkers, who were raised and remained throughout their lives traditionally halakhic, sought to apply the values and methods of the Enlightenment to traditional Jewish texts. They wrote philosophical and scientific tracts, primarily in Hebrew, which they applied, for example, to the Babylonian Talmud. Mendelssohn studied sacred texts with his rabbinic mentor as he began philosophical studies with these early *maskilim* (enlighteners).

Mendelssohn's first writings, in the 1750s, largely followed the themes and concerns of these early maskilim. He created the *Kohelet Musar*, a Hebrew journal, in which he eclectically cited and commented upon traditional texts in order to discuss modern issues. He was drawn to the rational texts of the Sephardim, particularly the biblical commentaries of the mepharshim and the philosophers. Given the Enlightenment's denigration of mystical experience, Mendelssohn's nearly complete neglect of kabbalistic texts is not entirely surprising. In 1760–61 he wrote a commentary on Maimonides' tract on logic; although he disagreed with Maimonides' Aristotelianism, he was drawn to Maimonides' attempt at philosophical systematization. In the late 1760s Mendelssohn began to write philosophical explanations (and defenses) of Judaism in German. By 1770, though, Mendelssohn once again redirected his energies.

For the next thirteen years Mendelssohn turned to translating and commenting on the Hebrew Bible. Dissatisfied with what he saw as sloppy Yiddish translations of the Hebrew text as well as with the overtly christological translations found in German Bibles (e.g., Luther's), he started with a new translation of the Psalms into German. In the course of this translation he began a second translation project, a collaborative translation and commentary on the Pentateuch.[6] Entitled *The Book of the Paths of Peace*, sometimes known in Hebrew as the *Biur* (Commentary), the latter project offered a full translation into German of the Pentateuch with accompanying commentary, all written in Hebrew script. This writing of German in Hebrew script, although by itself superficial, epitomizes the synthetic nature of the *Biur* and the tension at its core. Perhaps unsurprisingly, Mendelssohn and the other authors of the *Biur* much preferred the "scientific" methods of the traditional Andalusian Jewish biblical commentators, the mepharshim, to those found in classical midrash. They consistently cited grammatical and contextual support for their interpretations. Yet the *Biur's* authors are at times more conservative than the mepharshim. Where the mepharshim are comfortable discarding midrashic interpretations for new contextually based ones, the *Biur* consistently attempts to justify midrashic interpretations by means of the contextual approach. Mendelssohn is explicit on this point. Commenting on the twelfth-century biblical commentator Rashbam, Mendelssohn wrote, "Rashbam delved very deeply into *peshuto shel mikra'* [the simple, or contextual, meaning of the biblical text], sometimes more than was appropriate, such that in the love of the straightforward [interpretation] he sometimes deviated from the point of truth."[7] The *Biur* thus affirms the "genius" of the rabbinic interpretations of the Bible without condoning the assumptions and literary methods of midrash, which would have seemed foreign and off-putting to most of their readers, Jews and non-Jews alike.

In 1783, as he was wrapping up his translation projects (his own life would end three years later), he turned to a synthetic German work. *Jerusalem, or On Religious Power and Judaism*, became Mendelssohn's best-known work. It is a manifestly political document meant to advance the Jewish case for civic rights. In it he articulates an interpretation of Judaism and attempts to demonstrate the compatibility of Judaism (and Jews) with German civic society. His basic argument is that Judaism is fully compatible with the state. However obvious this conclusion might seem to us, it was a charged issue whose outcome was by no means clear in late-eighteenth-century Central and Western Europe. To Jews he had to argue that integration into the state did not pose a threat to what they saw as their traditional way of life. To Germans, who argued that Jewish beliefs and laws (e.g., observance of the Sabbath and the prohibition on intermarriage) were incompatible with full civic participation, he had to argue that distinctive Jewish practices were at least neutral in relation to civic rights. *Jerusalem* became one of the first modern works to wrestle seriously with justifying Jewish particularity within an egalitarian and "universal" society. German (or, for that matter, contemporary French or American) society, of course, was hardly universal or secular, frequently universalizing local Christian norms as natural morality or law. Whether or not Mendelssohn and his compatriots were aware that this was a potential line of attack (they probably did not), Mendelssohn sought to develop an argument that could convince both Jews and non-Jews.

Moses Mendelssohn understood Judaism as a religion. In *Jerusalem* Mendelssohn's argument is very much in dialogue with current Enlightenment ideas about the nature of religion. God was the universal creator, whose truths are eternal, natural, and accessible to all. "Religion," at its base, was "natural," an acknowledgment of and expression of gratitude to the beneficent, transcendent, and universal God. All monotheistic religions, including Judaism, thus stood as equal, and equally valid, expressions of this natural religion. Many people today continue to subscribe to this notion of religion, that all religions are *essentially* the same because they share the same eternal (often seen as moral) truths.

A consequence of this understanding of the nature of religion is that belief cannot differentiate one religion from another; all proper beliefs should be identical. "Judaism," he writes, "boasts of no *exclusive* revelation of eternal truths that are indispensable to salvation, of no revealed religion in the sense in which that term is usually understood."[8] Thus according to Mendelssohn what differentiates Judaism is historical truth. The Jews have a distinctive set of ritual, or ceremonial, legislation that embodies, in Mendelssohn's reading, the best of practical wisdom. "The ceremonial law itself is a kind of living script, rousing the mind and heart, full of meaning, never ceasing to inspire contemplation and to provide the occasion and opportunity for oral instruction."[9] A little later in *Jerusalem*, Mendelssohn expands on this notion. After demonstrating how faulty "permanent signs," that is, language and images, are for the preservation of the eternal truths of religion, he continues:

> In order to remedy these defects the lawgiver of this nation gave the *ceremonial law*. Religious and moral teachings were to be connected with men's everyday activities. The law, to be sure, did not impel them to engage in reflection; it prescribed only actions, only doing and not doing. The great maxim of this constitution seems to have been: *Men must be impelled to perform actions and only induced to engage in reflection.* Therefore, each of these prescribed actions, each practice, each ceremony had its meaning, its valid significance; each was closely related to the speculative knowledge of religion and the teachings of morality, and was an occasion for a man in search of truth to reflect on these sacred matters or to seek instruction from wise men.[10]

Sharing the same beliefs and ideas with all other genuinely "natural" religions, Judaism is distinguished by its store of practical knowledge, a collection of commandments, the mitzvot, whose observance helps to focus the subject on eternal truths. Much like Philo, who lived eighteen hundred years before him, Mendelssohn saw the purpose of each ceremonial law as some combination of pedagogical and symbolic, a condensed, physical sign of a metaphysical truth. The law is to add to the Jew's welfare (a position like Maimonides) while at the same time symbolizing something eternally true. Unlike Philo, Mendelssohn left unclear precisely how any particular commandment points toward an eternal truth.

Mendelssohn's understanding of Judaism was at once predictable and radical. It was, first and foremost, a product of its time. Mendelssohn drew deeply and explicitly from contemporary non-Jewish German thinkers in order to develop a modern idiom in which he could articulate a theology of Judaism. Mendelssohn's Judaism emerges as a religion that in essence was like all others. While never denying rabbinic authority, Mendelssohn shifts the traditional Ashkenazic focus on Talmudic studies to the Bible—a move no doubt informed by the emphasis that Protestants (and especially

Lutherans) placed on Scripture. It was also predictably rational, holding no place for mystical texts or practices. Reading traditional texts through his own historically contingent lens, Mendelssohn transformed Judaism into a modern religion.

Reaction to Mendelssohn's conception of Judaism was swift and harsh. Many European rabbis quickly condemned the *Biur*. This opposition led printers in the 1790s to recast the work more piously, removing critical notes and adding traditional commentaries; these later editions sold well, even in Eastern Europe. Traditionalists were also alarmed at an understanding that made the essence of Judaism universal. Not without some justification, they feared that by relegating the commandments to the role of pedagogical and symbolic, Mendelssohn's Judaism was a kind of flimsy tapestry that could too easily be cast aside in one's search for the universal essential truths; it did not hurt their argument that four out of Mendelssohn's six children converted to Christianity after his death.

The irony of these attacks is that Mendelssohn himself remained committed to both rabbinic authority and the mitzvot. Mendelssohn's intellectual shaping of Judaism, in his eyes, had few practical ramifications on daily practice. Mendelssohn remained, in all respects, a traditionally observant Jew. His commitment to rabbinic authority and the mitzvot, even while he was at the same time undermining the traditional modes of rabbinic interpretation (from which they derived their authority) and casting the mitzvot as "nonessential" to Judaism, for most intents and purposes made him superficially indistinguishable from the traditionalists who attacked him. For the *Biur* and some of his other works, in fact, he sought endorsements from the leading rabbis. To German intellectuals, who were becoming increasingly bold in drawing out the implications of Mendelssohn's thought, Mendelssohn himself appeared increasingly quaint.[11] By the end of the eighteenth and beginning of the nineteenth century, his legacy was being embraced or attacked by Jews who thought either that he compromised his Judaism too much or that his reforms did not go far enough.

Jews and non-Jews in the early nineteenth century were well-aware of the challenge that this new ideological understanding of Judaism posed for traditional concepts of Israel, that is, what it meant to be a Jew. The French perhaps saw the ramifications first. On September 28, 1791, less than a month after adopting a new constitution, the French National Assembly declared Jews to be full citizens of the Republic. This declaration was explicitly based on Enlightenment principles, primarily that all men (and, presumably, women) had equal access to civic participation. This, though, was hardly the end of the story. Fifteen years later Napoleon remained suspicious of the ability of Jews to fully participate in French society. In 1806 he convened an assembly of French rabbis and Jewish notables and posed to them a set of incisive and difficult questions. Among them, he asked: Is it lawful for Jews to marry more than one wife? Is divorce valid when not pronounced by courts of justice by virtue of laws in contradiction with those of the French code? Can a Jewess marry a Christian, and a Jew a Christian woman? Are Jews born in France bound to obey French laws and to conform to the dispositions of the civil code? The answers were at times as elusive as the questions were pointed, seeking to satisfy the state that "Judaism," like all other religions, was fully compatible with French identity while still preserving adherence to the "ceremonial law." Some of the answers of the "Paris Sanhedrin" were straightforward and honest: Although Moses does not explicitly ban polygamy, a decree from around 1000 CE forbade it to Jews in the West. Other questions posed more difficulty.[12] The Sanhedrin stated that there is no actual legal prohibition against intermarriage between Jews and Christians, although the rabbis disapprove of it: "In general they would be no more inclined to bless the union of a Jewess with a Christian, or of a Jew with a Christian woman, than Catholic priests themselves would be disposed to sanction unions of this kind."[13] Going on to state that the Jewish community could not penalize the civil marriage of a Jew and Christian, this answer equates Jews and Catholics as citizens of the state first with secondary affiliation in a religious community.

Here now was a definition of the Jew in line with the new definition of Judaism. All humans are linked by their common humanity and all citizens of a state by their common nationality. Religion is a separable voluntary association. Judaism is an ideology to which Jews can subscribe or not.[14]

The concrete ramifications of this new understanding throughout Western and Central Europe were almost immediate. Toward the end of 1817 a group of Jews in Hamburg created the New Israelite Temple Association and signed a constitution for a new "Temple" that was dedicated almost a year later. They saw themselves as restoring "public worship to its deserving dignity and importance." The new, dignified service of the Hamburg Temple, they wrote, should have "a German sermon, and choral singing to the accompaniment of an organ." Dignity, they continued, should also "apply to all those religious customs and acts of daily life which are sanctified by the church," including marriage and a new confirmation ceremony. Within three years the temple attracted a membership of about one hundred families, mainly middle-class merchants.

The liturgy used in the Hamburg Temple underscored its vision of Judaism as a religion that shared basic values with other religions. There were now German translations and prayers along with modifications in the traditional liturgy that deemphasized the desire to reinstate sacrifices. On the Sabbath they eliminated the reading from the Prophets and shortened the reading from the Torah to make more time for the sermon, which was delivered in German. Interestingly, the Hamburg Temple continued to seat men and women separately, placing women in the gallery.[15]

The response to these early reforms came from two directions. Politically, the rabbis of Hamburg attempted to assert their authority, appealing to the Hamburg assembly to transfer control of the temple to the "official" Jewish religious authorities. Although they won some minor concessions, this appeal failed. The controversy then spilled out of Hamburg and resulted in a condemnation, "These Are the Words of the Covenant," published by the Hamburg Rabbinical Court and signed by many of the leading rabbis of Central Europe. "These are the Words of the Covenant" singled out three "cardinal sins" of the Hamburg Temple: they changed the liturgy, they prayed in the vernacular (i.e., not in Hebrew), and they used a musical instrument on the Sabbath (even though it was played by a non-Jew). The text goes on to condemn their prayer book especially for deleting traditional references to the ingathering of the people Israel to Zion at the end of days and their liturgical practices, taking particular umbrage that the women of the Hamburg Temple were allowed to sing in public worship.

This earliest expression of reform was not a wholesale reevaluation of Judaism but an attempt to massage liturgical practices to make them relevant. Although still far short of formulating a coherent ideology, the early reformers clearly saw themselves as Jewish Germans, good Germans of the Jewish religion. Like all good Germans, they were pious; they worshipped on their Sabbath and held the Bible sacred. They sought decorum in their sanctuary and were uncomfortable with the rote recitation of Hebrew prayers they could not understand. Obviously, prayers that elevated Zion as the true promised land clashed with their own self-understanding as Germans. Because the bulk of the "ceremonial law" was postbiblical, it was also changeable. If traditional liturgical practices, for example, failed to accomplish their goals—as those goals were understood—they should be brought back into line with their original purpose.

For these early reformers, and in fact most Western and Central European Jews of all movements through the entire nineteenth century, liturgical practices were meant to solemnly honor the awesome, transcendent, and universal God. These early liturgical reforms were intended to streamline the service so that it might focus on and emphasize God's majesty. The use of an organ and choir invoked solemnity. New, polyphonic choral compositions for the synagogues were commissioned throughout the nineteenth century. Weddings, which have always had a chaotic edge and sexual charge to them, were domesticated, relegated to the synagogues, and given formal choral accompaniments. In 1847 Samuel Naumbourg, who was born in Germany but who composed much of the music used in the Consistory of Paris, published a two-volume collection of his compositions, *Chants Religieux des Israélites*, most of which are in a decidedly classical mode. Although the Hamburg Temple was most likely a modest space, synagogue architecture soon grew to match the grandeur of the music. In the 1860s grand synagogues opened in Berlin, Paris, and Budapest, among other major European centers. These synagogues frequently adopted a Moorish style, deliberately evoking the "Golden Age" of a rational Judaism in which Jews were seen as active creative participants in the larger culture. With their soaring architecture and hierarchical space, they were meant to emphasize the majesty of God rather than love and intimacy. This monumental architecture thus not only marked increased Jewish self-confidence and integration into European communities but also a theological stance that stretched across all of the emerging Jewish movements.

Only after the reforms of Hamburg would a coherent ideology arise to make sense of and justify them. In the 1830s Abraham Geiger began to formulate a vision of Judaism that would anchor the rise of the Reform movement. Raised in a traditional Jewish home in Frankfurt and having acquired both a "traditional" and secular education, Geiger was a prolific writer as well as a pulpit rabbi. Geiger's early scholarship focused on traditional rabbinic texts, such as the Mishnah and Talmud. The thrust of his scholarship was to show, in a manner consistent with the conclusions of the Wissenschaft des Judentums movement, that these texts were historically contingent, not simple and timeless statements of the divine will. Geiger believed that there was a powerful essence or spirit to Judaism that remained unchanged. Different Jewish communities, though, working within their historical contexts, would discover different ways to express this spirit. The ancient writings of the Rabbis were then expressions of the Jewish spirit, but not *privileged* expressions. For Geiger the spirit of Judaism was far more important than any of its texts or traditions. Rituals, for him, were instrumental, which can and should be adjusted if they failed to achieve their goals. This stance left little room for a theory of mitzvot. Subscribing to an ideal of personal autonomy popularized by Immanuel Kant, Geiger did not insist that the mitzvot—which he saw as historically contingent—were binding on all Jews. Like the Hamburg reformers and probably most German Jews of his day, he was uncomfortable with the notion of Zion as the promised land, and he too eliminated such references in the liturgies of the synagogues he served.

Geiger saw his project as regenerative. He sought not to tear down but to build up, to allow the true Jewish spirit, which had ossified in dry rabbinic texts and antiquated practices, to spring forth anew. Geiger had a notion of a true Jewish spirit of universal values and hopes, best expressed by the prophets of Israel. Just as the prophets preached doing good, helping the poor and needy, and striving toward universal peace, so too should the people Israel today. Ritual that does not lead to these ends (or to the pious worship of the sublime divinity) is, at best, meaningless.

Throughout the mid-nineteenth century Reform Judaism would be in intellectual ferment. By the end of the nineteenth century Reform Judaism in Germany would look surprisingly similar to Geiger's vision. This understanding of Reform Judaism, however, was from its very inception attacked by a more radical wing. These thinkers were, in a sense, merely taking Geiger's arguments one step further. Neatly summarizing their platform into three statements, for example, the Reformfreunde (Friends of Reform), a small group founded in Frankfurt in 1842, asserted:

1. We recognize in Mosaism the possibility of unlimited further development.
2. The collection called the Talmud, as well as all the rabbinic writings and statutes which rest upon it, possess no binding force for us either in dogma or practice.
3. We neither expect nor desire a messiah who is to lead the Israelites back to the land of Palestine; we recognize no fatherland other than that to which we belong by birth or civil status.[16]

Much of the third point was already well-established, although its explicit rejection of a personal messiah, implicitly in preference for a belief in a future messianic era of universal peace, was more controversial. Geiger would most likely have agreed with the substance of the second point, although its wording might have made him uncomfortable; he did see in these writings a genuine expression of the Jewish spirit. The first point, though, by carrying Geiger's formulation to its logical (but not necessary) conclusion, also highlighted its intrinsic flaw, namely, that it sets no limits. Reducing Judaism entirely to essence, grounded only by belief in a single transcendent God and universal values, the Reformfreunde were largely condemned by other Reform thinkers. The issue of limits, though, was not, and continues not to be, settled among Reform Jews. When some Reformers advocated the abolition of circumcision or moving the observance of Shabbat from Saturday to Sunday—both proposals roundly rejected by the Reform community—they may have been pushing the envelope, but they did have an ideological basis.

From the beginning of the Hamburg Temple, as we have seen, these reforms encountered stiff resistance. That resistance too, however, flowed from the same cultural context that produced the Reform movement; before long, both the reformers and their "orthodox" antagonists were speaking the same ideological language. The argument that reforms should not be made because of tradition, i.e., "this is how we have always done it," had little weight. Seeking to offer a response to the emerging Reform movement, "traditionalists" began to develop their own sophisticated justifications that drew as much on "secular" culture as did the writings of the reformers. The most prominent and articulate spokesman of this new traditionalist ideology was Samson Raphael Hirsch.

Hirsch was born in 1808 in Hamburg into a traditional family that was quite taken with Mendelssohn. He remained open to German secular culture throughout his life, even studying for a year at the University of Bonn. He served a rabbinical pulpit in Oldenburg, became the district rabbi of Moravia, and in 1851 was invited to take a pulpit in Frankfurt-am-Main, where he remained until his death in 1888. In a popular work published in German in 1836, Hirsch authored a direct attack on Reform Judaism, *The Nineteen Letters on Judaism*. He followed this book two years later with a more densely argued defense of what would become known as Modern Orthodoxy, entitled *Horeb: Essays on Israel's Duties in the Diaspora*. These works, together with his commentary on the Pentateuch, attempt to articulate a coherent ideological vision of Orthodox Judaism.[17]

Hirsch was uncompromising about the divine origin of halakhah. Like Mendelssohn and the Reformers, he understood Judaism to have a universal "essence" separable from the halakhah. The halakhot can be classified according to these higher values, such as justice, love, and education.

10.2 An Austrian menorah, made between 1880–1890.
Courtesy of the Abraham and Natalie Percelay Museum, Temple Emanu-El,
Providence, Rhode Island

Hirsch, however, refused to locate the value of the halakhah in its practical function or utility; it is not to be followed because it is good for the individual. Halakhah was binding because of its divine origin. Period. The law can be explained but it requires no justification, for it was not the creation of humans but of God.

Hirsch combined this strict approach to halakhah with perhaps a surprising openness to both secular knowledge and liturgical innovation. Hirsch believed that the ideal Jew was a *Mensch-Jissroel*, "Man-Israelite," who combined fidelity to the divine with proper social deportment and integration into the non-Jewish world. Hirsch himself appeared almost clean shaven, and at least one contemporary portrait shows him without a head covering. In his synagogues he instituted a German sermon and a choir, wore clerical robes, insisted on proper decorum, and eliminated the Kol Nidre prayer from the Yom Kippur liturgy because he felt that Christians would mock it. His rationale for these and other changes was to divide custom from law; law might be inviolate but its perimeters were bounded.

Like the Reformers he was fighting, Hirsch also put great emphasis on Scripture at the expense of rabbinic literature. In addition to his apologia, his commentaries on the Pentateuch, written in German, are best known. He edited a new prayer book with German translations and commentaries. He never eliminated references to a personal messiah and a return to Zion, as did the Reformers, but he clearly saw these ideas as secondary and infinitely deferred.

This "neo-Orthodoxy" flourished for a time in Frankfurt-am-Main, although it never attracted most Jews within Frankfurt-am-Main and was weak outside it. Feeling increasingly embattled, after 1876 Hirsch developed a more sectarian perspective, arguing for a legal corporate identity for the Orthodox community alone. This change in perspective put a tension into the heart of the movement, which now sought to embrace the outside world as it desired to separate from it.

Hirsh's neo-Orthodoxy was not the only backlash to Reform. In "These Are the Words of the Covenant" the voice of Rabbi Moses Sofer (1763–1839) rang louder than the others. The Hatam Sofer, as he came to be known, had established himself as a skilled Talmudist, having written many learned Talmudic commentaries and responsa.[18] Throughout the early nineteenth century he positioned himself as the stalwart defender of Judaism against the assaults of the Reformers. On specifics his opposition to the Reformers varied little from those of other traditionalists. He opposed changes in the liturgy, the use of German for prayers and sermons, use of an organ on Shabbat, and, of course, rejection of the Oral Torah. He also opposed translating the Bible into German as well as the study of modern philosophy, even as he embraced more practical forms of secular learning such as medicine and math since they had implications for solving halakhic problems. What set him apart from these other opponents of Reform was his theoretical edifice.

The Hatam Sofer understood the Reformers to be attacking not just specific aspects of the tradition but tradition itself. His response was to defend tradition writ large; each and every traditional idea and practice was to be thought of as if it derived from the Torah. Religious customs, *minhagim*, became law. One of his most forceful articulations of this idea came as a result of an incident that had little to do with Reform. A rabbinic court, upon which happened to sit some Reform sympathizers, issued a dispensation that Jewish soldiers fighting during Passover were permitted to eat legumes. From a juristic perspective, this ruling was undoubtedly correct. Not only is the prohibition of eating rice and legumes a custom that pertains only to Ashkenazic Jews, but for some of these soldiers such a dispensation was a matter of life or death. The Hatam Sofer, though, opposed it. The Ashkenazim, he argued were a single congregation, and any customs that they took upon themselves applied to the entire congregation and were eternally valid.

The Hatam Sofer's true legacy as an extreme traditionalist, however, is decidedly mixed. As the rabbi of Pressburg, the Hatam Sofer was constrained by a governmental policy that recognized only a single, Jewish communal organization in which were strong Reform voices as well as the more moderate views of his congregation. His more extreme statements, such as the famous "everything new is forbidden!" are thus more theoretical than practical, assertions of a distant "ought." At times envisioning a separatist Jewish community that shunned German and secular knowledge, expelled the Reform heretics, and could regulate itself according to the strict norms of tradition, as he understood it, he was also a pragmatist who issued rulings that went against each of these prescriptions.

The Hatam Sofer's extreme expressions of separatism were largely rhetorical. He and the other traditionalists, were fighting against a common enemy, the Reformers. By the 1860s, though, his words rang differently. By now Reform had developed into its own movement and, in the eyes of the traditionalists, had moved so far outside the pale that it was no longer considered threatening. For the Hatam Sofer's disciples, neo-Orthodoxy, with its attempt to justify the accommodation of tradition with modernity, was more threatening. They thus understood and marshaled the Hatam Sofer's rhetoric as an attack on the neo-Orthodox.

These traditionalist opponents of neo-Orthodoxy emerged as a new ideological group in Hungary in 1864–65.[19] The group quickly coalesced around a rabbinic ruling that sharply attacked positions espoused by the neo-Orthodox. This ruling, issued in 1865 in Michalowce and signed by twenty-five rabbis, forbade changes in traditional synagogue architecture or liturgical practice as well as preaching in German. Synagogues that instituted such changes were deemed "houses of heresy," and it was forbidden to enter into them. As the rift between these traditional Jews grew, the opponents of the neo-Orthodox increasingly attacked them as heretics worse than the Reform, modern-day Sadducees who deceived the masses with their traditional veneer but then plunged them into fatal error. They went as far as branding the neo-Orthodox as an 'erev rav, a mixed multitude. Their use of the term refers to a specific notion, found in Lurianic Kabbalah, that locates the souls of the "mixed multitude" in the sitra ahara, the other side. In their eyes the neo-Orthodox had become existentially evil.

Led by Akiva Joseph Schlesinger (1837–1922), this group developed an ideology to compete with that of neo-Orthodoxy. Starting from the Hatam Sofer's more extreme statements, Schlesinger argued for a new form of traditionalism. These neo-traditionalists radically expanded the scope of the halakhah. Non-normative traditions, like the contradictory aggadic passages that pepper classical rabbinic literature or even the Zohar, were now eclectically read as normative. Schlesinger, for example, took rabbinic statements against learning "Greek wisdom" as a blanket prohibition against learning all forms of secular knowledge, an unprecedented position. "Wherever the Talmud does not conflict with the Zohar, the halakhah is like the Zohar," he wrote.[20] This fundamentalist way of reading traditionally non-normative Jewish texts as normative, although having some historical precedent, lies at the heart of ultra-Orthodoxy to this day.

In addition to their expansion of the scope of halakhah, the neotraditionalists advocated Jewish social segregation. At a time when there were no Jewish nationalists, Schlesinger broke new ground. The foundation of all Jewish religious life (yahadus), he claimed, was the willingness of the Jewish community to separate from those around it. Jews were to remain distinctive in name, language, and dress. "Yiddish is, from the viewpoint of Jewish law, just like Hebrew," Schlesinger wrote, advocating an avoidance of other vernaculars.[21] Here Schlesinger again drew normative conclusions from aggadic texts; the selection of names, use of vernacular languages, and most aspects of dress were to that time unregulated in the halakhah. Typically, Schlesinger and some of his compatriots pushed this notion to the extreme. Without distinguishing oneself in name, language, and dress, one ceases not only to be a good Jew but even to be a Jew altogether. Like the other Jewish movements, neo-traditionalism (sometimes called ultra-Orthodoxy) grew as a response to modernity, complete with its own ideological justifications.

Given the later development of ultra-Orthodoxy, with its neutral if not hostile stance toward Zionism, it is perhaps ironic that Schlesinger is sometimes considered a proto-Zionist. He did, in fact, move to Israel, where he attempted to establish a number of educational institutions before he died there in 1922. His focus on the people Israel as single, national body held together by a supernatural essence drew somewhat from the ideas of Judah Halevi, but resembled more the modern Zionist movement. As we have seen, throughout the nineteenth century Western and Central European Jews of all kinds minimized, if they did not simply reject, the idea that Jews were better off in Zion, the promised land. One important catalyst for this rejection was the hope offered by the Enlightenment and the gradual political emancipation of the Jews, that they might become part of the larger body politic. By the end of the century, some Jews had despaired of this hope. "Normalization" of the Jews had moved so slowly and unevenly, they wondered if it would ever arrive or if Jews would forever be the foreigners in the midst of Europe.

The Dreyfus affair sparked a response to this growing Jewish unease. In 1894 a French army captain, Alfred Dreyfus, was wrongly convicted of treason. The case itself, as well as the public exchanges that followed in its wake, revealed a much deeper and darker anti-Semitic vein among the supposedly enlightened French elite than anyone ever imagined existing.

The Drefus affair prompted Theodor Herzl, an assimilated Jewish journalist sent from Austria to cover it, to write a manifesto, *Der Judenstaat* (*The Jewish State*). Often seen as the beginning of political Zionism, *The Jewish State* argues that Jews could never be at home in Europe. The answer, Herzl insisted, was an independent Jewish homeland, preferably but not necessarily in Palestine. Here Jews, under an aristocratic government, could live in peace as a nation, each immigrant community bringing its own language as, he claims, works in Switzerland. In Herzl's eyes Israel was a nation, no more and only slightly less than any other national group, such as Germans, Italians, or the French. His vision of the Jewish nation differed from these others, however, in that he curiously neglected to discuss the role of religion in this new nation. For Herzl Israel was a nation formed by the anti-Semite, a community pushed together by outside forces rather than having any positive forces internally that drew it together. Zionism was not a form of "Judaism" that was missing some elements; it was first and foremost a form of political nationalism, with little connection to the past. Zionism arose from European state nationalism.

Herzl's plan struck a nerve. Many Jews who shared his disillusionment with the "Jewish question" quickly came to support his ideas and helped to organize the first Zionist congress in 1897.[22] He was, though, quickly attacked on both flanks. Many European Jews were not as disillusioned as Herzl and continued to maintain that they could live rich lives as Jews and Europeans. The Reform movement attacked Herzl for what they saw as his rejection of the promise of the Enlightenment. The Orthodox rabbis joined the Reform rabbis in their attack on Zionism for being "antagonistic to the messianic promises of Judaism," although the two groups had different things in mind by this condemnation.[23] Many Orthodox groups, of all kinds, quickly grew to see the attempt to settle Palestine and form a Jewish state there prior to the messianic era as sacrilegious, a presumptive act against God's will. For these Jews, the "ingathering" of the Jews to Israel would take place only in the messianic era, and that would happen whenever God willed it; it was a passive eschatology in which humans had little role.[24]

Yet another modern Jewish movement traces its roots to nineteenth-century Germany. Heinrich Graetz was one of the most prominent practitioners of the influential but short-lived Wissenschaft des Judentums movement, a movement for the scientific study of Judaism. Encouraging the application of modern forms of analysis to traditional Jewish texts, this early nineteenth-century movement would eventually give rise to the modern academic study of Judaism. Unlike scholars of Judaism in the modern university, these early practitioners of Wissenschaft were never "disengaged"; they saw their program as a reshaping of Jewish identity by revealing its national essence. Graetz's history was a national one, meant to develop a story, as "scientific" and natural as any national history of its time, to which modern Jews could subscribe. On one level Graetz authored his history as an alternative to the sacred history of Israel—it would create a new imagined community among those who shared its new story.

The institutional success of the Wissenschaft des Judentums movement fell well short of the expectations of its founders. It was never able to develop a new "historical" Jewish identity, and many of its founders and their families eventually converted to Christianity. Zecharias Frankel (1801–1875), however, used elements of the Wissenschaft movement in a different combination. Frankel subscribed to the basic premise that Judaism had undergone, and continues to undergo, change in history. Breaking early with the Reformers, Frankel set his "party" against both the Reform and the Orthodox:

This party bases itself upon rational faith and recognizes that the task of Judaism is religious action, but it demands that this action shall not be empty of spirit and that it not become merely mechanical, expressing itself mainly in the form. It has also reached the view that religious activity itself must be brought up to a higher level through giving weight to the many meanings with which it should be endowed. . . . We must, it feels, take into consideration the opposition between faith and conditions of the time.[25]

For Frankel, true faith is eternal, constituting the essence of Judaism, although his understanding of the precise content and contours of this essence remained ambiguous. Much of the expression of this faith was, in his view, historically contingent, the result of continuing negotiation between scholars and the community. The scholars who wish to preserve Judaism's essence, or forms, cannot do so without the consent of the people. This is the kernel of his idea of "positive historical Judaism," that Jewish traditional texts should be subjected to critical and historical inquiry, but that all traditional aspects of Judaism be viewed as positive. This became the program of the Jüdisch-Theologisches Seminar in Breslau, which Frankel began to direct in 1854. The Jüdisch-Theologisches Seminar pioneered the combination of secular (historical) studies with study of traditional Jewish texts as part of a rabbinical education. To a great degree this new curriculum was a response to popular demand—by the 1840s a majority of rabbis in the major German cities held doctorates from secular universities, thus transforming the rabbinate.

For all their riotous variety, it is their emphasis on ideology that holds together these Jewish responses to modernity. Judaism was problematized: it needed to be explained and justified. The conditions of modernity compelled Jews to articulate self-consciously who they were as Jews. The Jewish philosophers of the Middle Ages, of course, had already tried this, but under different social conditions, for different reasons, and to an underwhelming response. The European attempt was much more systematic and had much higher stakes. Both non-Jews and Jews needed to be convinced that "Judaism" was modern and relevant.

The cost of this transformation was ideological splintering. There had always been sharp differences between Jews of the same community, but the reluctance to systematize those disputes as ideological differences had helped many of these communities to avoid fragmentation. Even in Spinoza's community, in which can be seen the very beginning of these processes of modernity, only "monstrous" ideas and deeds could spur the community to action. Ideologies lower the bar. Previously, Jewish communities could mark their customary differences through geography, for example, identifying as Ashkenazim and Sephardim. By the end of the nineteenth century, though, they were setting themselves off from each other by ideology. Even practice, or adherence to halakhah, lost its role as the lowest common denominator. Geiger, Frankel, and Hirsch all exhibited a similar adherence to halakhah; I doubt that they would have had any halakhic objection to eating in each other's houses. Yet they feuded bitterly over their abstract understanding of Judaism. What ideology gains in intellectual precision it loses in the notion of the unity of the people Israel.

Given the ideological and intellectual ferment of Western and Central Europe and the profound impact that these ideological developments had on Western understandings of Judaism, it is sometimes too easy to overlook the fact that in the eighteenth and nineteenth centuries 80 percent of the world's Jewish population lived in Eastern Europe. Like their Western brethren, these Eastern European Jews were Ashkenazic, tracing their ancestry back to Germany, and thus shared both a language (Yiddish) and dependence on the same group of Ashkenazic rabbinic authorities. Also like their Western brethren, they were confronted with the conditions of modernity. The shape of this confrontation, as well as their reaction to it, however, was very different.

Whereas Baruch Spinoza emerged from a community that was increasingly feeling the pressures and opportunities presented by a faith in reason, Eastern European Jews in the seventeenth and eighteenth centuries were being drawn to Kabbalah. Interest in the popularization of Kabbalah among Eastern European Jews exploded in the seventeenth century. In the wake of Sabbatai Zvi's messianic mission kabbalistic tracts flooded the Eastern European Jewish market, where if the number of printings and references to them are a reliable indicator they were widely circulated and studied. By the eighteenth century Kabbalah had gained such authority among Eastern European Jews that the leading rabbinic authorities consistently advocated its study and incorporated kabbalistic concepts and doctrines into their own halakhic writings. Even Rabbi Eliyahu ben Shlomo Zalman (1720–97), the "Vilna Gaon," unquestionably accepted the force and authority of Kabbalah.

Although scholars such as the Vilna Gaon wrestled with the esoteric and maddeningly complex mystical texts such as the Zohar, most Jews encountered Kabbalah in a more popular form. Kabbalistic tracts were written and translated into Yiddish for a less scholarly audience. Other abridged kabbalistic works that omitted the dense theosophic speculation of the Zohar circulated widely. Kabbalah so deeply penetrated Eastern European Jewry that it influenced religious practices.

One of the most noticeable areas of religious practice in which a popularized version of Kabbalah played a role was prayer, particularly the *tekhines*, popular supplications. Many of these supplications were authored by men and women, primarily in Yiddish, for a female audience and were very popular throughout Eastern Europe. They were to be recited primarily as part of the prototypically "female" rituals, such as immersion in the ritual bath following menstruation, the baking of bread, and the lighting of Shabbat candles. There were *tekhines* for other occasions as well, though, especially for life cycle events and for penitence, around the time of the High Holy Days. Some were also infused with watered-down kabbalistic concepts. One woman, for example, identified in the text as Shifrah, wrote a Yiddish supplication concerning the lighting of candles on the Sabbath:

> The commandment of Sabbath candles was given to the women of the holy people that they might kindle lights. The sages said that because Eve extinguished the light of the world and made the cosmos dark by her sin, [women] must kindle lights for the Sabbath. But this is the reason for it: Because the Shelter of Peace [= the Shekhinah] rests on us during the Sabbath, on the [Sabbath-]souls, it is therefore proper for us to do below, in this form, as it is done above [within the Godhead], to kindle the lights. Therefore, because the two souls shine on the Sabbath, they [women] must light two candles. . . . Therefore, by kindling the lamps for the holy Sabbath, we awaken great arousal in the upper world. And when the woman kindles the lights, it is fitting to her to kindle [them] with joy and with wholeheartedness, because it is in honor of the Shekhinah and in honor of the Sabbath and in honor of the extra [Sabbath] soul. Thus she will be privileged to have holy children. . . . And by this means she gives her husband long life.[26]

Shifrah rejects the traditional midrash that women today light Sabbath candles in order to gain atonement for Eve's sin. Instead, she draws from kabbalistic sources to show the supernal effects of lighting the candles; it creates desire in the upper world for unification with the Shekhinah. Lighting Sabbath candles has cosmic implications.

At the same time, it does not hurt that it helps one's family directly. This supplication also illustrates another, and perhaps the primary, interest in

Kabbalah among Eastern European Jews: its practical implications. Ultimately, most Eastern European Jews saw in Kabbalah practical arts to bring good fortune or ward off the evil eye. They were far less interested in theosophic speculation that would restore the Godhead into the form that would bring about the coming of the messiah and universal redemption than they were in healing their sick child *now*. Kabbalah became a way to harness the divine power against the cosmic forces of evil that ceaselessly lurked. It is, for example, for practical reasons that Eastern European Jews adapted the ceremony of the *upsherin*. This ceremony, literally "shearing," refers to the first haircut that a boy is to receive, when he turns three years old. It is first attested in kabbalistic sources from the sixteenth or early seventeenth century and was tightly linked to theosophic speculation. As practiced by Eastern European Jews, it was connected to a boy's initiation to Torah. At the same time that the boy lost his hair he began to don the *kippah* and *tallit katan*, the fringed four-cornered garment that he should always wear. He moves from an undifferentiated state into the state of being male—the act is in fact explicitly compared to *orlah*, literally an uncircumcised penis but also a fruit tree whose produce is prohibited until three years have passed. It will now be Torah and its symbols that protect the boy from the evil forces. The *upsherin* ushered a boy through the dangerous and liminal transformation, his long locks protecting him from the demons until he could don the kippah and tallit katan.

Practical Kabbalah flourished in this community precisely because of its underlying cosmology. This was a world in which evil was seen to have an ontologically independent existence: the demons hovered. Unlike most early rabbinic literature, the Zohar's mythology was congruent with this outlook on the world; neither Moses Mendelssohn nor Moses Maimonides would have recognized it. Kabbalah, that is, was attractive to many Eastern European Jews because it confirmed what they already thought they knew about the world and offered a solution to it. German Jews during the Enlightenment had a fundamentally different vision of the structure of the world, one that was very much at odds with the threatening, somewhat dualistic mythology of the Zohar.

The preference of Eastern European Jews for this relatively dark cosmology must be understood against their demographic and social situation. There never was any movement in Eastern Europe, unlike Western and Central Europe, to grant civic rights to the Jews. The Jews were often not oppressed, but neither were they fully integrated into their larger surroundings in Eastern Europe. Most Eastern European Jews in the eighteenth and nineteenth centuries lived in urban environments, and many cities had a large Jewish presence. Yet despite both their concentration (strength in numbers) and their relatively good relations with their Christian neighbors, they rarely felt entirely secure. They were economically integrated into the Polish state, but their actual safety often depended on the mercurial temperaments of Polish nobility. A cosmology that understands evil as omnipresent does help to make sense of an unstable world occasionally punctuated with acts of unspeakable terror.

It was also their demographic and social condition that made Eastern European Jews more receptive to the notion of an intrinsic Jewishness, as advocated by Judah Halevi and the Zohar. The Jew was thought to have a special soul; to be a Jew meant to possess this divine gift by virtue of one's birth. The acceptance of such a notion naturally causes theological problems accommodating the proselyte, but, given the scarcity of conversions to Judaism in Eastern Europe during the eighteenth and nineteenth centuries, this problem was marginal at best. Popularized Kabbalah thus also provided the resources from which these Jews could validate and even valorize their sense of separateness. As always, it would be incorrect to universalize by saying that all Jews or Jewish communities were committed to the notion of an intrinsic Jewish soul, but the concept became so widely circulated that the term *Jewish soul* found its way into popular short stories.

To understand the Jews of Eastern Europe purely as separatist, drawing from their tradition in order to react to the historical circumstances in which they found themselves, would be too simplistic. The majority of Jews in Eastern Europe lived in religiously and socially diverse environments. They had social and economic relationships with their non-Jewish neighbors. Polish Jews may have seen themselves as distinct, and not have been entirely trusted by non-Jews, but they were also Poles who shared many of the same cultural assumptions.[27] While much more scholarly work needs to be done in order to confirm this impression, Jews and non-Jews throughout Eastern Europe appeared to have shared many fundamental religious understandings. The Jewish stance toward practical Kabbalah, including prayers, practices, and amulets, looks similar to the kinds of things that contemporary non-Jews were doing in order to ward off the "other side." Both sets of practices, in fact, grew out of a shared cosmology that was nevertheless justified in radically different ways: whether it was the sitra ahara of the Kabbalah, the fallen angels and demons of the Catholic Church, or more generalized notions of the world as a dangerous place, Jews and non-Jews often shared a conceptual world. Similarly, Eastern Europeans,

Jewish and non-Jewish, shared basic understandings of gender roles and the permissible roles of women in public religion and both Jews and non-Jews went through a period of religious revival at roughly the same time in the eighteenth century.

Even the Jewish movement of ba'alei shem, "masters of the name," is best understood against this Eastern European, and especially Polish, background. These Jewish shamans, some itinerant and others not, offered their practical services to the populace. Like contemporary non-Jewish shamans, they asserted that they had access to divine powers, which they could then harness for the benefit of their clients. To do this, the ba'alei shem, as their appellation suggests, primarily used manipulations of the divine names, drawing on the hoary notion (repeated in the Zohar) that to know the true name of something is also to gain power over it. The ba'alei shem gained reputations as masters of the practical Kabbalah and were sometimes consulted even by non-Jews who sought to play it safe.

The most famous of these ba'alei shem, by far, was Israel ben Eliezer. The Ba'al Shem Tov, as he would later be known, was born in 1698 in Poland. Despite the existence of a vast hagiographical literature that arose following his death in 1760, we actually do not possess much historical knowledge of his life. Unlike most of the other ba'alei shem, Israel ben Eliezer was also part of a pietistic conventicle. These conventicles had been in existence in Ashkenazic Jewish communities since the Middle Ages; their members were known as Hasidim. At that time to be a Hasid, literally "pious," meant to be part of a small and local ascetic and mystical group. Structurally, although not organizationally, the Hasidim resembled monks, a highly cohesive ascetic (although not sexually abstinent) group of men who sought personal contact with the divine. Leading one such group of Hasidim must also have added prestige and authority to Israel's reputation as a ba'al shem, one who then applied this power for the good of others.

Israel ben Eliezer appears to have distinguished himself from these traditional Hasidim through his communal concern. The Ba'al Shem Tov prayed not only for his own benefit, or the benefit of his clients, but also for the entire community of Israel. For him to be a Hasid meant to utilize one's connection to the divine for the good of the entire community; the people Israel become his client.

The later legends about the Ba'al Shem Tov depict him as a charismatic religious enthusiast. He preached to all Jews that one need not be a scholar, or even literate, to live in the presence of God. More than the study of sacred texts or even the punctilious observance of halakhah, God requires sincere intention. The portrayal of the Ba'al Shem Tov as emphasizing inner intentions over external actions may, in fact, speak more about those who created and collected these legends than they do about the genuine teachings of Israel ben Eliezer. In any case, they reveal a community that was very much part of the religious revivalist movements active throughout Poland in the eighteenth century. These Christian movements too were reacting to the tension inherent in their religious institutions between inner intention and required external devotion, emphasizing the former over the latter. True religious devotion was open to all who had the proper desire.

To see Israel ben Eliezer as the founder of what would be transformed into modern-day Hasidism is anachronistic. The Ba'al Shem Tov himself left few written records, but his disciples created out of his teachings and practice a distinctive movement. Several of these men, such as Dov Ber of Mezeritch, gathered around themselves groups of younger disciples and attempted—some more successfully than others—to spread their version of the Ba'al Shem Tov's message. There were important differences between this new Hasidism spread by these various groups, but they shared several defining characteristics. While some Hasidic groups emphasized more than others the value of the study of the traditional Ashkenazic curriculum—mainly Talmud—they all highlighted the role of religious enthusiasm. This enthusiasm is encapsulated more completely in two theological propositions promoted by the Ba'al Shem Tov, pantheism and *devekut*. The teachings of the Baal Shem Tov and his early followers have an ambivalent relationship with Lurianic Kabbalah. Against it they prefer a mystical system that emphasizes God's all-enveloping presence—the Lurianic emphasis on divine emanation is devalued. This pulls much Hasidic thought toward pantheism and more psychological understandings of God's presence. God is everywhere, even within the human being. The proper response to God's presence is devekut, practices that lead to one's "cleaving" to the divine. These practices are primarily bodily and joyful and focus on the internal state of the believer more than on the formal characteristics of the practices.[28]

This, however, does not mean that early Hasidim abandoned Lurianic Kabbalah. They drew upon it to understand the cosmic consequences of their religious enthusiasm. Popularized notions of Lurianic Kabbalah provided a model for them to emphasize the role that ordinary Jews could play in repairing the divine and thus bringing about the redemptive age. By lifting the holy sparks and restoring them to their rightful place in the Godhead the Hasid is engaged in an active redemptive process. It held out to all Jews, however educated, the possibility of participation in this cosmic repair of the divine.

Not all Jews, however, were quite seen as equal. Among the more controversial Hasidic doctrines was that of the tzadik. Literally "righteous one," in earlier rabbinic literature the term applied vaguely to Jews who were considered exceptionally upright in their social and religious conduct. In the hands of the Hasidim of the late eighteenth and early nineteenth century, though, it came to denote the head of a Hasidic group. Instead of being assigned on the basis of merit as (in theory) was the case in rabbinic institutions, it was dynastic: The previous tzadik would appoint his successor, who was almost always a son or son-in-law. Drawing on the model of the Ba'al Shem Tov, the tzadik was seen as an intercessor with God on behalf of the Hasidic group. By virtue of birth and office, he lived on a higher spiritual plane; his prayers were more potent than those of his followers. Hasidic groups vary in how much power they ascribed (and continue to ascribe) to the tzadik, but some went so far as to seek to touch the tzadik or even his robe in order to brush up against divine power.[29]

Hasidic groups also began to develop distinctive ritual practices. Instead of using the standard Ashkenazic liturgy, they switched to the Sephardic, with the Lubavitch using the mystically tinged liturgy of Isaac Luria, the Ari. This liturgy contains mystical meditations that link some prayers to kabbalistic acts of tikkun. They encouraged physical movement and gesticulation during prayer if it would increase one's ability to focus.

By the late eighteenth century these Hasidic groups had respectable followings, and it is not difficult to see why. Hasidism tapped into both the wider religious revivalist spirit as well as the specifically Jewish popularization of Kabbalah. It combined the idea that humans can harness the divine powers for their own benefit with a far loftier notion that ordinary Jews could make a cosmic impact. Despite the power that Hasidism vested in all its adherents, it also maintained a tangible sign of divine access in the tzadik. The path to God for the Hasid did not run through long and arduous training in the Talmud but through his own heart. Their emerging ritual practices helped them to form a unique and distinctive community, fostering a feeling of chosenness within the people Israel.

Hasidism was certainly distinct, but it was not on any kind of natural or predetermined collision course with the rabbinic establishment. And had Hasidism not incensed the Vilna Gaon, these Hasidic circles might well have coexisted as yet another ill-defined group of Jews within traditional Jewish society. Through his sharp and relentless attacks on the emerging

Hasidic movement, though, the Vilna Gaon not only turned the power of the rabbinic establishment against it, but in so doing paradoxically helped both Hasidism and the *mitnagdim* ("the opponents" of Hasidism) to shape their own distinctive identities.

The Vilna Gaon was arguably the most well-known and respected rabbi of all Europe in the second half of the eighteenth century.[30] His status derived both from his prodigious knowledge of traditional rabbinic texts and his peculiar lifestyle. To the Vilna Gaon the highest worship of God was realized in the dialectical study of the Torah. Torah, in this sense, meant not only the Talmud and its commentaries but also kabbalistic writings. His mastery of the traditional curriculum was so renowned that scholars were said to have traveled long distances for an audience with him in order to elucidate textual and halakhic problems, only to find they sometimes had a hard time actually gaining that audience. Even if these accounts are later exaggerations, there is no doubting his prestige and influence. The Vilna Gaon had no rabbinic office, nor was he the head of any yeshiva or Jewish educational institution.[31] Instead, he was an old-style Hasid, a reclusive, ascetic mystic who immersed himself in study. He was said to have retired for long periods of seclusion, away from both family and community.

The Vilna Gaon should not, however, merely be seen as an exemplar of a traditional type of rabbinic authority. He was working within traditional molds, but he also transformed them. For the old-style Hasid, the goal was to orient the self to God; study was but one means toward that reshaping of the self. But the Vilna Gaon elevated study of the Torah as the primary vehicle to God. Study for its own sake, a value relentlessly articulated in classical rabbinic texts, was now lifted out of its context and given an almost ideological importance. This evaluation of the importance of study was in fact weakly parallel to the increasing importance that contemporary universities were placing on abstract and theoretical knowledge, knowledge for its own sake.

Although the later Haskalah thinkers of Eastern Europe would claim the Vilna Gaon as "one of them," his relationship to modern Enlightenment values was weak. He did advocate branches of secular education such as mathematics and some of the sciences, but only because this knowledge could help to elucidate problems found in rabbinic texts. Knowledge for its own sake, for the Vilna Gaon, never meant the study of modern metaphysics and philosophy, which he harshly condemned. The Vilna Gaon was neither a maskil nor a traditional rabbinic scholar.

According to legend, the Vilna Gaon's opposition to the new Hasidim primarily centered on their use of the liturgy of the Ari and on what he saw as foolish and disrespectful gestures during prayer. While these might in fact be the immediate causes of his hostility, there were clear underlying tensions. The Hasidim were moving in the opposite direction to that of the gaon, subordinating study to personal piety and opening the path to God to even the illiterate. Moreover, they did this under the banner of the Hasidim, which must have been especially galling to the gaon. According to one testimony, the gaon "said that it was a duty to repel [the Hasidim] and pursue them and reduce them and drive them from the land."[32]

The gaon's opposition to the Hasidim intensified the conflict. Ironically, it might also have helped the far-flung and diverse Hasidic circles to unify under the strain of persecution. Local and ad hoc customs were charged with the power of borderlines, and Hasidism, while maintaining its diversity, itself began to harden into a discernable movement. The gaon's ban unleashed communal persecutions of local Hasidim that succeeded in uniting them where the Hasidim themselves could not.

The gaon's ban also helped to unify those who saw themselves as his disciples. Those who wished to follow in the gaon's path could now identify as mitnagdim. Although not exactly an ideological platform, zealous opposition to the Hasidim served as an easily accessible way to find common ground with others who wished to signal their adherence to the gaon.

The gaon's more enduring legacy, however, found a deeper and more stable home in the development of the Lithuanian yeshiva. One of his preeminent disciples, Rabbi Hayyim, established a yeshiva in Volozhin in the early nineteenth century. The yeshiva, located about halfway between Vilna and Minsk, crafted an approach modeled after that of the gaon, at least as understood by Rabbi Hayyim. It soon developed a stellar reputation, attracting many students and serving as the model for other yeshivot throughout Eastern Europe. Following the lead of the gaon, the yeshiva emphasized Torah study for its own sake, an approach that led to increasingly theoretical speculation. This was an institutional culmination of a process that had been building over more than a century. The rise of Jewish printing allowed not only for the spread of popularized kabbalistic works but also for halakhic tracts. An unforeseen ramification of this explosion of printed rabbinic works was the weakening of the oral tradition and rabbinic power to adjudicate halakhic disputes. The rabbis themselves were well aware of this, and at the time they vociferously denounced the spread of these printed tracts, which they saw as undermining their own authority. Now, instead of consulting a rabbi for halakhic guidance, some Jews began to consult printed texts. Over the course of time the easy availability of halakhic tracts shifted the focus of rabbinic activity away from practical issues to more abstract and theoretical ones. Instead of reading a Talmudic passage for its halakhic or normative implications, the scholar became increasingly concerned with explaining the reasoning behind later commentaries on the passage.

Within the Volozhin Yeshiva and its offspring the tendency toward abstract analysis thrived. One of its most prominent advocates was Rabbi Hayyim of Brisk (1853–1918). He developed a rigorous analytical method that focused on the concepts underlying the halakhah. Seeking to explain how the halakhah worked rather than justifying it (who, after all, can understand the divine will?), the Brisker method sought to recover the conceptual underpinnings of the halakhah. This approach transforms halakhah from a somewhat messy set of norms for living in the real world into a perfect system ontologically rooted in the divine. Halakhah is to be both lived and studied for its own sake as a perfectly coherent and eternal system. Rabbi Hayyim's grandson, Rabbi Joseph Dov Soloveitchik, became the foremost proponent of this approach in America.

The students of the Volozhin Yeshiva were expected to pursue these questions with both intellectual and physical rigor. The intellectual approach was similar enough to modern modes of thinking that many of its later graduates easily found an intellectual home in the Haskalah movement in Eastern Europe. Despite many tensions between the yeshiva and the maskilim—due mostly to the yeshiva's steadfast opposition to including secular studies in its curriculum—many of the maskilim nevertheless spoke highly and fondly of their educational experience. This might be somewhat surprising considering the ascetic environment, in which students awoke at 3 AM to begin their studies, often not concluding until 10 PM or later.

The Volozhin Yeshiva was closed and reopened several times before eventually being shut down for good (at least officially) by the Russian government in 1892. Over the close to one hundred years of its existence, the Volozhin Yeshiva and the yeshivot modeled on it gave rise to a new form of Judaism sometimes known as yeshiva Judaism. Revolving around the institution of the yeshiva and granting authority to the *rosh yeshiva* (head of the yeshiva), these Jews made talmud Torah, as they understood it, the focus of their religious lives. For these Jews, this increasingly abstract and intensive study of the sacred texts becomes an all-encompassing activity. Such an outlook is fundamentally at odds with those of thinkers like Mendelssohn and Hirsch, who also saw value and truth in "secular" knowledge, and the Hasidim who saw such study as either besides the point or even harmful. For this emerging yeshiva Judaism, on the other hand, there was no truth, worth, or knowledge outside of Torah. The path to God was limited to the rigorous study of a canon of rabbinic texts and the austere life that was to accompany such study. Contemporary rabbis were themselves aware of the distinctiveness of this approach: "A Judaism without Torah is [to Eastern European Jews] what a Judaism without the divine service is to the German Jews," wrote Rabbi Yehiel Weinberg, an Eastern European luminary, in 1916.[33]

This approach, as the historian David Biale points out, should be considered not as the faithful continuation of a Jewish tradition that stretches back into antiquity, but, like Hasidism and other forms of Jewish religious expression emerging in the nineteenth century, "self-conscious articulations of traditional ways of life in the face of a changing world."[34] Like the ideological movements developing in Central and Western Europe, and the growing Haskalah movement in Eastern Europe in the late nineteenth century, the "Orthodox" forms of Judaism in Eastern Europe increasingly developed self-conscious identities. To be a member of a yeshiva in Lithuania increasingly meant *not* to be a Hasid, a follower of Hirsch, or—heaven forbid—a maskil. Ironically, the two primary means by which yeshiva Jews began to cement their self-identity as a distinctive and coherent conservative movement were quintessentially modern. In 1912, Agudat Yisrael was created as a political party of yeshiva Jews. It was active in Eastern Europe in the prewar period (even winning seats in the Polish parliament), in the Zionist movement, and continues to function (albeit much transformed) in the political life of the State of Israel. Additionally, yeshiva Jews created their own newspapers, often printed in Hebrew (the language of the maskilim), to compete in the marketplace of ideas.

Despite these attempts to make its ideas more accessible, yeshiva Judaism always was an elitist movement. Most Eastern European Jews had neither the inclination nor the ability to engage in such a rigorous intellectual life. Thus the abstract intellectual debates of the yeshiva by and large stayed in the yeshiva; they had little impact on the daily lives of most other Jews. These Jews, sometimes derisively referred to as *amkha* ("your people," a reference to God's people Israel) by the yeshiva elite, led more or less traditional but unself-consciously "Jewish" lives. That is, most Eastern European Jews through the nineteenth century observed core Jewish rituals (e.g., Shabbat, festivals, kashrut, basic life cycle rituals) mimetically; they did so in the ways and with the understandings of their parents and others in the communities in which they were raised. "Traditional" Jews had little place or patience for the printed strictures of the halakhah or the abstruse discussions of the yeshiva. They might have respected the learning of the yeshiva students or been attracted to the more accessible leanings of the Hasidim, but they lived as neither. As with the generations of Jews before them, they lived in symbiotic but uneasy tension with those elites who saw themselves as the guardians of the rabbinic tradition. Sometimes they would ignore exhortation for increased halakhic observance, while at other times—particularly in matters of observance of kashrut—they could exceed the halakhic minimum. What a book or rabbi told them mattered far less than what they saw in their parents' home. For these Jews "Torah" was a way of life rather than a book.

This description is not meant to perpetuate the myth of a golden age of Judaism in Eastern Europe. In her saccharine but complex autobiographical narrative, Pauline Wengeroff tells of the erosion of the traditional Judaism of her childhood. Traveling with her husband through the Pale in the late nineteenth century, she ends up in St. Petersburg. The Jewish community of St. Petersburg had been wracked with internal dissension as many Jews sought Western-style religious reforms. The community nevertheless remained strong enough to build a monumental synagogue, the Choral Synagogue, which seated twelve hundred and was opened in 1893. Wengeroff comments:

> The Jewish community of St. Petersburg possessed a large, splendid synagogue and two rabbis, one learned in modern studies and one Orthodox. But it had distanced itself considerably from Jewish custom and tradition. The most distinguished of the Jews adopted many foreign traditions and celebrated alien festivals such as Christmas. Of Jewish holidays they observed only *Yom Kippur* and *Pesah*—and even these were in a so-called modern manner. Many calmly arrived at the synagogue in a carriage and took their meals on *Yom Kippur* during the intermissions.[35]

She goes on to say that most Jews in St. Petersburg were, actually, faithful to tradition. Not her husband, however, whom she describes as forcing her to abandon the traditional ways that she had loved. Her account is complex to evaluate: Was she an unwilling victim of her husband's demands, or, as other passages of the memoir suggest, was she too an accomplice, forging a modern Jewish identity? And certainly she cannot be seen as representative of anything other than a minuscule segment of bourgeois, assimilated Russian Jews. In any event, Wengeroff, among others, testifies to deepening self-consciousness, and ruptures, in the traditional Judaism of Eastern Europe.

Against the odds, well into the twentieth century, this rich European Jewish life not only survived but thrived. In Warsaw in 1897, for example, the census counted 210,526 Jews, comprising 33.7 percent of the entire population of Warsaw—by 1939 the number of Jews in Warsaw had climbed to 375,000, although this represented only 29.1 percent of the total population.[36] Jews in Warsaw predominantly saw themselves as Poles, yet in 1897 five-sixths of them declared Yiddish as their first language. Despite the ability to assimilate, and a small vocal group of Jews who advocated assimilation, the Jews of Warsaw forged a distinctive Jewish identity.

Nor did the Communist persecutions seriously change traditional Jewish life. Central Russian authorities intervened with Jewish village, or *shtetl*, life in a variety of ways, ranging from taxes and prohibitions on ritually slaughtered meat to penalties for circumcision, but these were rarely effective. Jews in the Russian cities were more directly affected by these attempts at cultural homogenization. It was much easier to keep tabs on the Choral Synagogue in St. Petersburg than on the shtetl of Turov.[37]

The Shoah, of course, destroyed what assimilation and the new Communist government could not. The Russian photographer Roman Vishniac's pictorial record of Polish Jews (who had not yet lived under a Communist regime) on the eve of the Holocaust would seem almost quaint if it was not, in hindsight, so horrifying.[38] Along with the six million Jews murdered by the Nazis and their collaborators perished the fine threads of their culture, the rich tapestry of European Jewish life. Later depictions of this life, from *Fiddler on the Roof* to the writings of Isaac Bashevis Singer, and even the modern novelist Jonathan Safran Foer, might romanticize or excoriate it, but all recognize its loss.

Curiously, although nineteenth- and early twentieth-century European Jews created distinctively intellectual and book-based religious communities, their enduring legacy was not literary. Unlike Jewish communities before them, they did not add to the Jewish canon; Graetz's history never achieved the status of the Zohar and the fruit of all the intensive scholarship of Volozhin is not to be found in any authoritative and revered text. Perhaps in time some of the texts that these communities did produce will slowly acquire such an authority, but even the writings of the Vilna Gaon are today rarely studied and even less often have become the basis for supercommentaries. This is not to deny that these Jews produced texts that remain important to living Jewish communities. Shneur Zalman of Liady (1745–1813), the founder of Habad (Lubavitch) Hasidism, wrote in 1793 a systematic treatment of kabbalistic thought known as the *Tanya*; modern Lubavitch Hasidim continue to study and revere it. Israel Meir Kagan (1838–1933), a Polish rabbinic scholar also known as the Hafetz Hayyim, published a widely used commentary on the *Shulhan Arukh* that was called the *Mishnah Berurah*. Some Ashkenazic communities accept this commentary as halakhically authoritative. Neither these nor other literary works from this time, though, have received widespread acceptance among Jewish religious communities not associated with the groups from which their authors stemmed.

Instead of books, the legacy of European Jews of the nineteenth and early twentieth century has been their institutions. Whether the Jewish movements that thrive today in America, or the Hasidism of Williamsburg in Brooklyn or Kfar Habad in Israel, or the Haredi Judaism of Meah She'arim in Jerusalem or Lakewood, New Jersey, or secular Judaism, or the academic study of Judaism—all are descended from the European Jewish encounter with modernity. These institutions, both conceptually and materially, have been no less malleable than texts, with modern Jewish communities reshaping them in their own images.

EPILOGUE
Whither Judaism?

THIS BOOK BEGAN with a word. What is *Judaism?* Where did it come from, what does it signify, and how do we—Jews and non-Jews, religious and secular, academics and not—use it? However simple these questions might appear, the answers to them are anything but simple or straightforward. I have attempted to sketch my answers not merely as some abstract and theoretical formulation, but as it might look in practice. To define Judaism is to engage the messy realities of the Jews who continually recreate it.

Judaism, I have argued, cannot serve as the subject of a verb; it cannot "do" anything. Judaism neither believes nor prescribes, it does not think or say. Jews, not *Judaism,* have agency. Judaism cannot, therefore, be seen as possessing some transhistorical essence or single defining characteristic. To talk of the Judaism of a particular historical community makes far more sense than to refer to Judaism writ large.

This refusal to understand *Judaism* as more than a collection of religious communities that have only a family resemblance to each other should at the same time not obscure the fact that there *is* a family resemblance between them. If today many people overemphasize, even by implication, the universality of Judaism, others err on the other side by not taking seriously that Jewish communities have almost always seen themselves as part of the same family and have a variety of texts and practices that link them. These characteristics, which are hardly universal across time and space, nevertheless can be charted. One Jewish community might understand its claim to be "authentically" Israel to be rooted in genetics, while another community's claim might be made on the basis of religious faith; both, however, share their self-identification as Israel. Although Jewish communities, and the individuals within them, have widely diverse understandings of basic theological concepts, such as God and Torah, the vast majority share the assumption that to be authentic those beliefs must be grounded in "canonical" texts. If texts constitute one form of tradition, a set of practices constitute another. Some rituals have been remarkably persistent (although not always practiced—or practiced regularly—by the majority of a Jewish community), even if interpreted in radically different ways. Judaism constitutes a map of the ways in which real historical communities of Jews have defined themselves and struggled with their tradition.

This understanding of Judaism rejects the conceptual models that emphasize belief. Such an approach to the explanation of Judaism is as old as Judaism itself, which I have argued was largely forged in eighteenth- and nineteenth-century Germany. Judaism, like Christianity, was to be seen as defined by a finite number of meaningful essential beliefs. While it is true that the shared "authoritative" texts of the rabbinic tradition delimit the parameters of a conversation, the coordinates of the actual beliefs articulated within it are so vast as to be analytically meaningless. To say that "Judaism is monotheistic" is uncontroversial as long as one is willing to stretch the term *monotheistic* to include the divine pantheon lurking behind the biblical texts, the picture of Helios and his host on the synagogue floors of late antiquity, the dualism of the *Bahir* and the emanated God of the Zohar, and the pantheism of Mordechai Kaplan and the early Hasidic movement. The religion of Israel shares certain conceptual benchmarks such as God, Torah, and Israel, but the contents of these concepts are highly fluid.

I have also rejected the traditional assertion that it is the observance of the halakhah that serves as Judaism's essential core. It is simply not the case that all or most Jews prior to the Enlightenment either were halakhically observant or accepted in any straightforward way "the" halakhah, even in the many communities that *in principle* would have accepted rabbinic notions of halakhah. The concept of mitzvot has indeed always been important in most Jewish communities, and many practices (e.g., circumcision, Shabbat, kashrut, holidays) have been persistent. As we have seen, though, even rabbinic thinkers are divided about the purpose of the observance of the commandments, not to mention the actual details of the mitzvot. Until very recently there has been no direct line from a halakhic text or code to actual practice; this too has been a complex, tense, and negotiated relationship. Many Jews have striven, and continue to strive, to live their lives in accord with the will of God as expressed in the commandments, but here too this leads to enormous latitude in both conceptualization and practice.

Moreover, as scholars have long recognized, it is impossible to understand the religious life of a Jewish community without seeing it within the larger world in which it is situated. Jews do have a history as well as a textual tradition that has continued to build throughout time. But Judaism does not; a community's religious expression is a product of its refraction of historical experience, texts, and traditional practices through its own uniquely situated conceptual lens. Abraham Joshua Heschel once asserted that Judaism is a minimum of revelation and a maximum of interpretation. Heschel was referring to the human understanding and articulation of the awesome encounter with the divine on Sinai, but the phrase can also be seen as highlighting the important role of "interpretation" generally, of Jews continually remaking and recreating relevance out of the resources bequeathed to them.

Typically today, most analyses of Judaism ultimately drive toward an evaluation of Judaism's "strength." A chapter like this might normally be expected to make some kind of statement of Judaism's strength or weakness, whether it is gaining vitality or dying. I have argued here for a different kind of analysis that makes such an evaluation moot. Variety, multivocality, and interpretation have been hallmarks of the Jewish experience. One cannot measure the strength of a community's Judaism by the percentage of its members that observe one defined set of mitzvot, share particular beliefs, or intermarry. As in the past, Jewish communities continue to remake themselves in riotous diversity. Whether the different manifestations are "correct" or not I will discuss later in this chapter, but, if history is any guide, few of these manifestations will survive more than a generation or two. That is, if the model argued for here has any predictive value, it is that those forms of Judaism lacking a self-identity as Israel—participation (however defined) in the conversation informed by a traditional (if fluid) canon or recognition of a set of traditional practices—face a far higher bar. To the extent that they explicitly reject the conceptual maps of traditional Jewish texts, the secular Judaism of today, like the Yiddish-centered Bundist culture in America in the first half of the twentieth century, may have little historical staying power.

Similarly, there are no limits to the possibilities for the development of new religious practices. Jews have always created new practices and rituals, often without rabbinic sanction. The breaking of a glass under a wedding canopy, for example, which today is the symbol par excellence of a Jewish wedding, was bitterly opposed by medieval rabbis for centuries, before they grudgingly reinterpreted it from its function of scaring demons away to that of recalling the destruction of the Temple. An underdetermined practice allowed for its integration into a web of rabbinic meanings that contemporary Jews ultimately found more compelling. Heavy-handedly overdetermined rituals—those that are tightly linked to a single interpretation—have far less chance of survival than do those that emerge organically and are ultimately drawn into the canonical texts, where they can even lie dormant for years before being reinvigorated with new meaning, like the Tu b'Shevat seder.

Whither Judaism? I do not know if we are heading into a postmodern, post-Zionist, and postideological period or into one of increasingly strong fundamentalism; both currents are strong in the community in which I live. Even if Jews are being drawn away from ideology, the institutional and administrative structures of the Jewish movements in the United States will not shut down any time soon. They may "weaken" in some sense of this word and transform themselves, but like many such institutions they will continue to evolve. They, along with the American Jews who may or may not join them, will continue to have a rich set of traditional resources for living a nonideological Jewish life.

If, on the other hand, the Jewish communities of the United States and Israel become increasingly fundamentalist, riven by opposing ideologies and the demand to take sides, Jews will have yet another rich set of resources upon which to draw. Perhaps the racial theory of Judah Halevi will continue to climb in prestige and Maimonides' doctrinal litmus test will be revived.

My point, of course, is that religious development does not work in straight lines, and certainly not one that radiates from "tradition." There is no natural or logical ending point to the rabbinic tradition; it is sprawling, diverse, and malleable. The future of Judaism, of course, is not trapped in the either/or dichotomy presented above. Judaism is not going to become any single thing, and Jews will continue to struggle with their tradition, using these resources to construct meaningful Jewish life within cultures and societies that rarely are characterized by a single outlook. Judaism tomorrow will be like Judaism today and yesterday—a family of communities struggling to make sense of a common identity and tradition.

Judaism is not sui generis. The same model that I have developed in regard to Judaism applies, in one form or another, to all "religions." What does it mean, after all, to speak of *Christianity, Islam, Buddhism,* or *Hinduism,* not to mention the scores of other smaller religions? All developed in the nineteenth century from first-order definitions into terms that denote ideological and essentialized religions. *Christianity*, for example, has no more meaning than *Judaism*; it too is wildly diverse. Whether the model that looks at issues of identity, textual tradition, and persistent practices would be fruitful for unpacking Christian diversity has yet to be determined, but the problem is the same. As I mentioned in the introduction, my own understanding of Judaism draws upon Talal Asad's attempt to understand Islam—Islam is certainly no more unified than Judaism or Christianity. Hinduism, as scholars have long noted, is virtually a late nineteenth- and early twentieth-century fiction, an attempt by the colonizing British to make sense of the diversity of Indian religion, thus creating a model that many Hindus came to accept. Even otherwise self-reflective academics frequently invoke religion as if it were a self-explanatory category that is either identical with the canonical tradition or completely divorced from it. It's neither.

I have meant this book as an attempt to understand and explain the diverse religious practices of Israel and, by implication, of other religious traditions too. I have not attempted to offer a constructive argument, in the sense of arguing for a first-order definition of Judaism that I would like to replace existing definitions. Nevertheless, this book does raise pointed constructive issues that, in conclusion, need to be addressed. Here, rather than offering a detached argument written in the omnipotent and authoritative voice of the third person, I would prefer to speak more personally. Just as writers shape their materials and arguments, so too do the materials shape the writer. I have learned from the journey of researching and writing this book, and while others will quite legitimately draw different conclusions from the material presented here it might be worthwhile to reflect on my own constructive engagement with the argument.

One of the leitmotifs of this book has been the relationship between reason and revelation. How are we to understand revelation in light of the critical analysis of reason? What debt, if any, does reason owe to revelation? Or, put in more modern and relevant terms, does the academic and critical study of religion have anything to contribute to religion itself, and does religion offer anything to moderns who are secular or members of other faith communities?

When I go about my job as a scholar of religion, I bracket, to the extent possible, my own religious commitments. As a critical thinker, I work according to accepted scholarly conventions, attempting to persuade my readers on the basis of "reason," and try to follow my evidence honestly rather than shoehorning it in order to justify my own lifestyle and theological commitments. I am forced to see and grapple with the patent incoherence of the Torah, the relatively marginal place of the Rabbis in their society, the pseudepigraphic nature of the Zohar, and the malleability of tradition. I try to make sense of the rise and fall of rituals and even liturgies within a theological framework that, on occasion, claims divine authority and eternal relevance.

At times, though, when I am not writing or teaching or otherwise engaging in my professional responsibilities, the brackets fall away and I now must confront these same issues as a Jew. Such a confrontation is frequently challenging; how is one to "square the circle" of an understanding of the Torah as a redacted text with a commitment to the mitzvot? Are these two modes of looking at Judaism to be compartmentalized, left as mutually exclusive options? Or is there a way to "fuse the horizons," to use Hans-Georg Gadamer's phrase, to allow the tension between these perspectives to be creative rather than destructive?

I have found in the rabbinic tradition intellectual resources for my own encounter with this tension. For at least some of the Rabbis, divine truth was too full to be contained by language, all the more so by a single particular linguistic formulation. When read within the sprawling conversation comprised by their literature, the Rabbis offer the possibility of seeing truth in a proposition and its opposite, with everything in between. They offer conceptual maps of creative tensions. This is why rabbis themselves have opposed the codifications of belief and even halakhah; the rabbinic tradition leaves one uneasy with single, simple answers.

Modern ideological movements cut a straight path through the thicket of tradition. For many Jews this has been a good and necessary thing—in a world that values intellectual coherence, they package coherent, and marketable, versions of Judaism. In the process, though, they lose the tradition's tolerance for tensions and contradictions. In their domestication of Judaism, with the necessary highlighting of certain aspects of tradition and devaluing of others, I cannot help but feel that something is lost.

My life is complex, and not only on a cognitive level. I try to make my way through the world, delicately balancing my love for and responsibilities toward my wife, children, family, friends, students, country, and God with my professional life and own more personal needs. I struggle to balance the time and money equation, and sometimes simply to meet my bills.

I am nagged by self-doubt and the sense that I could and should do every-thing better. I suspect that I am fairly typical of middle-class, middle-aged, white Americans.

I struggle with these feelings every day, and while I have not yet found solutions to them I have also come to recognize that the tensions are themselves necessary; this is part of what defines me as a mature human being. For all of its problems, I want complexity in my life. And when I walk into a synagogue, read a popular Jewish book, listen to a sermon, or even turn to an article on religion in the local paper, I find something of-fensive in the sometimes implicit request that I turn off my critical facul-ties. My students begin every semester saying that religion is "personal" and a "matter of faith," having been conditioned to search only for the single and simplest truth in a religion immune from critical inquiries. Our society has put religion in a box.

I want my religion as complex and messy as the rest of my life. When my father died, I did not turn to religion for platitudinous comfort but for a structure for my grief and anger at God. The documentary hypothesis is rarely in the front of my mind when I listen to the weekly Torah reading, but every once in a while it rises from the depths to challenge me. To see the historical and structural parallels between Passover and Easter, or the halakhah and the Islamic *sharia* (Islamic law), adds another layer of under-standing and appreciation to my life as a Jew.

It is not helpful for either religious or secular people, Jews or not, to think of religion as pious naïveté. If such a stance lessens the humanity of the religious, it also deprives the secular of a rich set of human resources. The stories of Judaism, Christianity, Islam, and all other religions are not sto-ries of abstract, childish systems but of human beings wrestling with pro-foundly human problems. We do not have to accept the answers of a given faith community to find something useful in them, either as individuals or communities. When I, as an individual, confront the "big" questions of life, death, and evil, I want to see what answers are out there—all of them. When I, as a citizen, debate important matters of public policy, I want to hear dif-ferent perspectives. Just because I am a Jew who rejects the assertion that Christ is the son of God and who consistently votes for "pro-choice" can-didates does not mean that I do not want to be challenged by or learn from Catholic bishops insisting on the preciousness of all life. Some of these re-sources will be more useful to us than others, and some might be simply repellent. But to reject the answers of religious thinkers just because they are religious is to throw out the baby with the bathwater.

I raised the issue of judgment. Are all forms of Judaism equally "correct"? Can any Jewish community or ideology within it be said to be more authentic than another? Throughout this book I have tried to avoid this question, laying out some different portraits, for the most part empathetically, to allow the reader to judge for him or herself. Yet I also recognize that the lack of judgment can itself be read as a kind of judgment: By not making judgments am I not promoting relativism that recognizes as equally "authentic" any and all things that any Jewish community may do? Is there not a logically necessary slippage between the criteria by which I select my data (i.e., including all communities that identify themselves as Jewish) and the implied conclusion that they are all valid?

As a scholar, I have the responsibility to avoid judgments of religious authenticity. I can try to describe, explain, analyze, and critique, but it is not my job—and I believe strongly that it is not appropriate for any scholar of religion—to say who is actually "right" or "better." There is, admittedly, a degree of relativism inherent in this approach. At the same time, I do not consider myself a relativist. I think that there really is truth in the world, to at least some of which we have access. The problem is reconciling history, with its rich and complex record of Jewish communities recreating their religious understandings, with a conviction that all is *not* relative.

Again, it is the Rabbis, with their multivocal and organic perspective, who help me to grapple with this problem. Convinced that there is indeed religious truth, the Rabbis nevertheless see that truth as so full that it is unable to contain a single meaning. When I take off my scholarly hat, I do, admittedly, find some forms of Judaism more congenial than others. But I also believe, now as a committed Jew, that the competing claims to truth made by all these forms might well be correct—all manifestations of some larger, obscure, but single truth.

The qualifier in that last sentence, the *might*, is important to my own approach, both theological and intellectual. One need not be a relativist to admit that she or he cannot discern God's will. To pick one way of doing things does not necessarily mean that another way of doing things is wrong; this is a decision that I would prefer to leave in the hands of heaven. I can be a certain kind of Jew without believing that either my coreligionists, or the members of other faith communities, are "sinners." For me, religious truth claims that exclude the possibility that other religious truth claims might be correct are theologically presumptuous.

But recognition of the extraordinary diversity of Jewish religious life through history calls also for an intellectual posture of humility. No single work of scholarship can possibly begin to do justice to Jewish diversity through the ages; the sheer amount and complexity of the data, the linguistic skills that are necessary to make sense of the texts, and the theoretical sophistication needed to shape them into something coherent are all daunting. I have found writing this book to be a humbling experience, and every day it exposed ever clearer the depth of what I did not know.

For more than two and a half millennia, Jews have struggled to translate their traditions in order to make them comprehensible in and relevant to their own historical contexts, and they continue today to recreate their Judaism. This is not a story of some essentialized "Jewish spirit" but of the human spirit, of the ways in which humans create communities, mark those communities with difference, and use their own distinctive traditions within a historical context to struggle with universal problems.

GLOSSARY

Abulafia, Abraham (1240–ca. 1291): Jewish mystic, known for his messianism.

aggadah: All nonlegal rabbinic literature, e.g., stories. Often contrasted with halakhah.

Agudath Ha-Rabbanim: Founded in 1902, an organization of ultra-Orthodox rabbis.

agunah: "Anchored" woman, one whose husband can or will not grant her a divorce.

Alfasi, Rabbi Isaac ben Jacob (1013–1103): Also know as the Rif, head of the yeshiva in Lucena (Andalusia) and author of *Sefer Halakhot*.

aliyah: Literally, in Hebrew, "ascent," refers to moving to Israel. Can also refer in a synagogue to "ascent" to the *bimah* to say a blessing over the Torah reading.

Almohads: Conservative Muslims from North Africa who overthrew the Almoravids.

Almoravids: Berbers from the area of Morocco, conservative Muslims.

Am yisrael: "People of Israel," a concept of Israel as a cohesive social group.

amoraim: Rabbis who lived ca. 250 CE—500.

Amram ben Sheshna (mid-ninth century CE): One of the geonim; authored the earliest extant siddur.

Anan ben David (fl. 770 CE): Opposed the rabbinic notion of the Oral Torah, ultimately seen as the founder of Karaism.

Apocrypha: Collection of Jewish texts not included in the Tanak but accepted into the Catholic Bible.

Aramaic: Semitic language much like Hebrew; used as the official language of the Persian Empire.

Arba'ah Turim: Written by Rabbi Jacob ben Asher (ca. 1270–ca. 1343; Toledo), a law code upon which the *Shulhan Arukh* builds.

Aristobulus: Jewish-Greek philosopher who probably lived in the second or first centuries BCE.

Ashkenazim: Those Jews who trace their heritage back to medieval Germany (*Ashkenaz*).

ba'al shem: "Master of the name," Eastern European Jewish wonder worker.

Ba'al Shem Tov: "The Master of the Good Name," refers to Israel ben Eliezer (1698–1760), usually considered the founder of Hasidism.

Babylonian Talmud (Bavli): Redacted around 500 CE, a sprawling work of rabbinic literature containing commentary on the Mishnah, law, stories, and dialectical argumentation.

Bar Kokhba: "Son of the star," the name applied to the leader of a Jewish uprising in Palestine in 132 CE.

Bar, bat mitzvah: The marking (and sometimes celebration) of a Jewish child's attainment of the age of legal responsibility (twelve for a female, thirteen for a male).

bimah: Raised dais in a synagogue, on which either prayers are led or the Torah read.

Biur: Translation (finished 1783), led by Moses Mendelssohn, of the Torah into German, with commentary.

Book of Beliefs and Opinions: Philosophical tract written by Se'adyah Geon in 933.

brit milah: "Covenant of circumcision," circumcision of a Jewish boy when eight days old as a mark of God's covenant with Abraham and his descendents.

Cairo Geniza: Store of ancient Jewish texts found in the attic of the Ben Ezra Synagogue in Cairo.

Canonization: Process or act through which a text is designated as sacred.

Conservative Judaism: Modern ideological movement that seeks to maintain a traditional but flexible stance toward Jewish law.

creatio ex nihilo: Idea that God created the world from nothing; there was no preexistent matter.

Crescas, Hasdai ben Abraham (1340–1410): Jewish philosopher, author of *Light of the Lord*.

Dead Sea scrolls: Assorted ancient texts found near the Dead Sea that are thought to testify to a Jewish sect from the Second Temple period.

devekut: "Cleaving," used by Hasidim (drawing on Lurianic Kabbalah) to refer to a cleaving to God.

dhimmi: Islamic category of "protected minorities," referring to Jews and Christians.

Diaspora: Refers to the land outside of Palestine (land of Israel).

Ecclesiasticus (Ben Sirah): Biblical book found today in the Apocrypha.

Enoch: Minor biblical character around whom a strong apocalyptic tradition grew in the Second Temple period, resulting in pseudepigraphical books such as 1 Enoch.

eruv: Rabbinic legal institution that transforms a "public" space into a "private" one and thus allows a Jew to carry in it during Shabbat.

eschatology: Concept of the end of time.

Essenes: Jewish sect during the Second Temple period; perhaps the authors of the Dead Sea scrolls.

Essentialism: Idea that a thing has a unique essence.

etrog: Citron, used on Sukkot.

Eyn Sof: Concept of the infinite in kabbalistic thought, the source out of which the *sefirot* emanate.

exilarch: Political leader of the Jews in Babylonia; the office continued into the Muslim period.

Ezra: Biblical figure, said to lead exiles from Persia to Jerusalem (ca. 420 BCE); seems to have the Torah in his possession.

fatwa: Islamic legal responsum.

Frank, Jacob (1726–1791): Polish leader of an antinomian Jewish group known eponymously as the Frankists.

Frankel, Zacharias (1801–1875): German Jew who developed a school of historical Judaism, a forerunner to Conservative Judaism.

Geiger, Abraham (1810–1874): German rabbi whose writings were seminal for the development of the Reform movement.

Gemara: Rabbinic commentary on the Mishnah, which together with the Mishnah comprise the Talmud.

gematria: Interpretive technique of translating letters into numerical values and then back into other words that have the same value.

geonim: Leaders of the rabbinic academies from ca. 550 CE—1050.

Gersonides (Levi ben Gershom or the Ralbag; 1288–1344): Jewish philosopher and author of *The Wars of the Lord*.

get: Jewish document of divorce.

Graetz, Heinrich (1817–1891): German Jewish historian.

Guide of the Perplexed: Written in Arabic by Maimonides; finished in 1190.

Gush Emunim: Literally, "Block of the Faithful," a religious-Zionist movement in Israel.

hadith: Sayings of the prophet Muhammad.

Haggadah: Liturgy for the Passover seder.

halakhah: Jewish law.

Halakhot Gedolot: Geonic legal guide to the Babylonian Talmud.

Halakhot Pesukot: Geonic legal work that survives only in fragments.

halav yisrael: "Milk of an Israelite," the idea that kosher dairy products need to be produced and handled only by Jews.

Halevi, Judah (1075?–ca. 1140): Spanish poet and writer, author of the *Kuzari*.

Hannukah: Eight-day minor holiday commemorating of the rededication of the Temple in 165 BCE.

Haredi: "Trembler," refers today to an ultra-Orthodox Jew.

Hasidism: Revivalist movement that began in eighteenth-century Poland.

Haskalah: Jewish Enlightenment of the eighteenth and nineteenth centuries.

Hasmoneans: Descendant monarchs of the Maccabees.

havdalah: Ceremony marking the end of the Sabbath.

Havurah movement: Anti-institutional Jewish movement in the United States in the 1960s and 1970s.

Hebrew Union College. Founded in 1885 in Cincinnati; now, after merging with the Jewish Institute of Religion, the central seminary for the training of Reform rabbis in North America.

Hekhalot literature: Collection of texts from late antiquity or the geonic period that describe ascents to heaven.

Hellenism: Complex of linguistic, political, and cultural features that marked the Near East.

Herzl, Theodor (1860–1904): Austrian Jew who is credited with founding modern political Zionism.

Hirsh, Samson Raphael (1808–1888): German rabbi normally credited with founding "neo-Orthodoxy" or "Modern Orthodoxy."

Holocaust: Also known as the Shoah in Hebrew, refers to the murder of over six million Jews during World War II.

Hoshanna Rabba: The last day of Sukkot; thought to end the annual period of judgment.

Ibn Ezra, Abraham (1092–1167): Spanish commentator on the Tanak; notable for his philological interests.

Ibn Gabirol, Samuel (ca. 1021–ca. 1058): Jewish poet and philosopher, author of *Fons Vitae*.

Ibn Janah, Abulwalid Merwan (Rabbi Jonah; born ca. 990 CE): A native of Cordoba, author of *The Book of Embroidery* and *The Book of Roots*, some of the first works of Hebrew grammar.

Israel: Can refer to 1. Jacob, the biblical character; 2. Jacob's descendents (the "children of Israel"); 3. the land that the Torah promises to Abraham's descendents; 4. the modern political state.

Isserles, Rabbi Moses (1530–1572): Polish rabbi who glossed the *Shulhan Arukh* from an Ashkenazic perspective.

Jacob of Marvège (twelfth to thirteenth centuries): Author of *Responsa from Heaven*.

Jerusalem, or On Religious Power and Judaism: Moses Mendelssohn's best-known work (1783); a contemporary definition of Judaism and argument for Jewish civic rights.

Jewish Theological Seminary of America: Founded in 1887 in New York; now the central seminary for the training of Conservative rabbis in North America.

Josephus: Jewish historian who lived in the first century CE.

Judah, Rabbi, the Prince (or Patriarch): Redacted the Mishnah and served as some kind of Jewish communal leader.

Judenstaat, Der: *The Jewish State,* Theodor Herzl's Zionist manifesto.

Kabbalah: "Tradition," the distinctive Jewish mysticism that arose in the Middle Ages and was exemplified by the Zohar.

Kabbalat Shabbat: Collection of psalms and hymns recited immediately before Shabbat; added by Lurianic kabbalists in the sixteenth century.

Kagen, Rabbi Israel Meir (1838–1933): Polish rabbi known as the Hafetz Hayyim who authored an influential commentary on part of the *Shulhan Arukh*, the *Mishnah Berurah.*

Kaplan, Mordecai (1881–1983): American thinker whose ideas founded the Reconstructionist movement.

Karaism: Movement in the geonic period that rejected the Oral Torah and authority of the rabbis.

Karo, Rabbi Joseph (1488–1575): Author of the *Shulhan Arukh.*

kashrut, kosher: Jewish dietary laws.

kehillah: "Community," designating the local, semiautonomous Jewish communities of medieval Europe.

ketubbah: Refers primarily to the statutory payment that a husband (or his estate) owes to his wife on dissolution of the marriage; can also refer to the marriage contract itself.

kibbutz: Communal settlement in the modern State of Israel.

kippah (yarmulke): Form of head covering traditionally worn by some Eastern European men, and is now a standard custom.

Kol Nidre: Geonic prayer annulling all vows; traditionally recited the eve of the Day of Atonement.

Kook, Rabbi Abraham Isaac (1865–1935): Rabbi in Palestine well-known for his distinctive mystical theology that incorporated Zionism.

Kuzari: Written in Arabic by Judah Halevi, a purported dialogue between a king, a Jew, a Christian, a Muslim, and a philosopher.

Lekha Dodi: Kabbalistic hymn written in sixteenth century by Solomon Alkabez; now incorporated into most modern versions of *Kabbalat Shabbat*.

Leeser, Isaac (1806–1868): Spiritual leader of Mikve Israel in Philadelphia; retranslated the Hebrew Bible into English, published by the Jewish Publication Society.

Lubavitch Hasidim. Also known as Habad, a group of Hasidim.

lulav: Bunching of three species of foliage, waved together on Sukkot.

Luria, Isaac (1534–1572): Kabbalist in Safed, credited with developing a new kabbalistic system.

maamad: Council of lay leaders in Sephardic communities in Amsterdam and the New World.

Maccabean revolt: Uprising against the Seleucids led in 165 BCE by the Maccabee brothers.

Maccabees, Book 1: Court history of the Maccabees and the Hasmonean kings, probably originally written in Hebrew around 100 BCE and now in the Apocrypha.

Maccabees, Book 2: Theological account of the Macabean uprising, written in the Diaspora, probably in Greek, around 100 BCE and now in the Apocrypha.

Maimonides (1135–1204): Jewish philosopher and legal codifier.

mamzer: Child of an adulterous or incestuous union.

Marranos: "Pigs," the insulting term given in Spain to the Jewish converts to Christianity who continued to practice Judaism secretly.

maskilim: "Enlighteners," the active participants of the Haskalah.

Masoretes, Masoretic Text: The scribes who, during the geonic period, punctuated the Tanak, creating a stable Hebrew text.

matzah: The unleavened bread eaten on Pesach.

Mendelssohn, Moses (1729–1786): German Jewish philosopher and writer.

Mepharshim: Medieval rabbinic scholars whose comments on the Tanak generally followed the *peshat* method.

Messianic Jews: Modern-day Jews who accept Jesus as the messiah.

mechitza: A partition that separates men from women in a place of prayer.

Midrash: A distinctively rabbinic genre of biblical interpretation.

mikveh: A body of water, immersion in which can remove ritual impurity.

minhag: A local, Jewish custom.

minyan: A prayer quorum, either ten Jewish men, traditionally, or, in modern liberal Judaism, any combination of ten Jewish men and/or women.

Mishnah: Redacted ca. 220 CE, the first work of Oral Torah.

Mishneh Torah: Code of law written by Maimonides in Hebrew; completed in 1178.

mitnagdim: "Opponents," referring to those who opposed Hasidism.

Mitzvah, mitzvot (plural): Commandment.

Modern Orthodox Judaism: A movement founded by Samson Raphael Hirsch in nineteenth-century Germany, seeks to integrate secular knowledge with tradition.

Nahmanides (Rabbi Moses ben Nahman; 1194–ca. 1270): Wrote scriptural and halakhic commentaries; member of conservative kabbalistic circle in Catalonia.

Nebuchadnezzar: Babylonian king who destroyed the first Jerusalem Temple in 586 BCE.

niddah: Menstruant.

omer: Grain offering that immediately follows Passover and begins the seven week countdown to Pentecost (Shavuot).

Oral Torah: Rabbinic concept that God's revelation on Sinai included what would become the rabbinic tradition.

Orthodox Union: Founded in 1898 as the Orthodox Jewish Congregational Union of America, it is the central institution for Modern Orthodoxy in North America

Palestinian Talmud (Jerusalem Talmud, Yerushalmi): The Mishnah together with its amoraic commentary, redacted in Palestine about 400 CE.

Passover (*Pesach*): Festival of unleavened bread that also commemorates the exodus from Egypt.

Patrilineal descent: Refers to the Reform movement's decision in 1983 to recognize the children of Jewish fathers and non-Jewish mothers who are committed to Judaism as Jewish.

Paul: Jew from Asia Minor who believed that Jesus was the messiah.

Pentecost (*Shavuot*): Holiday that occurs fifty days after Passover.

peshat: "Contextual" approach to biblical interpretation that seeks to employ contemporary "scientific" techniques.

Pharisees: Jewish sect of the Second Temple period; perhaps predecessors of the Rabbis.

Philo (ca. 30 BCE–30 CE): Jewish philosopher writing in Greek in Alexandria, Egypt.

Pittsburgh Platform (1885): Important early codification of Reform Judaism in America.

piyyut: Form of Jewish liturgical poetry that begins in late antiquity.

polythetic: Method of categorizing things based on overlapping sets of shared characteristics.

priest (*kohen*): Officiated in the Temple when it stood, but now only observing vestigial functions. Thought to be a descendent of Aaron, through the father's line.

prophet: One who received a direct communication from God. The Rabbis thought that prophecy ceased during the Second Temple period.

Purim: Minor holiday marked by the reading of the book of Esther.

Qumran: The site near the Dead Sea where the Dead Sea scrolls were found.

Rabad (Rabbi Abraham ben David of Posquières; 1125–1198): Objected to Maimonides's codification of the *halakhah*.

Rabbanite: During the geonic period, a supporter of the rabbinic tradition and institutions, against the Karaites.

Rabbi Isaac Elchanan Theological Seminary (RIETS): Founded in New York in 1897 to train Orthodox rabbis; now part of Yeshiva University.

Rabbis: Refers to the authors of the classical rabbinic literature, ca. 70 CE—640; rabbi literally means "my teacher" and has been used as an official title from the rabbinic period to the present.

Rashi (Rabbi Shlomo ben Isaac; 1049–1105): Preeminent commentator on the Tanak and Talmud; lived in Provence.

rebbe: Leader of a Hasidic group (see also tzadik). "The rebbe" today often refers to Menachem Mendel Schneerson, the leader of Lubavitch, who died in 1994.

Reconstructionist Judaism: Modern ideological movement based on the ideas of Mordecai Kaplan.

Redaction: Process of editing separate documents to make them into a single text.

Reform Judaism: Modern ideological movement that began in nineteenth-century Germany. Today, the largest of the modern movements.

Rosh Hashanah: Holiday marking the Jewish new year and the beginning of the ten days of repentence. In the Torah called the holiday of trumpeting.

Sabbatai Zvi (1625–1676): "Failed messiah" who, toward the end of his life, converted to Islam.

Sadducees: Jewish sect from the Second Temple period.

Satmar Hasidim: Now settled primarily in New York, a Hasidic sect.

Schlesinger, Akiva Joseph (1837–1922): Leader of Haredi Judaism.

Se'adyah ben Joseph: Served as geon of Sura, 928–942.

seder: Ceremonial meal held on the first night (or, in the Diaspora, first two nights) of Passover. The Haggadah is read during it.

Sefer haBahir: "The Book of Illumination," written in twelfth- or thirteenth-century Provence, an early kabbalistic text.

Sefer HaRazim: Book of mystical (and "magical") formulae and experiences, written in late antiquity.

sefirah, sefirot: "sphere"; kabbalistic term for the emanations of the Godhead.

Seleucids: Hellenistic dynasty based in Syria and winning control over Palestine in 200 BCE.

Sephardim: Jews who trace their heritage back to medieval Spain (*Sepharad*).

Septuagint: Greek translation of the Torah (and ultimately the rest of the Tanak), prepared in Egypt about 200 BCE.

Shabbat: Jewish Sabbath, starting Friday at sunset and ending Saturday night.

shatnez: Biblical prohibition of mixing wool and linen in the same garment.

Shearith Israel: First Jewish congregation (1704; New York) founded in America.

Shechinah: God's "presence." Used by kabbalists to denote the last emanation, closest to humans, and God's feminine side.

sheloshim: Thirty-day period of mourning for a close relative; less restrictive than the *shiva*.

Shema: Deuteronomy 6:4, although can also refer to the paragraph that follows it together with some other biblical passages. Part of the traditional Jewish liturgy.

Shemini Atzeret: Semi-independent holiday immediately following Sukkot.

shiva: Seven-day period of intensive mourning for a close relative.

Shneur Zalman of Liady (1745–1813): Founder of Habad (Lubavitch) Hasidism and author of the *Tanya*.

shofar: Trumpet made from a ram's horn and associated especially with Rosh Hashanah.

Shulhan Arukh: Joseph Karo's sixteenth-century Jewish law code.

siddur: Literally, "order"; Jewish prayer book.

sitra ahara: "Other side"; used by kabbalists to refer to the power of evil.

Six-Day War: In a short war in 1967 Israel emerged victorious over her Arab neighbors and occupied Jerusalem, the Golan Heights, the West Bank, Gaza, and the Sinai Desert.

Sofer, Rabbi Moses (1763–1839): Also known as the Hatam Sofer, urged little accommodation of modernity.

Spinoza, Baruch (1632–1677): Jewish philosopher in Amsterdam.

sukkah: Booth in which Jews are to eat (and sleep) during the holiday of Sukkot.

synagogue: Jewish prayer house, usually permanently housing a scroll of the Torah.

takkanah: Rabbinic legal decree.

tallit: Four-cornered fringed shawl worn at Jewish prayer services.

tallit katan: Four-cornered fringed garment traditionally worn by men all the time, usually underneath one's shirt.

Talmud Torah: Activity of studying rabbinic texts, thought by the rabbis to be a religious obligation in its own right.

Tanak: Corresponds more or less to the "Old Testament." An acronym of its three parts, *T*orah, *N*evi'im (Prophets), and *K*etuvim (Writings).

tannaim: Rabbis who lived from 70 CE—ca. 250.

tekhines: Popular supplications, written mainly in Eastern Europe in the nineteenth and early twentieth centuries.

tefillin: phylacteries, leather boxes containing portions of the Torah that are worn by men during some prayer services as well as in private prayer.

Temple: Usually refers to the Temple in Jerusalem; now a frequent designation for a synagogue.

Temple Scroll: One of the Dead Sea scrolls; contains an idealized model of the Jerusalem Temple.

ten days of repentence: Period between Rosh Hashanah and Yom Kippur.

teshuvah: Can refer to "turning," the act of repentance, or to "response," denoting a rabbinic legal responsum.

theodicy: "Problem" of God's justice.

theurgy: Use of certain practices and verbal formulas to harness the divine power to do one's will.

thirteen principles of faith: Maimonides's codification of what he saw as the essential beliefs of Judaism.

tikkun: "Fixing"; concept in Lurianic Kabbalah that repairs defects in the Godhead.

Tisha b'Av: Minor holiday on the ninth day of the month of Av, a fast day, commemorating the destruction of both the First and Second Temples.

Torah: Can refer to the Pentateuch; the scroll on which it is written; or the entire and continuing content of God's revelation.

Tu b'Shevat: Fifteenth day of the month of Shevat, marking the "new year for the trees."

tzadik: "Righteous one"; Hasidim used this term to refer to their leader, whom they saw as exceptionally holy.

ulama: Islamic scholarly class.

Union of Reform Judaism: Union of North American Reform congregations.

upsherin: Eastern European custom of cutting the hair of a Jewish boy for the first time around his third birthday.

Vilna Gaon (Rabbi Eliyahu ben Shlomo Zalman; 1720–97): Legendary scholar and opponent of the emerging Hasidim.

Vulgate: Latin translation of the Bible produced by Jerome in the fifth-century CE.

Western Wall: Western retaining wall of the Jerusalem Temple, and today the most revered Jewish holy site.

Wise, Isaac Meyer (1819–1900): Early Reform rabbi in America, founded Hebrew Union College in 1875.

Wissenschaft des Judentums: "Science of Judaism," the German movement in the nineteenth century to study Judaism academically.

Yavneh: According to the Rabbis, the site of the first rabbinic academy.

YHWH: The tetragrammaton, the four-lettered name of God found in the Torah.

Yiddish: Jewish language that developed in medieval Germany but was used by Eastern European Jews well into the twentieth century.

yiddishkeit: Denotes Jewish culture in an Eastern European context.

Yigdal: Metrical Hebrew hymn based on Maimonides's thirteen principles of faith, written in 1404 and part of many modern Jewish liturgies

Yohanan ben Zakkai, Rabban: Credited with founding the rabbinic academy at Yavneh.

Yom Kippur: The Day of Atonement, a major fast day.

Zerubbabel son of Shealtiel: Established the foundations of the Second Temple ca. 515 BCE.

Zion: Another term for the Promised Land.

Zionism: The political movement to establish a Jewish country in Palestine.

Zohar: Mystical, Aramaic commentary on the Torah, attributed to Rabbi Shimon bar Yohai but probably written (or compiled) in the thirteenth century by Moses de Leon.

BIBLIOGRAPHICAL NOTES

INTRODUCTION

Despite the many books that claim to "introduce" Judaism, very few actually wrestle with the definitional issues, and the few that do tend to adopt an implicitly essentialist perspective. Among the best of these books are Michael Fishbane, *Judaism: Revelation and Its Traditions*, Religious Traditions of the World (San Francisco: Harper and Row, 1987); Nicholas de Lange, *An Introduction to Judaism* (Cambridge: Cambridge University Press, 2000); Jacob Neusner, *The Way of the Torah: An Introduction to Judaism*, Religious Life of Man (Belmont, Calif.: Wadsworth, 1988); and Dan Cohn-Sherbok, *Judaism: History, Belief, and Practice* (London: Routledge, 2003). My approach comes closest to Neusner's, but is also quite distinct from it. Robert M. Seltzer, *Jewish People, Jewish Thought: The Jewish Experience in History* (New York: Macmillan, 1980), remains a classic introduction to Jewish history and civilization. An excellent, edited survey of Jewish culture, in the largest sense of the term, is David Biale, ed., *Cultures of the Jews: A New History* (New York: Schocken, 2002).

1. Erwin Ramsdell Goodenough's massive study was published as *Jewish Symbols in the Greco-Roman Period*, Bollingen Series 37 (New York: Pantheon, 1953–1968). Jacob Neusner's abridged edition, with an excellent introduction, was published by Princeton University Press in 1988.
2. For an explanation of the polythetic approach to religion, see Jonathan Z. Smith, "Fences and Neighbors: Some Contours of Early Judaism," in his book, *Imagining Religion: From Babylon to Jonestown*, Chicago Studies in the History of Judaism (Chicago: University of Chicago Press, 1982), pp. 1–18.
3. Clifford Geertz, *The Interpretation of Cultures* (New York: Basic, 1973), pp. 87–125.
4. For the concept of imagined communities acting as a cohesive force in a society, see Benedict Anderson, *Imagined Communities: Reflections on the Origin and Spread of Nationalism*, rev. ed. (London: Verso, 1991).

5. The very definition of religion is contested by its scholars. See, for example, the essays in *Guide to the Study of Religion*, edited by Willi Braun and Russell T. Mc-Cutcheon (London: Cassell, 2000); and Jonathan Z. Smith, "Religion, Religions, Religious," in Mark C. Taylor, ed., *Critical Terms for Religious Studies* (Chicago: University of Chicago Press, 1998), pp. 269–284.

6. See Talal Asad, *The Idea of an Anthropology of Islam* (Washington, D.C.: Center for Contemporary Arab Studies, 1986).

7. Susan Starr Sered, *Women as Ritual Experts: The Religious Lives of Elderly Jewish Women in Jerusalem* (New York: Oxford University Press, 1992).

8. The National Jewish Population Survey, 2000–2001, can be found at http://www.ujc.org/content_display.html?ArticleID = 60346.

9. Haym Soloveitchik, "Rupture and Reconstruction: The Transformation of Contemporary Orthodoxy," *Tradition* 28.4 (1994): 64–130.

10. For a theory of ritual, see Catherine Bell, *Ritual Theory, Ritual Practice* (New York: Oxford University Press, 1992).

1. PROMISED LANDS

For a snapshot of American and Israeli Jews today, see Samuel G. Freedman, *Jew Versus Jew: The Struggle for the Soul of American Jewry* (New York: Simon and Schuster, 2000). Jack Wertheimer, *A People Divided: Judaism in Contemporary America* (New York: Basic, 1993) still offers an excellent picture of the state of the Jewish movements in America. Several ethnographic accounts of modern Jews are indispensable. Samuel C. Heilman's many works, especially *Synagogue Life: A Study in Symbolic Interaction* (Chicago: University of Chicago Press, 1976), remain classics. Several books offer sensitive sociological analyses of American and Israeli Judaism: Charles S. Liebman and Steven M. Cohen, *Two Worlds of Judaism: The Israeli and American Experiences* (New Haven: Yale University Press, 1990); Steven M. Cohen and Arnold M. Eisen, *The Jew Within: Self, Family, and Community in America* (Bloomington: Indiana University Press, 2000); and Charles S. Liebman and Elihu Katz, eds., *The Jewishness of Israelis: Responses to the Guttman Report* (Albany: State University of New York Press, 1997). For the history of American Jews in this chapter, I have relied heavily on Jonathan D. Sarna, *American Judaism: A History* (New Haven: Yale University Press, 1994).

1. Jewish population figures are notoriously difficult to pin down. The *American Jewish Yearbook* is a good source. Another good, but not unbiased, resource is the "Demography" Web site of the Department for Jewish Zionist Education of the Jewish Agency: http://www.jafi.org.il/education/100/concepts/demography/.

2. David and Tamar De Sola Pool, *An Old Faith in the New World: Portrait of Shearith Israel, 1654–1954* (New York: Columbia University Press, 1955), p. 220.

3. On the development of Reform Judaism, see Michael A. Meyer, *Response to Modernity: A History of the Reform Movement in Judaism* (New York: Oxford University Press, 1988); and Dana Evan Kaplan, *American Reform Judaism: An Introduction* (New Brunswick, N.J.: Rutgers University Press, 2003).

4. Platforms of the Reform movement can be found in the two books mentioned in note 3 above. They can also be found online at the Central Conference of American Rabbis Web site: http://data.ccarnet.org/platforms/.

5. For an old history of the Conservative movement, see Mordecai Waxman, *Tradition and Change: The Development of Conservative Judaism* (New York: Burning Bush, 1958). For a recent demographic profile, see Sidney Goldstein and Alice Goldstein, *Conservative Jewry in the United States: A Sociodemographic Profile* (New York: Jewish Theological Seminary of America, 1998). See also Jack Wertheimer, ed., *Jews in the Center: Conservative Synagogues and Their Members* (New Brunswick, N.J.: Rutgers University Press, 2000).

6. On Orthodox Judaism in America, see especially Jeffrey S. Gurock and Jacob J. Schachter, *A Modern Heretic and a Traditional Community: Mordecai M. Kaplan, Orthodoxy, and American Judaism* (New York: Columbia University Press, 1997).

7. The figures on American Jewish religious observance are from Sarna, *American Judaism*, pp. 224–225.

8. On the impact of the army experience on the development of American Judaism after 1945, see Deborah Dash Moore, *GI Jews: How World War II Changed a Generation* (Cambridge: Belknap Press of Harvard University Press, 2004).

9. Cf. Mordecai M. Kaplan, *Judaism as a Civilization: Toward a Reconstruction of American-Jewish Life*, reprint edition with a forward by Arnold Eisen (Philadelphia: Jewish Publication Society, 1994).

10. A journalistic account of the state of the Lubavitch movement today is Sue Fishkoff, *The Rebbe's Army: Inside the World of Chabad-Lubavitch* (New York: Schocken, 2003). For the current Orthodox attack on Lubavitch messianists, see David Berger, *The Rebbe, the Messiah, and the Scandal of Orthodox Indifference* (London: Littman Library of Jewish Civilization, 2001).

11. This article was mentioned in the introduction: Haym Soloveitchik, "Rupture and Reconstruction: The Transformation of Contemporary Orthodoxy," *Tradition* 28.4 (1994): 64–130.

12. On the issues surrounding female involvement in Orthodox (and other halakhic forms of) Judaism, see, in addition to the sources mentioned in the bibliographical notes to chapter 6, Rachel Adler, *Engendering Judaism: An Inclusive Theology and Ethics* (Philadelphia: Jewish Publication Society of America, 1998); and Tamar Ross, *Expanding the Palace of Torah: Orthodoxy and Feminism* (Hanover: Brandeis University Press/University Press of New England, 2004).

13. The Reform movement's resolution on "The Status of Children of Mixed Marriages" (March 15, 1983), is widely available on the Web. See the "Resolutions" section of the CCAR Web site, http://www.ccar.org.

14. For various approaches to the issues that homosexuality raises for the different religious movements in America, see Steven Greenberg, *Wrestling with God and Men: Homosexuality in the Jewish Tradition* (Madison: University of Wisconsin Press, 2004); Moshe Shokeid, *A Gay Synagogue in New York* (New York: Columbia University Press, 1995); Walter Jacob and Moseh Zemer, eds., *Gender Issues in*

Jewish Law: Essays and Responsa (New York: Berghahn, 2001); Gil Nativ, "Rabbi, Bar Kappara, and Homosexuality," *Conservative Judaism* 57.1 (2004): 87–94.

15. Mark Washofsky, *Jewish Living: A Guide to Contemporary Reform Practice* (New York: UAHC Press, 2001), p. 53.

16. The reports and data from the 2000–01 National Jewish Population Survey (NJPS) are available online. Summary reports are available on the United Jewish Communities Web site, http://www.ujc.org, and the full datasets at the North American Jewish Data Bank site; at this writing, http://www.jewishdatabank.org. NJPS has its critics. For a very different interpretation of the evidence, see Calvin Goldscheider, *Studying the Jewish Future*, Samuel and Althea Stroum Lectures in Jewish Studies (Seattle: University of Washington Press, 2004).

17. Steven M. Cohen and Arnold M. Eisen, *The Jew Within: Self, Family, and Community in America* (Bloomington: Indiana University Press, 2000), pp. 8–9.

18. Ibid., p. 187.

19. The history of the State of Israel is, of course, contested. See Howard M. Sacher, *A History of Israel: From the Rise of Zionism to Our Time* (New York: Knopf, 1991); Benny Morris, *Righteous Victims: A History of the Zionist-Arab Conflict, 1881–1999* (New York: Knopf, 1999). Given the fast pace of political development in the Middle East, there is no "up-to-date" summary of the situation, but for one popular and still relevant presentation, see Thomas L. Friedman, *From Beirut to Jerusalem* (New York: Doubleday, 1990).

20. This book was mentioned in the introduction: Susan Starr Sered, *Women as Ritual Experts: The Religious Lives of Elderly Jewish Women in Jerusalem* (New York: Oxford University Press, 1992).

21. For some selections of Kook's writings in English, see *The Essential Writings of Abraham Isaac Kook*, ed., trans., with an introduction by Ben Zion Bokser (Amity, N.Y.: Amity House, 1988). Aviezer Ravitzky, *Messianism, Zionism, and Jewish Religious Radicalism* (Chicago: University of Chicago Press, 1996) offers a good summary of the religious positions on Zionism.

2. CREATING JUDAISM

There are, of course, many introductions to the Hebrew Bible. At the same time, there are surprisingly few accessible and responsible guides to the religion of ancient Israel. The standard, although badly dated, histories of biblical Israel are Yehezkiel Kaufmann, *The Religion of Israel, from Its Beginnings to the Babylonian Exile,* trans. and abridged by Moshe Greenberg (Chicago: University of Chicago Press, 1960); and John Bright, *A History of Israel,* Westminster Aids to the Study of the Scriptures (Philadelphia: Westminster, 1959). Modified, and somewhat more accessible introductions can be found in the essays in Hershel Shanks, ed., *Ancient Israel: A Short History from Abraham to the Roman Destruction of the Temple,* 2d ed. (New Jersey: Prentice Hall, 1999). Richard Elliott Freedman, *Who Wrote the Bible* (San Francisco: HarperSanFrancisco, 1997), provides a highly readable, entertaining, and informative account of the creation of the Torah (Pentateuch) and the documentary hypothesis. Susan Niditch, *Ancient Israelite Religion* (New York: Oxford University Press, 1997), provides a good introduction to the religion of ancient Israel. Jon D. Levenson, *Sinai and Zion: An Entry into the Jewish Bible*, New Voices in Biblical Studies (Minneapolis: Winston, 1985), provides a highly accessible account of biblical theology. *The Jewish Study Bible: Tanakh Translation, Torah, Nevi'im, Kethuvim*, ed. Adele Berlin, Marc Zvi Brettler, and Michael Fishbane (New York: Oxford University Press, 2003), contains informative commentaries and essays. The approach that comes closest to the model of this book is Marc Z. Brettler, *How to Read the Bible* (Philadelphia: Jewish Publication Society, 2005). Translations of the biblical text used throughout this chapter are modified from *Tanak* (Philadelphia: Jewish Publication Society, 1985).

1. For an account of the trial of the Talmud, see Judah Rosenthal, "The Talmud on Trial," *Jewish Quarterly Review* 47 (1956–57): 58–76, 145–69. For Augustine's evaluation of Judaism, see the discussion by Jeremy Cohen, *Living Letters of the Law: Ideas of the Jew in Medieval Christianity* (Berkeley: University of California Press, 1999), pp. 19–65.

2. A popular book on the production of the King James Bible is Adam Nicolson, *God's Secretaries: The Making of the King James Bible* (New York: Harper Collins, 2003).

3. There is not much popular literature on Judaism during the early Second Temple (Persian) period. James D. Purvis, "Exile and Return," in Shanks, *Ancient Israel* offers a good overview essay. More specialized essays can be found in *The Cambridge History of Judaism*, vol. 1: *Introduction: The Persian Period*, ed. W. D. Davies and Louis Finkelstein (Cambridge: Cambridge University Press, 1984).

4. Most scholars today accept that the Torah is historically fictitious. There remains, however, much contention about the historicity of other parts of the Tanak. For an overview of this controversy, see Marc Brettler, "The Copenhagen School: The Historiographical Issues," *AJS Review* 27:1 (2003): 1–21.

5. Ronald S. Hendel, *Remembering Abraham :Culture, Memory, and History in the Hebrew Bible* (Oxford: Oxford University Press, 2005), offers a sophisticated account of the ways in which the redactors of the Torah constructed memory. He also has an essay, "Israel Among the Nations: Biblical Culture in the Ancient Near East," in Biale, *Cultures of the Jews*, pp. 42–75.

6. Israel Knohl, *The Divine Symphony* (Philadelphia: Jewish Publication Society, 2003), is a highly readable account of the theologies of the Bible. Jack Miles, *God: A Biography* (New York: Knopf, 1995), offers a intriguing literary and theological analysis of the God of the Hebrew Bible. Mark Smith, *The Early History of God: Yahweh and Other Deities in Ancient Israel* (New York: Harper and Row, 1990), has a more scholarly approach. See also James L. Kugel, *The God of Old: Inside the Lost World of the Bible* (New York: Free, 2003).

7. Ilana Pardes, *The Biography of Ancient Israel: National Narratives in the Bible,* Contraversions 14 (Berkeley: University of California Press, 2000), has a fruitful discussion of the Bible as a "national biography."

8. There are several excellent essays dealing with the Hebrew Bible's treatment of religious experience in Arthur Green, ed., *Jewish Spirituality,* World Spirituality 13 (New York: Crossroad, 1983). In that volume see the essays by Jon D. Levenson, "The Jerusalem Temple in Devotional and Visionary Experience," pp. 32–61; Michael Fishbane, "Biblical Prophecy as a Religious Phenomenon," pp. 62–81; and James L. Kugel, "Topics in the History of the Spirituality of the Psalms," pp. 113–144.

9. The story of Elephantine is told in Bezalel Porten, *Archives from Elephantine: The Life of an Ancient Jewish Military Colony* (Berkeley: University of California Press, 1968).

10. For an attempt to reconstruct the lives of Israelite women from the archaeological and meager textual evidence, see Carol Meyers, *Discovering Eve: Ancient Israelite Women in Context* (New York: Oxford University Press, 1988). For a variety of feminist approaches to the Hebrew Bible, see the many works of Athalya Brenner.

3. BETWEEN ATHENS AND JERUSALEM

There are several good introductions to this historical period. Shaye J. D. Cohen, *From the Maccabees to the Mishnah* (Philadelphia: Westminster, 1987); James C. VanderKam, *An Introduction to Early Judaism* (Grand Rapids: Eerdmans, 2001); John J. Collins, *Between Athens and Jerusalem: Jewish Identity in the Hellenistic Diaspora* (New York: Crossroad, 1983); Elias Joseph Bickerman, *The Jews in the Greek Age* (Cambridge: Harvard University Press, 1988); and Erich. S. Gruen, *Diaspora: Jews Amidst Greeks and Romans* (Cambridge: Harvard University Press, 2002). Gruen also surveys Jewish life outside the land of Israel during the Greco-Roman period in his essay "Hellenistic Judaism" in Biale, *Cultures of the Jews,* pp. 77–132.

The texts discussed in this chapter are all available in good English translations. Haggai, Zechariah, Daniel, Ecclesiastes, Esther, Ezra, and Nehemiah are all books from the Hebrew Bible. Any edition of the Apocrypha or the "Old Testament Apocrypha" (found separately or as part of a Catholic Bible) contains the books of Ben Sira (Ecclesiasticus) and 1 and 2 Maccabees. Pseudepigraphical books, such as the books of Enoch, along with the fragments of other Jewish writings in Greek (e.g., Aristobulus, Ezekiel the Tragedian, Letter of Aristeas, 4 Maccabees), can be found in James Charlesworth, ed., *The Old Testament Pseudepigrapha,* 2 vols. (Garden City, N.Y.: Doubleday, 1983–1985). The most readable translations of Philo and Josephus can be found in the appropriate editions of the Loeb Classical Library, published by Harvard University Press. There are many translations of the Dead Sea scrolls—that of Geza Vermes, *The Complete Dead Sea Scrolls in English* (New York: Penguin, 1998), is probably best for popular reading.

1. On Alexander's invasion of the Near East and the political struggles, a good introduction is offered by John H. Hayes and Sara R. Mandell, *The Jewish People in Classical Antiquity: From Alexander to Bar Kochba* (Louisville: Westminster John Knox, 1998). A dated, but still very important and accessible, study of the Maccabean revolt is Elias J. Bickerman, *The God of the Maccabees: Studies on the Meaning and Origin of the Maccabean Revolt*, trans. Horst R. Moehring, Studies in Judaism in Late Antiquity 32 (Leiden: Brill, 1979).

2. Philo, *Allegorical Works* 3.99, trans. F. H. Colson and G. H. Whitaker, Loeb Classical Library (Cambridge: Harvard University Press, 1968–1987), 1:367–369.

3. Aristobulus, fragment from Eusebius, *Praeparatio Evangelica* 8.10.2, trans. A. Yarbro Collins in Charlesworth, *The Old Testament Pseudepigrapha*, 2:838.

4. Ibid. 8.10.15, 2:839.

5. Philo, *The Special Laws*, 1.186, trans. F. H. Colson in the Loeb Classical Library edition, 7:205.

6. Apocalyptic tendencies are usually contrasted with the "Hellenistic Judaism" found outside the Land of Israel. This division is too simplistic. On apocalyptic works, John J. Collins, *The Apocalyptic Imagination: An Introduction to Jewish Apocalyptic Literature*, Biblical Resource Series (Grand Rapids: Eerdmans, 1998); Martha Himmelfarb, *Ascent to Heaven in Jewish and Christian Apocalypses* (New York: Oxford University Press, 1993).

7. On the rich literature and traditions regarding the figure of Enoch, see Gabriele Boccaccini, *Beyond the Essene Hypothesis: The Parting of Ways Between Qumran and Enochic Judaism* (Grand Rapids: Eerdmans, 1998), which has a provocative although controversial thesis.

8. For a grand survey of the exegetical life of Scripture in antiquity, see James L. Kugel, *The Bible as It Was* (Cambridge: Belknap Press of Harvard University Press, 1997).

9. On the Dead Sea scrolls and the community that produced them, see Lawrence H. Schiffman, *Reclaiming the Dead Sea Scrolls: The History of Judaism, the Background of Christianity, the Lost Library of Qumran* (Philadelphia: Jewish Publication Society, 1994); and James C. VanderKam, *The Dead Sea Scrolls Today* (Grand Rapids: Eerdmans, 1994).

10. One of the few modern (and responsible) book-length discussions of Jewish sectarianism during this period is Albert I. Baumgarten, *The Flourishing of Jewish Sects in the Maccabean Era: An Interpretation*, Supplements to the Journal for the Study of Judaism 55 (Leiden: Brill, 1997). Unsurprisingly, there is an enormous literature on the emergence of Christianity. For one such introduction, see Alan Segal, *Rebecca's Children: Judaism and Christianity in the Roman World* (Cambridge: Harvard University Press, 1986).

4. THE RABBIS

There is no book-length treatment of the Rabbis, their development, and their literature. There are, however, several excellent essays and articles that treat this topic. Two essays in Biale's *Cultures of the Jews* survey the social conditions in which the Rabbis worked in their two centers: Oded Irshai, "Confronting a Christian Empire: Jewish Culture in the World of Byzantium," pp. 180–221; and Isaiah Gafni, "Babylonian Rabbinic Culture," pp. 222–265. See also Gafni's essay, "The World of the Talmud: From the Mishnah to the Arab Conquest," in Hershel Shanks, ed., *Christianity and Rabbinic Judaism: A Parallel History of Their Origins and Early Development* (Washington, D.C.: Biblical Archaeology Society, 1992), pp. 225–265. One of the most recent and sophisticated evaluations of the Rabbis appears in Seth Schwartz, *Imperialism and Jewish Society, 200 B.C.E. to 640 C.E.*, Jews, Christians, and Muslims from the Ancient to the Modern World (Princeton: Princeton University Press, 2001), especially pp. 162–176. Some essays in Barry W. Holtz, ed., *Back to the Sources: Reading the Classic Jewish Texts* (New York: Summit, 1984) give fine introductions to some of the literature of the Rabbis: Robert Goldenberg, "Talmud," pp. 129–175; Barry W. Holtz, "Midrash," pp. 176–211. Milton Steinberg's novel, *As a Driven Leaf* (New York: Behrman House, 1996 [ca. 1939]) is entertaining and provides one of the more vivid, if historically inaccurate, portrayal of the early Rabbis.

1. For an interpretation of the causes of the "Great Revolt," see Martin Goodman, *The Ruling Class of Judaea: The Origins of the Jewish Revolt Against Rome A.D. 66–70* (Cambridge: Cambridge University Press, 1987).
2. 4 Ezra 3:32–36, trans. B.M. Metzger in *The Old Testament Pseudepigrapha*, 1:529.
3. Ibid. 4:26–30; 1:530–531.
4. Gedaliah Alon provocatively argues that Yavneh was actually a kind of POW camp. See his book, *The Jews in Their Land in the Talmudic Age, 70–640 CE*, ed. and trans. Gershon Levi (Jerusalem: Magnes, 1980), 1:86–118. On Jewish sectarianism and the emergence of the Rabbis, see Shaye J.D. Cohen, "The Significance of Yavneh: Pharisees, Rabbis, and the End of Jewish Sectarianism," *Hebrew Union College Annual* 55 (1984): 27–53.
5. On the Bar Kokhba revolt, see the essays in Peter Schäfer, ed., *The Bar Kokhba War Reconsidered: New Perspectives on the Second Jewish Revolt Against Rome*, Texte und Studien zum antiken Judentum 100 (Tübingen: Mohr Siebeck, 2003).
6. The extent to which the Rabbis were shaped by their Greco-Roman environment remains an area of scholarly disagreement. I more fully develop the parallel between Rabbis and philosophers in my article, "'And on the Earth You Shall Sleep': Talmud Torah and Rabbinic Asceticism," *Journal of Religion* 83 (2003): 204–225. On the Mishnah as a legal textbook, see Abraham Goldberg, "The Mishna—A Study Book of Halakha," in Shmuel Safrai, ed., *The Literature of the Sages*, Compendia Rerum Iudaicarum ad Novum Testamentum 2.1 (Philadelphia: Fortress Press, 1987), pp. 211–262.
7. Another good introductory essay on midrash is by James L. Kugel, in James L. Kugel and Rowan A. Greer, eds., *Early Biblical Interpretation*, Library of Early Christianity (Philadelphia: Westminster, 1986). For a fascinating case study of

the evolution of a midrash, see Shalom Spiegel, *The Last Trial: On the Legends and Lore of the Command to Abraham to Offer Isaac as a Sacrifice*, trans. with an introduction by Judah Goldin (New York: Schocken, 1967).

8. The midrash is taken from the *Mekhilta d'Rabbi Ishmael*, section *BaHodesh* 4. A full English translation of the midrash can be found in Jacob Z. Lauterbach, *Mekilta de-Rabbi Ishmael*, 3 vols. (Philadelphia: Jewish Publication Society of America, 1933).

9. Translation from *Judaism on Trial: Jewish-Christian Disputations in the Middle Ages*, ed. and trans. Hyam Maccoby (London: Littman Library of Jewish Civilization, 1993), p. 115.

10. The major collections of tannaitic midrash and their English translations are the *Mekhilta d'Rabbi Ishmael* on Exodus (see the translation of Lauterbach, cited above); the *Sifra* on Leviticus, trans. Jacob Neusner, *Sifra, an Analytical Translation*, Brown Judaic Studies 138–140 (Atlanta: Scholars, 1988); *Sifre to Numbers: An American Translation and Explanation*, ed. and trans. Jacob Neusner, Brown Judaic Studies 118–119 (Atlanta: Scholars, 1986); and *Sifre on Deuteronomy*, trans. Reuven Hammer, Yale Judaica Series 24 (New Haven: Yale University Press, 1986).

11. Marc Hirshman, *A Rivalry of Genius: Jewish and Christian Biblical Interpretation in Late Antiquity*, trans. Batya Stein (Albany: State University of New York Press, 1996), discusses several midrashic passages that appear to respond directly to Christian attacks.

12. The primary collections of amoraic midrash are found in the Rabbah collection, but do not include all of the books in it. Genesis, Leviticus, Deuteronomy, Ecclesiastes, Ruth, Lamentations, and Song of Songs in particular are considered amoraic (the rest date from a later period). These collections are all translated in H. Freedman and Maurice Simon, eds., *Midrash Rabba* (London: Soncino, 1939).

13. On the Rabbis of Babylonia, see the essay by Gafni in Biale, *Cultures of the Jews*; and Jeffrey L. Rubenstein, *The Culture of the Babylonian Talmud* (Baltimore: Johns Hopkins University Press, 2003).

14. The best translation of the entire Babylonian Talmud remains that of the Soncino Press. Parts of the Steinsaltz Talmud are translated into English; they have a very helpful commentary. The Schottenstein edition of the Talmud, part of the Artscroll series (Brooklyn: Mesorah, 1990–2005), too easily renders the original languages in accordance with preconceived theological notions. On the printing of the Babylonian Talmud, see Marvin J. Heller, *Printing the Talmud: A History of the Earliest Printed Editions of the Talmud* (Brooklyn, N.Y.: Am Hasefer, 1992).

5. RABBINIC CONCEPTS

There are several discussions of what the Rabbis "believe," although most of them treat rabbinic thought selectively by minimizing those aspects that are less relevant to modern sensibilities. David S. Ariel, *What Do Jews Believe? The Spiritual Foundations of Judaism* (New York: Schocken, 1995), provides a balanced, if partisan, treatment. Older studies include George Foot Moore, *Judaism in the First Centuries of the Christian Era: The Age of the Tannaim* (Cambridge: Harvard University Press, 1927–1930); and Ephraim E. Urbach, *The Sages: Their Concepts and Beliefs*, trans. Israel Abrahams (Cambridge: Harvard University Press, 1979). Solomon Schechter, *Aspects of Rabbinic Theology* (Woodstock, VT: Jewish Lights, 1993 [New York: Schocken, 1961]) is still worthwhile reading. The notion of "organic" theology that I use in this chapter derives from Max Kaddushin, *Organic Thinking: A Study in Rabbinic Thought* (New York: Bloch, 1938), which remains a difficult book.

1. On the development of notions of Jewishness, see Shaye J. D. Cohen, *The Beginnings of Jewishness: Boundaries, Varieties, Uncertainties* (Berkeley: University of California Press, 1999).
2. On the concept of the mitzvot, see Elliot N. Dorff, *A Living Tree: The Roots and Growth of Jewish Law* (Albany: State University of New York Press, 1988).

6. MITZVOT

There are several modern guides to the mitzvot, most of which align relatively strongly with an ideological movement. A popular Orthodox guide is Hayim Donin, *To Be a Jew: A Guide to Jewish Observance in Contemporary Life* (New York: Basic, 1972). Some of the positions of the Conservative movement are detailed in Isaac Klein, *A Guide to Jewish Religious Practice*, Moreshet Series 6 (New York: Jewish Theological Seminary of America, 1979), although much has changed since its publication. Mark Washofsky, *Jewish Living: A Guide to Contemporary Reform Practice* (New York: UAHC Press, 2001), has recently produced a guide to the mitzvot for Reform Jews.

Again, perhaps surprisingly, the halakhah of the Rabbis of antiquity themselves has never been treated synthetically and comprehensively, and the isolated discussions of it are rarely accessible to a nonscholarly audience. Lawrence H. Schiffman, "Was There a Galilean Halakhah?" in Lee I. Levine, ed., *The Galilee in Late Antiquity* (New York: Jewish Theological Seminary of America, 1992), pp. 143–156, gives a general account of some religious customs peculiar to the Galilee.

1. For Abraham Joshua Heschel's idea of sacred time, see his book, *The Sabbath: Its Meaning for Modern Man* (New York: Farrar, Staus and Young, 1951).
2. On one aspect of the dietary laws, see David C. Kraemer, "Separating the Dishes: The History of a Jewish Eating Practice," *Studies in Jewish Civilization* 15 (2005): 235–256.
3. Mary Douglas, *Purity and Danger: An Analysis of Concepts of Pollution and Taboo* (Harmondworth: Penguin, 1970). She has significantly modified her position in *Leviticus as Literature* (Oxford: Oxford University Press, 1999).
4. In his unconventional book, Keith Hopkins, *A World Full of Gods: Pagans, Jews*

and Christians in the Roman Empire (London: Weidenfeld and Nicolson, 1999), attempts to evoke the flavor of this religious world.

5. Phillip Goodman has edited a series of books that offer nice collections of original sources in English translation on most of the Jewish holidays. These anthologies have been published by the Jewish Publication Society of America. An interesting analysis of the evolution of Passover can be found in Baruch M. Bokser, *The Origins of the Seder: The Passover Rite and Early Rabbinic Judaism* (Berkeley: University of California Press, 1984).

6. For his understanding of life cycle events, see Arnold van Gennep, *The Rites of Passage*, trans. Monika B. Vizedom and Gabrielle L. Caffee (Chicago: University of Chicago Press, 1960).

7. For some studies of Jewish life cycles, seen from different perspectives, see Harvey E. Goldberg, *Jewish Passages: Cycles of Jewish Life* (Berkeley: University of California Press, 2003); and Ivan G. Marcus, *The Jewish Life Cycle* (Seattle: Washington University Press, 2004).

8. On rabbinic sexuality, see Daniel Boyarin, *Carnal Israel: Reading Sex in Talmudic Culture* (Berkeley: University of California Press, 1993). On marriage, Michael L. Satlow, *Jewish Marriage in Antiquity* (Princeton: Princeton University Press, 2001).

9. The books on women in the Talmudic period almost all foreground modern concerns, offering more of a feminist analysis than historical reconstruction. See Blu Greenberg, *On Women and Judaism: A View from Tradition* (Philadelphia: Jewish Publication Society of America, 1981); Rachel Biale, *Women and Jewish Law: An Exploration of Women's Issues in Halakhic Sources* (New York: Schocken, 1984); and Judith Hauptman, *Rereading the Rabbis: A Woman's Voice* (Boulder: Westview, 1998).

10. Jeremy Cohen, *"Be Fertile and Increase, Fill the Earth and Master It": The Ancient and Medieval Career of a Biblical Text* (Ithaca: Cornell University Press, 1989), offers an excellent account of the rabbinic approach to procreation.

7. THE RISE OF REASON

On Jews in this period, see generally Reuven Firestone, "Jewish Culture in the Formative Period of Islam," in Biale, *Cultures of the Jews*, pp. 267–302, who deals more with Jews during the time of Mohammad. This chapter relies heavily on Robert Brody, *The Geonim of Babylonia and the Shaping of Medieval Jewish Culture* (New Haven: Yale University Press, 1998).

1. On the relationship of Christians and Jews in antiquity, see Irshai, "Confronting a Christian Empire," in Biale, *Cultures of the Jews*. Irshai reflects the scholarly consensus that the Jews were more or less left alone by the Christian rulers.

2. *Codex Theodosianus* 16:8:25, translated in Amnon Linder, ed., *The Jews in Roman Imperial Legislation* (Detroit: Wayne State University Press, 1987), p. 288.

3. *Theodosius II, Novella* 3, ibid., p. 332.

4. On the incident in Minorca, see Scott Bradbury, ed. and trans., *Letter on the Conversion of the Jews, Severus of Minorca*, Oxford Early Christian Texts (Oxford: Clarendon, 1996).

5. Comment on Psalm 119:1 by Japheth b. Eli, translation in Daniel Frank, ed., *Search Scripture Well: Karaite Exegetes and the Origins of the Jewish Bible Commentary in the Islamic East* (Leiden: Brill, 2004), p. 29 (with some stylistic modifications).

6. Stylistically modified translation from Leon Nemoy, *Karaite Anthology*, Yale Judaica Series 7 (New Haven: Yale University Press, 1952), pp. 17–18.

7. On Islamic scripturalism and its relationship to Karaism, see Michael Cook, "Anan and Islam: The Origins of Karaite Scripturalism," *Jerusalem Studies in Arabic and Islam* 9 (1987): 161–183.

8. Quoted from Brody, *The Geonim of Babylonia*, p. 114.

9. On the competition between Palestinian and Babylonian rabbis in the period of the Rabbis, see Isaiah M. Gafni, *Land, Center, and Diaspora: Jewish Constructs in Late Antiquity*, Journal for the Study of the Pseudepigrapha Supplement Series 21 (Sheffield: Sheffield Academic, 1997).

10. Several translations of *piyyutim* can be found in T. Carmi, *The Penguin Book of Hebrew Verse* (Harmondsworth: Penguin, 1981). On the geonic production of standardized prayer texts, see Lawrence A. Hoffman, *The Canonization of the Synagogue Service* (Notre Dame: University of Notre Dame Press, 1979).

11. Quoted from Brody, *The Geonim of Babylonia*, p. 254.

12. Quoted from Gideon Libson, "Halakhah and the Law in the Period of the Geonim," in N. S. Hecht, B. S. Jackson, S. M. Passamaneck, Daniela Piattelli, and Alfredo Rabello, eds., *An Introduction to the History and Sources of Jewish Law* (Oxford: Oxford University Press, 1996), p. 236.

13. Quoted from Brody, *The Geonim of Babylonia*, pp. 288–289.

14. Quoted from the translation of Alexander Altmann of the *Book of Doctrines and Beliefs*, in Hans Lewy, Alexander Altmann, and Isaak Heinemann, eds., *Three Jewish Philosophers* (New York: Atheneum, 1973), p. 122.

15. Ibid., pp. 137–138.

16. Ibid.

17. Ibid., p. 101.

18. Ibid., p. 171.

19. Quoted from Brody, *The Geonim of Babylonia*, p. 320.

20. Ibid., p. 305.

8. FROM MOSES TO MOSES

There is an enormous and rich literature on Andalusia, Andalusian Jews, and Maimonides specifically. The standard, introduction to the Jews of medieval Spain is Yitzhak Baer, *A History of the Jews in Christian Spain*, trans. Louis Schoffman (Philadelphia: Jewish Publication Society, 1961), although it is dated and focuses on the experience in Christian Spain. More recent discussions include Jane S. Gerber, *The Jews of Spain: A History of the Sephardic Experience* (New York: Free, 1992); and Raymond P. Scheindlin, *Wine, Women, and Death: Medieval Hebrew Poems on the Good Life* (Philadelphia: Jewish Publication Society, 1986). Scheindlin also has an excellent essay, "Merchants and Intellectuals, Rabbis and Poets: Judeo-Arabic Culture in the Golden Age of Islam," in Biale, *Cultures of the Jews*, pp. 313–386. Maria Rosa Menocal, *The Ornament of the Word: How Muslims, Jews, and Christians Created a Culture of Tolerance in Medieval Spain* (Boston: Little, Brown, 2002), paints a beautiful portrait of cultural and religious interaction in Andalusia.

My readings of Maimonides' philosophy have been most influenced by the various works of Menahem Kellner, especially *Maimonides on Judaism and the Jewish People*, SUNY Series in Jewish Philosophy (Albany: State University of New York Press, 1991), and *Must a Jew Believe Anything?* Littman Library of Jewish Civilization (London: Littman Library of Jewish Civilization, 1999). Isadore Twersky's work on Maimonides' legal writings remains fundamental. See especially Isadore Twersky, *Introduction to the Code of Maimonides (Mishneh Torah)*, Yale Judaica Series 22 (New Haven: Yale University Press, 1980). For translations of Maimonides' writings, the main sources are Isadore Twersky, ed., *A Maimonides Reader* (New York: Behrman House, 1972); and Shlomo Pines, ed. and trans., *The Guide of the Perplexed*, 2 vols. (Chicago: University of Chicago Press, 1963). The *Mishneh Torah* is translated in the Yale Judaica Series.

1. Two essays in Holtz, *Back to the Sources*, offer excellent introductions to the literature discussed here, Edward L. Greenstein, "Medieval Bible Commentaries," pp. 212–259; and Norbert M. Samuelson, "Medieval Jewish Philosophy," pp. 260–303.

2. *Guide* 3.51, translation in Pines, *The Guide of the Perplexed*, 2.618.

3. Ibid.1.54; 1:128.

4. Ibid. 3.27; 2:510.

5. For a survey of Jewish legal activity in medieval Spain, see Eliav Shochetman, "Jewish Law in Spain and the Halakhic Activity of Its Scholars Before 1300," in N. S. Hecht, B. S. Jackson, S. M. Passamaneck, Daniela Piattelli, and Alfredo Rabello, eds., *An Introduction to the History and Sources of Jewish Law* (Oxford: Oxford University Press, 1996), pp. 271–298.

6. The translation of the passage from Ibn Ezra is taken from H. Norman Strickman and Arthur M. Silver, trans., *Ibn Ezra's Commentary on the Pentateuch*, vol. 2, *Exodus (Shemot)* (New York: Menorah, 1996), pp. 504–507.

7. Judah Halevi, *Kuzari* 1.11, trans. Isaak Heinemann in Hans Lewy, Alexander Altmann, and Isaak Heinemann, eds., *Three Jewish Philosophers* (New York: Atheneum, 1973), p. 33, and 1.12 for the continuation.

8. Ibid. 1.25; p. 35.

9. Ibid. 1.63; p. 37.

10. Ibid., 1.115.

11. Ibid., 3.7; p. 90.

12. Maimonides, *Epistle on Martyrdom*, trans. Abraham Halkin, *Crisis and Leadership: Epistles of Maimonides*, with discussions by David Hartman (Philadelphia: Jewish Publication Society of America, 1985), p. 16.
13. Ibid., p. 30.
14. Ibid., p. 31.
15. Maimonides, *Commentary on the Mishnah*, Sanhedrin 10:1, in Twersky, *A Maimonides Reader*, p. 404.
16. Ibid., p. 410.
17. Ibid., p. 412.
18. Ibid., p. 422.
19. Maimonides, "Introduction to the *Mishneh Torah*," in Twersky, *A Maimonides Reader*, p. 40.
20. Maimonides, *Guide*, introduction to part 1, in Pines, *The Guide of the Perplexed*, 1:5.
21. Leo Strauss famously suggested that the *Guide* is written in a kind of esoteric code, so that it means one thing to the casual reader but conveys a more radical message to initiates. Leo Strauss, *Persecution and the Art of Writing* (Glencoe, Ill.: Free, 1952), especially pp. 38–94.
22. A useful introduction to medieval Jewish philosophy is Colette Sirat, *A History of Jewish Philosophy in the Middle Ages* (Cambridge: Cambridge University Press, 1985).
23. An annotated English translation of Levi ben Gershom's major philosophical work is available as Seymour Feldman, trans., *The Wars of the Lord*, 3 vols. (Philadelphia: Jewish Publication Society of America, 1984–1999).

9. SEEING GOD

Gershom Scholem pioneered the modern study of Jewish mysticism and his works remain deeply relevant. See especially his collections of essays, *Major Trends in Jewish Mysticism*, rev. ed. (New York: Schocken, 1946), and *The Messianic Idea in Judaism, and Other Essays on Jewish Spirituality* (New York: Schocken, 1971). Kabbalah has been receiving increased attention in recent years, both popular and academic. In English, Moshe Idel's books, *Kabbalah: New Perspectives* (New Haven: Yale University Press, 1988), and *Messianic Mystics* (New Haven: Yale University Press, 1998), attempt to revise some of Scholem's positions. Especially readable entrances into Kabbalah are Arthur Green, *A Guide to the Zohar* (Stanford: Stanford University Press, 2004); and the essay by Lawrence Fine, "Kabbalistic Texts" in Holtz, *Back to the Sources*, pp. 305–359. A short selection of texts can be found in Daniel C. Matt, ed., *The Essential Kabbalah: The Heart of Jewish Mysticism* (San Francisco: HarperSanFrancisco, 1995); and a much longer, well-annotated selection in Isaiah Tishby, ed., *The Wisdom of the Zohar: An Anthology of Texts*, trans. David Goldstein, Littman Library of Jewish Civilization (Oxford: Oxford University Press for Littman Library, 1989).

1. Joseph Karo, *Maggid Mesharim*, trans. in Louis Jacobs, ed., *The Schocken Book of Jewish Mystical Testimonies* (New York: Schocken, 1976), p. 144.

2. Ibid., p. 141.

3. Ibid., p. 138.

4. On sixteenth-century Safed and the Jewish community there, see the vivid essay by Solomon Schechter, "Safed in the Sixteenth Century. A City of Legists and Mystics," in his *Studies in Judaism*, 2d series (Philadelphia: Jewish Publication Society of America, 1908), pp. 202–285.

5. Jacob of Marvège, *She'elot u'Teshuvot min ha-shamayim*, trans. Jacobs, *The Schocken Book of Jewish Mystical Testimonies*, p. 93.

6. *The Zohar,* ed. and trans. Daniel Matt (Stanford: Stanford University Press, 2004), 1:127–28 (= 1:17a). There are several English translations of the Zohar, but the best is that of Matt. Only the first two volumes have been published, and the translation is still in process.

7. Zohar 1:17b; *The Zohar*, trans. Matt, 1:132.

8. Ibid. 1:147a; 2:321.

9. Ibid. 1:73a; 1:432.

10. On Abraham Abulafia, see Moshe Idel, *Abraham Abulafia: An Ecstatic Kabbalist: Two Studies* (Lancaster, Calif.: Labyrinthos, 2002).

11. On the possible links between kabbalistic and medieval Christian ideas, see Peter Schäfer, *Mirror of His Beauty: Feminine Images of God from the Bible to the Early Kabbala,* Jews, Christians, and Muslims from the Ancient to the Modern World (Princeton: Princeton University Press, 2002). Arthur Green has a long essay on this topic, "Shekhinah, the Virgin Mary, and the Song of Songs: Reflections on a Kabbalistic Symbol in Its Historical Context," *AJS Review* 26.1 (2002): 1–52.

12. For an entrance into Christian mysticism, see Bernard McGinn and John Moyendorff, eds., in collaboration with Jean Leclercq, *Christian Spirituality: Origins to the Twelfth Century,* World Spirituality 16 (New York: Crossroad, 1992).

13. From the *P'ri Etz Hadar*, translated in Miles Krassen, "New Year's Day for Fruit of the Tree," in *Judaism in Practice from the Middle Ages Through the Early Modern Period*, ed. Lawrence Fine, Princeton Readings in Religion (Princeton: Princeton University Press, 2001), p. 91.

14. Gershom Scholem, *Major Trends*, p. 263.

15. On Sabbatai Zvi, see the pioneering study of Gershom Scholem, *Sabbatai Sevi: The Mystical Messiah, 1626–1676*, trans. R. J. Zwi Werblowsky, Bollingen Series 93 (Princeton: Princeton University Press, 1975).

10. EAST AND WEST

The topics that this chapter takes up have a vast primary and secondary literature. The essays in Biale, *Cultures of the Jews,* are excellent: Richard I. Cohen, "Urban Visibility and Biblical Visions: Jewish Culture in Western and Central Europe in the Modern

Age," pp. 731–796; David Biale, "A Journey Between Worlds: East European Jewish Culture from the Partitions of Poland to the Holocaust," pp. 799–860; and, especially, Moshe Rosman, "Innovative Tradition: Jewish Culture in the Polish-Lithuanian Commonwealth," pp. 519–570. Selections of many of the relevant primary documents can be found in Paul Mendes-Flohr and Jehuda Reinharz, *The Jew in the Modern World: A Documentary History*, 2d ed. (New York: Oxford University Press, 1995).

1. A good introduction to Heinrich Graetz and his conception of history can be found in Heinrich Graetz, *The Structure of Jewish History, and Other Essays*, ed., trans., with an introduction by Ismar Schorsch, Moreshet Series 3 (New York: Jewish Theological Seminary of America, 1975). See also Ismar Schorsch, *From Text to Context: The Turn to History in Modern Judaism* (Hanover: Brandeis University Press, 1994).

2. Quotations from Heinrich Graetz, *History of the Jews*, 6 vols. (Philadelphia: Jewish Publication Society of America, 1967): "Through its constant use . . ." (4:22–23); "Messianic enthusiasm . . . " (4:18–19); "perverted the verses . . . " (4:23).

3. My discussion of Spinoza relies heavily on the books by Steven Nadler, particularly *Spinoza: A Life* (Cambridge: Cambridge University Press, 1999), and *Spinoza's Heresy: Immortality and the Jewish Mind* (Oxford: Clarendon, 1999). There are several translations of Spinoza's works; see *The Collected Works of Spinoza*, ed. and trans. Edwin Curley (Princeton: Princeton University Press, 1985).

4. Quoted from Nadler, *Spinoza's Heresy*, p. 180.

5. On Moses Mendelssohn and the context of his life, see David Sorkin, *Moses Mendelssohn and the Religious Enlightenment* (Berkeley: University of California Press, 1996); and Allan Arkush, *Moses Mendelssohn and the Enlightenment*, SUNY Series in Judaica (Albany: State University of New York Press, 1994).

6. For the Haskalah's engagement with Scripture, see Edward Breuer, *The Limits of Enlightenment: Jews, Germans, and the Eighteenth-Century Study of Scripture* (Cambridge: Harvard University Center for Jewish Studies, 1996).

7. Ibid., p. 220.

8. Moses Mendelssohn, *Jerusalem, or, On Religious Power and Judaism*, trans. Allan Arkush (Hanover: Brandeis University Press, 1983), p. 97.

9. Ibid., pp. 102–310.

10. Ibid., pp. 118–119.

11. On the Jewish Enlightenment, see Shmuel Feiner, *The Jewish Enlightenment*, trans. Chaya Naor, Jewish Culture and Contexts (Philadelphia: University of Pennsylvania Press, 2004).

12. For a history of French Jewry, see Paula Hyman, *The Jews of Modern France*, Jewish Communities in the Modern World 1 (Berkeley: University of California Press, 1998). Selections of the answers of the Paris Sanhedrin to Napoleon (1806) can be found in Mendes-Flohr and Reinharz, *The Jew in the Modern World*, pp. 128–133.

13. Quoted from Mendes-Flohr and Reinharz, *The Jew in the Modern World*, p. 129.

14. On the birth of Jewish ideological movements in nineteenth-century Germany, see especially Michael A. Meyer, *Response to Modernity: A History of the Reform Movement in Judaism* (New York: Oxford University Press, 1988); David Ellenson, *Rabbi Esriel Hildesheimer and the Creation of Modern Jewish Orthodoxy*, Judaic Studies Series (Tuscaloosa: University of Alabama Press, 1990).

15. For the Constitution of the Hamburg Temple (1817), see Mendes-Flohr and Reinharz, *The Jew in the Modern World*, p. 161.

16. Quoted in Meyer, *Response to Modernity*, p. 122.

17. Samson Raphael Hirsch's most well-known writings are *Horeb: A Philosophy of Jewish Laws and Observances*, trans. I. Grunfeld (London: Soncino, 1962), and the more popular *The Nineteen Letters on Judaism*, ed. Jacob Breuer (New York: Feldheim, 1960).

18. For a sketch of Hatam Sofer's life, see Jacob Katz, "Towards a Biography of the Hatam Sofer," in *Profiles in Diversity: Jews in a Changing Europe 1750–1870*, ed. Frances Malino and David Sorkin (Detroit: Wayne State University Press, 1998), pp. 223–226.

19. On the neo-traditionalism of the ultra-Orthodox, see Michael K. Silber, "The Emergence of Ultra-Orthodoxy: The Invention of Tradition," in Jack Wertheimer, ed., *The Uses of Tradition: Jewish Continuity in the Modern Era* (New York: Jewish Theological Seminary of America, 1992), pp. 23–84. Jacob Katz is generally credited with the distinction between "traditional" and ideological Jewish communities. See especially, Jacob Katz, *Out of the Ghetto: The Social Background of Jewish Emancipation, 1770–1870* (Cambridge: Harvard University Press, 1973).

20. Quoted in Silber, "The Emergence of Ultra-Orthodoxy," p. 60, note 77.

21. Akiba Joseph Schlesinger, "An Ultra-Orthodox Position" (1864), cited from Mendes-Flohr and Reinharz, *The Jew in the Modern World*, p. 203.

22. A standard history of Zionism can be found in Walter Laqueur, *A History of Zionism* (New York: Holt, Reinhard, and Winston, 1972).

23. From the "Protestrabbiner," published in 1897 and quoted in Mendes-Flohr and Reinharz, *The Jew in the Modern World*, p. 539.

24. The rabbinic positions on Zionism are discussed by Aviezer Ravitzky, *Messianism, Zionism, and Jewish Religious Radicalism* (Chicago: University of Chicago Press, 1996).

25. Zecharias Frankel, "On Changes in Judaism" (1845), quoted in Mendes-Flohr and Reinharz, *The Jew in the Modern World*, p. 195.

26. Translation from Chava Weissler, *Voices of the Matriarchs: Listening to the Prayers of Early Modern Jewish Women* (Boston: Beacon, 1998), p. 97.

27. On the Jewish situation in Poland, see Gershon David Hundert, *Jews in Poland-Lithuania in the Eighteenth Century: A Genealogy of Modernity*, S. Mark Taper Foundation Imprint in Jewish Studies (Berkeley: University of California Press, 2004).

28. There is, again, an enormous literature on Hasidism. An entrance into the scholarly study of Hasidism can be found in Gershon David Hundert, *Essential Papers*

on Hasidism: Origins to Present (New York: New York University Press, 1991). A fascinating biographical portrait of one of the earliest Hasidic rebbes can be found in Arthur Green, *Tormented Master: A Life of Rabbi Nahman of Bratslav,* Judaic Studies Series 9 (University: University of Alabama Press, 1979).

29. Martin Buber, ed., *Tales of the Hasidim*, trans. Olga Marx (New York: Schocken, 1947–48), offers a fascinating if historically completely unreliable glimpse into at least how early twentieth-century German Jews viewed the Hasidic legends. For a more sober analysis of the life of Israel Baal Shem Tov, see Moshe Rosman, *Founder of Hasidism: A Quest for the Historical Baal Shem Tov,* Contraversions 5 (Berkeley: University of California Press, 1996).

30. On the Vilna Gaon and his legacy, see Immanuel Etkes, *The Gaon of Vilna: The Man and His Image*, trans. Jeffrey M. Green, S. Mark Taper Foundation Imprint in Jewish Studies (Berkeley: University of California Press, 2002).

31. On Yeshiva Judaism as a response to modernity, see David Biale, "A Journey Between Worlds," in Biale, *Cultures of the Jews.*

32. Quoted in Etkes, *The Gaon of Vilna*, p. 88.

33. Modified from the quotation in Marc Shapiro, *Between the Yeshiva World and Modern Orthodoxy: The Life and Works of Rabbi Jehiel Jacob Weinberg, 1884–1966* (London: Littman Library of Jewish Civilization, 1999), p. 63 and note 70 on the same page.

34. Biale, "A Journey Between Worlds," p. 819.

35. Pauline Wengeroff, *Rememberings: The World of a Russian-Jewish Woman in the Nineteenth Century*, trans. Henny Wenkart (Bethesda: University Press of Maryland, 2000), pp. 206–207.

36. For the population figures of the Jews of Warsaw, see Stephen D. Corrsin, "Aspects of Population Change and of Acculturation in Jewish Warsaw at the End of the Nineteenth Century: The Censuses of 1882 and 1897," in Wladyslaw T. Bartoszewski and Antony Polonsky, *The Jews in Warsaw: A History* (Oxford and Cambridge, Mass.: Blackwell in association with the Institute for Polish-Jewish Studies, 1991), pp. 214 and 221, and, in the same volume, the essay of Edward D. Wynot Jr., "Jews in the Society and Politics of Inter-war Warsaw," p. 292.

37. On the shtetl of Turov, see Leonid Smilovitskii, "A Belorussian Border Shtetl in the 1920s and 1930s: The Case of Turov," *Jews in Russia and Eastern Europe* 1.50 (2003): 109–137.

38. For the famous and haunting photos of Roman Vishniac, see, among others, his collection *A Vanished World* (Harmondsworth: Penguin, 1986).

INDEX

Design Matters
Creating Powerful Images for Worship

Jason Moore and Len Wilson

Abingdon Press
Nashville, TN

Library of Congress Cataloging-in-Publication Data

Moore, Jason, 1976–
  Design matters : creating powerful imagery for worship / Jason Moore and Len Wilson.
    p. cm.
  Includes bibliographical references.
  ISBN 0-68749446-X
  1. Public worship—Audio-visual aids.   I. Wilson, Len, 1970–   II. Title.

BV288.M66 2006
246—dc22

2006001684

Scripture quotations marked (NIV) are taken from the HOLY BIBLE, NEW INTERNATIONAL VERSION® NIV® Copyright © 1973, 1978, 1984 by International Bible Society. Used by permission of Zondervan Publishing House. All rights reserved.

Portions of this book first appeared in Church Production magazine.

06 07 08 09 10 11 12 13 14 15—10 9 8 7 6 5 4 3 2 1

MANUFACTURED IN THE UNITED STATES OF AMERICA

Contents

Acknowledgments

The basis for this book germinated from the spores of our teaching ministry as we began to meet eager pastors, worship leaders, and media ministers who had more passion than professional training about the work of actually creating images. There has been much about the theory of images in worship, and little design. This crack in the soil became the basis for our ministry, Midnight Oil Productions.

One of the primary reasons our ministry continues is because of the risks that dozens of church leaders, paid and volunteer, have taken in hosting our teaching seminars. Without their faith, Midnight Oil would wither. The same is true for all those who purchase our resources and who take time to encourage us to keep on doing what we're doing. We want to thank you for watering our soil and allowing us to fertilize yours.

Jim Kumorek and Brian Blackmore of *Church Production* magazine gave us a venue for writing a series of articles that became this book, which would not have come together without their regular deadlines. Paul Franklyn at Abingdon Press continues to be open to publishing our ideas, and Rebecca Burgoyne ensures they get collected and processed on time. To all of you, thanks for keeping us on track and helping harvest this book. We appreciate your work.

A special thanks to Phil Cooke for taking time out of a busy weekend shoot schedule to write a wonderful Foreword that just nails the importance of design. Phil, you get it.

We as the Church have a lot of learning to do when it comes to design. Our hope is that what we've learned can play a small part in growing the seeds of image in worship and ministry.

Len: When I began full-time media ministry in 1995, my original mission statement was to make media integral to church life, to make it excellent, and to increase media literacy in ministry such that people could create their own digital media productions like they create their own Microsoft Word documents. I was encouraged to dream big, but this is a goal far more audacious than one person can achieve in a lifetime. Through my partnership with Jason, though, we together are able to do more than I can ever do alone in making our dreams into reality. Thank you, brother, for your commitment to our work. Your design skills just keep getting better. While many designers guard their craft as their greatest asset, you graciously share yours, and I'm better because of you. You make the mission a joy.

Thanks also to Joe Carmichael and the creative team of Community of Hope in Mansfield, Texas, including my wife Shar, the team's creative director, for giving me an environment for creative expression. Shar, you help me in so many ways I cannot enumerate. But I would definitely start with your superior offspring management skills. Speaking of, my contribution to this project is dedicated to two children who have entered our lives with great rejoicing in the time since I last wrote an acknowledgements page, Christian Wayne Wilson and Joslyn Grace Wilson. I look at you and I see reasons for continuing to sow the seeds of ministry in our digital culture.

Jason: Garfield the cat, created by cartoonist Jim Davis, changed my life. In third grade I discovered that I could take a handful of crayons and some paper and could make people smile just by sketching out what I saw in front of me. Somehow, that lazy, lasagna-eating cat became my trademark, and by the end of that year I had drawn Garfield for just about everyone in my class. I liked the way creating "art" made me and those around me feel. At the age of eight, I began planning my career as "an artist" (whatever that meant). From those early experiences, I wandered from opportunity to opportunity encountering people who have helped me figure that out.

Thankfully, The Creator got a hold of me in junior high and I realized that I needed to use this gift to bring glory to Him and not me. Thanks God, for giving me, and all of us, the incredible ability to think creatively. This gift has brought meaning and purpose to my life, and I will forever be thankful for the supernatural presence of the Holy Spirit who guides my hands as I create.

I have had many instructors and critique partners over the years, skilled and unskilled, who have helped me continue to perfect this craft. Chief among those is my wife and companion Michele who, whether she knows it or not, makes me better at what I do. One or two comments can send me on a sometimes long but worthwhile quest to get it just right. I love you and thank you for making me a better artist.

To Len, my partner and best friend, I can't express in words how much you mean to me. You are iron sharpening me as we walk this path together. You have taught me more than you'll ever know.

To the 97/98 staff at the School of Advertising Art—particularly Tim Potter, Michael Bonilla, Cindy Lash, and Perry Edwards—thanks for all of the great instruction. I didn't always understand back then why you were so hard on us, but I get it now!

Thanks to Jim Siegel for teaching me how important color is to an image. I don't paint on canvas anymore, but the lessons I learned have made my digital paintings better.

I'd like to dedicate my contribution to Design Matters to my son Ethan Robert Moore. These past five months your smiles have brought your mom and me so much joy. What an incredible gift you are to me. I hope that in all of daddy's busyness you always know how much I love you.

The Language of a Generation

"Aesthetics, or styling, has become an accepted unique selling point—on a global basis. In a crowded marketplace, aesthetics is often the only way to make a product stand out."
—Virginia Postral
  —*The Substance of Style: How the Rise of Aesthetic Value Is Remaking Commerce, Culture, and Consciousness*

Few things are powerful enough to unite an entire culture. Governments, dictators, business leaders, and global influencers of all kinds have spent centuries trying to discover how to bring together organizations, communities, and nations; and time and time again, they've found one answer.

Design

Early in the life of the church, the Christian community discovered the transforming power of images. From Byzantine paintings and mosaics, to the great art of the Middle Ages and Renaissance, to the icons of Eastern Orthodoxy, the church presented its message through the narrative storytelling of images. Under Communism, Lenin exploited the influence of propaganda posters, and it didn't take long for the kings of American business to investigate the power of advertising images. For good or bad, since the earliest days of recorded history, the power of design has influenced millions.

And now, once again, design has united a generation.

From the intense graphic design of video games, to the pioneering special effects of major motion pictures, to the storyboards of music videos and commercials and high definition television, young people today speak the language of design. My daughters could retouch digital photos while in elementary school and by middle school were accomplished web designers.

Today, we live in a design driven generation, and if the Church is going to make an impact, design is the language we must learn.

In Western culture, content has always been king. From the earliest days of the Hebrew scriptures to the spread of Christianity across Western Europe and eventually America, we've been a "word based" people. William Tyndale's translation of the Bible into English sparked a revolution of literacy in the sixteenth century, and the greatest missionary efforts of the last few centuries have been the goals of translating and distributing the Biblical text to every culture and people group on the planet.

As a result—and rightly so—<u>content</u> has been far more important than <u>form</u> in our art, writing, media, music, and architecture. But today, we live in a <u>design</u> culture, and form has become a critical key to connecting with the public. So while Biblical literacy can never been taken for granted, we now face a new challenge: presenting a message of hope to a generation that's more visually sophisticated than any generation in history.

It's not hard to see, because the evidence is everywhere. Just check out the unique design features of new computers or the interior design of coffee shops. Cell phones, automobiles, software, movies—all are examples of a design driven culture. Better design isn't just decoration, it's "connection." Designer Charles Eames said, "Design is a plan for action."

Sure, sixteenth century Pope Julius could have painted the Vatican's Sistine Chapel a nice solid color, but he chose to give Michelangelo a little creative challenge. We Christians should have learned something, but today we build churches in metal buildings, design boring websites, and create tacky book and tape covers. As a producer and media consultant, I have spent decades encouraging clients to realize the power of design for connecting with customers and recognizing its influence on getting a message heard. I recommend they reconsider worship graphics and images, product packaging, television programming, websites, publications—anything they create with a new attitude toward design. Rethinking the design elements of a project isn't just a "cosmetic" issue—it's a fundamental issue about something that connects with the audience or customer on a very deep and significant basis.

But how can we do it? How can we teach thousands of pastors and ministry leaders the power of design? How can we instill the passion that drives a visual generation in these seminary graduates who have spent their careers focused on text-based messages alone?

Jason Moore and Len Wilson have made an incredible contribution toward helping us start that journey. In this remarkable book, they have not only shown the need for effective design in the work of ministry, but have given us a practical, easy to understand roadmap for making a visual impact.

Don't toss out your Bibles, commentaries, reference books, charts, or tables. The power of text will always be critical in telling the eternal story of our faith experience. But now you have a new tool to help you capture a new generation.

Simply put, if you're interested in creating a ministry outreach that presents the gospel in a compelling way that will capture the hearts and minds of the mainstream audience, this is the book for you.

Prepare to discover how to speak the language of this culture. Become a catalyst for telling the greatest story ever told, in a language and style this generation understands.

Welcome to the powerful world of design.

Phil Cooke
President and Creative Director
Cooke Pictures
Santa Monica, California

Why Design Matters

It is no longer sufficient to simply build a better mousetrap. That mousetrap had better look good. The rise of Design with a capital "D" is the cover story of the decade, according to Wired, Newsweek, Business Week, *and* Fast Company. *In every story, the bottom line is that design matters.*

At seminars, we begin the day by showing a video clip that asks people why they do or don't go to church. Some of the answers are typical: "because I believe in God"; "because I'm a spiritual person"; and "church is good for you." The overwhelming majority of responses, though, focus on the reasons that people don't go to church. Some of the answers, in fact, can be hard to hear: "it doesn't relate to me"; "the church tends to alienate people"; and "it's boring."

Although some of the answers in the video clip address issues beyond how congregations communicate in worship, the clip reveals that the forms of communication used are important, often playing a major part in why people think church is not relevant, why it alienates people, and why it is boring. (To view a streaming version of the clip, go to http://www.midnightoilproductions.com/reading/?p=4.)

Most churches have visual technology. Recent estimates show that the majority of churches in North America are now using screens in worship. For those who have been longtime advocates of visual communication in ministry, this is cause for celebration—at last, the need to communicate to our visual culture is taken seriously.

Unfortunately, by simply adding a screen and projector in a sanctuary a church does not guarantee growth or vitality. Just because we build it, it doesn't mean they'll come. Or with respect to screens in worship, just because we show, it doesn't mean they'll grow.

Perhaps we overlook the significant difference between technology and culture. As proposed in *Digital Storytellers*,[1] congregations often adopt new media but retain old mindsets, using digital technology as decoration on the same old tree without realizing that an entirely different medium necessitates a different way of thinking about the audience and communicating with the culture.

Adding a screen to worship but not changing the culture of mission in the congregation will reach few new disciples. After the turmoil of the transition into digital technology has passed, the congregation realizes that nothing is really different after all. Perhaps worship services now have a visual version of the bulletin, hymnal, and prayer book overlaid above nature scenes or abstract blobs of color, requiring more work on the part of worship planners, but that's about it. It invariably disappoints those who paid for the technology in the first place.

Poor utilization of the screen can overshadow the most meticulously planned dramas, music, and messages—no matter how much effort is given to these other elements of worship. Weak visuals stick out like a giant sore thumb. They can do more harm than good, resulting in worship that is not only unimproved from the old way but is often worse.

---

[1] Wilson, Len and Moore, Jason. *Digital Storytellers: The Art of Communicating the Gospel in Worship* (Abingdon Press: 2002), p. 19.

Are Screens a Fad?

Some pundits are predicting that the screen is a fad or trend in contemporary worship, destined to fade once its novelty passes. We met with a pastor and friend who has used media as an integral part of ministry for years. We were stunned by his question: "So, do you think media is just a fad? Because everything I'm hearing is moving away from media in worship."

The question is important because it is risky to make absolute statements about a technology in worship that is driven by cultural relevance. Continually attempting to cast the Gospel in the spirit of the times is at the same time a worthy evangelistic endeavor and a dangerous activity, as the culture is a slippery devil. There's a fine line between capturing the spirit of the times and chasing the zeitgeist, or running after relevance, and on occasion some have perhaps been guilty of trying a little too hard to be hip. Ministry using digital technology in worship is more than being about "relevance."

Another group of media innovators asked the same question at the end of the fifteenth century. Gutenberg's radical new media machine had persisted for fifty years and a new trade called "publishing" had developed. But the industry hit a wall. The initial goal of publishers was to reissue all of the world's useful manuscripts as books, by using Gutenberg's invention. But they were running out of useful manuscripts. What was left to print?

Around the same time, Christopher Columbus returned and needed a way to disseminate his discovery of a New World. He chose books and printed letters, which were quickly distributed around Europe. The new class of literates—people who had been reading books—applied the reading knowledge they had gained in incredible, fast-changing ways. As Columbus and others used the press not merely to repeat the known but also to reveal the unknown, a gulf in learning emerged between the old guard of teachers and the new class of learners. A radical thing happened: publishers began to print books containing original ideas. Rather than a technology that archived old knowledge, the printing press forced a truly revolutionary change in the very way people approached questions about faith and reason. "A gulf, practically unbridgeable, grew between [literates] and their teachers, who still belonged, mentally, to the preliterate age. Within a century after Gutenberg, most of the old moral and religious structures of the preliterate age fell into ruins."[2]

As many have pointed out, the parallels between the time following Gutenberg's invention and our current introduction to the era of digital technology are remarkable.

So, as our friend asked, are screens in worship just a fad? Another friend of ours, this one in the worship media industry, stated that he thought media was going to be "the next praise and worship;" that is, not just a fad but a trend that will drive changes in worship style for the next twenty to thirty years.

Although the second friend is a bit more optimistic about media's role in worship than the first, maybe neither grasps the magnitude of what is just beginning. Perhaps what many currently call "worship media" doesn't completely reflect the coming changes to how we do worship, because we are just beginning the journey of learning to think in image.

We believe that digital technology in worship, and the use of image, is a permanent shift in the culture of the church. This shift will be misunderstood for the designer who merely throws up random images on the screen with no understanding of image in worship. To that sort of approach, the screen is probably a fad. But there is something deeper than typing lyrics and sermon points into PowerPoint, finding a trendy background, learning the latest acronyms for gear and software applications, and making sure the projector fires up every Sunday.

Until church leaders and worship designers, including the pastor, learn to think in image, the technology will probably be a substitute for the printed word.

---

[2] Van Doren, Charles. *A History of Knowledge* (Ballatine: 1991), p. 377.

Text to Image

Church leaders are often advised that they should become "students of the culture."[3] Where that statement may fall short is in not getting specific enough about what exactly being a "student of the culture" means. Simply observing the surrounding world can be a great aid in making one's communication of the Gospel more relevant, but effective use of screens in worship requires something more.

Most of us who proclaim the gospel today are products of modern-era training.[4] Our education systems in public and private schools, in seminaries, Bible schools, and in congregations are very much rooted in text. By the time we have graduated, we have learned to agonize over the meaning and context of every word. We are able to consider the nuances of different synonyms and what effect each might have on our intended meaning. We have learned to compose vast collections of words into books to convey what we intend to express.

Even oral communication passes through this textual filter when we construct worship scripts, prayers, and sermon manuscripts, before we ever speak them out loud. For the most part, we are a highly literate society that understands "text" well. We are operating within the current cultural context of five-hundred years of development for the primary emphasis of the printed word.

In worship, the use of "text" is highly refined, whether or not the congregation calls its worship "traditional" or "contemporary." However, we are dealing now with a different medium, as is the culture around us.

As a medium, the screen is about image, not about text. Just as there are rules for the formation of text, such as those described in Strunk and White's *The Elements of Style*, there are also rules for the formation of

---

[3] Wilson, Len. *The Wired Church* (Abingdon Press: 1999), p. 23ff.
[4] By "modern-era" we are not referring to "modern" as in the latest or most advanced development but "modern-era" as in a period of history characterized by forms of communication that are rapidly fading.

images. Image rules are rarely considered. But the screen isn't a large piece of paper. It's a new medium, which requires a new mind. It is imperative that worship designers make the move from text to image. This is not to say that text does not have a place in worship but that pastors and worship designers need to move beyond modern, literate forms of thought about the use of text if they are to capture the spirit and potential of their screens.

The Power of Image

The potential for images in worship is amazing. Effective use can initiate incredible growth and transformation in a church's culture and in the lives of individuals who are assimilated into the secular, visual culture. The screen can be a catalyst for adopting styles of worship that are more indigenous, connecting to local communities in powerfully fresh, missional ways.

But the key to such transformation is in understanding that the screen is a visual medium, not a textual medium. Worship design teams, media ministers, and pastors alike must learn to think and create in image, in order to communicate the gospel, enact transformation, and make disciples in a visual culture. They must learn visual design if the new technologies that congregations have incorporated into sanctuaries are going to work for the mission of the church and not against it.

If we are going to use screens in worship, as most churches now aspire to do, then we must not be content with merely communicating in text. We must learn visual literacy. We must acquire "graphicacy."[5]

Part of the movement toward image is an acknowledgement that the medium is at least as important as the intended message. In fact, form and content are inseparable. Over time, the integration of the form and content of text has occurred so seamlessly that we are no longer aware of the medium or the communication that is occurring. The shift to communication through image and metaphor can seem jarring to those used to worship in text.

---

[5] Wilson, Len. *The Wired Church* (Abingdon: 1999), p. 10.

The shift to the screen requires a group of persons to create a "production." The extra effort is then more visible and held in suspicion, which is why some critics of the screen assert that it detracts or entertains, that it is shallow or "dumbs down," that it requires churches to abandon their traditions, or (mostly) that it just requires too many people and money resources. Old forms, or the means by which communication occurs, are so routine that they are for all purposes transparent. New forms become visible. Worshippers don't think about books, but they are highly aware of the screen.

Jesus addresses this problem in his parable of new wine and old wineskins in Matthew 9:16-17. Old skins, filled with new wine, will burst. The wine, or the Christ, needs to be presented in a new communication form that won't break down before it gets to the eyes and ears of those who hear it.

Learning to understand the nuance of image in worship is vital to ministry in our dominant digital culture. It also fits with how the gospel has been communicated historically. Jesus' use of story and parable in the first century fits with popular culture's use of image to communicate in story and metaphor today. Paul's ability to engage his culture and use its latest media, from writing to roads, fits with our digital technology's present ubiquity. Pope Gregory's blessing on stained glass as the "Bible for the illiterate" fits with the projection screen's facility to bring post-literate people to an experience of the Word. The explosion of innovation and change that occurred in the church during the Reformation, concurrent with the rise of the printing press, parallels the explosion in cultural change occurring today, concurrent with the rise of digital technology.

Implicit in this understanding of the screen's purpose is that worship has a missional purpose. Tom Bandy states it well in *The Uncommon Lectionary*:

> [W]orship is a form of mission. It employs the indigenous cultural forms of any given micro-culture, in order to introduce seekers to Christ. Or, it employs whatever learning methodologies are most effective in any given micro-culture, in order to motivate disciples to witness, serve, and model authentic Christian faith…worship is not intended by God or planning teams to send people to coffee, refreshments, and conversation with

their friends. It is intended to help people drink deeply from the
fountain of grace, and send them to bring living water to the
rest of the world.[6]

Preachers and worship designers already know that it is not sufficient to
stop with exegesis, or interpretation of the biblical text, while planning
worship. Even a literate sermon moves from understanding the biblical
text to understanding the world. Now the world is constructed visually
through image. There are new rules to learn.

Learning the Rules of Image

The purpose of the following chapters is to move use of media in worship from simply projecting headshots, song lyrics, bullet points, and
nature backgrounds to something that captures the spirit of how the
culture communicates. Using powerful art in today's most popular artistic styles, excellent design, and cultural references is a must for making
worship connect in the digital age. Whether you are a church pastor or
administrator, musician, producer, or artist, knowing a few principles for
design can go a long way in helping you become more effective in
reaching a lost world with good news.

The remainder of this book, and the accompanying DVD, will address
time-tested principles for design that may open your eyes to new ways
of thinking when creating powerful graphics for worship. Its goal is to
help you begin the journey of learning to think in image. If you employ
these techniques, you'll begin to see a difference in the way people
respond to the screen and, more importantly, the way they respond to
the offer of grace and forgiveness.

---

[6] Bandy, Tom. *The Uncommon Lectionary* (Abingdon Press: 2006), p. 9.

Chapter 1
Building Doorways to Truth

Design Principle: Creativity and Metaphor

The first principle for good design has little to do with design skills, software proficiency, or even artistic ability. Before a designer ever puts pen to paper or mouse to mouse pad, he or she must develop a concept that will effectively and clearly communicate the message.

Each of us is creative—even those who might claim that the creativity gene skipped a generation. In the creation story of Genesis 1, God models the creative process, demonstrating that good things take time. Although God could have made all of creation happen in an instant, instead God demonstrates meticulous intentionality and the importance of design.

How does creativity emerge? There are many different forms that creativity can take, but one of the most powerful, if not the most powerful, forms is through a focus on metaphor.

What exactly is a metaphor? Simply put, metaphor is a tangible way to express a story, thought, or idea. The metaphor becomes tangible because it uses familiar symbols to compare and contrast one thing or idea with another. Comparing or contrasting familiar objects, stories, and situations can make difficult concepts more accessible to the listener or viewer.

Metaphor is a doorway through which the viewer can enter into a truth. A metaphor is a comparison between two seemingly unrelated objects, where one's characteristics are transferred onto another. For example, "God is a roaring lion."[7] If we are not obsessed with a literal interperation of the texts of the Bible, as if seeking to define truth through a set of propositions, we know that God is not really a lion (or a bull who was worshipped by some people in Israel). But we know that God seemingly behaves like a lion, which is a powerful, royal symbol for a ruler. The characteristics of a lion are suggested for the purpose of imparting understanding and truth. This truth still has room for ambiguity and mystery, because God is and God is not a lion.

Few beings or things seem more abstract than a God somewhere "up there"? Perhaps that's why God repeatedly shows up in the Bible through metaphor, from a burning bush to a pillar of cloud and, ultimately, as a Body. Even after God comes Incarnate in Jesus, God's Spirit appears as a dove, or tongues of fire, or a rushing wind. The stories of faith in God are told with and through metaphor.

This ancient wisdom wasn't limited to God's people, either. Aristotle wrote in 322 BCE, "The greatest thing by far is to be a master of metaphor. It is a sign of genius, since a good metaphor implies an eye for resemblance."[8]

In fact, it could be argued that the world has a much better handle on metaphor in the present time than the church. Metaphor is immersed

---

[7] C.S. Lewis, in *The Lion, the Witch, and the Wardrobe*, portrays the ruler of Narnia as Aslan, the regal lion. This metaphor for God is at the heart of the Chronicles of Narnia.
[8] Aristotle, *De Poetica*, Mckeon, Richard (ed.), *The Basic Works of Aristotle* (Random House: 1941), p. 1479.

throughout the increasingly digital culture, both as a form of expression, more fundamentally, as a way of understanding truth.

An Experiment in Metaphor

As an experiment, one morning as Len left the house he decided to monitor his experience of metaphor. His wife had left the car radio on the adult contemporary station the previous day, so the first song he heard when he pulled out of the driveway was called "White Flag," by the artist Dido. In it, Dido laments the end of a relationship in which she still loves her significant other. She uses the white flag, and a distressed ship, as metaphors for her feelings. Next was the contemporary classic by Elton John, "Candle in the Wind." In it the songwriter compares the life and death of the American celebrity Marilyn Monroe to a fragile candle who was too easily blown out by destructive forces around her. After two melancholy love songs, Len was feeling a little nauseated so he switched to an alternative rock station, The Edge, whose name itself is a metaphor. They were playing a popular song by Coldplay, "Clocks." As you might imagine, the song was not literally about clocks. The first four experiences of his day were metaphorical.

Later that day as he worked on a database, he was struck by the number of churches whose very identity is rooted in metaphor. There were records for churches called The River, The Journey, Crossroads, The Oasis, Pathways, True North, and more. The congregation of the modern era sought to find meaning in linear fashion by naming itself the "First Church" of its respective community. The congregation of the digital era seeks meaning instead through metaphor.

Three Reasons Why Metaphor Is Important

In addition to its ubiquity in culture, there are three fundamental reasons why focusing creativity on metaphor is important.

First, metaphor makes the message easier to understand. When there are elements of a biblical story that are hard to connect with, or there is language that doesn't make sense in today's culture, metaphor opens a door into surprising possibilities.

At one congregation, we were part of a worship design team that developed a service around the story of John the Baptist, who was preparing for the coming of Christ as told in Luke 3:16-17. The team expressed concern that many of the elements in the passage are foreign and confusing to a non-agricultural, urban society. John uses language such as "thong," (which means something *completely different* today than it did in Jesus' day), "winnowing fork," "threshing floor," and "chaff"—all objects with which suburbians might not be familiar. Beyond the confusing language, the crux of John's message is purity. The team didn't want the message to get lost in translation.

So, the team focused its creativity on designing a metaphor that would connect John's message with this present culture, and we settled on one of today's most pervasive beverages: coffee. The filter plays the part of the winnowing fork that separates the wheat (or flavor of the coffee) from the chaff (or grinds). When the water passes through a filter full of ground coffee beans, the result is a pure cup of coffee. The grinds are tossed away. John's message reconnects in a way that many people can understand.

It's unlikely that the worshippers would retain their awareness of purity if we had shown a staged video clip of an actual threshing floor. The resemblances for a daily understanding of sin and evil would evaporate before the projector is turned off. But with coffee, something happens after worship is over on the weekend. On Monday morning, most of the viewers rise and make coffee. Suddenly, in daily life their routine behaviors become reminders of the Gospel; in this case, what it means to be pure.

Second, metaphor is the glue that makes the message stick. This glue, retention, is the second reason to use metaphor. When a metaphor is employed and the hard work of redeeming the metaphor is done, people will carry the message with them for much longer than they would have otherwise.

Consider another worship service design with a youth pastor, on the subject of racial reconciliation. While designing the service, the African-American youth pastor shared a personal story about his time at a small, mostly Caucasian, Christian college. As he familiarized himself with his new surroundings, he was disturbed by some of the art in one of the buildings on campus. A very large mural depicting heaven filled one of the cathedral ceilings.

Efrem scanned the painting back and forth and was frustrated by what he saw. This representation of heaven left something out. It was filled only with European faces in angelic poses. He wrestled with this painting as he asked himself, "Do I fit into a heaven like that?" His internal response was, "I don't think this is what heaven will look like at all. All who believe will dwell there together, regardless of race, gender, or socioeconomic status."

His sermon argued that if segregation has no place in heaven and if believers will live in heaven together in harmony, then they should strive to do the same on earth. So the worship design team developed the theme of "A Preview of Heaven" and the metaphor of movie previews. Just as Movie trailers give the viewer a sense of what the upcoming movie will be like before they see it, so should the earthly expression of the kingdom of God give the world a preview of heaven, where no one is excluded.

Jason created an animation to start worship that mimicked the style of the cheesy clips that run between the trailers and the feature, filled with dancing refreshments, crying babies, and ringing cell phones. The sanctuary was decked out with theater decorations (including a row of theater seats on stage). The team served popcorn to worshipers as they entered the room. The worship graphics had a movie preview theme.

Six months after that worship celebration a woman from the congregation said, "Jason, I've got to tell you something. You've ruined my movie going experience." She went on to explain, "It's actually a good thing. Every time I go to the movies now and I see that cheesy animation that runs before the movie starts, I leave the theater with a renewed passion for living a preview for heaven on Earth." She continued, "And it hasn't just happened once, it happens every time I go."

We knew that metaphors made the message easier to understand, but until then, we had not realized how it helped worshipers recall the message, with a certain degree of depth, even a long time later. When worship planners use metaphors from the culture and do the hard work of redeeming them, the culture becomes a reminder of the Gospel. This means that the Gospel becomes inescapable because culture is inescapable. Not all metaphors from the culture are redeemable, though. Be careful what you choose!

Third, and perhaps most importantly, metaphor is a key part of the design process because it was Jesus' model for public ministry. Mark 4 tells a story from the early part of Jesus' public ministry, in which he tells the parable of the sower. It's a long parable (vv. 3-9). Afterwards, when the crowds had left and the disciples were alone with Jesus, they revealed to him that they had no clue what he had been saying. Possibly frustrated at their lack of understanding, Jesus took the time to explain the entire parable to them, actually spending more time on the explanation than he had on the parable itself (vv. 10-20).

Instead of concluding that such a creative presentation of the Gospel didn't work, and returning to the religious rhetoric he had learned in the Temple (Luke 2:41-52), Jesus continued to speak in parables, telling the parables of lamp on the stand (Luke 8:16-18), the growing seed (Luke 8:5-8), and the mustard seed (Luke 13:18-19). "With many similar parables Jesus spoke the word to them, as much as they could understand. He did not say anything to them without using a parable. But when he was alone with his own disciples, he explained everything" (Mark 4:33-34).

Parables were Jesus' exclusive public style! He didn't simply use parables as an alternative for the dumb ones in the crowd. Metaphorical teaching was his only public method. Jesus understood that, to communicate ideas with effectiveness, he had to present his teaching in a medium that made sense to his audience.

People in our time still listen best when spoken to in a familiar language. This is the essence of metaphor.

The same is true in visual design. It is not sufficient simply to use the screen to present text in worship, however creatively treated; the best designs use visual metaphors to communicate basic ideas and thoughts. The presence of metaphor is at the core of learning to think in image. It is what separates good design from bad because it is the primary means with which we can express creativity.

How does this translate into designing graphics for worship? This is a question that we're still learning to answer, too. We're not certain that anyone has our image future in worship figured out yet. And we're not alone: the media industry experiments, too. Those who are behind the times in the advertising industry are in a panic because one of its key target audiences, the eighteen- to thirty-four-year old male, is so attuned to interactive technologies such as TiVo that they are choosing to delete or ignore traditional advertising (known as features and benefits, or F&B, ads) because it's "boring"—i.e., they don't communicate through metaphor. David Art Wales of Ministry of Culture, a New York advertising consulting firm, says, "There's a huge lure to obscurity. That's one of the keys—giving people something to discover, which is the antithesis of the way most advertising works."[9] As designers of worship, don't underestimate your congregation's ability to decipher meaning through image. Make sure though, that you actually have a metaphor in the first place.

Even without realizing it, novices often don't completely understand how metaphor works. The word *metaphor* is often used incorrectly as a generic term to describe anything visual. Metaphor is something very specific that is achieved through much effort.

To know if you have a metaphor, fill in the blank to this statement: This message, idea, or passage is like _____. For instance you could say the idea of a spiritual life without regular prayer and Christian community is like living off of fast food. A person is technically eating but not doing himself or herself any good with such a diet. You might call the worship service "Fast Food Faith."

---

[9] Frank Rose, "The Lost Boys," *Wired Magazine* (August 2004).

Metaphors should also be quickly and easily understood without detailed explanation. Worship designers should be able to write how a metaphor connects to a biblical idea in a sentence. Often a four to seven word title phrase (or theme sentence) on a graphic is enough of a description to make the metaphor clear. Additionally, since the purpose is to create images, the metaphor cannot simply be wordplay but must be visual in nature.

Examples:
- Fast Food Faith, on discipleship, with the image of some food in fast food packages, or a drive-through menu board

- King of the Jungle, on God, with the image of a strong lion, à la Lion King or Chronicles of Narnia

- Pure to the Last Drop, on purity, with the image of a cup of coffee

- Can You Hear Me Now?, on prayer, with the image of a mobile phone

- Metamorphosis, on spiritual transformation, with the image of a butterfly

- Restored, on salvation, with the image of a car being restored in a garage setting

- The Whole Truth and Nothing But, on truth, with the image of a lie detector

As you begin to design, look for ways to communicate ideas through visual metaphors. Tap into your creativity. Think about visual equivalents. Avoid prepositions and move toward experiential words and objects. Brainstorm about everything from current pop culture references to pithy sayings. And, unlike the list of examples above (which are appropriate to a book genre), stay away from bullets on the screen because bullet points are best left to BULLET-ins.

Terms to Learn:

Each chapter closes with a few "terms to learn," or words and phrases that are helpful to know while learning to think in image.

Hook—A creative interpretation of a theme. It is helpful for artwork to have some sort of "hook" or some way to express themes that are understandable and memorable.

Metaphor—A tangible way to express a story, thought, or idea using resemblance and contrast.

Theme—The title, tagline, or named representation of the metaphor for an image or service, ideally four to seven words long. In the context of worship, preferably the words of the theme have both cultural and theological connections.

Chapter 2
Using The Best of Design Culture

Design Principle: References

One of the urban legends in the movie business concerns Steven Spielberg's beginnings as a film director. Allegedly, Spielberg snuck onto the Universal lot at the age of sixteen, acquired an office, gave his name to the switchboard so he could get calls, and hung around until he established himself. He "faked it 'til he made it." Even if it turns out that the legend is mostly romanticized myth,[10] there is empowerment in that story.

As a college student in the early 90s, Len felt a call to communicate the Gospel by using the language of film and TV (the Internet came later). Len found that experience in the professional production world was hard to obtain. So he often "faked it." This feeling, of not really being technically up to the task, lasted even into his first full-time media ministry position at Ginghamsburg Church. He had convinced others of his expertise and suddenly had to deliver—and not occasionally but every week!

---

[10] See [http://www.snopes.com/movies/other/spielberg.asp for a detailed take on this myth.

With no art school education and little experience, one of the ways Len "faked it" through those first days as a local church media minister was by watching television. If whle watching TV or a movie at home, he saw a video treatment or edit sequence or shot selection that looked cool, he would punch record on the VCR or scribble a storyboard down in a notepad. If it was on tape, he would take the clip to the church, digitize it into the computer, and then watch it forwards and backwards, frame by frame, to try to figure out what exactly had happened that made watching it so very engaging.

This survival technique was actually being taught at the same time to Jason in art school. Finding inspiration from the media culture, or in other words *finding references*, is the second principle for design. It is part of the daily grind for artists in ad agencies, movie studios, and web companies all over the world.

Finding the Best of Design Culture

Perhaps there are no original ideas. Every creative concept or some version of it has already been done. While that might be slightly overstated, it definitely seems that many good ideas have already been snatched up. Truly innovative creations pop up from time to time, such as the "bullet time" effect used in the Matrix films or the silhouetted dancing music lovers in the Apple iPod commercials. But for the most part, high impact design is achieved by finding inspiration in the look and feel already present in the current culture of design. The good news is that it is not necessary to revolutionize the design world with every click of the mouse. Often, creativity and originality can be found in simply finding good references.

Figures 1A and 1B show a recent ad for a computer input device called a Wacom tablet that was used as a reference for an image for worship. Notice that while the image says something completely different, the reference provided ideas for the layout and color scheme.

When Jason was in art school (at a school specifically geared toward commercial art), it was a requirement to turn in a reference with each project. A typical project might begin with a client, such as Nike. Some copy and a logo would

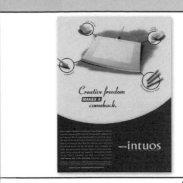

Figure 1A

be all that was provided as a starting point. A concept would then be developed, and then Jason and the other students would have to search through a large book called *A Design Annual* for a design reference. This book contained all of the top designs for the year. Before moving ahead with the ad, he had to decide on a reference that complimented the concept, copy, and company profile.

For the longest time this requirement for a reference made no sense to Jason or many of the other students. Why couldn't they just be creative on their own without design references? With a few years of experience, Jason began to realize that when he saw other designers fail to use references, their work might speak to them and a handful of others, but many times it was stylistically esoteric, failing to speak to a larger audience.

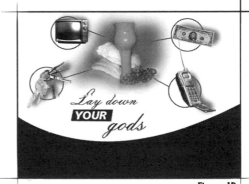

Figure 1B

By using references, designers retain or achieve connection with the current culture. There are trends that we need to incorporate into our work if we want to speak to the dominant part of our culture that is engaged by commercial art.

The idea of using references isn't a new one. From music to movies, to furniture, clothing, and electronics, contemporary culture is a swirl of design folding back in on itself. Look at the way computers are designed. Apple changed the beige world of computers in 1997 with the introduction of the iMac. Now there are toasters, irons, trashcans, and more designed with the same grape, blueberry, and tangerine colors. Recall the joke about your closet: "Hang on to that shirt a while longer— it will come back in style." Retro is always in. The current decade is being called the "Mashup" by publications such as *Wired* for its cultural stir fry in mixing various artistic sources together.[11]

The first commercial spot that Len created as a media minister was a Christmas ad in 1996. He took a colleague's photo of a baby on hay and accompanying copy for a print ad, which was called "The Day God Got Personally Involved," and created a single sequence that descended from space as words about God's "distance" flashed on the screen. The words popped and stuttered and then smoothed out as the end of the shot revealed the baby Jesus. Len had taken the idea for the text treatments from the opening credits to the film *Seven*, a dark film about a serial killer. The ad was a big hit. (Those same opening credits were influencing a lot of people in the industry at that time, and the jumping text look is still a trend in design.)

Homage or Plagiarism?

Some might be concerned that all of this sounds at the very least unorig-inal, or at the worst, plagiarism. There is a line between ripping off some-one's design and referencing it to create a new work. To better understand the nature of using references, and in continuing the shift from text to image, compare the process of writing. In school, when given an assignment to write an essay on a particular topic, the student is taught how go to the library and conduct some research. A little dig-ging usually reveals previous essays on the same subject.

Now, if the student simply copies what he or she has read verbatim and claims it as original, then he or she plagiarizes another's work, vio-lates copyright, and is in danger of expulsion. The correct research process involves reading others' thoughts, digesting them, and creat-ing, at the least, summations of different theories regarding the topic

---

[11] Daniel Terdiman, "Mashup Artists Face the Music", *Wired Magazine* (April 2004).

and, at best, an original angle no one else has yet explored. In either case, he or she references other works and then creates something new. Referencing a body of work creates something that is both original and connected to current thought.

This doesn't stop at graduation. Authors and researchers ("text professionals") know that they must stay connected to current trends for their work to have any influence. The same is true in a visual language. By using references, designers acquire a voice in the current culture. There are trends that designers need to incorporate into their work if they want to speak to the dominant part of the culture that is engaged by commercial art.

Design on a Dime

The good news is that references free a designer to raise the bar on his or her work with less effort than might be expected. It costs nothing to become a student of the culture. The industry surrounding commercial art spends time, energy, and money figuring out how to rise above the din of media messages in society. A person doesn't need to be an incredibly creative and talented designer to create some really great images. Merely look at other designs with an eye for detail, asking what would make it useful or not useful to the project at hand

It's not hard to adapt a design from something in print or on TV with a little practice. One of the favorite activities from our respective childhoods was *Weekly Reader* magazine. Among other fun things to do on the Activities Page was a section with two grids, each containing nine sections [see Figure 2]. One grid, typically on the left, had a picture in it. The other grid was empty. The reader was encouraged to examine the image on the left and recreate the image in the empty grid on the right by using the gridlines as markers. The same concept can be applied to any source material, as references can come from any design source.

References for screen graphics can be found by looking at websites, TV, and even print brochures. It's important to keep in mind, however, that references must be adapted to the desired medium. For example, when finding sources from just about anywhere other than television, it is necessary to adapt the *aspect ratio*. The aspect ratio is just a fancy term for the way the screen is shaped. Most screens currently have a 4:3 aspect ratio. That's 4 parts wide by 3 parts high. If you as the designer are fortunate enough to have widescreen, then there are several options available, the most common being 16:9.

Some print designers are excellent at creating brochures, mailers, and other print projects, but the screen presents new challenges that are difficult for an old hand to overcome. The leap from paper to screen can be difficult if the designer does not consider the canvas.

Unlike a brochure, which can be designed in a variety of shapes in a process called die cutting, the screen is a fixed size. Sometimes that 4:3 box feels like a jail cell. It is awkward to take a well-designed piece, created for print, and stick it in the middle of a blank screen. Nine times out of ten it does not work. Graphics for the screen must be designed with the canvas in mind. This sometimes creates unique challenges, especially when it comes to sermon illustrations.

Figure 2

Imagine that Sunday's message calls for a story on Mother Theresa. It would make sense to put a picture of her on the screen to further the telling of the story. But what happens when the designer is unable to find an image that works with a 4:3 canvas? What to do?

The lazy designer simply puts the image in the middle of the screen with black on either side [Figure 3A]. This however, isn't a good solution for the screen. It is the visual equivalent of receiving a brochure in the mail on an $8^1/_2$ x $5^1/_2$ piece of cardstock with printing only in the middle. Imagine receiving someone's business card printed on a 3x5 card with printing only in the middle. Leaving the paper (and the screen for that matter) blank on the edges becomes the message, and it is a blank message.

Pay attention to investigative report shows on television such as *Dateline NBC*. Watch what happens when they put up a photo or document on the screen. Instead of displaying the document with black on either side of the photo or document, designers employ techniques such as a blurred repeat of the photo, or some sort of background consistent with the look of the program behind it. So, as a solution, put the picture of Mother Theresa on

Figure 3A

Figure 3B

top of a scaled up, blurred, and muted version of the same photo [Figure 3B]. Or better yet, place the photo over top of a muted version of the thematic background for the day [Figure 3C]. This will fill the canvas and make better use of the space without any unwanted "black holes."

Finding Good References

Begin by starting a reference library. Collect appealing designs from the worlds of film, television, and advertising. Start in the living room. What magazines do you subscribe? What TV shows do you watch? What sites do you surf? Look at this media with a

Figure 3C

critical eye. Identify not only what is cool, but begin to analyze why it is compelling. Anything visual qualifies. We have digitized scenes from movies, DVD interfaces, and TV shows to understand why something worked well. We have even taken apart flash files and animated GIFs. If while reading a magazine, you see an ad you like, tear it out (make sure it's your magazine first!) and save it for future reference. Do the same with creative direct mail cards, movie posters, CD sleeves, and maybe even something from the newspaper. If you don't know how, learn to take a screen capture on your computer. This comes in handy while surfing the web. Visit http://www.macromedia.com/ and visit their showcase section. Subscribe to *Wired* magazine, which may be the best-designed magazine in print. Be conscious of design decisions made in the media you consume. Is there anything you find inspiring? Over time, looking for references can become an almost unconscious exercise. Always be on the lookout for great references to communicate the Gospel in ways that connect with the current culture.

Terms to Learn:

Aspect ratio—The ratio of the width of the image to the height of the image. For most screen images the current aspect ratio is 4:3. HDTV uses an aspect ratio of 16:9, and many designers will be forced to adapt to this standard for worship in the future as congregations convert their visual setups.

Die cut—A cut made with a die, i.e., the sharpened edge of a thin strip of steel rule. A specialized technique for creating unique shapes in boxes, folders, brochures, and other print works.

Plagiarism—The false presentation of another person's work as one's own, without acknowledging or giving the source of the ideas and expressions. It happens when an artist uses references without adapting them to his or her own style.

Reference—A work that provides inspiration to an artist.

Chapter 3
The Basics of Design

Design Principle: Composition

At the foundation of any powerful image is its composition. Understanding this principle and its underpinnings is not optional for those who want to create inspirational media that encapsulates and propels the Gospel message.

Without composition, art would be a collection of random colors, shapes, and objects, tossed together with little hope of engaging anyone. Many beginners fail to recognize this and don't realize that composition is at the core of design. Think of *design* and *composition* as interchangeable words.

When professional photographers practice their artistic craft, they always have composition on the mind. For example, when a family goes to a studio for a portrait, they are made to stand in all sorts of seemingly strange poses. When they ask the dad to lean his head in toward his wife or when they ask the daughter to put her foot on a box, with one elbow on her knee, they are determining the best composition. Even though the family may feel like a twisted pretzel while in the session, their photos usually come back with a very pleasing layout.

Composition is the order in which all of the elements in a completed work (or image) are arranged. These elements aren't limited to, but may include, lines, shapes, colors, shading, text, people, and other objects. Arranging them in the most visually pleasing way is the key to the successful transmission of an intended idea. An artist can never be sure how people will react to and interpret art, but putting an emphasis on the process of composing the image helps achieve purpose with a greater degree of success.

From a conceptual standpoint, the best images are those centered on one primary idea. This means that one element (the one that communicates a message the best) becomes the focal point of good design. The rest of the image then (in many instances) becomes "eye candy" that supports the main subject of the image. The focal point in the image is equivalent to a main idea in a paragraph. In the world of text, the other sentences in a paragraph support the main idea so that meaning is communicated clearly.

Many budding media ministers will begin their understanding of design while working within Microsoft PowerPoint (which is a presentation rather than a design application). Photographs in PowerPoint are often presented over a gradient color background, as seen in Figure 1A. We'll call this the "eighth grade collage" look. While this look may be artful on poster boards for class or in scrapbooks, it doesn't work as well with images for the screen. The eye doesn't know where to go. The result is an amateurish and ineffective image. Good composition positions elements so that the eye can naturally flow from one part of the image to the other in a way that makes visual sense, while knowing what is primary and what is secondary.

There are many ways to emphasize one primary element over others, including placing it in a dominant position on the screen, enlarging it to contrast against the size of other elements, and using the other elements as a visual frame. The image should always be composed in such a way as to draw the eyes to the area of highest importance.

The secondary elements provide a richness that brings depth and additional visual interest to an image, as seen in Figure 1B. After the eye is drawn to the primary element, it will then begin to detect other, more subtle elements. Notice how the same elements from figure 1A have been rearranged to highlight the cross and the man with his head in his hands. Whereas in 1A we see a generic montage of "mission" type images, in 1B we see a man praying in the shadow of the cross, surrounded by the struggles of the world. The secondary photographs work together with the primary photograph to create not just a snapshot but also an idea. The presence of the idea—functioning as a "grace period" to others—is more prominent in 1B than 1A.

Composition furthers the objective of communicating the Gospel in a visual language. Composing images with multiple levels of visual interest will help images stand up to extended and/or multiple-viewings. When design decisions are made correctly, congregations won't get bored, but will want to further explore the image.

Figure 1A

GRACE PERIOD

Figure 1B

The ultimate goal in creating an image is balance. Harmonizing between primary and secondary elements can be tricky, and finding the right proportions to please the eye can take time. Images with good balance and composition are obvious immediately. Unfortunately there is no exact checklist to figure out if an image is composed and balanced properly. This is a subjective decision to be offered by the artist, and it often becomes clearer with experience.

Composition Guidelines

1. Create asymmetrical images.

Most images don't work when they're created in symmetry. It is much more interesting to create asymmetrical layouts where elements aren't centered. Placing objects in the center is very dull.

2. Don't split the image into halves.

Avoid creating a strong vertical or horizontal line in the center of an image. If photographing a landscape, don't put the horizon (a strong horizontal line) in the center of the image. Similarly, if photographing a telephone pole (a strong vertical line), don't put it in the center of the image. This rule also applies to artificially created lines. When centered, vertical and horizontal lines split the image into halves and confuse the viewer as to what is most important.

3. Lead the eye into the image.

Don't arrange images in such a manner that they lead the eye out of the frame. In other words, with a photo of a woman walking to the right, place her on the left of the frame so that she will lead the eye into the image.

4. Type is important.

Remember that adding a theme line (or title) to the image equates to adding another element of significant importance. In an image, letters become visual objects. Text on the screen often gets the short end of the stick. Place type with the same degree of intentionality that accompanies the other visual elements of an image. It is a part of the image, not something to be added "on top." (For more on type, see Chapter 8.)

5. Choose elements sparingly.

Clutter is a killer of design. Don't be afraid to leave some open space. For example, if doing an image with a "Back to School" theme, stick with something simple, such as a chalkboard, or an apple on a desk. It is cluttered to include a backpack, school bus, lunchbox, flagpole, yellow #2 pencils, chalkboard, and apple, all in the same image.

6. The Rule of Thirds.

This classic rule has been around much longer than screens in worship. The image in Figure 2A has been overlaid with a simple grid in Figure 2B. This grid, which resembles a tic-tac-toe board, provides guidelines for composing images. The horizontal and vertical lines provide areas of emphasis for the frame, with the greatest areas of emphasis occurring at the intersections of the lines. Notice how the glass of milk, which is the most important element in the frame, is centered on the right line. The rule of thirds helps artists create asymmetrical images, as mentioned above, while still framing elements in a cohesive way.

Figure 2A

While a helpful guide, avoid strict adherence to these lines. The lines of pixels along the grid, and the four points of intersection, are not the exact points to position elements. They are merely clues to the

Figure 2B

47

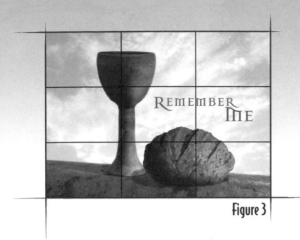

REMEMBER ME

Figure 3

general location of elements. In Figure 3, the most important part of the image, the cup, is not directly on the left line but is very close.

Watch for the use of the Rule of Thirds in television programs. Often, news magazine shows zoom in at the most intimate moment on an interviewee's face so tightly that the top of his or her head is cut off. Of all of the facial features, the eyes communicate the most. The videographer wants to capture the moment by featuring the eyes, without losing the mouth. The hairline, which is unimportant, is lost. This technique for capturing relationship through a visual language works because the subject's eyes remain on the upper horizontal line of the Rule of Thirds. In fact, this upper horizontal line is so important in composition that it is often called the Golden Line.

Knowing the rules for good composition is important, but breaking them is also part of the process. Once the basic rules for composition are mastered, opportunities will arise when the creative process calls for something a little different. This isn't an excuse to not learn the rules, but it becomes an opportunity to build on them.

When done with respect, breaking the rules can open the doors to some amazing things . The results often produce a creative tension that feels very fresh and (when done successfully) right.

One of our favorite examples of breaking the rules and getting away with it was from a Snapple tea ad from the 1990s. In the spot, one avid Snapple drinker shares all of her praises for the popular fruit drink. Using some of the strangest framing we've ever seen, her head and shoulders barely take up the very bottom right eighth of the screen as she goes on and on about the wonders of Snapple. The shot primarily captures the blank wall behind and above the woman. For some intangible reason, this temporary break from the rules of composition worked.

As you begin your next graphic for worship, we encourage you to spend some extra time on composition. You may even find it helpful to create several thumbnail sketches on paper to plan out where elements are going to go. Once the composition is determined, you'll have fun moving on to the next few principles.

Terms to Learn:

Composition—The ordering of elements within a frame when creating an image, either still or moving, with the intention of communicating ideas and feelings with the viewer.

Focal point—A specific area, element, or principle that dominates a work of art. The viewer's eye is usually drawn first to a focal point. Contrast, location, isolation, convergence, and the unusual are used to create focal points. In photography, the focal point also refers to the optical center of a lens when it is focused on infinity.

Guides—A set of lines in Adobe Photoshop that help the user position images or elements precisely. Guides appear as nonprinting lines that float over the image.

Rule of Thirds—A general composition guideline that divides an image into thirds horizontally and vertically, like a tic-tac-toe grid. The lines indicate areas of visual interest for placement of elements, with the points of intersection between the lines providing the greatest areas of visual interest.

Thumbnail sketch—A small-scale, low detail sketch done before actually creating a graphic, done for the purpose of fleshing out concepts.

Storyboard—A series of panels roughly depicting scenes, copy, and shots proposed for an animated or video production.

Chapter 4
Spicing Up Basic Imagery

Design Principle: Treatment

If graphic design is something like cooking, then treatment would be the spices that make it fun to eat. It's not very difficult to cook a basic pot of chilli, but making it stand out above the rest takes what popular chef Emeril Lagasse calls "kicking it up a notch."

The first three design principles are about the fundamentals of good design. The next three principles are about making images into visually appetizing feasts.

Treatment usually happens at or near the end of the production process. Once the references are established, graphic elements have been found, and the composition finished, the next step is to treat the image in some way.

There is a plethora of treatment styles to choose from, but knowing how and when to use certain treatments takes practice. References often provide the designer with suggestions and possibilities for treatments. Sometimes these can be effective. But choosing a proper treatment takes careful consideration. The question is, does the treatment fit the overall intended theme and tone of the image?

The first tendency of the budding graphic designer is to apply treatments inconsistent with the design's theme or to go crazy with the "toys." Design-leading application Adobe Photoshop comes with a variety of filters that enable the user to make images look like anything, such as an impressionist painting, a neon sign, a cardboard cutout, and more. Because there is such a wide variety of possibilities, the temptation is to use them—sometimes all at once. The results can be disastrous. Just because a budding designer can make a photo look like it was run over by a car tire doesn't mean he or she should. Next Mother's Day, avoid "grunge filters." And if you're doing a high tech graphic, don't make it look like an oil painting.

When chosen wisely, however, treatment adds additional levels of artistic depth, visual interest, and drama. Sometimes it can even add meaning to an image. For instance, if communicating the Holy Spirit as fuel for faith, a picture of an old gas pump might look even more interesting and nostalgic if treated as a sepia tone, an old brownish and aged photo look [Figure 1]. The image of a puppy is a great lead-in to discussions around

Figure 1

Figure 2

devotion. When treated to look like a pencil drawing hand-rendered by an artist [Figure 2], the viewer is drawn deeper into the image through more interesting visuals. Lastly, to represent the Word being "the lamp unto our feet and light unto our path," a day-for-night treatment might be

used [Figure 3] to create contrast between light and dark, emphasize the streetlight over the path, and provide more drama to the image.

Figure 3

Through treatment, images can even begin to express deep theological truth to a congregation. Some of the most powerful metaphors for faith, suggested by the Bible, are basically visual in nature, such as the idea of light and dark. Well-designed images can illustrate these symbols in ways that are more compelling than reading about them or hearing someone talk about them. While designing, consider the basic truth of the image and ways in which treatment might help communicate that truth.

Some photographers may think that the idea of treating their images in some additional way is an insult to their work, and in some cases we agree. Photography is a distinct art form. One would not need to treat an Ansel Adams photograph, for example. Unfortunately, not many of us possess the skills (and equipment) to take pictures that measure up to Ansel Adams. If you have those skills, you might be less inclined to think about treatment.

For the rest of us, however, treatment is a great way to create professional level, finished pieces from not so professional level snapshots. Of course the rules of composition still apply when in the field creating source imagery for a finished graphic, and designers should constantly strive to improve their skill level in production, but the old saying "fix it in post" is true in that treatments applied in front of the computer can make amateur images look professional.

You'll quickly begin to see a big improvement in your designs as you begin to incorporate different types of treatments, both in the quality of your images and in their ability to communicate the Gospel. The more you practice and play with various styles, the better you will get at it. For more on treatment, check out our free step-by-step tutorials at http://www.midnightoilproductions.com/training/, where we have a growing collection of tutorials that enable anyone to learn to apply high quality treatments to source images of any kind.

Terms to Learn:

Treatment—The application of effects to a source image for the purpose of creating enhanced visual appeal to a final work. Treatment in a finished piece helps to visually communicate the intended theme and tone of the designer.

Chapter 5
Can't Touch This

Design Principle: Texture

One of the most visceral senses in human beings is the sense of touch. The tactile world around us is a playground for the senses, and every day we experience it in powerful yet sometimes subtle ways. From architecture and landscaping to culinary arts and even clothing, texture is a part of any good designer's palette.

There are two types of texture often discussed in art school.

The first type is tactile texture. Tactile simply means the sense of touch. Tactile texture refers to tangible surfaces incorporated into a piece of art that one can touch. Tactile texture is physical and can be handled by the viewer. A piece of art might incorporate heavy buildup of paint, cardboard, felt, sandpaper, as well as other elements.

The second type is called visual texture and is the impression of actual textures. Visual texture creates the illusion of the world around us by attempting to reproduce the color and contrast found in real objects. Sometimes these textures can be abstract, and at other times they can be clearly recognized.

Although both types of texture are important, we as digital artists are more likely to concentrate on visual texture. When we create graphics for the screen (or even on paper) texture should always be considered.

There are exceptions to every rule, but generally speaking, flat or solid color is boring. This is why most PowerPoint gradients and templates don't sustain interest. Texture frees an artist from the dull rut of flat, uninteresting backgrounds. When artists incorporate texture into designs, they can take stark solid backgrounds that often throw off the balance of images to a place that creates much more visual appeal.

Though it is crucial, texture, however, cannot save every design. Texture has the power to make an image more interesting, but it isn't powerful enough to make up for bad composition. So after creating a compelling layout, texture can be used to take the image to the next level. The more a designer begins to use texture in him or her work, the better he or she will become at making choices about what works and what doesn't work.

Seasoned designers recognize that different textures affect the image, and the viewer's reaction to the image, in varied ways. Some textures are inviting, such as the cloth and shading in the Sacred Covenant image [Figure 1]. Others are repellent, such as the splattered blood in the Broken

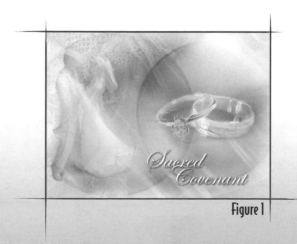

Figure 1

Figure 2

image [Figure 2]. An invitation by the artist to explore texture can increase the visual interest in a composition by adding variety without changing the overall color or spatial relationships within the image. When it works, it can be spectacular, and when it doesn't, it can ruin an image.

Some images don't require and won't benefit from the addition of texture. Texture should always be considered, but it will not always be the solution. Think of it as something to add to the artist's "bag of tricks."

Figure 3

Sometimes an image may look like it would be fine without texture, only to be enhanced by the addition of it. Notice the Home Builders image [Figure 3]. Prior to the texture of the blueprints, it seemed to be complete. It was interesting, but the addition of the blueprints at the top and bottom rounded off this image in a way that made it better.

Textures, such as the blueprints, take an image from a simple graphic to a concept or an idea. The worship designer strives for communication of the Gospel through image, which is at the heart of the use of images— not just eye candy or abstract, meaningless "art" but a medium to com-

grains of truth

Figure 4

municate the Gospel. In this case, texture helps convey part of the process of the home construction by showing the planning stage. Textures can add subtle nuances to an image that will bring a more complete concept in front of the image—in this case, using the metaphor of home construction when imagining the work of building spiritual foundations. Create imagery that tells a story.

Texture Guidelines

1. Repeat a primary element or a part of it in the background.

The silos are repeated as a texture in this Grains of Truth image [Figure 4]. This is a simple solution that works most of the time. It works because the primary image has relevant components and matching colors, so an artist can be reasonably assured that the composition is complementary. Try not to overuse this technique, or clutter will emerge.

Figure 5

2. Use photos as texture.

In the Grace Period image referenced earlier [Figure 5], seven photos have been used at varying opacities to create a rich visual texture. When using photos as texture, it is important to maintain the proper balance so that textures don't overtake the primary focus of the image. Using too much texture can create an imbalance between primary and secondary elements. In this image the viewer might not realize that there are seven different photos being used to create texture but only see one idea because the texture and other elements are balanced.

Figure 6A

The Grace Period image is an extreme example of photo texture. The use of photos as texture can be a more advanced technique, as is shown here, but one can also use a single photograph.

3. Use abstract colors and contrast.

A small portion of virtually any photo (approximately 75 pixels by 75 pixels) can be enlarged to full screen (720 by 540 or whatever output is set to), blurred and then colorized to make a great abstract textured background. Figure 6 illustrates this technique. A tutorial is also included on the DVD.

Figure 6B

Figure 7

Figure 8

4. Lines and shapes.

Using seemingly random lines, shapes, and shading can also create nice textures. The Counting Down image [Figure 7] contains a series of lines and shapes that add to the overall feel and visual appeal of the image.

5. Type as texture.

Sometimes type can make an interesting texture when it doesn't compete with the readability of the main theme or other text on the image. In the Crossing Over image [Figure 8], a series of type layers with the words " crossing over" further adds to the richness of the image. Some type layers are readable but don't compete with the main layer of type, and other layers are blurred to where they cannot be read.

Next time you're tempted to use a solid color background or a simple gradient, remember the importance of texture. Although it can be one of the more subtle design elements, it can make an image richer and more engaging. It's important to keep that in mind as we are communicating the most important message people will ever receive through our work as artists.

Terms to Learn:

Texture—The tactile quality of a surface or the representation by appearance of such a surface quality.

Chapter 6
Adding Meaning to Imagery

Design Principle: Colors

In the opening scenes of the classic film *The Wizard of Oz*, we're invited into the world of Dorothy, who longs to escape from her family farm to something more adventurous and thrilling. Kansas is a boring place through her eyes—dull and colorless. Shot on black and white film, the lack of color expresses the lifeless feelings that Dorothy experiences.

But then Dorothy is swept off by a tornado and lands in the Land of Oz. From the first glimpse of this magical place, it's obvious that this is the adventure of which Dorothy has been dreaming. Vibrant colors leap from the screen, signifying to the viewer that, as Dorothy says shortly after arriving, "We're not in Kansas anymore." The colorful canvas of Oz, contrasted with the dreary black and white of farm life in Kansas, tells Dorothy's story in a stunning contrast.

Simply put, color evokes feeling. This next principal for design enables artists to bring sometimes subtle and other times overwhelming emotion to imagery. Although often not realized, colors communicate. At an almost subconscious level, certain colors can make one feel happy, passionate, angry, or uneasy, while other colors might make one sad, lonely, cold, or scared. Understanding how color affects art is an important part of becoming a better artist.

Ever wonder why Eeyore, the melancholic donkey from *Winnie the Pooh*, is blue? Or why green means *go* but red means *stop*? Why in *Star Wars* films do Jedi (good guys) fight primarily with blue and green light sabers while the Sith (bad guys) fight with red? The answers to those and other artistic color choices can be found in the understanding of color symbolism.

Color symbolism is just one of the tools an artist can use to add emotional depth to imagery. Rather than picking random colors, choose colors with intentionally. Within art, various colors across the spectrum have well established meanings.

Red for instance, symbolizes (among other things) power, anger, energy, heat, love, violence, passion, and intensity. One could think of red as a color that resonates with strong or intense feelings of any kind. Orange, on the other hand, can imply balance and warmth but also vibrancy and flamboyance. Yellow may have widely varied meanings such as joy, happiness, imagination, cowardice, hope, and idealism. Blue may signify peace, technology, cleanliness, water, trust, and depression. Green can mean health, good luck, youth, nature, envy, and generosity. Purple can imply royalty, intelligence, nobility, and mystery.

Of course, many viewers won't realize these emotive decisions at a conscious level. But choosing the right color adds a subtle layer of meaning that, along with other techniques such as texture and treatment, further communicates ideas within imagery. Often powerful imagery works consciously and subconsciously. Color symbolism can have a powerful impact on the viewer when chosen with thoughtful consideration. When designing a new image, identify what emotions are important, then choose colors that fit that emotion. When worshippers are asked in a group to render an opinion about the image, if there are competing critical appraisals, color might be at work subconsciously, bringing diverse and very subjective emotions to the surface.

The story of the prodigal son (Luke 15:11-32) may be seen from the view-point of the older brother (the "good" one) who does not squander his father's inheritance. The older brother perceives that his younger brother gets his half of the wealth, wastes it, and returns home—only to have a party thrown in his honor. Perhaps the older brother is annoyed by this injustice. He may be very angry. Consider an image to express what was happening in this story, through the eyes of the firstborn. The result is a graphic, "A Mind Blowing Experience" [Figure 1]. The somewhat cartoon-ish outward representation of the internal emotion of anger might express how the "good" brother felt.

Figure 1

The image of the man with the blown mind was treated to bump up the red tones in his skin, which enhanced the more literal physical reaction to anger. What is more important from a color perspective, though, is the red text. As stated above, red symbolizes anger. This image is intentionally "light" on color. The stark white background helps to emphasize the red and black type as it provides a contrast for the saturation and luminance present in the type.

Color can be measured by these values: hue, saturation, and luminance. Hue is basically a synonym for color. When one asks what color something is, they're really asking what the hue is. Saturation is the intensity of the color.

So a cherry red sports car has a lot of saturation, whereas a red pastel shirt has very little saturation. Luminance is how light or dark the color is. Adding white to a color (or increasing the lightness) augments the luminance and adding black (or decreasing the lightness) diminishes the luminance.

Programmers have worked out mathematical explanations for how hue, saturation, and luminance work. While understanding the terminology is very helpful, most artists discover that playing around with image creation tools will quickly make finding the right color easy.

In addition to the symbolism contained within color, it's important to learn the basics of color theory. The color wheel [Figure 2], a grade school staple, is a visual representation of how color is formed from a theoretical perspective.

There are three primary colors: red, yellow, and blue. All colors on the color wheel are made up of these three colors. Next to those colors are secondary colors. Secondary colors are made up of equal parts of the primary colors. The primary color blue for example, when mixed with green, results in the secondary color blue-green.

The color wheel can be useful at times by helping an artist determine a color scheme for his or her work. A color scheme is simply a palette of color that an artist uses while working on any piece of art. Two well-known color schemes are built into the color wheel, to create color harmony.

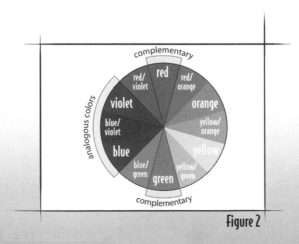

Figure 2

Color harmony is simply a grouping of colors arranged and applied in the most visually pleasing way. Good color harmony creates balance in an image and engages the viewer in an experience of the art. The lack of color harmony can either bore the viewer through under-stimulation, or it can repel the viewer through overuse or misuse of color. Skilled designers present colors within imagery in a logical, ordered, and structured fashion. Here are a few formulas for color harmony:

Color Guidelines

1. Complementary colors.

A complementary color scheme uses colors from the wheel that are directly across each other. The standard Christmas colors of red and green complement one another well because they are opposites on the wheel. In the Spirit of Peace image [Figure 3], a purple-blue/orange-yellow color scheme works well against white and black.

SPIRIT OF PEACE

Figure 3

2. Analogous colors.

Any color and its two adjacent neighbors are analogous. Analogous color schemes tend to work well together because the colors within them are so closely related. For example, a blue, blue-violet, and violet combination should look great together because they share like colors in their makeup. You can see in the Remember Me image [Figure 4] an analogous red, red-orange, orange color scheme.

3. Monochromatic colors.

Monochromatic schemes use shades of the same color. Take any color from the color wheel and add white or black to make a monochromatic scheme, as shown in The Master Conductor [Figure 5], which is all based on the color blue with darker and lighter shades applied to create various colors in the image.

Figure 4

Figure 5

4. Red, white, and blue.

For those who live in the USA, red, white, and blue color schemes signify patriotism, freedom, honor, and pride. Sometimes the use of these colors adds a subliminal message to an image, as seen in the Major League Baseball logo, for example. A viewer might be more inclined to think of baseball as the "All-American sport," simply because of the colors in the logo. It is important to understand that color symbolism can be both universal and culture-specific. Some color schemes in art have more, less, different, or no meaning outside the cultures in which they are created. Be careful when using this scheme not to confuse patriotism and faith in God, which are different things.

5. Black and white.

Sometimes the lack of color can make a powerful statement, as exemplified with the Wizard of Oz example earlier. In the Desert Detour image [Figure 6], the feeling of loneliness is enhanced by the lack of color.

Figure 6

6. Selective color.

When an image is predominantly black and white, the selective use of a single color gives the viewer a strong focal point. In the Living Water image [Figure 7], the water appears to be even more alive and vibrant since all of the color has been removed from the surrounding rocks.

7. Warm and cool colors.

Note also that there are differences in the color wheel between warm and cool colors. The type of color one chooses will influence how an image is perceived. Cool colors include green through violet. They tend to have a calming effect on the viewer and range from soothing and nurturing on one end of the spectrum to cold and sterile on the other.

Figure 7

Warm colors, on the other hand, get the blood boiling—literally. Many studies have shown that blood pressure can actually rise when staring at warm colors, which include red through yellow-green. The emotions initiated by these colors range from passionate love to anger and violence. A mixture of warm and cold colors can clash but can also create balance. Warm colors tend to overpower cool colors, even when applied in equal amounts. Red, for instance, has more visual weight than blue when added to the same design even if portions are fairly similar. That may be fine for some designs, but for others it may not work. Always try to maintain balance when working with a mixture of warm and cool colors.

8. Color models.

The color wheel is used primarily by painters for mixing color, but it is also helpful for creating visual harmonies and color schemes.

Those who work in digital environments may be confused by the difference between the classic primary colors (red, yellow, and blue) and another color mode called RGB, which stands for red, green, and blue. Most of the equipment one uses to create and display media, such as computer monitors, digital cameras, scanners, projectors and televisions, are based on RGB.

RGB is the color mode of the human eye. This method of looking at color, which is called additive color synthesis, is a detailed process where all colors are derivatives of red, green, and blue. Although RGB is newer and is technically a more accurate way of describing the relationship of color, the color wheel, which was invented by Isaac Newton, remains an important part of design. For more information about the difference between primary colors and RGB colors, search on the phrase "RGB color theory" in your web browser.

To further complicate things, there is yet another color scheme called the CMY or CMYK method. CMYK stands for Cyan, Magenta, Yellow, and Black. It is actually based on RGB color theory. Whereas RGB is the primary color space for digital imagery, CMYK is the main color mode for all things printed. Generally speaking, when no special printing processes are employed, all colors in any finished full color piece (such as magazines, direct mail cards, etc.) are made up of CMYK ink that is applied to a printed surface. RGB = screen graphics, and CMYK = printed graphics. Again, go to the web for more details on CMYK color theory.

Experimentation is really the key to strong color in design, and many times even the most well planned color scheme will change over the course of the design process. Incorporating color with intentionality can make anyone's art better, but most importantly it allows an artist to communicate the Gospel message with emotion and greater conceptual depth. In every image, say more with color!

Terms to Learn:

Analogous—Colors that are closely related in hue(s). They are usually adjacent to each other on the color wheel.

CMYK—The acronym for the four basic ink colors used in "process" color printing: Cyan, Magenta, Yellow, and Black. Images designed for print output must be developed in this color mode within an image creation program.

Color symbolism—The various meanings often associated with specific colors in the spectrum. Color symbolism can influence an artist's decisions while creating images.

Color wheel—A circular diagram of colors where primary colors (red, blue, or yellow) are on one side and secondary colors, which are made by mixing two primary colors, appear on the other. A color wheel is used to identify, mix, and select colors.

Complementary—Two colors that are directly opposite each other on the color wheel.

Duotone—A two-color reproduction of a monochromatic original image, usually a black and white photograph. A two-color image based on the tonal values from a monochromatic source photo. Any two colors can be chosen and mixed to create a duotone.

Gradient—A blend from one color to another color.

Grayscale—An image representation in which each pixel is represented by a single sample value representing overall luminance. Grayscale is synonymous with black and white.

Hue—One of the three attributes of color, the other two being saturation and luminance (also referred to as brightness). It is a specific color classification given to an object based on the seven colors found in the spectrum; red, orange yellow, green, blue, indigo, or violet. The hue refers to the wavelength of the color (not the intensity or saturation of the color). For example, a blue hue can look navy at a very low saturation level and sky blue at a very high saturation level.

Luminance—One of the three attributes of color, the other two being hue and saturation. Luminance refers to the brightness of the color.

Monochromatic—A color scheme limited to variations of one hue, a hue with its tints and/or shades.

Pantone—An industry standard color-matching system used by printers and graphic designers for inks, papers, and other materials. A Pantone Matching System© color is a standard color defined by percentage mixtures of different primary inks.

RGB—An acronym that means Red, Green, and Blue. RGB is the basic additive color model used for color video display, as on a computer monitor.

Saturation—One of the three attributes of color, the other two being luminance and hue. Saturation refers to the intensity of the color.

Selective—The use of a single contrasting color in a predominantly monochromatic image for the purpose of creating a strong focal point.

Tritone—Like a duotone but made up of three colors based on a monochromatic photo. An image produced by taking a black-and-white picture and printing it on top of itself in three different colors of ink to produce a subtle range of tones.

Chapter 7
Adding Depth

Design Principle: Light and Shadow

"Lights, camera, action!"

Many directors might think it is pretentious to actually say this on a set, but the famous saying in film reveals much about the process. In making pictures, use of light is one of the most important things the artist must consider.

Since a camera's eye is different than a human eye, what may look one way in reality may look very different in the frame. For example, take someone sitting in a room in the middle of the day. The room contains natural sunlight from a window and incandescent light from a floor lamp. The human eye, which is infinitely more advanced than the best camera, has the capability to adjust these varying light sources. The person is not aware that the room's light actually has competing light sources (sunlight is a harsh blue and incandescent light is a soft yellow). The camera cannot make such adjustments, however. If the camera is balanced for indoor lighting, then a framing of such a room might reveal a bluish, washed out person. One can't simply photograph the real thing and have it look as real on screen.

Therefore, artists must control light and shadow to create a false "reality" in the frame that tells the story. This means learning to see beyond how we are accustomed to seeing with our own eyes.

For example, we created an interpretation of the Christmas story of the shepherds in the fields at night. So we visited a field with a generator at night and quickly discovered that with every light we projected at full power our set was still woefully insufficient to shoot a scene. What we could easily see with our own eyes was not visible through the camera's eye. Vimos Zsigmond says that, "The eye sees deep into darkness and far into highlights. No film or digital technology can 'see' the way the eye sees, so cinematographers must know how to create light."[12]

Many times, light in a digitally created image is "hyper" real, or more real than reality. Recreating what the human eye perceives as light and shadow for the screen takes a degree of skill that comes through studying the way light and shadow exist in the real world. Because of the limitations of digital image processing, artists often fake light and shadow in imagery.

We learned from our earlier nighttime lighting experiments that creating night shots regularly requires starting with imagery acquired during the daytime. The process of converting a daytime image to one that appears to be shot at night is known as "day for night." This type of treatment shifts the color tones present in an image to blue-purple hues and adjusts the brightness and contrast to much darker levels. In addition, artificial shading and highlighting are often added to create moonlight and a sense of depth.

As shared in Chapter 4 on treatment, we created a visual representation of Psalm 119:105 ("Your word is a lamp unto my feet/ and a light unto my path"), so we started with a compelling daytime shot and added shadow

---

[12] Jon Silberg, "Master of Light," *American Cinematographer* (Oct 2004), p. 56.

and light to make the image much more interesting and dramatic [Figure 1]. The addition of moonlight on the buildings and trees adds realism to the image.

Figure 1a

Such moonlight shots are an example of hyper-real lighting in that they are more exaggerated than what the eye would see in reality. Real moonlight is much more subtle, but the audience accepts this as "real" because it is a normal convention and is often seen in both moving and still images.

Light couldn't exist without shadow. Although they are opposites, they work together in tandem. Artists learn to contrast the two in creative ways. Film noir is a classic genre that makes exagger-

Figure 1b

ated, effective use of light and shadow. A suspect sits in a dark room, intimidated by his interrogators with only a single, bare light bulb dangling over his head. A down-on-his-luck man sits at a bar with a single beam of light cutting through his cigarette smoke and whiskey glass. The effect of the light against a mostly darkened room adds tension to the scene. Lighting affects mood in powerful ways. The Unshackled image [Figure 2] is a great example of this.

In addition to the emotional undertones of an image, lighting and shadow (or shading) help define and give character to objects within an image. Without shading, most of what we see would be very dull and

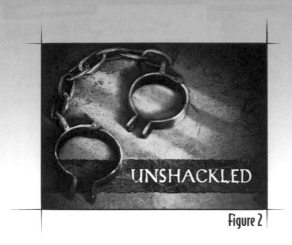

UNSHACKLED

Figure 2

somewhat shapeless. When shading is incorporated into certain design elements, shape information can be maximized to create visual distinctions from other elements within a design. In other words, shading can make objects more or less important in any given composition. Shading can be the result of real lighting, or it can be applied in the computer.

The play of light on an object is what makes it dull or interesting. As light flows over an object, it creates areas of shadow and highlight. This enables the viewer to identify it and appreciate its aesthetic beauty.

In the real world, when one lights an object to be used in a graphic, it is best to create dramatic lighting. Most of the time, flat lighting is uninteresting. Try lighting an object from different angles. One might find that backlighting or using more than one light source could make the object even more visually interesting.

Generally speaking, the more contrast one achieves when lighting an object, the more it will visually pop off the screen. High contrast lighting can also assist in providing a focal point in a finished design. The less contrast, the more cartoon-like (or flat) it can become. This applies to both computer-generated lighting and real world lighting.

Two different types of shadows are used in creating imagery: drop shadows and cast shadows. Each provide depth in an image.

Drop shadows.

Drop shadows are often associated with text or other objects that are flat in appearance. Drop shadows lift or separate these elements from the background or the secondary aspects of a design. They are the same shape as the layer for which they are providing a shadow. In the Metamorphosis image [Figure 3] a drop shadow behind the theme text helps to lift it off the butterfly. The butterfly also has a drop shadow applied to separate it from the background elements.

Figure 3

Cast shadows.

Cast shadows are typically created naturally when a scene is acquired with a camera. These are the shadows created when an object or subject blocks light. On a sunny day, when people see their shadow stretched out on the ground, they are looking at a cast shadow. Cast shadows provide important visual clues to where objects reside in three dimensional space. They help create depth.

Besides telling the viewer how close or far away an object is from the camera, they also tell where objects are in relation to other elements in a scene. Learning to create cast shadows will help an artist expand his or her options. All of the shading and cast shadows in the Unshackled image [Figure 2] were created artificially using Adobe Photoshop.

Adding shadows can be as effective in creating a mood as adding highlights. By darkening certain parts of an image, other parts look brighter by comparison. By selecting a large soft brush loaded with black (in Adobe Photoshop) and painting around the edges of a graphic, a designer can provide depth and highlight to the center portions of an image. In the Restored image [Figure 4], this soft black shading (or

Figure 4

depth frame) creates a more realistic lighting scheme for an old garage, and it focuses the eye on the photos in the center of the table.

Figure 5

The Lighthouse graphic tutorial contained on the DVD provides an opportunity to learn about applying light and shadow to an image. This tutorial is created around the construction of a lighthouse image, casting a beam into night sky, offering hope to sailors on the rough waters of the ocean [Figure 5]. By working from a daylight image of a lighthouse, the tutorial details step-by-step instruction for applying a "day for night" treatment and varying shadows and lights to create the final image.

Terms to Learn:

Cast shadow—The dark area that occurs on a surface as a result of an object obscuring the light source in front of the surface.

Drop shadow—A colored or shaded box or character offset and placed behind an identical box or character to give a shadow effect.

Glow—The opposite of a shadow in that it creates a surrounding highlight of an image. A high radiance creates a soft, subtle glow, but a low radiance creates a hard, bright glow, such as a neon glow.

Shading—Applying a darker value to an object or background to create the illusion of space and depth. Shading can also be used to further enhance, or point the eye toward, the focal point of an image.

Chapter 8
Treating Letters as Images

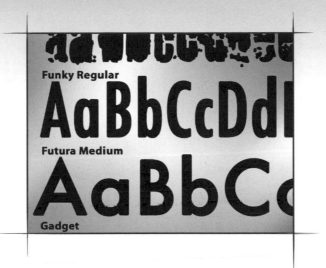

Design Principle: Fonts

It starts with a blank screen. Then, some brainstorming. Next comes the layout, followed by color, texture, and treatment. But before finishing an image, each designer must face one of the most important moments in the design process—choosing a font (or typestyle).

Sadly, designers frequently treat fonts as the "unwanted stepchildren" of design, giving them little thought. Those who make this mistake can destroy the power of what would otherwise be an inspiring image by randomly choosing a font and slapping on text at the last moment. Many powerful worship images have been ruined by unconscious font selection. Fonts are one of the most significant elements in design, so choose them with careful consideration, keeping in mind the overall tone and theme of the graphic.

Although graphic designers for worship should be advocates for more imagery, text does have a valuable place. For example, graphic images are often designed to set up a theme for worship, and they probably include a title, which may be the same as the sermon title. The words of the title must be displayed with a specific font, which when present has as much if not more power to communicate the theme as any of the other principles for design.

Novice designers may focus on the symbolic content in the words in the title. However, in a graphic image, letters have a more powerful role to play. They become visual objects. It is not sufficient to rely on the textual meaning of the letters because, in the context of a graphic image, the look and feel of the font selection contains an additional layer of symbolic meaning beyond what the letters signify in rational thought.

This added meaning is part of the tension between text and image. These two meanings—the rational meaning and the symbolic (imagistic) meaning—should complement rather than compete with one another. One website, http://www.bancomicsans.com, asserts that, "Type is a voice; its very qualities and characteristics communicate to readers a meaning beyond mere syntax." Letters don't go on top of the graphic; they are *part of* the graphic.

Each font that a designer chooses to put on the screen (or in print) speaks with a voice that should compliment the theme. Many fonts evoke feelings, and those feelings can eclipse the syntactical meaning of the text. For a Mother's Day image expressing the love and connection

Figure 1

between a mother and her child, a calligraphic font would work well as pictured in Figure 1, but not the grunge font as pictured in Figure 2. The grunge font speaks in a much louder voice, communicating rough, dirty, and edgy feelings, overshadowing the image and the meaning of the text.

Font Guidelines

1. Two types of fonts.

When working with type it's helpful to know that there are two types of fonts: Display and Body.

Display fonts, sometimes called headline fonts, as seen in Figure 3A, draw attention to important lines of text and are usually more artistically complex. Use them primarily for small blocks of text like sermon points and theme lines. Display fonts are typically not legible in large bodies of text. For example, the display fonts in the song lyrics image in Figure 3B will overwhelm the eye of the viewer.

Body fonts, sometimes called copy fonts, such as the one pictured in Figure 4, are readable in large blocks. They are also easier to read when smaller (like the letters that you're reading now). A rule of thumb for screen use is not to go below thirty points, but there are always exceptions to the rule, depending on the design of a particular font. Contrary to popular belief, body fonts need not be artistically dull to be

Figure 2

Figure 3A

Figure 3B

Figure 4

effective. They can be script-like, have a techno feel, or even have a slight grunge feel. Readability is important, but choosing a body font only for readability's sake is not an excuse to pull out Helvetica, Arial, and the other "frigid fonts." (See below.) In some cases, certain fonts will work as display and/or body fonts.

Try to pick one of each type of font for a set of graphics (a set meaning a collection of images to be seen over the course of one worship service). As stated above, some fonts will work for both, but most of the time it is best to pick one of each. When building graphics for a worship series, try to stick with the same fonts throughout. After picking the font set, don't veer from it. Staying consistent is much better from a design perspective. Use the font set for scripture reading, sermon points, song lyrics, and so forth.

One exception to this principle would be to use another font for an occasional illustration.

2. Finding the right font.

Choosing the ideal set of fonts is an art in and of itself. From cereal boxes to road signs, one can find a perfect font for every image. Finding that font takes time and usually means ditching the fifteen or twenty fonts that come pre-installed on every computer (the "frigid fonts"). Most of the time, this collection include such classics as Arial, Helvetica, Times New Roman, Courier, and others. These fonts were not created for graphic design but instead serve more functional purposes, such as reading email or writing a report.

This base collection of fonts has become trite, like an overused metaphor. One particular base font is probably the worst thing to happen to graphic design since Microsoft PowerPoint clipart—Comic Sans. This font, although cute and more creative than the others, has been used in many inappropriate ways and is often inconsistent with the theme. If the goal is to create a superhero theme, or a comic book look, it makes sense, but displaying Comic Sans over an image of the Crucifixion is wrong. (We've actually seen this.) Ban Comic Sans—unless it works with the theme.

If the pre-installed fonts are inadequate, then where does a worship designer go for new and more creative solutions? Hundreds of fresh and eye-catching fonts can be downloaded on the web, some of which cost money and others that are free. Check out www.1001freefonts.com, www.dafont.com, and www.fontfreak.com for some excellent free fonts. Other productive sources for fonts are: www.fonts.com, www.myfonts.com, www.emigre.com, www.fontheads.com and www.t26.com. The fees at these sites are are worth the cost; they are extremely well designed.

Figure 5

Become more aware of the way fonts are used by the pros in the commercial art world. Take note of the fonts used in magazine ads, on billboards, and on movie posters. One popular font, Trajan [Figure 5], is used frequently by Hollywood in movie trailers and on posters, such as *Gladiator*, *War of the Worlds*, *Cast Away*, *A Beautiful Mind*, and countless other well-known titles. Use of that font, when appropriate, can give images a "bigger than life" feel because of the associations with film. Other fonts used in advertising can, on occasion, give graphics a boost just by the visual association they have with how they're used in the commercial art world.

How does one find a specific font such as Trajan? Two services help designers identify and obtain fonts that are seen on websites, printed on a poster, or elsewhere. Check out www.identifont.com for an easy to use, step-by-step survey to help name that cool font on the movie trailer. This image-based questionnaire asks a series of questions about various aspects of the font and, when finished, lists several possible matches.

Also, look at www.whatthefont.com. An even more advanced font identification service, *What the Font* asks the user to upload a small JPG image of the font in question and, through an amazing process of identifying each character in the uploaded image, lists many possible matches. Both of these services are free.

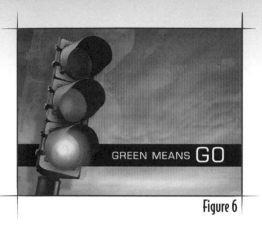

Figure 6

3. Build a library of fonts.

It's hard to avoid, but don't fall in love with a particular font. Using the same fonts over and over makes for a dull and less visually stimulating graphic viewing experience. Also, don't just use a font because it's cool. It's a well-known fact that Jason is more of a Star Wars fan than any normal human should be. On his system is a font called Star Jedi—a font that looks strikingly similar to the Star Wars logo. Yet, as much as he likes the films, he has never been able to use it in a graphic. Whether Star Jedi, Comic Sans, or Dirty Type-writer, the question should always be, is this font appropriate to the image?

There are some fonts that seem to work for everything, but it's important to change things on a regular basis, which is why the "pick two for each graphic set" idea is handy. It prevents designers from getting into a rut.

4. Integrating type into the image.

Each design should be built with versatility in mind as it pertains to text. As stated before, the main graphic for the day [Figure 6] will likely have a theme (or title) line. Designers will often add to the text by the use of some sort of backing bar or box as illustrated with the black bar behind the theme, Green Means Go. This bar also comes in handy for sermon points. Always integrate sermon points (or sermon notes) into the design, as seen in Figure 7.

One popular problem is to place sermon points randomly along a single straight line across the middle of the image in Arial or some other system font. As stated, in such cases the designer is incorrectly thinking of the image as background to type, whereas in reality the letters are part of the image, not "above" it. Although the letters need to stand out from the rest of the image, they are still a part of the image. This is a subtle but important distinction to learn.

Figure 7

Point bars are great, but they are not the only option and should not be overused. Glows, drop shadows, and strokes can also create depth or special highlighting of the text within the image. It makes sense to make a muted, low contrast version of the image for large bodies of text, such as the scripture in Figure 8, to keep the theme going.

Song lyrics are graphics too! Although not very visually inspiring, their purpose is to aid in the inspiration that comes from joining together in song. This is not an excuse to temporarily ignore design. Stay consistent with the font set when it comes to "praise and worship" times. (We also recommend sustaining a consistent background with the theme for the day.) Adding a two pixel stroke and a drop shadow to song lyrics will make them much more readable and keeping the point size, or the size of the font, consistent throughout the music set.

One designer (the church shall remain nameless) produced a set of song lyrics graphics where every slide had a different point size. Many of the slides were a single line of lyrics, made as big as possible for the amount of text on the screen, so flipping from one to the next was visually jarring—like staring at a Las Vegas casino marquee for too long.

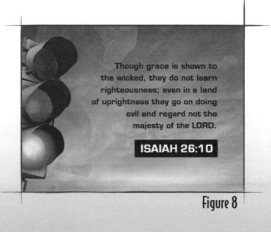

Figure 8

Top Ten Rules for Typography

There are many other rules and aspects of typography, but here are ten core guidelines to keep in mind (some of which summarize earlier comments):

1. Stick with the same point size throughout the whole set. Sermon points may be larger, but consistency is the rule.

2. Most fonts should be at least thirty point for the screen.

3. Avoid serif fonts. A serif is a fine line finishing off the main strokes of a letter, such as at the top and bottom of "M." Most serifs are too thin for the screen and may flicker.

4. There are two types of fonts: display (sometimes called headline) and body (sometimes called copy). Generally, it is best to pick one of each for every graphic set. Some fonts work as both display and body. Display fonts are good for theme lines, sermon points, and small bodies of text. Body fonts are good for song lyrics, scripture, and any other large bodies of text.

5. Don't use fonts outside of the selected set unless making an illustration. Keep the visual thread going throughout the set, even with fonts, and avoid veering off in an unnecessary direction.

6. Keep sermon points short. We recommend four to seven words or less. An old advertising rule is to keep slogans under seven words. This is a good rule for sermon points too.

7. Choose appropriate fonts. No grungy typewriter fonts on Mother's Day or script fonts on a Super Bowl football graphic [Figure 6]. Always ask the question: Does this font fit the overall feel and theme of this image?

8. Limit text on the screen because it is a visual medium. Say it with imagery rather than with text whenever possible.

9. No Comic Sans or Times New Roman (unless you're doing a comic book graphic or newspaper illustration or some other appropriate use).

10. Have fun!

Type is an integral part of most finished designs, so treat it with the same respect as the other principles. Fonts can be dangerous in the hands of the ignorant, but when chosen with intentionality and careful consideration, they can be the icing on the cake. Create a rich visual experience by using the perfect font.

Terms to Learn:

Ascenders—The portion of any character that extends above the height of a lower case "m."

Baseline—The invisible line on which letters and numbers sit.

Body fonts—Fonts that work well for body copy, which is main (non-headline) text. It is the text of stories and articles. Body fonts are usually highly readable in large blocks.

Bold—Short for boldface. A set of letters that is heavier (thicker or darker) than the normal set of the same font.

Bullet—A typographical symbol or glyph, most commonly a dot, used to introduce items in a list.

Centered justification—When blocks of text are aligned in the center.

Condensed font—A narrow version of a font.

Copy—The written part of a completed design, particularly in commercial art and advertising. Effective copy is critically important, especially in visually oriented messages.

Copy fonts—Another term for body fonts.

Descenders—The part of a lowercase letter that descends below the baseline. The lower case letters g, j, p, q and y have descenders.

Display/headline fonts—Fonts that draw attention to important lines of text and are usually more artistically complex. Primarily used for small areas of text like sermon points and theme lines. Display fonts are typically not legible in large bodies of text.

Font/typeface—A graphical design applied to all numerals, symbols, and characters in the alphabet. A font usually comes in different sizes and provides different styles, such as bold, italic, and under-lining for emphasizing text.

Grunge fonts—A term used for the trend of freeform, dirtied, almost graffiti-like fonts, in which letters appear distressed, organic, or purposely break typeface rules. Grunge fonts, such as Dirty Type-writer with all of its rough and broken edges, have been en vogue since the mid 90s.

Italic—A version of a typeface that is slanted and script-like.

Justification—To align text so that all the lines begin and/or end at the same place. Justifications can be along the right side of the page, the left side, down the middle (center justification), or set to evenly distribute text across the page (full justification).

Kerning—The amount of space between any two characters in a word, initially determined by the design of the font. To kern is to adjust this space. Kerning between the letters "a" and "s" in the word "fast" would look like this: fa st. See below for tracking.

Leading—Pronounced "ledding." The space between lines of type in a block of text. Leading is specified in points and includes the point size of the text; so for example, 12 point type set with 9 point lead-ing would have the lines of type touching each other. Standard leading is typically 120% or about 2 points larger than the type point size; for example 10 point type by default (in many programs) would have a leading of 12 points.

Left justification—When blocks of text are aligned to the left.

Oblique—A version of a typeface similar to italic in that it is slanted, but distinct in that it lacks script.

Point size—The measurement of the vertical size of a font. A point is about 1/72 of an inch.

Right justification—When blocks of text are aligned to the right.

San serif font—A font that is straight without extending strokes at the top and bottoms of letters. Typical san serif fonts include Helvetica and Arial.

Script fonts—A general term for a type of font that mimics cursive or calligraphic handwriting.

Serif font—A font with small adornments, or finishing strokes, at the tops and bottoms of letters. Typical serif fonts include Times New Roman and Palatino.

Tracking—The uniform space between all glyphs (characters) in a block of text. It is commonly confused with kerning. Kerning can be thought of as space between two letters, and tracking as space between all letters. Tracking is sometimes called character spacing or letter spacing, especially in reference to computer typesetting. (and is often a tactic in typesetting to fit copy on a specific line of text). Tracking all of the letters in the word would look like this: f a s t. See above for kerning.

Chapter 9
Putting A Graphic Together

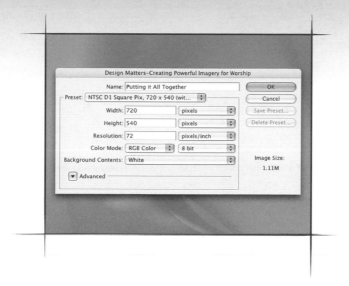

Having learned the eight principles for design, it's time to put your own graphic together. This chapter will walk you through the basic details of building powerful imagery for worship. Note that it is important to read this chapter before diving into the tutorials on the DVD, as you'll save much time by understanding the integration of these concepts.

Pre-Planning

1. Identifying a concept.

Before the first pixel is painted on screen, it is important to have a strong concept. Brainstorming is an important pre-step to the design process. Skimping on the creativity results in an image that isn't very compelling, even if it is well designed. It's like going to a movie with great special effects but a weak plot. There may be a wow factor initially, but it won't be long until the wow has faded into boredom.

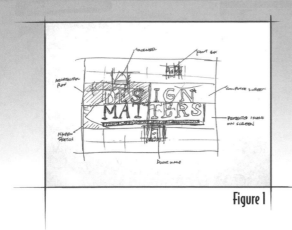

Figure 1

2. Making thumbnail sketches.

With a great concept in place, one might think the next step is to sit down in front of the computer with mouse in hand. A better starting place however, involves a few sheets of copier paper and a felt-tipped pen to construct a thumbnail sketch.

Thumbnail sketches [Figure 1] are handy tools for any artist, regardless of skill level. These sketches are abbreviated drawings, usually about an inch or two high. Usually they are done very quickly, without edits or corrections. Pen is the most common medium used because it forces the artist to get ideas down without a lot of fine-tuning. The natural ability to draw is a plus, but it isn't a necessity. Basic shapes can go a long way in representing more complex objects.

There are many advantages to creating thumbnail sketches as opposed to just diving in to the computer. First, an artist can quickly experiment with composition. Simply sketching major design elements, then adjusting their placement, will aid in the discovery of multiple layouts in a shorter period of time. Possibilities that may have never been tried in the computer are often found quickly on paper.

Another reason for starting with sketches is that it saves potential wandering in the wrong direction. If an artist is working as part of a team and the team is trying to decide upon a certain look or feel for the graphic, a thumbnail sketch can often help determine the final direction. This saves the artist the potential problem of time-consuming redesigns. On more than one occasion, worship planning teams have discovered late in the process that the image is "all wrong."

In some situations, thumbnails may be turned into more complete, larger scale sketches before going to the computer. This idea is more likely to play out when the image producer has natural drawing abilities.

Production

With the metaphor and basic layout ideas in place, you can finally hit the drawing board, so to speak. There are many things to keep in mind when beginning graphics production:

Two types of graphics.

There are two different formats for creating graphics: raster graphics and vector graphics.

Raster-based graphics are what most people think of when creating images for the screen. This type of image maps bits directly to a fixed canvas (and is sometimes called a bitmap). This means that the data that exists cannot be scaled larger without the computer program having to interpolate the enlargement. Even with today's most advanced software, this isn't a task that is very easily accomplished. Images scaled beyond about 130% tend to break down and become pixilated (or "jaggie").

Software to create raster graphics are often referred to as "paint programs." They are extremely powerful and can be learned intuitively by many users. Among the leaders in the market are Adobe Photoshop, Adobe Elements, and Corel Paint Shop Pro.

Vector graphics are math based geometric shapes. Their greatest strength is that the images are infinitely scaleable with no degradation. They are commonly used to create logos and very crisp looking artwork. The well-known Flash format, made popular on the web, is vector-based. So are very large works, such as billboard art.

Most of the time, images created for the screen are not vector-based, but on occasion there may be reason to use them. Adobe Illustrator, Corel Draw, and Macromedia Freehand are the top three vector art programs on the market. Learning to create vector-based art requires a much higher learning curve than raster art. For most artists whose focus is on designing graphics for the screen, it is an unnecessary skill to develop.

Square vs. Non-Square Pixels.

Computers break images down into series of very small elements called pixels. Basically pixels are the dots that make up a digital picture. In the world of computers, pixels are square (as wide as they are high). Video on the other hand contains non-square pixels. Problems can arise when square pixel graphics interface with non-square video, in that they stretch to be non-square. This problem requires much more space than can fit in this book, so for more reading, check out *Creating Motion Graphics* (CMP) books or search "square vs. non-square pixels" on the Internet.

Which Application to use.

Once all the principles for design sink in and creative concepts begin to flow, choosing the right image creation program is the next big step. The decision of which program to use is often dictated by budget. If $650 is not a barrier, then there is no better choice than Adobe Photoshop.

Photoshop has been the de-facto standard since it was released in 1990. It is capable of doing basically anything a designer can think of, but its learning curve can be steep. Its standard feature sets are unmatched by any other program on the market. Its pricetag is out of reach for most worship designers, but for more advanced users it's a price worth paying. To learn more and download a fully functioning demo version, visit www.adobe.com.

The good news is that Adobe has given the lower end design world a gift that can only be described as amazing. In 2001, Adobe released a scaled down version of Photoshop called "Elements." Adobe Elements has many of the most used Photoshop's features and is apparently much more user friendly. The catch is that although it can open print-based CMYK images, Adobe Elements cannot edit in this mode. Its use is solely for screen and web. With a discounted price ranging from $50 to $75, Photoshop Elements is well within most budgets. To download a demo version visit www.adobe.com.

Another of the leading programs is Corel's Paint Shop Pro. Some reviewers assert that Paint Shop is close to Photoshop, without the learning curve. Paint Shop is a good choice for the beginner and advanced user, a claim that is not often made about Adobe's programs. Paint Shop Pro is usually priced at $100. Visit www.corel.com to learn more and to try it out.

Those with no budget whatsoever still have an option. GIMP (GNU Image Manipulation Program), originally developed as freeware by two University of California Berkeley students, has been added to and refined by volunteers since its 1996 release. Numerous plug-ins and extensions let this software do a lot of what professional programs can do. It has been called "polished and user-friendly," and the best part is that it is a free download at www.gimp.org/.

The programs listed above would all fall under the raster graphic category. Although vector graphic programs are less often used for image creation for the screen, it may be helpful to know what's available.

Adobe Illustrator is probably the most mature and well known of the bunch. Those familiar with Adobe's suite of products will feel more at home with Illustrator than its competitors, but the learning curve is very steep. Illustrator at this writing is priced at $500; see the demo at www.adobe.com.

If Illustrator has an archrival, it would be Macromedia Freehand. These two programs have competed for market dominance since they were both in their earliest incarnations. Freehand's features and toolsets are very similar to Illustrator. If choosing on price alone, Freehand is twenty percent cheaper at this writing. Visit www.macromedia.com for a complete working demo.

CorelDraw, a consumer level program, is a powerful program for approximately $300. Its features and toolsets are also very similar to its more expensive competitors. Visit www.corel.com for a free trial version.
There is a free vector-based graphics program available too. The open source vector graphics editor, Inkscape, has been in development since 2003. Although it lacks many of the more advanced features of the lead-

ing proprietary software titles, the latest version provides a large portion of the basic vector editing capabilities found in them. Inkscape can be downloaded at www.inkscape.org.

Choosing Source Material.

To create imagery, many artists begin with pre produced, or "stock photography." There are at least two different categories of "stock photos."

The most economical type is called "royalty free." Royalty free images have little to no restrictions on them, once purchased. They can be manipulated and used in a variety of ways. Royalty free images can be very reasonably priced, from $2 per image to more than $100 an image. Some popular sites for individual royalty free photos, free and/or inexpensive, include:

> http://sxc.hu/ - an artists' image exchange with many free, high quality photos. The individual copyright holders determine rights.
> http://www.istockphoto.com/ - Many strong graphics for only a dollar or two.
> http://www.dreamstime.com/ - Requires an initial buy-in of credits, which act as currency for images. We spent $20 on credits, but only used 1 credit for the graphic we wanted.

Another even cheaper option for royalty free stock photos is to join a subscription service such as www.photospin.com. Services like this offer thousands of images for a relatively small fee of approximately $200 a year.

Rights managed photos, the second type, are typically much higher in quality, but you get what you pay for. They start in the range of $250 to $500, and they go much higher too. In addition to price, the other drawback is that they are usually licensed for a fixed period of time, such as five years. After that, the artist must "re-up" and pay fees again.

Browsing stock photo libraries can be inspiring and can generate ideas. Once a photo is found, a free comp version can be downloaded that can be used for placement, approval, or just to collect for future ideas. These comp photos usually come with a logo or watermark on them. It is unlawful to remove the watermark and use the image without paying for it. Even the images that are not watermarked must be paid for, so please respect the ownership of the copyright holder.

A third option, which is only usable on a limited basis, is simply to use an image search engine such as Google. Copyright provides some protections for images from other sites. For more information, read on. A warning, though: make sure you set your Google preferences to ignore adult material.

See the list at the end of this chapter for additional sites.

No Clipart!

Contrary to what Microsoft PowerPoint might suggest by the inclusion of a clipart gallery, clipart Is not good for the screen! Remember the principle covered in chapter on references about filling the canvas.

Most clipart is cheesy. In nearly every case, it is more detraction than enhancement. The original purpose for such art was to dress up printed newsletters. The idea worked fairly well for its original intention. Newsletter designers would clip out these small pieces of line art, or simple shaded drawings, and then paste them around text to dress up the final product. Remember that the screen is a visual medium, so these print tactics don't apply.

Copyright.

Copyright matters when it comes to creating powerful imagery for worship. It is also a field of law that is changing frequently in light of rapid advances in digital technology and Congressional pressure from lobbyists such as Jack Valenti and the Motion Picture Association.

As of the writing of this book, churches retain some limited rights in regards to the use of still images. As outlined in *The Wired Church*,[13] according to Section 110(3) of the Copyright Act of 1976, a church may legally use any still image from any source in worship without violation of copyright as long as that image is used only in a single worship

---

[13] Wilson, Len. *The Wired Church* (Abingdon Press: 1999), pp. 158–160.

service. Any use beyond the live worship event though is a violation of copyright, and any use of a "sequence of images," e.g., video, is a violation of copyright, unless prior permission is obtained. This is good news for a designer who wants to use source material such as a cover from *Newsweek* or *Time* for a sermon illustration, for example. But it is not a blanket umbrella for making unethical decisions, such as downloading "comp" images from stock photo sites and removing the watermark, as mentioned earlier.

We must make the disclaimer that we're not lawyers; this is what lawyers have told us. For more information about copyright and images in worship, consult an attorney or a service such as the Church Copyright Association at http://www.churchca.com/.

Resolution.

Mastering all of the principles for design and applying them to a finished image is all for naught if it is built at the wrong size. Resolution is an important aspect in the image creation process.

Basically, any screen, be it a telephone LCD screen, television, projector, or computer monitor, can only display images at 72 ppi (pixels per inch). Anything over that is "wasted" digital information. In a way, that's a good thing because it makes finding sources easier. There is an abundance of images on the web that exist at this resolution, and the lower resolution stock photos are cheaper.

When it comes to building graphics for the screen, it's best to create them at whatever size your presentation software will project. The resolution will still be 72 dpi, but the pixel count should always be as high as it can for the program that will be displaying the image.

For instance, Microsoft PowerPoint by default creates slides at 720 by 540 (NTSC 601 Square Pixels) at 72 dpi. If the application's settings are not changed, graphics should be built at these specs. A common size for projectors is 1024 by 768, so some designers build for this size and change the presentation software to match. Check to see what the default specs are for the program you'll be using.

As stated in the raster graphics description, it's important not to over-enlarge an image for the screen. A postage-stamp sized graphic cannot be scaled to the size of a movie poster. The rule of thumb to keep in mind is that 130% is the limit to a successful enlargement.

Building a Set of Images for Worship

There are a few types of images that should be included in every set. Most of the time, effort, and energy will be spend on a primary image. This is the default image that sets up the theme for the day. It signals the theme to worshipers and then becomes a sign that they don't need to look as intently as the screen. This image ensures that the screen never goes black. Going to black, or raising and lowering the screen, are both very distracting and should be avoided unless done with a very obvious artistic purpose.

Next, song backgrounds come in very handy during the service. The best song backgrounds are based on the primary graphic. They are often heavily muted or blurred so that lyrics or other text can easily be read.

Sermon point graphics will also be very useful. Be as intentional on the font choice and placement as on the primary image. Point bars and drop shadows can be used to separate the text from the background.

Build a background for scripture references. This may be similar or exactly the same as the song background. Just remember to make it match the set visually. Keep text to a minimum on scripture references, as the screen is a visual medium.

Refer to the DVD for some sample sets of worship graphics, a more complete description of the types of graphics to create, and a step-by-step process for making a ready-to-present set of images.

Terms to Learn:

Clip art—Generic images, designs, and artwork originally developed with desktop publishing that was designed to be literally "clipped out" and used for illustrations. Mostly used by amateur artists; clip art is best used very sparingly.

DPI/PPI—Dots per inch (pixels per inch). A measure of the resolution of a digital image. 72 dpi/ppi is screen resolution.

Megapixel—One million pixels; a measure for the resolution of a digital camera.

Non-square pixel—See pixel next. Pixels in the graphics world are square, but pixels in the digital video signal are non-square. Designers creating images for video must compensate for non-square pixels. Adobe Photoshop includes the ability to correct pixel aspect ratio for non-square pixels.

Pixel—The basic unit of the composition of an image on a television screen, computer monitor, or similar display. Screens are rated by their number of horizontal and vertical pixels; for example, 1024 by 768 means 1024 pixels are displayed in each row, and there are 768 rows (lines).

Raster graphics—A graphic image composed as an arrangement of screen dots, or pixels. It is used by contrast to the term vector graphics, which breaks down when scaled upward. Common types are GIF (.gif), JPEG (.jpg/.jpeg), Photoshop (.psd), TIFF (.tif /.tiff), PNG (.png), and BMP (.bmp). Programs that create and manipulate raster graphics are often referred to as "paint programs."

Resolution—The basic measurement of the amount of information on a display. Many computer monitors now display a standard resolution of 1024 by 768.

Rights-managed—A type of licensing agreement that protects image copyright holders. Non-exclusive rights allow buyers to pay a fee each time they use the image, but other buyers can also purchase and use the image under the same license. Exclusive rights allow buyers exclusive use of an image under the terms of the license for a fee.

Royalty-free—As opposed to rights-managed, royalty free licensing allows buyers to pay a single fee for unlimited usage of an image. This is the preferred method for most (non-commercial) designers because it provides more freedom and is usually less expensive.

Square pixel—See pixel above. Pixels in the graphics world are square, but pixels in the digital video signal are non-square. Designers creating images for video must compensate for non-square pixels. Adobe Photoshop includes the ability to correct pixel aspect ratio from non-square to square pixels.

Vector graphic—A type of image that makes use of geometrical primitives such as points, lines, curves, and polygons to represent image. Vector graphics are visual representations of mathematical formulas, which make them infinitely scaleable with no degradation to the image. It is used by contrast to the term raster graphics. Programs that create and manipulate vector graphics are often referred to as "draw programs."

File Formats

AI—A file format native to Adobe Illustrator. Art is saved in vector format, which are comprised of mathematically defined shapes. Used for creating high-resolution, scalable images.

AVI—An acronym for Audio Video Interleave, which is a multimedia container format introduced by Microsoft as part of the Video for Windows technology. AVI files contain both audio and video data in a standard container that allows simultaneous playback. The audio/visual data can be encoded or decoded by a software module called a codec and can work with many compression schemes.

BMP—The proprietary image format developed by Microsoft Windows, which is our preferred format for displaying graphics on screens due to its relatively lossless compression.

DV—An acronym for Digital Video and a format for capturing and storing video in digital format. The DV format is an international standard for consumer use created in 1995 by a consortium of companies. Most digital camcorders record in some form of the DV format.

EPS—An acronym that means Encapsulated PostScript; a file format that supports both vector graphics and bitmap images (and is most common to the printing industry).

JPG—An acronym for Joint Photographic Experts Group. A standardized image compression mechanism designed for compressing either full-color or grayscale photographic images, often for use on the Web. JPG is "lossy," meaning that the decompressed image is not quite of the same quality as the original image.

MOV—Apple's QuickTime movie file format. Can play both video and audio files. The audio/visual data can be encoded or decoded by a software module called a codec and can work with many compression schemes.

MPG—The file extension that denotes a file that is in MPEG-1 digital video format. MPEG stands for Moving Picture Experts Group and is the name given to a set of standards used for coding media files in a digital compressed format. MPEG files are generally much smaller than original source files yet maintain similar quality. Current standards that exist include: MPEG-1, MPEG-2, MPEG-3, and MPEG-4, with MPEG-1 the most universally used.

PDF—An acronym that means Portable Document Format. A now ubiquitous file format invented by Adobe that captures, or "prints," all the elements of a document as an electronic image.

SWF—A version of the Macromedia Flash Player vector-based graphics format. It is ideal for presenting vector-based interactive and animated graphics with sound for the Web. Because a SWF file is vector-based, its graphics are scalable and play back smoothly on any screen size and across multiple platforms.

TIF—An acronym that means "Tagged Image File." It is an industry standard, lossless raster graphic or image format and is well suited for accurately storing scanned images.

Websites for Source Material

Corbis—http://pro.corbis.com/
iStock Photo—http://www.istockphoto.com/
Dreamstime—http://www.dreamstime.com/
Digital Juice—http://www.digitaljuice.com/
European Space Telescope—http://www.spacetelescope.org/
Free Fotos—http://www.freefoto.com/
Free Images (from the UK)—http://www.freeimages.co.uk/
Getty Images—http://creative.gettyimages.com/
The Image Exchange—http://sxc.hu/
NASA NIX Media Library—http://nix.nasa.gov/
NASA TERRA Space Photo Library—http://terra.nasa.gov/
NOAA Government Photo Library—http://www.photolib.noaa.gov/
Photospin—http://www.photospin.com/
Picture Quest—http://www.picturequest.com/
USDA Online photo center—http://www.usda.gov/oc/photo/-opclibra.htm

Chapter 10
Growth Matters

Since its 1964 debut, the Ford Motor Company's Mustang has consistently been a top seller because of its unique design and performance features. A company with such a long-running favorite model as the Mustang might be tempted to rest on its laurels and resist making changes to what has traditionally been such a successful automobile. In fact, some Mustang enthusiasts might argue that throughout the years Ford has done just that, on occasion making poor design choices and losing sight of what makes a Mustang truly a Mustang. Certainly various model years could be cited where the combination of design and performance fell below standards previously set.

However, in 2005, Ford overhauled the look and feel of the Mustang car, celebrating forty years of design innovation. The new model, with its retro-edgy feel, is removing fuel from detractor's fires. It infuses some of best aesthetic and mechanical attributes of the past with design features that are purely contemporary in style. The biggest acknowledged problem with the new Mustang so far is that it has been nearly impossible to keep in stock!

The reason dealerships all over the country can't keep up with demand for the Mustang is that Ford has finally demonstrated that it both values good design and understands the need to continually build on its design successes. Ford knows that in this age of good design they can't afford to let their designs get "rusty" or their competition will take over the market.

Car manufacturers across the board are returning to their collective past and innovating for the future with good design that is catching the public's eye.

The last principle for design centers on the idea of engaging in continual growth. As designers we can learn much from the Ford Mustang. We might not be designing the next great sports car each week when we put together graphics for worship, but it is imperative that we continue to learn, practice, and grow as visual communicators of the Gospel. If we don't, darker forces will "take over the market" of those we're trying to reach. Just like Ford Motor Company, we can't afford to get rusty.

#1- Develop a Design Standard.

Once an artist figures out what works, he or she should use it to advantage. A good artist develops a personal style, or design standard, and then learns to stick to it.

What is a design standard? Although the exact composition of a design standard varies between fields of study, basically it is a set of styles that is imagined as a system (such as for worship images each week or in the design of a website). Design standards include elements such as shapes, sizes, layouts, colors, typography, and use of symbols and icons. Think of a design standard as a personal set of rules developed over time that are to remain unchanged. A designer's standard is like a personal constitution that encompasses all of the rules that he or she will follow in his or her creative endeavors. This helps create a personal style but also creates a consistency in his or her work.

For example, perhaps you favor the use of photographs as texture. You prefer to create images using complementary colors. You like to treat photos by highlighting important lines and shapes. On the other hand, you may vow never to use certain fonts, such as Comic Sans, on the screen.

You might also decide that clip art is not part of your design palette. You may choose only to use certain types of images or treatments. These are all artistic decisions that give your work a distinct look. Such distinctions should be developed and nurtured as part of what makes the work "yours." Finding where the line is on certain aspects of design and then showing restraint in not crossing these lines can create a creative tension that will make your work stand out above the work of others.

After a designer raises the bar, it's not a good idea to go back to the old way of doing things. Figuring out what works and then adding that to an ever-growing palette helps to ensure future success. Think of the additions as adding amendments to the core constitution.

In addition to having a personal design standard, it is necessary to create a design standard for each graphics set you create. A good goal for wor ship is to make each graphic set have its own visual identity (even when doing a message series). This will make visuals and the biblical truth connected to them more memorable. It will also reduce the chance that one week's message is confused with another message.

The weekly design standard plays out in the font choices, text layout, sermon point placement, and much more. Song backgrounds, illustrations, and any other image put on the screen should adhere to the standard for the week. You might even take a moment to write down or create a sample of "the standard" before completing a set of graphics. This is especially helpful if more than one artist is working on graphic production. A design standard list might look like this:

> Body font: Baker Signet, 28 point
> Display font: Trajan Bold, 40 point
> Song background: blurred muted version of the primary
>   image
> Sermon points: use same bar as theme line for all points
> Scripture: should be made to look as if they are on a high-
>   way sign
> Color scheme: Green, Yellow, Red
> Drop shadow: 45° angle, softness 50%
> Filters used for illustrations: Cutout at 30% opacity

The design standard becomes a set of rules that ensure consistency throughout a worship graphics set. Consistency is one of the most important but commonly overlooked aspects of design. Consistency allows the artist to create a visual thread that starts at the beginning of worship and continues throughout, making a much more lasting impression on worshippers. The graphics set should looks as if it all came from one family or body of work, even when illustrations are used. This avoids a "potpourri" look, which can be visually jarring. Sermon points, song lyrics, and illustrations should ideally follow the same rules each time they are displayed, unless there is a good reason to stray from the standard to create visual tension.

Each week the rules should be defined according to the style of the graphic being used, but they should not conflict with an artist's own design standard. A physics theme would have rules very different from a pastel Mother's Day theme or an early flight metaphor. Asking what is at the essence of a particular look or style then finding ways to communicate that through the treatment of text and illustrations will take graphic sets to the next level.

#2- Balance Design Standard and References.

Once the standard is in place, there is a balance that must be found between a) sticking to a personal style and b) looking to the culture for reference and inspiration. For example, the Ford Mustang has a look and style that is all its own, but when compared to other manufacturer models, regardless of year, one can see the influences of other car companies. In other words, Ford developed a style with the Mustang and stayed with it while at the same time following trends present in the automotive design world of the time. They would have had little success if they had kept building the 1964 design for the last forty years.

This is a delicate balance to maintain. The second generation of Mustangs, from 1967-1968, included what has become one of the most sought after collectibles on the market, the 1967 Shelby Mustang. In fact, this is the model that was the strongest historical reference for the designers of the 2005 model. Ford designers were successful in tapping into the emerging muscle car market while creating a look that was distinctly their own. On the other hand, some of the Mustang's least popular model years occurred when this balance became askew in the 1970s. Its fifth generation redesign, nicknamed the Mustang II, marked a low point in its illustrious record. The benefit of history shows a car maker that lost sight of what truly constituted a Mustang.

This can happen to worship media designers, as well. When the latest craze comes out, it's tempting to want to learn the processes behind the technique. Often such continual desire for improvement is a good thing because it expands our palette. But be careful that the latest trends in design don't interfere with personal design standards. If an artist is known for clean lines and solid colors, then appropriating the "grunge" look entirely may not be in that artist's best interests.

If done in moderation, a stylized look like "grunge," or any other trend, can add freshness to a standard. Adding it to the standard (the thing by which all graphics are created from) would be a mistake, however. It may be helpful to refer to the core constitution/amendment analogy here.

#3- Don't Rest on Past Successes.

For every artist, there comes a point in time that supernatural creativity occurs in the design and execution of his or her art, when every element falls perfectly into place and chattering voices echo praises about the work. It is natural to celebrate these times. The danger, however, just like a car company that sticks with a design until it has lost its edge, is in letting the joy of success become an excuse to do the same thing over and over. Once success starts to come on a more regular basis, the tendency to rest on past laurels can be hard to pass up.

We've been to individual churches where the graphics, designs, and treatments look nearly identical from one week to the next. It's almost as if the artists are plugging in new titles and colors for each week but sticking with the same treatments and design elements that have previously worked. The style might have a real impact when singled out, but when overused (most every week), a rut forms, and innovation grinds to a halt. This is bad for the artist, but more importantly, it is sad for congregations who endure the same basic look every week.

The irony is that many artists volunteer their work for worship out of a personal desire to reinvigorate what they perceive to be inert forms and liturgies, only to create new inertia by producing similar images and designs every week. Images in worship can become stagnant just as words can become stagnant in rubrics and liturgies.

#4- Keep Doing the Hard Work.

Another temptation for an artist, similar to the temptation to rest on past success, is to rely on a standard palette of tips and tricks when creating new work. The lack of inspiration and the time constraints can some-times lead to a recycling of what has worked previously. It can also occur when the artist begins to take on an attitude of having "arrived."

Although Jason is admittedly almost completely right-brained, Len has more of a balance of left and right. This means that for Jason, design imagination comes more naturally, but for Len, initial inspirations are often great, and final pieces are frequently acceptable, but the journey in between can be difficult. Creating art is hard work. If for whatever reason he doesn't want to go to the trouble of dealing with that anguish, Len has been around long enough in the design and production world to know a few tips and techniques, and he has enough buttons on his com-puter screen to be able to whip out a "standard" worship graphic, for example, without too much work. But with little effort comes too little response. If the artwork doesn't move the artist, then it's almost a guar-antee that it won't move an audience.

Over time, both of us in our own ways have discovered that there is a spiritual discipline to designing art for worship. Keeping up the hard work of going someplace new and not relying on known tricks is a nec-essary part of good design that moves people.

Even after producing many successful designs, always strive to maintain an attitude of not yet knowing everything there is to know about creat-ing powerful visuals.

#5- Always Be a Student of Design.

Continuing education is vital. Read books, subscribe to design maga-zines, and join design organizations, such as the National Association of

Photoshop Professionals (http://www.photoshopuser.com). Search the Internet and bookmark sites with great online tutorials.

It's worth repeating here that one of the earlier principles, finding references, is at the core of growing as an artist. Staying on top of popular styles, fonts, colors, and treatments in culture will ensure that new creations are relevant. Whenever an artist has a bout with "designer's block," references act as a wrecking ball that is sure to take down the creative hurdle. Open a magazine, turn on the television, or visit the web during these frustrating times.

#6- Work with Other Artists.

Find a critique partner, or another artist, as a great way to leap forward as a worship designer. The more honest you allow a critique partner to be, the better your work will become. Being an artist requires the development of a thick skin. "Thick-skinned artist" is often an oxymoron. It is helpful to remember that criticism (when given from the right person) is an opportunity for improvement, not a personal attack. Learning to accept criticism is one of the keys to becoming an effective artist.

#7- Evaluate Your Work.

One of the best ways to improve is to establish an evaluation schedule. Setting up some type of monthly or quarterly review can be very helpful. This may or may not involve critique partners.

As a part of the review, analyze every piece completed during that time, including successes and failures. What caused the successes? What contributed to the failures? Pay particular attention to the appropriation of new techniques and the adherence to a personal design standard.

Looking at previous success and failures can make future designs better. As much as one might like to avoid looking at the less successful endeavors, it is important to do so. They provide some of the most valuable lessons that will make for future successes.

Design matters, and growth matters too. Finding ways to sharpen your skills will make you a powerful visual communicator of the Gospel.

Appendix – Additional Terms to Learn

Aliasing–The appearance of jagged distortions in curves and diagonal lines in an image because the resolution is limited or diminished or there is insufficient data. Called the "stair-step" effect.

Alpha channel–A portion of each pixel's data that is reserved for transparency information. 32-bit graphics systems contain four channels — three 8-bit channels for red, green, and blue (RGB) and one 8-bit alpha channel. The alpha channel is really a mask — it specifies how the pixel's colors should be merged with another pixel when the two are overlaid, one on top of the other.

Anti-aliasing–The process of removing or reducing the jagged distortions in curves and diagonal lines so that the lines appear smooth or smoother.

Animation–The act of imparting life, motion, or activity. In the world of digital media, it refers to the process of giving motion to still images, whether cartoon or photographic.

Bevel–A three-dimensional edge effect applied to the border of a graphic. Adding a beveled effect to a graphic image gives the image a raised appearance by applying highlight colors and shadow colors to the inside and outside edges.

Bleed–When setting up images to be printed, the portion of an illustration or image which extends beyond the trimmed page.

CCLI–The copyright service that allows a church to display copy written song lyrics on screens during worship without violation of applicable law.

Cell based animation–A form of animation that requires every individual frame of video or film to be individually hand drawn, at rates of usually twenty-four or thirty frames per second.

Codec—An acronym for "compression/decompression." Also, an algorithm or specialized computer program that encodes, or reduces, the number of bytes consumed by large files. Files encoded with a specific codec require the same codec for decoding. Programs such as QuickTime, Photoshop, and Windows Media use codecs to reduce the size of media files.

Compression—A technology that reduces the size of a file by removing redundant and/or non-critical information. Uncompressed, or lossless, images are quite large, particularly when working with print resolution images and in video, thus necessitating the need for compression formats to make work more manageable.

CVLI—The companion organization to CCLI (see above), which allows congregations to use videos in worship without violation of applicable copyright law.

Emboss—To create raised surfaces on an object. A technique for creating a raised surface on a piece of paper by pressing into it from behind, which was originally done by hand and now by digital effect.

Fields—Interlaced images and video consist of two fields that must be rendered independently and combined into one frame. Each field contains half the scan lines (either even or odd) and is a separate file. One can either render to fields or to frames.

Filters—In image editing programs, a filter is a special effect that can be applied to an image to create interesting visual treatments.

Interlaced—A method of refreshing an image on a monitor. Instead of refreshing the entire image (progressive scan), an interlaced monitor refreshes the odd-numbered scan lines first, and then refreshes the even-numbered scan lines on a second "pass." In standard (NTSC) video, a field is refreshed sixty times per second, creating thirty distinct images every second.

Interpolation-based animation—A form of animation that uses keyframes, or markers, to indicate motion over time and relies on computer algorithms to create movement from one time/space to another.

Landscape—An image where the width is greater than the height.

Letterbox—The image of a wide-screen picture on a standard 4:3 aspect ratio television screen, typically with black bars above and below. It is used to maintain the original aspect ratio of the original source (usually a theatrical motion picture of 16:9 aspect ratio or wider). Also a design technique that simulates the look of a letterboxed image.

Marching ants—The "technical term" in the Adobe Photoshop manual for the marquee, or the moving, dashed line that indicates a selection.

Mask—The unselected part of the image in Photoshop, which is protected from editing. Masking is a technique used in Photoshop to apply color changes, filters, or other effects to portions of an image.

Opacity—The degree to which an image is transparent, allowing images behind to visually show through.

Plug-in—A software module that "plugs into" an application in order to give it a specific, additional functionality. Plug-ins are most commonly used to create special treatment effects.

Portrait—An image where the height is greater than the width.

Progressive—A non-interlaced method of refreshing an image on a monitor. Where each line scans in progression from the top to the bottom of the monitor.

What's on the *Design Matters* DVD

Experiencing the DVD is a must for getting the most out of *Design Matters: Creating Powerful Imagery for Worship*. It contains a number of elements that will illuminate and illustrate concepts discussed in the book. These are:

All of the figure illustrations referenced in the book. It's a challenge to discuss graphic design in colorless printed form. These full-color renditions of all of the examples are helpful in understanding techniques, especially for the color chapter.

"The 7 Principles of Design." This video feature summarizes the core of the book, with graphics and video illustrations, and is both a good introduction to the book or refresher lecture, depending on if you're more likely to crack open the pages or the disc sleeve first.

Video tutorials. Three full-length, step-by-step tutorials show Jason building graphics in Adobe Photoshop. These are designed not just to teach the image being constructed, but also to show image manipulation concepts that can apply to other projects as well. We hope that the tutorials act as lessons in a class on designing worship graphics, giving you a basis for applying the principles of design.

Source material for these tutorials, as well as print versions in the PDF format, are on the data portion of the disk. In addition, the disk also contains four bonus tutorials in PDF format with accompanying source images. The four bonus tutorials are also available online at http://www.midnightoilproductions.com/training/. These may be accessed by inserting the disc into a DVD-ROM equipped computer.

Free media. Use some samples from our Midnight Oil library to begin to incorporate powerful media in worship right away. These are included without restriction in regard to worship. You may play these directly off the DVD. If you like them and want more, we'd love to see you online at http://www.midnightoilproductions.com/.

Notes

Notes

Notes

Notes

Notes

Notes